Becoming Critical

Becoming Critical

THE EMERGENCE OF
SOCIAL JUSTICE SCHOLARS

Edited by

FELECIA M. BRISCOE

and

MUHAMMAD A. KHALIFA

Published by
STATE UNIVERSITY OF NEW YORK PRESS
Albany

© 2015 Felecia M. Briscoe and Muhammad A. Khalifa

Printed in the United States of America

For information, contact
State University of New York Press
www.sunypress.edu

Production, Laurie D. Searl
Marketing, Kate R. Seburyamo

Library of Congress Cataloging-in-Publication Data

Becoming critical : the emergence of social justice scholars / edited by
Felecia M. Briscoe and Muhammad A. Khalifa.
    pages cm
Includes bibliographical references and index.
ISBN 978-1-4384-5655-3 (hardcover : alk. paper)
ISBN 978-1-4384-5656-0 (e-book)
    1. Social justice—Study and teaching (Higher)   2. Critical pedagogy. 3.
Minorities in higher education—United States.   4. Minorities in higher
education—United States—Biography.   5. Teachers—Training of—Social
aspects—United States.   I. Briscoe, Felecia, editor of compilation.
II. Khalifa, Muhammad A., 1975–
    HM671.B44 2015
    378.008—dc23   2014027593

10 9 8 7 6 5 4 3 2 1

First, we thank and acknowledge all of the courageous authors who have contributed to this book.

We also thank our research assistants, who have been invaluable: Sara Harrington, Elizabeth Gil, and Carol Gines.

Contents

Section I
Introduction and Overview of Book

Section II
Critical Race Autoethnographic Case Studies

Section III
Critical Feminist Autoethnographic Case Studies

Section IV
Critical Intersectional Autoethnographic Case Studies

Introduction and Overview of Book

CHAPTER ONE

Introduction and Conceptual Framework

·•——·•·

Critical Theory, Social Justice, Power, and Autoethnography

FELECIA M. BRISCOE AND MUHAMMAD A. KHALIFA

We, Felecia and Muhammad, began our academic careers as middle school science teachers in Las Vegas, Nevada, and Detroit, Michigan, respectively. Our teaching experiences led us to become deeply troubled by the systemic practices that disadvantaged minority and low-income students in these two very different cities. One of our primary goals in earning our doctoral degrees was to help develop knowledge that would create a more equitable educational system. Yet, more than 20 years after teaching in the public schools, I (Felecia) received the following e-mail from one of my brightest and most highly motivated teacher education students:

> You ever been in a place, where everybody is real depressed, but they don't really know it. It is where the tedious and mundane are worshipped . . . The least bit of creativity and inspiration has been excised. People rule through fear and intimidation. The staff is treated like children. People wonder what is wrong with our kids. We aren't doing them any favors, except making them sick of school. We have tested them to death. When we aren't testing them, we are pre-testing them or teaching them test strategies. Richmond worships at the altar of standardized testing. There is no room for heretics or non-believers. (A. Jackson, personal communication, September 16, 2008)

Mr. Jackson, an African American man, was one of the most creative and motivated students I have encountered in my more than 20 years of teaching in higher education. He wrote the letter during his third year of teaching in an urban majority Black elementary school. I reflected a long time on this e-mail, asking myself questions about what had happened to this very promising teacher and how such an environment was affecting the lives of the children he taught. I came to the conclusion that somewhere we had taken a wrong turn in our understanding of what an equitable school system should look like. The current punitive approach of standardized testing, fear, intimidation, and so forth was the result of neoliberal accountability policies and was supposedly done in the name of achieving equity.

Muhammad had similar experiences both personally and through his own children's education. When he first began his teaching career on the east side of Detroit in the late 1990s, he encountered such an intense culture of standardized test fraud that he thought it was just part of the way that education *really* happened. The rationale he was given for cheating on the Michigan Educational Assessment Program, or MEAP, was that "the wealthy White suburbs cheat on the MEAP, so we cannot compete unless we do it." The same culture that caused despondency in Felecia's students led, on the one hand, to conformity with a high-stakes neoliberal reform imposed on Detroiters. Ironically, this was followed by a resistance to the neoliberal reform, ultimately through an elaborate culture of staff working behind the scenes to increase the MEAP scores of Detroit students.

We have spent many hours discussing what different kinds of understandings might help our educational system to actually become equitable. We would also like it to become one in which teaching and learning occur, not within a technical-rational testing framework, but within a framework that encouraged the intrinsic joys of teaching and learning. Those discussions led to our present objectives. The first segment of this chapter focuses on the book's objectives. The second segment describes our conceptual framework. Finally, we present an overview of the book's organization and content.

Objectives

Our objective is to develop an understanding of the different paths taken by people of various races/ethnicities, socioeconomic backgrounds, national origins, abilities, and genders in their development as critical scholars. We develop this understanding through a qualitative meta-analysis. These auto-ethnographies delineate key events and points in our lives that have shaped us into the critical scholars we are today. As critical autoethnographies, they focus on power relations embedded in those events and the authors' responses to colonizing relationships of power. Despite being positioned in different spaces, all the authors have developed critical perspectives in their teaching and/or research. There are two levels of findings and two levels of critical social theory development. Each of the 11 authors conducts the first level of analysis on her or his own life using and expanding on current critical theories. We, the editors, conduct a second level of analysis by identifying common and divergent themes and the relationship of those themes among the 11 case studies. Thus, this book contributes to the development of critical theories—especially as they pertain to identities—and qualitative methodologies, as well as the literature on social justice education. Accordingly, we analyze the autoethnographies, delineating relationships in the commonalities and differences in the paths taken by the different authors in becoming critical scholars for social justice. Therefore, this book can be read in its entirety, or any one of the autoethnographic case studies and be read alone and on its own terms.

Why These Objectives?
New Perspectives from Different Social Spaces

There are a number of important reasons for writing this book that relate to the development of critical theory and research methodologies. However, and perhaps more importantly, this book applies to the practical and ethical challenges faced by teacher educators, pre-service teachers, educational researchers, and educational practitioners. Increasing numbers of teacher education programs are emphasizing social justice or critical perspectives in their curricula (Cochran-Smith, et al., 2009). At the same time, the university and public schools are becoming increasingly diverse: "By the year 2020, minority students will account for 45 percent of the nation's public high-school graduates, up from 38 percent in 2009" (Hoover, 2013, para. 2). This diversity presents a number of opportunities and challenges for teacher education programs, educational practitioners, and those interested in social justice. Unlike recent uses of the word, by *diverse* we include all races/ethnicities (not just people of color), genders, economic classes, (dis) abilities, and sexual orientations. These challenges have arisen because, traditionally, the practices and policies of public schools (including institutions of higher education) have enacted the cultural values, norms, and otherwise privileged White (e.g., Spring, 2006), male (e.g., Cannela & Perez, 2012), and middle-upper class students (e.g., Gandara, 1995).

At the beginning of the nineteenth century, Max Weber (1902/1992) predicted that Western society was developing into an iron cage of technical-rationality, wherein people were embedded in a quantifiable accounting-type system and had little to no freedom to use their own judgment or express their unique personality. A number of scholars have described neoliberal educational policies as the embodiment of this iron cage of technical-ationality (e.g., Hill, 2009; Mirowski, 2013; Samier, 2002). Other scholars have found that the neoliberal iron cage provides a colorblind façade of equity while continuing to disenfranchise groups that have historically suffered from oppression (Briscoe & Khalifa, 2013, Lipman, 2011). In addition to its inimical effects on disadvantaged groups, the neoliberal iron cage of technical-rationality has produced an increasingly sterile, alienated environment for the privileged (Baudrillard, 2005; Case, 2013). The voices of groups that have been marginalized may offer new understandings that help change the direction of schools and society into a more humane one.

The challenges presented by neoliberal versions of lingering traditional practices and policies of schools in the midst of increasing diversity are realized through inquiries such as a) Are the curriculum, practices, and norms of teacher education and public schools relevant to the increasingly diverse pool of teacher educators, pre-service teachers, practitioners, and students? b) Are the increasingly diverse students in higher education, including White, middle-class men, able to see the relevancy of social justice education and/or critical research in their lives and work? c) Are scholars, teacher educators, pre-service students, and educational practitioners aware of the diverse perspectives in society? d) Are all of the foregoing groups aware of the different paths available to diverse people in becoming critical?

This book provides information to help teacher educators, scholars, students, and public school practitioners address those challenges. In addition to addressing the above challenges, this book contributes to the development of critical theory and qualitative research methodologies. In doing so, it necessarily provides epistemological perspectives from those who have traditionally been excluded, silenced, or otherwise oppressed in our schools and society (e.g., Dixson & Rousseau, 2006).

Furthermore, people who have been silenced, excluded, or otherwise oppressed have all too often had their stories told by those of the dominant group (middle-class, European-American males)—and all too often those stories have constructed negative identities for those who have been traditionally oppressed (e.g., Briscoe, 2005). When critical educational researchers and/or practitioners from diverse social spaces and places tell their own stories, they produce counter-narratives, which not only resist the deficit identities that have been constructed in the dominant discourse (Delgado-Gaitan, 1994), but also develop new practices, epistemologies, and social theories (e.g., Collins, 2002; Duncan, 2005). These new understandings have the potential to help people engage in new forms of social justice activities.

As several scholars (e.g., Haraway, 1991) have noted, historically middle-class White males have conducted research and developed theories about oppressed groups. Most of this research and theorizing is colonizing, as it is still mired in European ways of seeing, understanding, and knowing the world (Tuwihai-Smith, 2012). Historically, such colonizing and colonized research has constructed deficit identities for marginalized groups. These constructions are part of an oppressive colonizing force. Dei (2006) finds that colonizing forces seek

> to impose the will of one people on another and to use the resources of the imposed people for the benefit of the imposer. Nothing is sacred in such a system as it powers its way toward the extinction of the wills of the imposed upon with one objective in mind: the ultimate subjection of the will to resist. An effective system of colonialism reduces the imposed upon to a shell of a human who is incapable of thinking in a subjective way of his or her own interest. In everything the person becomes like the imposer; thus in desires wishes, visions, purposes, styles, structures, values, and especially the values of education, the person operates against his or her own interest. Colonialism does not engender creativity; it stifles it, suppresses it under the cloak of assistance when in fact it is creating the conditions that make it impossible for humans to effectively resist. And yet there has always been resistance and there are new methods of resistance gaining ground each day.

One way to resist the colonizing forces of academic production and the unequal relationships of power it engenders is to have those of us who have been traditionally marginalized create and write our own stories, our own ethnographies. As Chang (2011) has noted, "[a]utoethnography is a qualitative research method that enables researchers to use their autobiographical and contextual data to gain a hermeneutical understanding of the societal context, and in turn, a sociocultural meaning of self (p. 13).

Furthermore, Denzin (2003) has found that "performance [auto] ethnography is more than a tool of liberation. It is a way of being moral and political in the world" (p. 258). This book articulates and embodies not only the way that autoethnography can inform critical thought, but also how it can be practically used to impact local change.

Autoethnographies have emerged in scholarly journals over the past decade or so. Carolyn Ellis (1997, 2004) and scholars like bell hooks (2003) and Gloria Anzaldúa (1999) have produced autoethnographies that have reflexively explored subjectivity, gender, and class in the context of a heteronormative, racialized, gendered, and classed society. Autoethnography challenges the criticism of traditional positivist epistemologies regarding "objectivity, absolute truth, and 'validity.'" We argue that we can tell our stories and project our "truths" using the tools only we, as native research-ers, have to interpret our lived experiences and the intellectual, emotional, and material effects of these experiences. By doing so, we help to develop new ways of knowing and acting in the world.

There is a third resonance to criticality. Pennycook (2001) describes this resonance as a crucial turning point, as in reaching a critical mass. The United States, indeed the world, is approaching a critical point in several areas, if it has not already reached that point. These critical points would include an increasingly disproportionate share of wealth and resources both between and within nation-states (e.g., Irvin, 2008; Rapley, 2004); increas-ing unrest, especially within nations with a smaller share of resources (de Oliver, 2008); and the degrading environment and depletion of natural resources (e.g., Climate Institute, 2011). It would seem that the conceptual frameworks that have informed the perspectives through which we make decisions locally, nationally, and globally have led us amiss in some way. By integrating the critical voices and epistemologies of those who have been silenced or otherwise marginalized, perhaps a more complete and holistic perspective will emerge. It is our hope that the emerging critical social theory from this book will help develop such a perspective.

Our work is relevant and unique for a number of reasons. For one, our project focuses on *educators* and their lived experiences that led them to become critical researchers and/or educators. We also found no works that focus exclusively on the experiences of critical scholars. Secondly, none of the extant autoethnographic projects brings a *number of collective voices* together. To date, they have all been single persons who have shared their stories. This book brings many critical autoethnographic voices into a single project and then draws lessons, similarities, reflections, and conclusions from individuals and the collective. This, we believe, has the transformational power to push our field forward—both methodologically and epistemologi-cally. And finally, our work is unique in that it focuses on how educa-tors and researchers trace their history into becoming *critical*. This journey pushes conversations both in and about education forward, particularly in an age when researchers are increasingly expected to be more deeply reflec-tive about their own journeys. Indeed, it is this "critical" edge that allows researchers and educators to be good, yet *different*, at what they do.

Conceptual Framework

In this section, we present the conceptual framework for *Becoming Critical: The Emergence of Social Justice Scholars*. It offers the logic and organizing principles of critical theories, power, and emerging identities as they apply to the epistemological challenges presented by race, class, gender, and other key social positionings. We contextualize the book as part of a larger plan aimed at developing the capacity of future teachers, administrators, and other practitioners as well as scholars to understand the different ways in which they and others can become critical; giving practitioners a broader and more diverse understanding of what it means to teach for social justice and the different paths that might be taken; and, finally, providing researchers with examples of innovative methods and new theoretical paths that can help us develop knowledge to advance the goals of equity and an appreciation of diversity.

Critical theory, social justice, power, and autoethnography provide the structure of the conceptual framework used in this study. Thus, we define and link each of these concepts together. Our definitions are very broad, allowing for a diversity of specific understandings as utilized by the variety of authors. We do this to simplify the use of these concepts and to provide a conceptual framework encompassing their meanings simultaneously. We begin by describing what we mean by the term *critical*, linking it to critical theory and social justice; then we provide examples of both critical theory and social justice. We then turn to the concept of power as it relates to both critical theories and social justice. Finally, we describe how critical autoethnography relates to the foregoing concepts and why autoethnography is integral to the book's objectives.

This book provides a range of understandings and commonalities in what is meant by social justice and by being critical. Some have argued that the concept of social justice is ambiguous and unclear (e.g., McDonald & Zwiechner, 2008; North, 2006). But we maintain that having a range of meaning for social justice and criticality is desirable, as different meanings may prove more useful in different and complex settings: Rather than expecting one meaning to apply to every situation, being able to select the meaning that best fits one's context may be more useful. Thus, throughout this book we often refer to these terms in the plural form. We, like many others (e.g., Collins, 2002; Pennycook, 2001), understand that there is no one universal critical theory or praxis (Freire, 2008), but rather many different ones that help us to understand and act in the different social, political, economic, and educational realities that we navigate in our lives.

Critical Social Theories and How They Relate to Social Justice

The critical aspect of our framework means that we are concerned with developing understandings of existing oppressive power relationships. As Pennycook (2001, p. 4) notes, "the most significant aspect of critical work is an engagement with the political critiques of social relations." For us, such knowledge should promote educational, social, and economic equity.

By equity, we do not mean equal conditions, but rather conditions that offer a diverse people equal opportunities for success, which includes an appreciation for diversity rather than a desire for uniformity. For example, in a classroom, if all students were taught in Farsi, the conditions would be equal for all. However, these conditions mean that students who speak Farsi will have a much greater opportunity for success than those who do not. Nor would such a classroom engender an appreciation for diversity in either the teachers or the students. Thus, although equal, the conditions would not be equitable.

Critical theories are theories that are developed and used to understand and investigate oppressive power relationships to help advance toward equity in all aspects of life. Currently, there are a variety of critical theories, ranging from Jürgen Habermas's *Knowledge and Human Interests* (1968), to Patricia Hill Collins's *Black Feminist Thought* (2002), to Dixson and Rousseau's *Critical Race Theory in Education* (2006), to Tuhiwai-Smith's *Decolonizing Methodologies: Research and Indigenous Peoples* (2012).

What these diverse critical scholars have in common is a critique of society or some aspect of society, with an effort to determine the following questions: Who is being oppressed? How are they being oppressed? What sorts of power relations reproduce that oppression? And how can that oppression be eliminated or at least ameliorated? Social justice is the praxis of bringing about greater social, political, and economic equity. Thus, we understand critical theories as the theoretical part of social justice praxis. However, the distinction between the two concepts may be more blurred than this simple categorization suggests; indeed, many scholars write about social justice theories—while others consider the development and dissemination of critical understandings as a form of praxis (e.g., Foucault, 1980a). These two terms coalesce in defining critical scholars. Critical scholars are those who use their critical understandings to teach and produce scholarship for social justice.

Clearly, critical scholarship and critical education (i.e., educating for social justice) are complementary aspects of one coherent effort to connect critical theories to the context in which one works—whether that work is teaching, researching, administering, or cooking. In making this connection, as a praxis of social justice, one can argue for and implement changes in institutional practices to bring about greater equity. Critical education attempts to build skills "for reflexive analysis of the educational process itself . . . [including] focus shifts from critique of existing practices to exploration and even advocacy of possible alternatives" (Fairclough, 1992, p. 221). Critical education, in other words, is a form of social justice praxis, as it consists of teaching people to understand and apply critical theories in their domains of practice. Such applications can be a tremendous force for transforming unequal power relations that privilege some while disadvantaging others. Thus, the concepts of critical theory and social justice are both integral to praxes for transforming our schools and society into more equitable ones.

Public schools are one of the few remaining public institutions that are charged with providing equal opportunities for students from different social spaces to develop into citizens with the knowledge and skills to effectively participate in a democratic society. Accordingly, we do not seek to condemn public schools, but to improve them. Rather than seeking to eliminate or privatize them, we see them as integral to the development of an egalitarian society. If our schools are to help bring about a more egalitarian society, we must be able to identify the specific aspects of our educational systems that act to oppress and marginalize various groups. To identify these aspects, we must first understand how power operates on these various groups within schools, including higher education.

Power, Colonizing Forces, and Identity

Power is one of those diffuse concepts that everyone uses and seems to vaguely understand, but for which there is no one, clear, agreed-on definition. We provide a working description, which we use in our introduction and in the summative chapter. However, a wonderful caveat is that our conception of power is deepened by the critical autoethnographies written by the variety of authors in this book. Foucault's explicit analyses of power[3] are found in *Discipline and Punish* (1977), *Power/Knowledge: Selected Interviews and Other Writings* (1980a), and *The History of Sexuality: Volume I* (1980b). These provide a tool kit for analyzing the relationship between power embedded in and enacted through social practices and identities. For Foucault (1980a; 1980b), power is that which influences the actions of others and operates around conflicts or potential conflicts. Foucault (1980a; 1980b) claims that power operates through everyday social practices (e.g., pledging allegiance to the flag), which act on an individual even as the individual enacts those social practices; power relations are reproduced or challenged in these enactments.

In addition, power is diffuse rather than concentrated in one person or center: "Power is never localized here or there. . . . [Rather, it] is employed and exercised through a net-like organization" (Foucault, 1980a, p. 98). "One doesn't have here a power which is totally in the hands of one person who can exercise it alone and totally over the others. . . . [But] everyone doesn't occupy the same position: certain positions preponderate and permit an effect of supremacy to be produced" (Foucault, 1980a, p. 156). On this construction, power relations act to oppress some while elevating others to reap the benefit of those oppressed. However, according to Foucault (1980a; 1980b), wherever there is power there is resistance. In the interplay between power and resistance that people carve out and perform their identities (e.g., Butler, 2003). "[Individuals] are always in the position of simultaneously undergoing and exercising this power" (Foucault, 1980a, p. 98). In this book we focus on colonizing forces, which is power operating to shape people's identities into colonizer/colonized.

We examine this interplay of power in the development of critical scholar identities. However, this book is unique in that the owners of those identities individually describe and make meaning of their own identities and experiences related to those identities. Thus, the power relations involved with the developing epistemologies are more equal than in most collective case studies. Because the editors do not pick out which parts of the contributors' narratives to include, the focus of each case study is the author of the case studies. As such, the contributing authors have lengthy periods of reflection to determine not only the wording they wish to convey their experiences, but indeed which aspects of their experiences they deem appropriate to keep private (see, e.g., Giles in Chapter 4). At the same time, the contributors of this book are more vulnerable than typical participants of case studies in that their identities are not kept confidential but rather are put on display for all to see and judge.

Many contributing authors described the difficulty they experienced in writing their autoethnographies. As they described to us (the editors) in e-mails and in person, reliving and writing down these events in their lives was both painful and cathartic. However, many said that they had developed new critical understandings of themselves and society. Tuck and Yang (2013) note that much of the qualitative research on those in different social spaces simply produces pain narratives, which act to construct damaged identities. They encourage moving beyond such spectacle-based, victim-only type of representations to "speaking in a voice of resistance" (Tuck & Yang, 2013, p. 230). These narratives all move beyond pain to voices of resistance. All authors hoped that their stories would advance equity for the increasingly diverse students and teachers in public schools and higher education. The contributing authors hoped to advance social justice by helping those in educational institutions become more aware of the difficulties faced by diverse students and develop appropriate frames for understanding their experiences and making educational decisions. Critical autoethnographies help develop these understandings of and practices in educational and social systems by drawing from the experiences and perspectives of those who traditionally have been silenced, excluded, and/or marginalized in the production and dissemination of knowledge about how people in different spaces experience our schools and society.

The Goals of Critical Autoethnographies

Autoethnographies as emerging qualitative methodologies provide for non-traditional ways of knowing. As it is an emerging field, its exact parameters are also widely contested. Denzin (2006) lists six different definitions of autoethnography. We embrace this same notion of multiplicity, but if we had to give a single definition to autoethnography it would be Stacy Holman Jones's (2005):

> Autoethnography is a blurred genre . . . a response to the call . . . it is setting a scene, telling a story, weaving intricate connections between life and art . . . making a text present . . . refusing categorization . . . believing that words matter and writing toward the moment when the point of creating autoethnographic texts is to change the world. (765)

Likewise, critical autoethnography is neither monolithic nor monolingual. Humans are complex beings and have multiple identities and realities. Adams and Jones (2011) demonstrate this well, as they bring autoethnography to Queer Theory. In their articulation of these bodies merging, they write, "[t]aking seriously autoethnography's and queer theory's commitment to uncertain, fluid, and becoming subjectivities, multiple forms of knowledge and representations, and research as an agent of change, we write a series of reflexively queer personal texts" (p. 108). Yet their work indicates—and this book confirms—that autoethnography can be merged with other critical frameworks that respond to unique realities. Thus, a primary goal of the critical autoethnographies in this book is to change the world by helping to create greater equity.

Autoethnography, as a nontraditional way of knowing, allows us to represent knowledge outside a traditional European framework that positions social change and progress in a linear fashion, from point A to point B. Most of our knowledge, methodologies for producing knowledge, and practices associated with the dissemination of knowledge have been constrained by traditions developed by upper middle-class White men. Thus, the knowledge produced under those traditional constraints necessarily follows White middle-class male norms. A rhizome approach, adapted from the work of Deleuze and Guattari (1984, 1987), understands the emergence and existence of knowledge as expanding in multiple directions of a given historical social system, weaving through various forms of knowledge, experiences, and subjectivities of a society. Although each of these autoethnographies is necessarily unique—as they are written by authors in different social spaces, focusing on different aspects of educational and social processes—they are at the same time related through rhizomatic sensitivity. Autoethnographies express rhizomatic sensitivity because stories find each other in some way, bringing together a wide diversity of voices, perspectives, and subjectivities that provide alternatives to the traditional essentialized identities many of us have been coerced into assuming during the current neoliberal period of late capitalism.

Through this autoethnographic project, our counter-stories come together in a rhizomatic fashion and are linked by key experiences that share similarities, dancing across ethnic, racial, gender, and economic class realities. Critical autoethnographies capitalize on autoethnography's promise of developing social theories in directions delegitimized by traditional research methods, but they do so critically. That is, the direction of the development is aimed toward the eradication of colonizing power relations and the pain brought on by those forces (see Pennycook, 2001).

Overview of the Book

The rest of the book is divided into five sections. The middle three sections are composed of the 11 autoethnographies. The authors include women and men who are African American and Black, Latino and Chicano, and European American; those from the middle, working and poverty classes; as well as those from a variety of religious faiths. The fourth remaining section of the book discusses the findings from our meta-analysis of the 11 autoethnographies as well as the theoretical implications of our meta-analysis. The professional biographies of the contributors make up the final section of the book.

The Autoethnographies in Sections II, III, and IV

While all 11 of the autoethnographic chapters focus on more than one aspect of the author's social locations, Section II primarily focuses on racism and Section III on sexism. The autoethnographies in Section IV focus on the intersections of multiple aspects of identity.

Section II consists of five critical race autoethnographies that use race as the primary focus of their analysis and critiques of their life experiences. These autoethnographies examine the authors' resistance to the oppressive colonizing forces that act on their identities. In Chapter 2, Michael E. Jennings, an African American male college professor who works at a large, research-oriented university, analyzes his early childhood experiences. In Chapter 3, Nosakhere Griffin-EL adds to the discourse on the contradictory lives of Black students within predominately White educational spaces. In Chapter 4, Mark Giles makes meaning of his academic experiences through the specific life events, cultural identity, and cultural relevance of a Black man teaching in higher education settings. In Chapter 5, Drs. Brenda G. Juárez and Cleveland Hayes analyze the importance of race in their respective stories of becoming critical educators. In Chapter 6, Joy Howard deconstructs how she, as a White woman, was shaped by racist colorblind discourse.

The two chapters of Section III examine the oppressive colonizing forces that act around gender. Although the authors examine women's situations in different countries (Kenya and the United States), they both come from singularly patriarchal cultures. Felecia M. Briscoe traces the conflicting truths about women that she learned in school/society and at home in a polygamous community. Damaris Choti describes an oppressive situation that surrounds the lives of girls and women in most societies in the world.

Section IV contains four autoethnographies that have more than one primary focus. In the first one, Dr. de la Portilla describes the complexities of her intersecting Chicana and working-class identity dimensions: how her earlier family experiences provided her with an understanding of the oppression she experienced in her doctoral program, as well as methods of resistance. Dr. Khalifa then explains the particular types of oppression he experienced as a Black man and his resistance to the identities ascribed to him. Subsequently, Drs. El-Amin, Henry, and Laura focus specifically on the hyphens that make up their intersecting identities and how many of the important dimensions of their identities were simply ignored, especially as a focus for research. Finally, Dr. de Oliver describes how the different dimensions of his identity became salient depending on the space he occupied and how even his identity as a professor was morphing as the university became increasingly neoliberal.

Concluding Chapters

Chapter 13 presents patterns and divergences found in the autoethnographies and the implications of these patterns. Chapter 14 presents advancements in critical social theory by examining the implications of these patterns and divergences and a model of the development of criticality suggested by the collective case study of these autoethnographies. Our book advances critical theory by presenting our understanding of the way the processes of schooling and society affect people from different social spaces. We also hope that it is an interesting and informative read for those who are not scholars, but who may have lived in spaces that isolate them from the lived reality of many.

SECTION II

Critical Race Autoethnographic Case Studies

Autoethnography and Critical Race Theory

.•——•.

Muhammad A. Khalifa

Understanding race and racial oppression in the United States has always been complex. This is true because racial oppression has taken so many forms, and shapes across the multiple eras in U.S. history. Though the geno-cide of indigenous peoples and the brutal enslavement of Africans in the Trans-Atlantic slave trade were never truly remedied, there at least were some ostensible constitutional and legal advances that broadened opportuni-ties for minority people. Yet even after genocide and slavery, scholars have studied the racially oppressive histories of illegal re-enslavement and lynch-ing, Jim Crow policy and practice, redlining and racial housing covenants, urban disinvestment and deindustrialization followed by racialized gentrifica-tion, Hoover's racially targeted COINTELPRO, mass incarceration, and now the disproportionality of school discipline resulting in the school-to-prison pipeline. These historical narratives are all a part of the exact same story, only with revised markings; they all complicate and complexitize narratives of racial harmony and progress so popular in the American imagination. The autoethnographies in this section all push narratives of race and racialized experiences in their personal and professional lives. Like the authors, we see a thorough understanding and usage of Critical Race Theory (CRT) as paramount to the ethnographies in this section.

Perhaps the biggest benefit of using CRT is the acceptance of racism as normality. According to Crenshaw (1995), "critical race theory embrac-es a movement of left scholars—mostly scholars of color situated in law schools—whose works challenged the ways in which race and racial power are constructed and represented in America legal culture and more generally in American Society as a whole" (p. xiii). Other scholars have pointed out that racism is endemic in everything from the macro systemic structures that disparately confer privileges to Whites while denying them to minoritized peoples down to the everyday microaggressions in the workplaces and personal spaces (Bell, 1995; Crenshaw, 1995; Delgado & Stefanic, 2012).

This normality of racism has profound and deep implications for life in the United States; because it is so pervasive, it becomes routine and eventually invisiblized. This causes people to take a colorblind (Bonilla-Silva, 2013) posture toward policies and practices that have been highly shaped by racial oppression. In this section, we analyze experiences in our lives using CRT to critique our encounters with racism, whether victims or unaware perpetrators of it. CRT historicizes the forgotten and racializes the invisible in ways that arrest colorblind ideology. These collective auto-ethnographies offer a clearer understanding of how racism evokes and leads to criticality. After our acknowledgements and encounters with racism, we began to resist in our own unique ways. In outgrowths of CRT, the collective ethnographies in this section rupture and upend White supremacy and privilege. The authors ask questions such as "When is it appropriate to challenge or confirm our own marginalization under the White gazes?" "How do I navigate White expectations of me along with my commitments to my community?" "How has colorblindness impacted my life and those whom I serve?" With the knowledge history that within the past 30 years, these regimes of racism have morphed into yet other new—and likely more sophisticated and inconspicuous—form, these scholars use their experiences and CRT to identify, situate, contest, and resist racial oppression. Following are brief descriptions of the chapters in Section II, as written by their authors.

In Chapter 2, Michael E. Jennings, an African-American male college professor who works at a large, research-oriented university, analyzes his early experiences. Specifically, his individual narrative challenges the master narrative that: a) early educational experiences are "race neutral"; and conversely b) posits that African-American males in the U.S. educational system confront racial bias and inequality while navigating the terrain of early childhood education and the primary grades (pre-K through third grade). His narrative forms a counter-story to these beliefs and uses CRT to analyze the role of race in one individual's early schooling experience within the context of the U.S. private educational system.

In Chapter 3, Nosakhere Griffin-EL adds to the discourse on the contradictory lives of Black students within predominately White educational spaces. Understanding these contradictions creates the possibility of moving beyond them by using the powerful tool of love. He uses the *Chappellian Contradiction* to understand the phenomenon of Black students *keeping it real*. Keeping it real is when a Black person resists an oppressive situation by saying what is on his or her mind regardless of the consequence. Conversely, not keeping it real is when a Black person fails to address an oppressive situation out of fear of negative consequences. Dr. Griffen-EL analyze two oppressive educational experiences he had as a graduate student that led to his becoming the critical scholar he is today—one who keeps it real in a loving way.

In Chapter 4, Mark Giles makes meaning of his academic experiences through his specific life events, cultural identity, and the cultural relevance of a Black man teaching in higher education settings. Dr. Giles theorizes the dynamics of educational access, opportunity, worthiness, and privilege and suggests a discourse on navigating racialized educational environments. He shares personalized ways of living and being in academic spaces with critical consciousness that challenge master narratives of academe. His development as a critical scholar is imbued with his attempt to bring his whole, Black, blue-collar self into these academic spaces.

In Chapter 5, Drs. Brenda G. Juárez and Cleveland Hayes present and analyze their respective stories of becoming critical educators. They examine their personal and professional experiences, investigating the ways that White racial domination within U.S. teacher education has structured their professional identities and opportunities. Tracking the points of inter-section between the historical privileging of Whites' collective interests and their daily work as teacher educators, the authors highlight representative moments in their struggles against Whiteness to illustrate how their respec-tive physical and symbolic removal and silencing are institutionally autho-rized and enacted as part of the maintenance of White supremacy.

In Chapter 6, Joy Howard examines colorblind Discourse/discourse. Her analytical framework incorporates Critical Race Theory, critical geog-raphy, and feminist standpoint theory. She conducts a narrative and poetic analysis of her formative and transformative experiences with colorblind D/discourse, using 12 years of written data. From her analysis, *Unbecom-ing . . .* emerges as a representation of her socially informed self-identifi-cation and rejection of colorblindness. Dr. Howard develops a model and tools for conducting critical autoethnographic research. Finally, she presents lessons learned by applying her experiential learning to her work as a teacher with regard to teaching racial literacy.

CHAPTER TWO

Auditioning for Whiteness

.•+————+•.

Autoethnography and Critical Race Theory in the
Early Schooling Experiences of an African-American Man

MICHAEL E. JENNINGS

Carla, a three-year-old child, is preparing herself for resting time. She
picks up her cot and starts to move it to the other side of the classroom.
A teacher asks what she is doing. "I need to move this," explains Carla.
"Why?" asks the teacher. "Because I can't sleep next to a nigger," Carla
says, pointing to Nicole, a four-year-old Black child on a cot nearby.
"Niggers are stinky. I can't sleep next to one." Stunned, the teacher,
who is White, tells Carla to move her cot back and not to use "hurting
words." Carla looks amused but complies.

—Van Ausdale and Feagin, 2001, p. 1

Although it has become fashionable in some circles to discuss the decline of
race and the subsequent rise of a "post-racial" society, racism still maintains
its place as a central facet in the education of African-Americans (Howard
& Flennaugh, 2011). This autoethnography explores the power of race in
the early schooling experiences of one individual. Autoethnography is utilized because of its potential for connecting personal narrative with issues of
race, power, identity, and the sociopolitical meanings that undergird these
constructs. Additionally, autoethnography has the ability to offer a robust
critique of society from the margins, something that is often difficult to
achieve for marginalized peoples who seek access to discourses of power.
For this reason, autoethnography (like memoir) may be the "ultimate multicultural act" (Adiele, 2010).

This chapter begins with an examination of Critical Race Theory (CRT), the theoretical lens that frames the autoethnography that is presented. Next is a discussion delineating autoethnography as a form of counter-story that challenges established master narratives about African-American male students. Following this is a discussion of early childhood education and its development as a social construct. Next is the presentation of an autoethnographic section that explores my experiences as an early childhood student in an urban-based Catholic school. Following this, I examine early childhood education and its development as a social construct. Next, I explore my experiences as an early childhood student in an urban-based Catholic school. A concluding section discusses the autoethnography that has been presented and its connections to larger constructs of race, identity, and education in American society.

Critical Race Theory as Theoretical Lens

In this autoethnography, I utilize CRT as my primary theoretical lens. CRT has evolved as an important construct in the study of education because of its strong focus on "centering" the concept of race in education in a sociocultural context that challenges dominant discourses (Ladson-Billings, 2005). Additionally, CRT has become an important component of the critical analysis of race in education because of its development and use of critical research methodologies. These methodologies are of primary importance because they challenge mainstream ideas regarding the "subjectivity vs. objectivity" binary that structures a great deal of educational research (Bernal, 2002; Parker & Lynn, 2002).

In the mid-1990s, educational researchers began making extensive use of CRT in their analysis of the American educational system (Dixson, 2006; Ladson-Billings & Tate, 1995). Since that time, scholars in education have worked to explore the theoretical and methodological significance of CRT and its role in, as well as its links to, educational theory and practice. Lynn & Parker (2006) asserted that, historically, CRT scholars (and those who preceded them) have established four key features of CRT about the basic nature of race in society.

First, CRT sees racism as being pervasive in the United States and representing "a normal fact of daily life in U.S. society" (Taylor, 2009, p. 5). Racism threads through the ideologies and assumptions of White supremacy, ingrained in the political, legal, and educational structures in ways that make them almost unrecognizable (Delgado, 1995, as cited in Taylor, 2009). Second, while the structure of White supremacy has a profound effect on the world, representing an "all-encompassing and omnipresent" (p. 4) system of privilege, power, and opportunities, it is generally invisible to its own beneficiaries (Taylor, 2009). Third, CRT strongly critiques liberalism as an ideology, questioning its ability to support the development of a just and equal society. CRT offers a sustained critique of traditional government institutions' ability and will to create an equitable and just society. CRT scholars are skeptical that the current paradigms utilized by government institutions can be catalysts for social change given their ingrained emphasis on incrementalism (Ladson-Billings, 1999). CRT adherents argue that government institutions such as courts and schools **do not** function as "neutral" entities in a society where constructs like race, class, gender, and sexual orientation remain powerful paradigms for oppression (Marx, 2008). Fourth, oppositional scholarship is a desirable outcome of CRT research and teaching. CRT challenges traditional notions of scholarly objectivity by promoting a radical scholarship that goes beyond the experience of Whites as the normative standard. Instead, it grounds its conceptual framework in the distinctive historical context that places an emphasis on the experiences of people of color (Taylor, 1998). CRT researchers and scholars often use "nontraditional" methods of research, such as narrative, storytelling, and autoethnography, to challenge existing constructions of race (Ladson-Billings, 1999).

Narrative as Counter-Story

Thus, central to CRT is the use of narrative and storytelling to challenge prevailing ideas and assumptions by "telling the stories of those people whose experiences are often not told" (Solorzano & Yosso, 2002). These stories represent an important "counter-narrative" that challenges racist ideology that creates, maintains, and justifies oppressive master narratives (Solorzano & Yosso, 2002). Given that the concept of race is a central focus in the dilemma facing African-American males, it is necessary to utilize a theoretical lens and methodology that has the ability to develop a counter-narrative that fully comprehends this dilemma and helps to advance a viable solution.

Autobiography has always been a major component of the literature created by African-Americans since at least the late eighteenth century (Fisch, 2007; Franklin, 1995; Stepto, 1991). African-Americans have been relegated to "the margins" of society but at the same time allowed limited access to society's "mainstream" workings. This phenomenon has created an "outsider/insider" paradox (Collins, 1991) that has forced people of color to become "subdued ethnographers." That is, being a "subordinate other" in American society has placed people of color in the unique position of becoming "native" ethnographers who observe and analyze the cultural norms and behaviors of Whites as a means of survival. In reflecting upon our own experiences, communities of color have informally and formally codified this ethnographic experience in several ways. One of the most important is through the use of autoethnography. Autoethnography (like ethnography) considers the individual in relation to the entire environment, but places greater emphasis on considering the life experiences and thoughts of the observer as well.

Autoethnography is often codified in a written form that has been described/labeled as an autobiography. With this in mind, the terms *auto-ethnography* and *autobiography* are used interchangeably throughout this chapter. One reason that autobiography has occupied an important place in the African-American experience is its emphasis on the intersection of personal experience and collective identity. Thus, historian V. P. Franklin (1995) describes autobiography as the most important genre in the African-American intellectual tradition.

Today, as in the past, autobiography gives African-Americans a chance to challenge and resist the degradation of racism so prevalent in American society (Stover, 2005). The evolution of autoethnography and its connection to CRT provides an account of the evolving struggle between the "self" and society that permeates African-American existence. Thus, autoethnography and the experiences it explores are of prime importance to those researching the experiences of marginalized peoples in the American educational system.

Early Childhood Education and Whiteness

Early childhood education is difficult to define, because both nationally and internationally there are no agreed-upon parameters regarding which age limits and terminology should define it (Turja, Endepohls-Ulpe, & Chatoney, 2009). Furthermore, existing definitions of early childhood are fluid in nature and have evolved within a variety of cultural and historical contexts (Chamboredon & Prevot, 1975; Kamerman, 2006). My autoethnography is reflective of a U.S. context. Thus, I am using the definition set forth by the National Association for the Education of Young Children (NAEYC). The NAEYC describes itself as "the world's largest organization working on behalf of young children" and has defined early childhood as being birth through age eight (NAEYC, 2009).

Mintz (2004) asserts that childhood is "not an unchanging biological stage of life but is, rather, a social and cultural construct that has changed radically over time" (p. viii). Anthropologist Sharon Stephens (1995) likens the social construction of childhood to the discourses created around race, class, or gender. Her research on the concept of childhood led her to conclude that the hierarchal relations created by the rigid dichotomy between children and adults, like other binaries in Western society, have helped to support the establishment of modern capitalism (as cited in Shepler, 2003). As the concept of early childhood education has expanded and evolved over the past 20 years, it has become integrated into the growing neoliberal discourse that has come to define U.S. education (Dahlberg & Moss, 2005). This discourse promotes the institutionalization of childhood and what Dahlberg and Moss (2005) refer to as an increased concern for the "effective governing of children" (p. vi). They further assert that neoliberalism's quest to increase the governing of young bodies is not new, but reflects an ever more efficient "regime of truth about early childhood education and care as a technology for ensuring social regulation and economic success, in which the young child is constructed as a redemptive agent who can be programmed to become the future solution to our current problems" (Dalhberg & Moss, 2005, p. 7). This concept of child as redemptive agent is especially important for the few African-American children who are granted access to elite educational programs and institutions. This access links the next generation of African-American students with the present reality of racial oppression and the future reality of a U.S. society in which Black and brown people will emerge as the majority. The neoliberal desire for ever more control of the young child lies in the power of early childhood education to strongly influence the programming of their "racial self." This desire to shape the racial self reflects neoliberal capitalism's efforts to maintain hegemonic structures in society by cultivating a group of schooled individuals of color who perpetuate the status quo while being touted as good examples of a meritocratic system.

Contrary to the "popular" belief held by many teachers, young children are quite aware of racial constructs (Van Ausdale & Feagin, 2001). As far back as the 1930s, academic research has examined the racial awareness of children in early childhood settings (Horowitz, 1938). Teitler (2008), after 70 years of research on racial perceptions of young children, has concluded that White children have a tendency to favor other Whites while harboring bias toward African-Americans, whereas African-American students tended to favor lighter skinned individuals and non–African-American individuals. Van Ausdale and Feagin's (2001) ethnographic research suggests that a hostile and discriminatory environment exists for children of color in early childhood institutional settings. They asserted:

> What is especially critical is the harm that accrues to children who are the targets of hostile comments, emotions, and discriminatory behavior. Racist behavior, intentional or not, usually causes harm to its target. Often the damage is not apparent immediately. The accumulation of damage over years of exposure to racial mistreatment will become more apparent as we investigate how racism has an impact on social relations in the lives of preschoolers. (p. 9)

Because early childhood institutional settings are locations for race discrimination, study is needed on how early childhood classrooms construct students of color as "others" (Earick, 2009; MacNaughton, David, & Smith, 2010). Connected to the construction of students of color as the other is the elevation of White students to a privileged position while simultaneously oppressing and devaluing students of color. In other words, it is "a system that bestows power and privilege on those who become identified as White and bestows disempowerment and disprivileges on those who become identified as People of Color" (Allen, 2002, p. xi).

Although issues of race, power, and privilege are endemic in U.S. education generally, and in early childhood education in particular, there has been little autoethnographic exploration of the experience of African-American students in early childhood settings. One of the obvious reasons for this is the issue of memory. In her discussion of autobiographical memory, Nelson (1993) examines memory in early childhood and describes these memories as often unreliable; however, she notes that memories associated with specific important events (moves, disruptions, trauma, etc.) can be more accurate. Furthermore, she explores the onset of these autobiographical memories in early childhood, describing them as the potential basis for one's personal life story (Nelson, 1993). With that in mind, the story that follows has come to frame much of the context of my life.

Pre-kindergarten and the Lasting Effects of a "Troublesome Word"

Some of my earliest memories as a child are related to school. I grew up in Philadelphia and attended both private and public schools. My mother did not feel that the local public elementary school would provide an adequate education, so she endeavored to send me to a private school to get me the "best" education possible. Paying for this education didn't come easy for my mother. She was divorced from my father and did not have a college degree or a full-time job until later in life. She relied on my paternal grandfather and grandmother to pay for my tuition. Thus, private school became possible for me despite coming from a family with a limited income.

Some of my earliest remembrances of schooling involved my family talking negatively about the local school system, while praising the education that I was getting in the private Catholic school that I attended. It didn't take long for me to learn the binary: public education in Philadelphia was equated with low performance and negativity, while private schools, run mostly by religious organizations, were equated with academic excellence and superior facilities. This segregation of schooling (public vs. private) also reflected the larger discourse on race and class in the city. This discourse reflected notions of racialized urban space that located my school in a traditionally wealthy section of the city known for its exclusivity, which stood in stark contrast to the African-American working-class community that I called home. The area around my school was seen as "clean," "safe," "beautiful," and a generally wonderful place to live and raise a family. By contrast, the area that I lived in was seen as "gritty," "unsafe," less than desirable, and overly crowded. In short, although my school was only about a 15-minute drive from the working-class Black neighborhood that I grew up in, it might as well have been 100 miles away. This reflected the heavy racial and economic segregation that still continues in the city of Philadelphia.

Unlike most Catholic schools in Philadelphia, the one I attended was not a part of a particular Catholic parish (i.e., church) and therefore was not overseen by the Archdiocese of Philadelphia. Schools run by the Archdiocese (at least those located inside the city limits) tended to have strong connections to the working class. My school was different. It was run by an order of Catholic nuns called the Sisters of St. Joseph. The school itself was far more expensive than the local parish school and served mostly White, upper middle-class Catholic families who lived in upscale suburban areas around Philadelphia. These patterns of schooling not only reinforced existing patterns of racial segregation but also reflected existing patterns of economic stratification that separated working-class Whites from their middle- and upper-class counterparts in the city.

I entered the school's Montessori preschool program in the early 1970s and graduated eighth grade at the age of fourteen in 1984. Despite the differences in my background, my memories of those early years of schooling were mostly positive. I liked my teachers, and I had several friends whom I played with regularly. However, I remember one particular instance that I can't easily forget that occurred when I was in pre-kindergarten. Although I don't recall all of the circumstances surrounding the event, I do remember the outcome: one of my classmates called me a "nigger." Although I was very young, I already knew that this was considered the ultimate insult for a Black person to endure. Hearing that word upset me deeply, and I told my mother about it soon after. As Van Ausdale & Feagin (2001) indicated, for better or worse, my experiences with race as a young child had provided me with insight into the White supremacist context of early childhood education.

My understanding of the demeaning slur directed at me was shaped not only by my experience of its use by Whites, but also by my observation of its use in the African-American community. I had heard this same word used several times by African-Americans in a different, yet still negative context. In this particular context, I remember the word being used as a marker to distinguish one's self as an African-American from "other" African-Americans who were identified as embodying behaviors and attitudes that were seen as an embarrassment to the larger African-American community. The commonality of both uses of this word was uniformly negative. Not only did I feel demeaned when the little boy in my class referred to me as a "nigger," but I also knew that I was now publicly marked as an outsider: as an "other" among my classmates and possibly in my own community.

I told my mother about being referred to as a nigger, and she was understandably upset. She immediately requested a meeting with the principal and explained to her the gravity of the situation. The principal promised to talk to the boy's parents. I don't remember if there were any immediate repercussions, but I do know that the boy did not return to the school the next year. Although his absence was a blessing, my racial innocence was lost.

This "troublesome word" (Kennedy, 2002) thus became important as a marker of difference or disdain by the White community, but also as a demarcation within my own community that highlighted "good" African-Americans and separated them from other African-Americans who were deemed to be "bad." The next several years of my life were very happy in many ways. However, this time period was one of confusion regarding my own identity and my place in a world where Whiteness was valued and Blackness was degraded. It was a world that I could never fully escape, no matter how much I tried.

One of the ways in which this degradation manifested itself was in the curriculum of the school. In some ways, a more accurate assessment would point toward what the school failed to teach in its curriculum. The "null curriculum" (Flinders, Noddings, & Thornton, 1986) of the school excluded regular discussions of African-American history and literature. These forms of history and literature only made brief appearances during "Black History Month" each year. Furthermore, our study of these subjects rarely went beyond typically bland rehashing of select portions of speeches given by Martin Luther King Jr. or listening to West African folktales. McCarthy (1988) describes this type of multiculturalism as a sort "benign pluralism" that does little to illuminate or challenge systemic issues of inequality. Instead, attempts at multiculturalism in my school seemed to exist in order to make White teachers and students feel good about the "differences" that existed at the school. For the few African-American students, the limited expression of multiculturalism offered in the school amounted to a form of social control that advocated cultural understanding and empathy while ignoring the politics of race and domination (Olneck, 1990). This type of multiculturalism, rather than helping to eradicate racism, sought to minimize the existence of racism by defining its existence as an unstructured set of individual acts of racial prejudice. This effectively ignored larger constructs of White supremacy and hegemony while rendering racism as an invisible entity that barely exists in a meritocratic society (McLaren, 1997).

Acting White: Prelude to an Audition

One of the most prolific proponents of the deficit perspective that character-izes research on African-American students was John Ogbu, a now deceased anthropologist from the University of California, Berkeley. Ogbu (2004) essentially argues that African-Americans hold negative views of schooling and the ability of schooling to enhance opportunity. Specifically, this ideol-ogy asserts that African-Americans do not believe that the racial barriers to success that they face in society can be overcome through sustained aca-demic achievement (Carter, 2008). Ogbu (2004) argued that in the face of oppression, rather than working toward academic success, African-American students developed an "oppositional collective identity" (p. 174) that chal-lenged "perceived" racism in the language and curriculum of the school.

Fordham & Ogbu (1986) extend this thesis further by discussing the phenomenon of "acting White" as a variable in their discussion of academic disengagement among Black students. Their research has been used to theo-rize that African-American students often disengage from behaviors leading to academic achievement because such behaviors are viewed by their Afri-can-American peers as "acting White" (Tyson, Darity, & Castilleno, 2005).

My own experience as a student in early childhood settings reflects some of the conclusions that have appeared in Fordham's work (Fordham, 1991; Fordham & Ogbu, 1986). As a young elementary school student, I sought to cope with the racism I experienced in school by adopting a persona that can best be described as an attempt at racelessness. I did this because I realized early on that being Black meant being different and being "less than" those who structured and dominated the school culture that I was immersed in. In short, I recognized that there were tangible rewards to affiliating with Whiteness, and I wanted to find a way to access those benefits just like my peers. This attempt seemed to work well during my early years in school. I managed to maintain excellent grades, and I seemed to be well liked by most of my classmates. Despite this, I still had a gnaw-ing feeling that I just didn't "fit in" with the rest of my classmates. Perhaps more importantly, I noticed that I no longer seemed to fit in with the other kids in my neighborhood.

As I matriculated through my primary grade years, I realized that I was moving further and further away from my neighborhood peers. Formerly I had felt a strong kinship with the other kids in my neighborhood and with the neighborhood itself. I regularly took to the streets to run and play with the other kids my age and participated in all the typical activities for boys my age. However, there were some differences. I was never very athletic, and I seemed to get picked less and less for the various teams that formed in the neighborhood to play athletically oriented games and sports. Also, I noticed that my speech pattern was different from the rest of my neighbor-hood peers. While growing up, my parents had emphasized the importance of what I now call "Standard American English." At the time, my parents referred to this pattern of speaking as simply "proper" or "correct" English. I don't remember them telling me at that age why it was important to speak a certain way, but I know that it was important to them. Looking back, I realize that they wanted me to have access to a specific form of cultural capital that would allow me to understand and access the "codes of power" (Delpit, 1988) necessary to successfully navigate my school environment. Using this form of English separated me from my peers and signaled that I was different. Looking back, I find myself thinking of this issue as a form of cultural loss. However, I also have to consider if I could have actually "lost" a linguistic code that I may have never truly possessed in the first place. In either case, I believe that linguist Joshua Fishman (1996) appropriately contextualizes these types of experiences with language when he asks the question: "What do you lose when you lose your language? [You pay] the price for it one way or another" (quoted in Dowdy, 2002, p. 1).

Conclusion—Auditioning for Whiteness

In many ways, the price I paid was a steep one. It is true that I have earned valuable credentials through my success in the American schooling process. This success has given me a certain legitimacy in American society and helped me to enter the ranks of the American upper middle class. How-ever, the price that I've paid has been my constant struggle to maintain a sense of self as a person of color in a world that requires me to expertly navigate White spaces while simultaneously negating the legitimacy of my own culture, history, and identity as a person of color.

To help reconcile this tension, I've struggled with various theoretical concepts that would help me to explain this struggle. Many of these con-cepts, such as the DuBois notion of double consciousness (DuBois, 1903), have been helpful in terms of analyzing my experiences within the context of broader social phenomena. However, especially helpful for me in under-standing and analyzing my experiences in early childhood education is a notion that I name "auditioning for Whiteness." My idea comes at least partially from the work of CRT scholar John O. Calmore (2005). Calmore (2005) discusses "Whiteness as audition and Blackness as performance" (p. 99) within the context of CRT and its analysis of the historical importance of Whiteness. Utilizing elements of Calmore's (2005) research, I have fash-ioned an academic metaphor that combines Black performance with the authoritarian gaze of Whiteness in education to coin the term, "auditioning for Whiteness."

In the last part of the nineteenth century and the first half of the twentieth, immigrants to the United States had to prove their Whiteness as a prerequisite for obtaining citizenship. This led to the idea that immigrants had to demonstrate or "audition" for a chance to participate in Whiteness as a form of privilege that had emerged in American jurisprudence as a legal prerequisite for citizenship. In discussing the importance or race in American life, Calmore (2005) relies on the work of Charles Mills (1997), whose writings on the "racial contract" emphasize the primacy of structural racism and its integral role in the development of Western society. Calmore (2005) discusses the continuing importance of this concept by stating that "under these circumstances . . . White performance was the quid pro quo for White privilege. Today, this is still largely the *quid* pro quo, but this is a bad bargain for people of color" (p. 102). This type of bargain was implicitly made available to me as part of my audition for Whiteness, starting at the very beginning of my formal education. Given that early childhood education is often the first contact that students have with the formalized educational system, it has the power to make a powerful first impression on students.

However, early childhood students also have an opportunity to make a clear impression on the system by challenging the status quo. Unfortunately, these challenges to the status quo may manifest themselves in ways that are subject to serious disciplinary penalties by school officials (Gilliam, 2005). As the first formalized contact with schools, elite early childhood programs thus represent a sort of first level training ground for those who will eventually access the highest levels of formal education and power in the American educational system. Participation in elite early childhood programs for people of color is rare given the racial and economic realities of American society. Furthermore, those few people of color who participate in such programs are implicitly being trained and monitored as part of an implicit audition for Whiteness. Those who do not appear able or willing to accept the bargain offered by the White terrain are eventually identified and targeted for marginalization. Those who succeed at the audition receive tangible benefits (e.g., academic credentials) and the ability to access social and cultural capital that is highly valued and therefore financially rewarded in capitalist societies. However, as seen in my own case and as Calmore (2005) points out, this bargain is very problematic for people of color.

For me, the tangible benefits received from my success in early childhood educational settings represent a sort of Faustian bargain. In this bargain, I benefited greatly from an enormous amount of cultural capital that came following my success as a student in an early childhood setting. Lareau (2000) and Ciabattari (2010) engage the notion of cultural capital in schools and refer to this type of cultural capital as the "cultural knowledge and social networks" (p. 1) used by middle- and upper-income parents to help improve the educational experiences of their own children. Although I benefited from acquiring this cultural capital, I lost something in the bargain as well: I became culturally alienated from my community and a strong supporter of the status quo. By my community, I refer both to the Black neighborhood of my youth and the academic community that I entered in my youth and adulthood. In using the term *cultural alienation*, I am referring to what Miller et al. (2009) have defined as "a person's rejection or sense of dissociation and detachment from prevailing social norms and values" (p. 4). The key word in this definition is the term *prevailing*. Within the early childhood program where I matriculated, the prevailing social norms and values reflected those of the White middle- and upper-class teachers and students who dominated the school. However, at home and in my community, a working-class/lower middle-class African-American culture prevailed. Although the distance between these cultures was dynamic and fluid, it was clear in school that my community culture was not the "norm."

In analyzing my experiences as a student during my early childhood education, it became clear to me that issues of race, identity, and power played a major role in how I experienced and understood the concept of schooling. Employing the lens of CRT, I view the structures of early childhood education as reflecting the dominance of White supremacy. As previously described, this White supremacy was reflected in the economic barriers to the school, the curriculum, and so on. When White supremacy is publicly identified as a component of the educational system, it is frequently met with a forceful reaction often based on anger, denial, and blame. To counter critical examinations of the ways in which power, privilege, and race have negatively affected African-American education, prominent public figures from the Black community are often given broad media attention for their willingness to discuss problematic issues around African-American educational attainment as the inevitable outgrowths of cultural deficiencies that are seen as rampant in the African-American community (Cosby, 2007). Reactions such as these reflect the all-consuming and ever present hegemonic system of privilege and power that works against African-Americans while simultaneously benefiting Whites (Taylor, 2009).

My own experiences reflect the reality that even when African-American men gain access to the privileged world of elite private schooling, they are still negatively affected by racism. At these types of institutions, students of color face White supremacy in unique and intimate ways that provide outstanding school credentials and skills while isolating them and attacking their self-esteem and sense of identity (Fordham, 1991; Perry, 1988). With this in mind, it is difficult to believe that educational institutions (public or private) will ever be able to play a major role in the creation of a just and equitable society. This pessimism is based on the fact that these institutions are strongly ingrained in incrementalism and face little serious pressure to make sweeping changes that would benefit people of color and poor Whites. In fact, it can be argued that social justice was never the intent of these institutions, but rather their primary purpose and effect has been to create and maintain paradigms of oppression such as race, class, gender, and sexual orientation by supporting and extending the existing institutional arrangements (Marx, 2008; Spring, 2010).

Given these realities, this autoethnographic chapter represents a counter-narrative to the story that society and schools tell about African-Americans. The stories commonly communicated about African-American students reflect a master narrative that portrays these students as lazy, incompetent, and anti-intellectual individuals who care little about education (Cokely, 2003). On the contrary, my own narrative regarding my experiences in early childhood education (and beyond) reflect the experience of an African-American student who cultivated an intense intellectual curiosity and a readiness to participate in the hard work that comes with pursing the "life of the mind." Thus, my counter-narrative resists the master narratives about African-Americans in education in two ways: by countering the academic identity constructed for African-Americans and by countering the image of U.S. schooling as universally beneficial or even neutral with regard to all racialized groups. Critical race autoethnographies highlight the struggles against racism by individual African-Americans who both embody and challenge the educational status quo in multiple and complex ways. The construction of such counter-narratives is important because it exposes the dominant story and suggests how things might be different (Harris, Carney, & Fine, 2001) while simultaneously representing what Bamberg (2004) describes as "the flip side of being complicit" (p. 351).

CHAPTER THREE

To Keep It Real or Not to Keep It Real

.•———•.

The Dialectics of the Chapellian Contradiction

NOSAKHERE GRIFFIN-EL

In the early 2000s, Comedy Central aired a variety show named after contro-versial Black comedian David Chappelle, which featured satirical skits that sought to promote dialogue on race relations in America. *Chappelle's Show* aired a skit titled "When Keeping It Real Goes Wrong," which addressed the dialectical dilemma African Americans face when oppressed within White-dominated educational spaces. White-dominated educational spaces refers to learning environments that implicitly or explicitly uphold Eurocentric thought and practice as the standard of being. For Chappelle, *keeping it real* meant reacting out of anger to racially insensitive comments (within the White-dominated educational spaces) made by White classmates, which result in Blacks being severely penalized by their employers and/or teachers. Chappelle offered two options for African Americans to learn how to keep it real: "pick your spots" or learn how to act phony. Thus, the *Chappellian Contradiction* seeks to understand whether Black people in White-dominated spaces will live as subjects, who confront oppressive actions regardless of the consequences, or as objects, who adapt to and accept oppressive action out of fear of the consequences.

The "When Keeping It Real Goes Wrong" skit starts with the nar-rator giving a biography of a successful Black businessman named Vernon Franklin. Franklin's life began in a poverty-stricken community where many members of his family and community were addicted to drugs. In spite of societal ills that plagued his family and community, Franklin focused on education and eventually became the first person in his family to go to college. During his graduation, he was honored as valedictorian of his class.

37

After college, Franklin got a job in corporate America, where he continued life as an overachiever. Consequently, he was named vice president of the company. Although Franklin was a successful businessman, he struggled with life within this White-dominated space.

One day, as a meeting was concluding, an incident between Franklin and his boss occurred that changed Franklin's life forever. Franklin's boss congratulated him on a job well done by saying, "Give me some skin, huh?" Franklin deemed this comment culturally insensitive and had to choose to confront (keep it real) or not to confront his boss (not keep it real). The confrontation between the two went as follows:

> VERNON FRANKLIN: Get your motherfuckin' hands out my face. You heard me motherfucker get your hands out of my face. What you think this is, shake my hand like a man. I gotta give you some five on the Black hand side . . . crazy jive, that's bullshit. . . .

> VERNON FRANKLIN'S BOSS: This is not the Vernon I know.

> VERNON FRANKLIN: Allow me to reintroduce myself—my name is Hov (Chappelle, Breanan, and Armour, 2004)!

Franklin's verbally violent confrontation got him fired from his job. Subsequently, he sought and found a new job at a gas station. It is important to note that Chappelle's skit is an extreme reaction to a racially insensitive comment within White-dominated spaces, but the consequence that Franklin faced for keeping it real is an authentic fear of African Americans. Chappelle's skit offers an important concept to Black-led confrontation within White-dominated spaces—how to keep it real.

Problem Statement

When oppressed by Whites, Black students have to decide to either confront or not confront. These two options force Black students to decide to either adapt to oppression or to become an agent of change who struggles to eradicate it. The fear of keeping it real *for* Black students with whom I went to school was that confronting the perpetrators of oppression could result in undesired social and/or academic consequences, such as immediate or eventual dismissal from their educational institution. Thus, keeping it real was not a popular decision for me or the Black students with whom I went to graduate school. Instead, many of us opted not to keep it real, which meant adapting to the culture of educational oppression. As a graduate student, I frequently had choose whether to keep it real, which meant confronting individuals or people who oppressed me or created an oppressive classroom environment, or not keep it real, which meant internalizing anger and adapting to the culture of oppression. Throughout my graduate experience, I engaged in the practice of not keeping it real because I feared academic and social consequences. Although not a consistent theme within my graduate experience, there were times when I chose to keep it real. This paper highlights two experiences when I chose to keep it real in individual and group settings. The intention of sharing these stories is to display the confrontation as a complex process that could contribute to the transformation of educational space by those who are victims and victimizers in systems of oppression. The two complex confrontational processes I analyze in this paper were pivotal in my development into the critical scholar that I am today.

Inquiry Questions

1. What is the process of keeping it real?

2. What are the risks and benefits of keeping it real?

3. How should Black students keep it real within individual and group settings?

4. How can autobiographical reflection assist Black students in confronting oppression within educational spaces?

Conceptual Framework

During my dissertation process, I developed a philosophical framework titled "Transconceptualization." I developed this framework inspired by Freire's work around the subject-object contradiction among oppressor and oppressed groups; his work talks about and at times emphasizes love, but he does not dig deep into the notion. While King's work digs deep into the notion of love, he does not discuss the role of love in education. Thus, I synergize the two authors' works and create Transconceptualization.

Transconceptualization is a philosophical framework that seeks to understand limitations and possibilities of life in the personal, educational, and societal contexts; this chapter seeks to address all of the contexts in developing an understanding of how to keep it real. This transconceptual framework offers five conceptual tools for understanding the process of keeping it real within White-dominated educational spaces: dehumanization, autobiographical reflection, forgiveness, confrontation, dialogue, and transformative action. I use these tools to analyze the stages of the confrontational experiences I had to endure to keep it real. This framework draws on the philosophical works of Paulo Freire and Martin Luther King, Jr. (1967). However, these scholars' works are not strictly adhered to within this paper; instead, their works assist in the inspiration of Transconceptualization. In sum, my transconceptual framework uses concepts from the aforementioned authors to make meaning of my graduate experiences.

Dehumanization is a process in which one is caught in an absolute subject-object contradiction in life. Within the Freirean discourse, this contradiction is expressed between the oppressor class and the oppressed class. On the one hand, the oppressor class is the absolute subject in society; on the other hand, its oppressed class counterparts are the absolute objects of the same society. Existing as an absolute subject in the societal contradiction implies that the oppressor class has the ability of imagining and building its ideal society, while the oppressed class accepts, adapts to, and assists in building the oppressor class' ideal society. The ability to reflect and act on the reflection is the foundation of what it means to be human, while the inability to engage in the aforementioned is a melancholy existence known as oppression. Freire (2008) notes that dehumanization is marked by "those whose humanity has been stolen" and by "those who have stolen it," which leads to both oppressed and oppressor living a dehumanizer (subject) and dehumanized (object) contradiction, which prevents both classes from developing their full potential as human beings (p. 44). People who restrict human beings from reaching their full human potential are oppressors, while those whose humanity is limited are the oppressed. Freire (2007) declares that dehumanization is a process that reduces the oppressed to the state of animals:

> If man is incapable of changing reality, he adjusts himself. Adaptation is behavior characteristic of the animal sphere; exhibited by man, it is symptomatic of his dehumanization. Throughout history, men have attempted to overcome the factors, which make them accommodate or adjust. (p. 4)

People who are oppressed exist as adapted beings and accept the unjust society as predestined. The oppressor class will never act in a manner that transforms the societal contradiction without pressure from the oppressed. Their reform of society at best provides a more benevolent form of oppression but never eradicates it; this is what Freire calls false generosity. Societal reforms by oppressors tend to make life easier for the oppressed class while substantially leaving the systemic oppression in place and maintaining an unjust order (Freire 2007). Dehumanization is a process that socializes the oppressed to live as objects and their oppressors to live as subjects, creating a societal contradiction.

Autobiographical reflection is a process that allows the oppressed class to become conscious of its oppression. Autobiographical reflection allows the oppressed to articulate experiences as a person and member of a specific group—based on class, gender, race, or all of the above (Hall 2009; Smith 1993). For Smith, autobiography is a time when the oppressed "restages their subjectivity" in society, while developing a "strategy for resisting" societal oppression (p. 156). When the oppressed class engages in autobiographical reflection, it engages in what she calls "autobiographical manifesto" (Smith, 2007, p. 157). Smith discusses autobiographical manifesto in the following way:

> Purposeful, bold, contentious, the autobiographical manifesto contests the old inscription, the old histories, the old politics, the *ancien regime*, by working to dislodge the hold of the universal subject through an expressly political collocation of a new "I." (p. 157)

The purpose of autobiographical reflection for oppressed people, who are conscious of their oppression, is to become "revolutionary subjects" while framing their identities as tools to connect to their fellow oppressed brethren. Furthermore, when oppressed people, who are conscious of their oppression, engage in autobiographical reflection, they are not just resisting dehumanization as individuals, but they are also using their experience as a "call" to assist in the development of a movement to transform society or institutional spaces (Smith, 1993). Hall (2009) suggests that the autobiographical manifesto is a tool that "critiques [. . .] various forces of oppression—social psychological, economic, and political—at work in society" (pp. 91–92). Hall, who writes about the autobiographical reflections of African American journalists, declares, "African-American autobiography of the individual life story has always been representative of something greater" (p. 92). Furthermore, he emphasizes that African American autobiographers who write from the autobiographical manifesto perspective tend to see themselves as a members of a marginalized group, so their stories seek to present personalized issues in a collective context (Hall, 2009). Hall and Smith both discuss autobiographical reflection as a tool to understand and critique oppression in their past experiences. I add to their notion of autobiographical reflection, in that I believe that the oppressed must engage in it to become conscious of past and present oppression; in addition, autobiographical reflection helps oppressors to become conscious of their actions that might oppress or contribute to an environment of oppression. When the oppressed class becomes conscious of its contradictions, it becomes possible for it to love its oppressor through the act of forgiveness.

Forgiveness, as an act of love, requires the oppressed class to understand that it and the oppressor class are human beings, living in constant contradiction. Understanding that it and the oppressor class are flawed by nature creates the potential for the oppressed class to develop love for the oppressor class and vice versa. The potential for love develops through the mutual realization that both the oppressor and oppressed have good and evil residing in both of them. In his sermon "Loving your enemy," Dr. King (2010) said, "When we look beneath the surface, beneath the impulsive evil deed, we see within our enemy-neighbor a measure of goodness and know that the viciousness and evilness of his acts are not quite representative of all that he is" (p. 45). Seeing the oppressor class as not the sum of the actions of its members creates the possibility for the oppressed to see good in them. For that reason, the oppressed have to develop the capacity to love by forgiving the oppressor class, because oppressed people, too, are flawed and fall short of perfection every day. Engaging in the act of forgiveness enables those in the oppressed class to abandon the burden of pain for a struggle to free themselves and their oppressor of dehumanizing practices of the past and present. Thus, the benefit of forgiveness lies in a stronger desire to assist themselves and the oppressor class in living a more humane life while assisting in the development of a better world. It is important to note that loving by forgiving is a difficult task, but it is a necessary prerequisite for a confrontation with the oppressor class.

Confrontation is essential to the oppressed class transforming itself into beings of praxis who become subjects of their thinking and actions. This does not infer that the burden of praxis lies only on the oppressed class; instead, it asserts that for change to occur within dehumanizing spaces, the oppressed class has to initiate the struggle. Freire's and King's works differ on whether confrontation should violent or nonviolent. However, both Freire and King view confrontation as an act of love that is essential to societal transformation. Freire's method of confrontation involves using violence to resolve the contradiction between the oppressed and oppressor classes (Freire, 2008, p. 56). He believed that when the oppressed use violence to end their oppression, it was an "act of love" that ridded both classes of oppression (Freire, 2008). King would agree that confrontation by the oppressed to end their oppression is an "act of love" for both classes, but he would assert that it would only be a loving act in the absence of violence. Here we see a major distinction between these individuals—nonviolent versus violent confrontation. King believed the use of violence by the oppressed to free themselves from oppression would "bring only temporary victories" and create more problems (King, 2010, p. 7). Thus, King believed the essential goal of nonviolent confrontation was not to destroy or harm the oppressor class, but to "oppose an unjust system" and "love perpetuators of the systems" (King, 2010, p. 8). Nonviolent confrontation creates the possibility of eradicating the absolute contradiction that creates oppressed and oppressor classes. Although King and Freire discussed the physical component of violence, this chapter discusses the verbal component of violence. For instance, Chappelle's skit about Vernon Franklin is an example of verbal violence used to confront a dehumanizing experience. Before the subject-object contradiction between the oppressor class and oppressed class can be permanently eradicated, dialogue between the classes has to occur.

Dialogue is the process that occurs between human beings who speak and listen to each other with the intention of understanding the world that was and naming the world that will be. Dialogue is not a contentious exchange of ideas with the purpose of intellectual domination; rather, it is the process where individuals are articulating ideas and listening to each others' ideas with the intention of developing solutions to human problems in a micro-context—home, community, institutional, or local levels; or macro-context—state, regional, national, or global levels (Freire, 2008, p. 89). Dialogue is a human activity done *with people, not to or for people.* Even though dialogue is a process where people collectively reflect on issues pertaining to the human experience, the outcome is not an intellectual articulation of what the *world should be* (Freire, 2008). Instead, dialogue is a collective process where individuals discover problems through a thematic investigation of the issues in society with the intention of eradicating the aforementioned. If those engaged in this reflection process have no desire to act, their words are intellectual chatter that has no effect on their world; thus, they engage in verbal anti-praxis, reflecting with no intention of acting (Freire 2008). Dialogue is a representative of a true desire to transform the world.

Transformative action, within the context of this paper, is collective action, seeking to assist in the development of better institutions and systems. This action, just as dialogue, is done *with people*, not *for people* (Freire, 2008, p. 167). For example, acting for the oppressed changes the appearance of oppression but does not aid the oppressed in acting with others to make a better world (Freire, 2008). In other words, transformative action is not a dialectical struggle, where some people are players in the game of life while others are on the sidelines cheerleading the team to victory. Nor is it a competition among players of the same team attempting to prove who should be ahead in the struggle. Transformation is a process where players, who have different skills and experiences, become teammates by working together for the ultimate victory—the defeat or eradication of oppression or oppressive conditions within institutional spaces. Transformative action is a collective struggle *with* human beings to end the societal contradiction by uniting the formerly oppressed and oppressor classes in common work to develop a new world. In the development of this new world, both classes have to be committed to loving each other even when the respective group is acting unlovable. It is important to note that love is an integral element in the process of maintaining, strengthening, and advancing a new society, because without it a new society is not possible.

The description of the concepts listed above offers Black students a process for keeping it real. First, the oppressed must understand the definition and be able to apply the concept of dehumanization. Second, students have to engage in autobiographical reflection to become conscious of the oppressive environmental conditions and the contradictions that exist within themselves, such as the whether they have a hopeful or fatalistic perception of the future. Third, students have to love by forgiving their oppressors for their actions. Fourth, students have to engage in nonviolent, verbal confrontation with individuals who have created or maintained the oppressive educational environment. Fifth, the post-confrontation experience should consist of students engaging in dialogue with those who have oppressed them with the intention of transforming the environment. Lastly, oppressed Black students have to work with other students and individuals who are creators or maintainers of oppressive educational space to make a new space free from the contradictions of the past. In sum, the Transconceptual framework incorporates conceptual tools that will aid Black students in their struggle to keep it real.

Keeping It Real in the Individual Context

In the fall of 2008, I was enrolled in the History of School Reform class. Each class started with the professor handing out printouts with weekly C-SPAN's Book TV schedules. After handing out the schedules, he would discuss the previous week's episodes. When he was finished discussing Book TV, he lectured on the weekly themes from the readings. After lecturing, he invited the class to present our required weekly position papers on the readings.

One day, I presented my position paper, which declared that it was pointless to reform the American educational system without reforming society. In the middle of my presentation, a young White woman with blond hair and blue eyes named Elizabeth interrupted me. She said, "You make me sick when you talk about transforming society." Her eyes were filled with viciousness, and her face was pink with anger. She ended her comment with a cold stare, and I returned it with an uncomfortable pause. The class quickly picked up the conversation, and they acted as if nothing had happened. As soon as there was a chance for me to speak again, I spoke. I rearticulated my argument in a clear and concise way, hoping she would understand this time. After I restated my position, I fell into a painful reflective silence.

I was in a class with students who claimed to be social justice advocates, yet no one stood up for me. One student was a critical race theorist, two students were progressives basing their work on the theories of John Dewey, one student was doing research on race, one student was a liberal democrat, and the professor was a self-proclaimed socialist. None of the left-leaning social justice advocates took the risk of critiquing this young lady for her dehumanizing comment. Even the professor failed to stand up for my right to speak in class. I realized in this moment that it was easy for people to talk about noble theories pertaining to social injustice and transforming the world, but it was much harder for individuals to stand up in the face of such injustice. After class, many of the classmates came up to me and said things about Elizabeth like, "She's young and immature" or "Her comment was a reflection on her, not you." Still, I had the same questions running through my head after each conversation: Why didn't they stand up for me during class? What if I would have reacted fully instead of pausing? If I had I responded in class, would I have been the talk of the School of Education?

If I had responded to Elizabeth's comment by going on a profane verbal tirade, I knew no one would have referenced her words directly; they merely would have said how disrespectful I had been toward her. As a Black man, I faced the Black standard, which essentially affirms that when Blacks act aggressively, it is a result of our innate anger; conversely, the *White standard* affirms White aggression and anger as reasonable because it is not in their nature to be upset. As a result of not wanting to match up to the White standard and fearing being verbally attacked again without support from classmates or my professor, I decided to speak less and less in class because I believed that what I said didn't matter to my classmates. Later that semester, I saw Elizabeth in the library, and she and I had a long conversation and about her comment in class. I expressed how the comment hurt me. She responded by apologizing and telling me a story. When she was a child, she had been a part of a church that had a mission to make the world a better place. Elizabeth's father had been an active member of the church, and upon his death, her family was left dependent on the church. However, the church didn't live up to its mission. This experience assisted her in developing an adverse perception of anyone who articulated ideals pertaining to societal transformation. Thus, my comments had invoked feelings she had suppressed in her subconscious. At the end of our conversation, I forgave her, but I hadn't forgiven those social justice advocates who stood by and said nothing.

Keeping It Real in Group Settings

In the spring of 2010, I went to Dr. Hull and asked her if could I co-teach one of the sections of the Social Foundations in Education course. Dr. Hull was known for being the *social justice advocate* in the School of Education, and the students she advised were known as social justice advocates. Two of the students whom she advised were in the History of School Reform class. Dr. Hull granted my request to co-teach one of the sections, but she requested that I enroll in the College Teaching course, which was a class where we could debrief and discuss the weekly issues of that came up in the course we taught. I was excited for two reasons. First, I was going to teach a college course while receiving feedback from a professor and classmates. Second, this was going to be a great semester, because I would learn if I was cut out to be a professor.

During this semester, I came to class ready and willing to engage in dialogue with my classmates. For this class, there was no textbook or syllabus. The class was based on the dialogical, meaning it was based on students engaging in dialogue with each other on issues we raised organically. I was excited about this class because I would be in an environment where students were willing to engage in dialogue.

Unfortunately, my experience in this class was as troubling as my prior experiences. Quickly, I learned that four students in the class had a prior academic relationship with Dr. Hull. Four students were either current or former teaching fellows for the Social Foundations course that Dr. Hull supervised. During class discussions, I felt like she and the former and current teaching fellows engaged in full with each other. At first, I found it difficult to keep up because they used unfamiliar terminology from an educational discourse centered on the works of John Dewey, in which Dr. Hull had trained these four students in previous classes. It was almost as if they were speaking another language. I spent the first few weeks listening and learning how they spoke to one another. As a rule, I spoke sparingly. The semester progressed, and I slowly built the courage to speak regardless of my inability to speak their shared language.

My classmates and professor spoke about the "other" (which is a reference to individuals who are oppressed) and social justice issues pertaining to race, gender, class, and sexual orientation throughout the classroom discussions. However, when I spoke in class about either race or class, my classmates' and Dr. Hull's feedback and comments were superficial at best. At worst, they returned my comments with disinterested stares. Upon the completion of my thoughts, the class would return to the regular flow as if I hadn't spoken. This frustrated me. After class, I would frequently head to my friend Eliada's office, where I would express my frustrations about my classmates never responding to my comments in class. She always responded with a simple question: "Do you ever ask them why they don't respond to your comments?" My answer was "Naw." She listened to my rants about feeling like a second-class citizen in a class full of social justicers. With her calm demeanor, she would return to her original question, and I would offer the same response. The truth was that I didn't know how to express my feelings in a nondestructive manner, and I wanted to keep it real by cussing them out for not engaging in dialogue with me. But I feared that expressing my real feelings could place my graduate career in jeopardy. Thus, I decided to remain quiet in class.

I hated going to this class every Thursday. I always arrived late on purpose. When we went on breaks, I would wander around the hallways and return to class five to ten minutes later as a necessary escape. At the end of class, I was the first one to head out the door. Whenever I was in class, a melancholic feeling pervaded my whole body. I would sit and watch my classmates engaging each other in a full dialogue and providing detailed feedback to each other. I couldn't help but feel jealous. Why couldn't I be pushed and supported in the same manner by my peers? This frustration grew and grew, and I just wished that the semester would end.

Each week, one student was responsible for presenting a paper that dealt with an idea related to college teaching. One week, most of the students in the class fell ill, which meant there were only a few of us in class. Those students who were absent made a request to Dr. Hull to push back the current student-presenter to the following week because they were very interested in her topic. Dr. Hull granted their request. The rescheduling of the student's presentation coincided with my first full day of teaching class independent of the other co-instructor in the Social Foundations course. When I arrived at class, Dr. Hull announced that most of our class had called out sick and that she had granted their request to for the other student-presenter to present next week. Consequently, my presentation would be pushed back two weeks. I was fine with the schedule change because I believed that it would give me more time to prepare my presentation. Dr. Hull turned to me and asked whether I wanted to discuss the lesson I taught today in class. Excitedly, I said yes and ran to my office to find my teaching materials and the lesson plans I had completed for the class. Then I discussed what I had done in class, the rationale behind my lesson plan, and the students' responses to my class. I received some feedback from my professor and classmates, which I thought was great. I left class that day imagining that I was going to present in two weeks on a different topic and receive feedback from my classmates.

The next week Terry presented, and at the end of her presentation, Dr. Hull looked at her schedule of presenters and did not call my name. I quickly corrected her and informed her that I was supposed to go the following week. She responded by saying:

DR. HULL: You presented last week.

ME: Yeah, but it was impromptu. I only presented because no one was here and everyone wanted to hear Terry's presentation.

DR. HULL: It was a good presentation.

ME: Yeah, but that was not what I wanted to present and get feedback on.

DR. HULL: What did you want to get feedback on?

ME: I am working on a paper that I am going to use for my teaching philosophy.

DR. HULL: Send it around. We'll look at it.

The class ended with me not being able to present the following week. I thought this schedule change was unfair. I was working on a paper, and I was imagining that I would be given the same chance to present my work that my classmates had received. The presentation that I had given felt like a commercial break. In fact, whenever I spoke in class, I felt like I was a *human-commercial*. Over the course of the next few weeks, I would fall into a critical silence, where I would dissect every word my classmates said in my head, but I never verbalized in class.

Toward the end of the semester, I saw Dr. Hull as I was walking through the hallway. She and I exchanged pleasantries. Her concluding remarks were, "Stop by my office, I am concerned about your performance in the class." I was confused, so I merely responded by accepting her request. We met later that week, and in the meeting, I finally used the advice from Eliada. I told Dr. Hull how I was feeling.

DR. HULL: Nosakhere, I am concerned with your performance in the class.

ME: [I pause] Well, DR. HULL, I feel like I am not valued in class. Whenever I speak in class, no one responds to any of my comments, but when other people respond there is a rich discourse between students.

DR. HULL: Do you think you could make your comments a little more inviting?

ME: Inviting?

DR. HULL: Yes, sometimes you say things in class and we don't know what to say.

ME: I just feel like the point of talking in class is for students to ask me questions, so I can express my thoughts more clearly or make comments on points of contention.

DR. HULL: I think if you bring this up to your classmates; it would be interesting to hear their responses.

ME: Ok.

I left the meeting still thinking it was meaningless to speak in the class. Also, I was happy that the class was nearing an end. I figured I wasn't going to speak in class because none of my classmates would listen. Therefore, I was content with not keeping it real, an educational stance I would take in our last class.

For the last class, Dr. Hull bought pizza, soda, cookies, and other snacks. We ate and then we gave her feedback on the class. In my mind, I thought all I had to do was get through these last few hours, and the class would be over. Everyone in the class shared a story affirming a common theme among my classmates: "This was the best class I ever had in my graduate experience." After everyone spoke, there was an uncomfortable silence, and Dr. Hull ended with a question directed at me: "Nosakhere, do you have anything to say?" I paused, and I allowed the nervousness to move from my heart throughout my body. With a clearing of my throat and President Obama's introductory phrase of "Well," I would lay out my severe discontentment with the class and my classmates.

ME: I sat in this class all semester. I have to admit this was one of the worst experiences I have ever had in graduate school. In most of my classes, students and professors have ignored my comments as if I have said nothing. But, this class, I had different expectations because you all are the social justice advocates in the School of Education. I hear you all talk about social justice, but haven't seen you all do social justice. Throughout this whole class, you have treated me like a dog, but I can't even say that because I see how some people treat dogs. You all treat me like a stray dog that walks near you, and you refuse to give it eye contact because you think it would bite you. When I speak in class, you never respond, and you never give me eye contact. After I finish talking, you return to talking as if I never spoke. When I spoke in this class, I felt like a commercial break, but not like a Super Bowl commercial because people pay attention to those. I felt like a commercial break on a regular show.

You know, when it comes on you run to the bathroom or the fridge? That one.

ME: [I pause] This class felt like a TV show that had a script and main characters on it. In fact, the class reminded me of *Seinfeld*. In that show, there are four main characters: Jerry, Elaine, George, and Kramer. The whole show is about these four people. At times, there are people who make guest appearances, but, for the most part, the show is about the four characters. When I sat in this class, it felt like the class was only about a selected few. A few of us weren't a part of the main narrative. We were sometimes allowed a chance to make a guest appearance, but for the most part the show was about the four main characters. For me, I was not a main character or a guest star who made an appearance, I was a commercial break that no one paid attention to when it came on.

ME: [I pause] Throughout this class, I heard many of you all talk about social justice, but I never have seen you all enact it or do it. For example, a few years ago, I sat in a class where a student turned to me and said that I made her "sick." [I was referring to the incident between Elizabeth and me in the History of School Reform class] She straight up disrespected me and infringed upon my right to speak freely in class. I was the "Other" that you all talk about, but none of y'all stood up for me. Lawrence and Sally, both of you were there, and you said nothing. Even Kevin was in the class, and he said nothing, too. However, if we read something or a topic comes up in class everyone is ready to speak about how it is oppressive. But, when oppression is in y'all's face, y'all don't say anything.

ME: [I pause] This class reminds me of my favorite movie when I was a kid, *Friday*. In the movie there was a guy name Debo, who was the oppressor of the movie. Then, you had Smokie, played by Chris Tucker, and Craig played by the rapper Ice Cube. In one scene, Smokie is in the street selling drugs to two Mexicans. He looks down the street and runs back to Craig's porch, and he says, "Debo," and Craig says, "What?" Smokie says, "Debo!" Smokie and Craig take off the jewelry and put it in a little box and hide it. Red, who was also sitting with Craig and Smokie on the porch says, "I'm just gonna tuck mine in" [referring to a gold chain he's wearing]. Debo comes up to the step and says, "What y'all got on my forty?" He was referring to a 40 oz. of liquor that people in working-class communities drink. Essentially, Debo wanted them to pay for his alcohol for the day. Everyone responds to him by denying that they had any money. Debo walks over to Smokie and grabs his pockets to check if he has any money. He turns to Red and asks him same question, "What do you got on my forty?" Red says, "Nothing." Debo pulls his collar back and sees the chain, and he snatches it off of his neck, and then he leaves.

ME: [I pause] Smokie stand up and says, "Let's jump 'em." and Craig says, "Sit down!" Smokie says, "I got mind control over Debo. He be like shut up, when he leave, I be talkin' again. I be talkin' again. I be talkin' again."

ME: [I pause] When that incident happened, many of you all came up to me and said many things, but none of you said anything in class. When he leave, I be talkin' again. When he leave, I be talkin' again. But, when the oppressor was in the room, nobody said anything, that's not social justice. I'm telling you about something I have done. I stood up many times knowing that when I did I was risking everything. I'm saying y'all gotta do that. I am saying live up to your social justice ideas. Do social justice. Don't just talk about it.

After I spoke, my classmates expressed their joy at having me in the class. Some expressed remorse for my feeling the way I felt. Others posed the question: What could they have done in that situation? I remember thinking it's not my responsibility to tell an individual how to act justly. It is up to them to discern the proper action, and to ensure that action is in line with their words and personal philosophy. The class ended with people asking me if they could talk to me privately, which I was open to. Other people were mad and thereafter only spoke to me in the hallways as a defensive mechanism.

Analysis

This section presents the results of my analysis of the above experiences especially as they relate to resolving the Chapellian Contradiction. I begin with dehumanization, which explains the anger as well as the need to resist.

DEHUMANIZATION

As a Black male within this White-dominated educational space, I adjusted to the oppressive environment. In the beginning, my adjustment to this oppressive educational space prevented me from engaging a struggle to eradicate it. In Freire's terms, I had "internalized" the oppressive cultural practices in the educational environment and become "fearful of freedom" (Freire, 2008, p. 47). I was an object within this educational space, and to move beyond this position, I had to "eject" the oppressive cultural practice from my being and replace it with the desire to be free (Freire, 2008). When I decided to eject the oppressive practices from my being, I became ready to become a subject within my educational space. This mental readiness created the opportunity for me to engage in a purposeful autobiographical reflection to understand the specific examples of dehumanization in the educational environment.

AUTOBIOGRAPHICAL REFLECTION

My autobiographical reflection assisted me in moving from object to subject of my graduate experience. As a subject, I became conscious of the specific examples of my oppression in the History of School Reform class and College Teaching classes. In my reflection on these experiences, I sought to "denounce" the oppressive classroom experiences and instead "announce" how individuals should be treated within the graduate educational space (Smith, 1993, p. 159). In the midst of this reflection, I always saw myself as a part of the Black graduate student body, which remained voiceless within this White-dominated educational space; thus, my reflection was a part of a larger narrative that rarely became public in this educational environment. My autobiographical reflection created the possibility for me to move to the next phase of the process—forgiveness as an act of love.

FORGIVENESS

Forgiveness is an intentional effort by the oppressed student to love the oppressor student because the oppressed student realizes that both are unfinished human beings. King declared that there is a "civil war" going on within all of us, which attempts to bring closer to "good or evil." And because all individuals are fighting an internal civil war, he asserts that the oppressed have to "find the good" in the oppressor student even though he or she would like to hate the latter. When my classmates oppressed me, I had to reject the feelings of hatred and make an intentional effort to love them by forgiving them for their actions. Forgiveness became a possibility only when

I realized my own unfinishedness. In other words, I was only able to forgive my oppressors when I realized that I am not perfect. The Freirean discourse offers a way to forgive the oppressor through his notion of "true generosity." He asserts that "true generosity" is the struggle to "destroy the causes" that prevent oppressed and oppressor from pursuing their full humanity (Freire, 2008, p. 47). For the oppressed student, forgiveness prior to a confrontation is the only way to produce fruitful results.

Nonviolent Verbal Confrontation

The oppressed student has to engage in a nonviolent verbal confrontation with the oppressor student. According to King (1967), a violent confrontation would not produce the desired results, he declared, "you can murder a lie, but you can't establish truth," he went on to say, "Darkness cannot put out darkness, only light can do that" (King, "Where Do We Go From Here," para. 43). The oppressed student who decides to confront the oppressor student has to commit himself to nonviolent verbal confrontation, because it is not the individual or the group that he seeks to destroy, as stated earlier, but rather the environment that socialized and produced students who oppress. The oppressed student has to be more concerned with building a new educational environment free of the oppression. When I confronted my classmates, I was very intentional with confrontation; I carefully chose the stories I would tell and attempted to fully explain the stories as they related to my experience. Although I might have had the right to lash out in a verbally violent tirade or to be more emotional in my confrontation, I decided to present my grievance as a "light" that would allow us to walk out of the "darkness" of the oppressive educational space that had been created.

Dialogue and Transformative Action

Upon confronting the oppressor student, the oppressed student has to engage in dialogue leading to transformative action in educational space. Freire discussed the notion of praxis within his work. For Freire, dialogue was a form of reflection in which two or more people engaged with the intention of acting. Without the intention of acting, dialogue would be collective chatter (Freire, 2008). The oppressed and oppressor students have to engage in dialogue to understand the issues within the educational space and have to commit to working together, not as members of the oppressed or oppressor classes, but as members of a new class of students—those who seek to eradicate oppression and create a new educational space where all can be free to pursue their educational dreams. In other words, Freire believed that the highest aspiration was for oppressed and oppressor to unite and engage in a new a new form of praxis to create the world that should be. My graduate experience varied with regard to dialogue; during my interaction with Elizabeth, I confronted her and we began to engage in dialogue about the in-class argument. The outcome of the dialogue resulted in us acting civilly toward one another. With regard to my College Teaching classmates, I was unable to engage in dialogue or transformative action. Although I didn't, I learned valuable lessons on how to do so in the future.

Recommendations for Keeping It Real

In the process of moving beyond the Chappellian Contradiction, Black students must understand the role of timing. Students' reflection on when to keep it real is pivotal, as it will have an impact on their classmates and themselves. Within this context, students have a choice whether to keep it real or not keep it real. Both choices have positive and negative consequences. This section seeks to provide a few risks and benefits of immediate confrontation and delayed confrontation and how to keep it real within individual and group settings.

The Risks and Benefits of Immediate and Delayed Confrontation

The first risk of delayed confrontation is that a student could commit verbal anti-praxis. When a student engages in verbal anti-praxis, he or she speaks about an incident with no intention of acting on the incident. Praxis is a synergistic process whereby a person's reflections are connected to his or her actions. When an oppressed student reflects on an incident in class with no intention of acting (which, in the context of the Chappellian Contradiction, would take the form of confronting his or her classmates), he or she is engaging in verbal anti-praxis. During my experience in the College Teaching class, I engaged in verbal anti-praxis because I constantly reflected on my oppressive educational experiences with my friends, namely Eliada, but I refused to confront my classmates. If Dr. Hull had not asked me to discuss my experience in the class, I would have never confronted my classmates. The oppressed student who engages in delayed confrontation risks never confronting his or her classmates unless prompted.

One benefit of delayed confrontation is that it provides time to construct a solid argument. A delayed response allows the oppressed student the chance to use the class experience to collect data through participant-observations that can affirm or disconfirm his or her feelings. For example, in numerous in-class situations, I observed my classmates doing three things with one another: (1) providing feedback on papers, (2) posing well-thought-out questions during in-class dialogue, and (3) giving eye contact to the speaker to show their full attention. Conversely, my experience as a participant in this class was oppressively different. My classmates habitually ignored my comments or mentally zoned out when I was speaking, provided me with shallow feedback, and rarely maintained eye contact with me when I was speaking. Delaying the confrontation with my classmates provided me the opportunity to collect data through my in-class experience and gave me time to construct a solid argument to address my concerns.

Delayed confrontation also allows oppressed students to emotionally compose themselves. An oppressed student who is emotionally composed can present a well-thought-out response. For example, after Elizabeth's comment in the History of School Reform class, I was extremely upset. As a Black male from inner-city Philadelphia, I wanted to return her comment with a profane tirade like Vernon Franklin in Chappelle's skit. However, the time between the incident and my confrontation with Elizabeth allowed me to calm down. Calming down gave me the strength to confront her in the library, which enabled us to have a productive dialogue, giving us the chance to understand each other's respective positions. This dialogue also enabled us to have to civil and meaningful interactions in future classroom experiences.

One of the risks of immediate confrontations is a misclassification of the oppressor classmates. For example, when Elizabeth disrespected me in class, I automatically thought that she was a racist. However, my perception of her changed when I spoke with her in the library. This conversation provided me with a chance to see her as a complex individual. Her disrespectful comments were still unacceptable, but I realized her comments had less to do with race and more to with a painful personal experience. Moreover, immediate confrontation would have resulted my calling Elizabeth a racist, which would have been an incorrect observation. Had I done so, then my reputation would have been seriously damaged. I would have been defined as the *mad Black guy* who thought all White people are racist. The oppressed student who engages in immediate confrontation runs the risk of misclassifying his or her colleague, which could take attention away from the original harm done to the oppressed student.

The second risk of immediate confrontation is jeopardizing the oppressed student's education. As I stated in the Elizabeth story, my fear of immediately reacting to her disrespect was that I would be judged by the Black standard. If White professors perceive a Black student as being mad, it could have deleterious impact on how he or she is evaluated during coursework and/or the dissertation process. I thought that professors would judge my work, in covert ways, with an extra-critical eye, which, at best, could have resulted in a lower grade than I deserved or at worst a failing grade. Additionally, covert forms of educational oppression could occur during the dissertation process, which could seriously delay its completion. I remembered other Black students who, while writing their dissertations, spoke of the arbitrary nature of the process. My inability to immediately emotionally compose myself and the risks of covert forms of educational oppression strongly discouraged me from engaging in immediate confrontation with my White classmates for fear of suffering the same fate as Vernon Franklin.

A benefit of immediate confrontation is that it prevents the development of fatalistic perceptions of one's classmates and the situation. During the semester in the College Teaching course, I developed fatalistic perceptions of my classmates; I believed they could not change. In reality, I had internalized the pain from the oppressive situation and begun to see them as predetermined beings. I was the embodiment of fatalism. Fatalism inhibits the oppressed person from fully experiencing the learning environment. However, the immediate confrontation offers the oppressed student the chance to fully experience the learning environment by presenting an oppressive in-class situation as a topic for discussion. A potential result of discussing the aforementioned is an opportunity for the development of a collective healing process. Healing together has the power to end both the oppression and the fatalistic perceptions of one's classmates.

Keeping It Real in Individual and Group Settings

The second phase of resolving the Chappellian Contradiction is selecting the environment in which to keep it real. First, keeping it real in a one-on-one situation requires that the oppressed student engage the oppressor student in conversation about the situation. Secondly, keeping it real in a group situation requires that the oppressed student engage his classmates in dialogue. In sum, this section seeks to understand the resolution of the Chappellian Contradiction as a practice that incorporates conversation and dialogue.

In the individual context, keeping it real is a process. First, the oppressed student has to confront his or her colleague about the oppressive behavior. The oppressed student should revisit the situation and express his or her feelings in a respectful manner. Upon expressing his or her feelings, he or she should listen and pose questions for understanding. If the oppressor student and oppressed student realize that the behavior is racist, they both should brainstorm informal and formal educative experiences to assist the oppressor student in undergoing a process to become a nonracist. Next, the oppressed student should work with his or her colleague to resolve the problem. At best, the two individuals can understand each other's respective positions and come together to end the oppression; at worst, the two individuals should agree to be civil toward each other. Last, love as an act of forgiveness should be pre- and post-conditions for one-on-one conversations; the oppressed student unloads the burden of pain by forgiving the oppressor student before and after the dialogue.

After the oppressive situation in the History of School Reform class, I had to keep it real by going through the above process. When I saw Elizabeth in the library, I made a decision to initiate a conversation with her. During our conversation, I retraced the incident that triggered her outburst and allowed her the chance to express her feeling about the incident. As the conversation progressed, I tentatively listened and asked questions, which allowed me to understand her position. We were able to resolve our problem, and we both left with an appreciation for each other, which resulted in us acting civilly toward each other in our subsequent classes. Last, I had to struggle with the notion of love by forgiving her for disrespecting me; this struggle was difficult, but had I not done so, a dialogue with her would have been impossible.

In the group context, keeping it real is also a process. First, the oppressed student must confront his or her classmates for their oppressive treatment. This can occur through the oppressed student arranging for time to speak in class about an incident or incidents when his or her classmates exhibited oppressive behavior. Second, he or she should revisit the issue and provide examples of the oppressive behavior and its impact on him or her. In addition, the oppressed student should provide examples from scholarly journal articles, books, and popular cultural artifact (e.g., music, movies, or television shows) that connect to his or her experience in the classroom. Third, the oppressed student should actively listen to his or her classmates. Active listening requires the oppressed student to receive his or her classmates' comments while making comments and posing questions to confirm he or she understands his or her classmates' perspectives. Fourth, the oppressed student should work with his or her classmates to create a process that resolves the problem. For example, the group could decide to start a reading group around themes raised within the group dialogue, or they could create forums to address the themes. Last, the oppressed student has to forgive his/her colleague for their oppressive behavior as both a pre- and post-condition of dialogue. Even though oppressed students might have the best intentions for confronting the oppressor student, they have to realize that it might not produce the desired results. The oppressor student might act hostile toward the oppressed student and reject the issues presented, but this should not deter him or her from struggling to eradicate oppressive conditions. The oppressed student has to develop innovative strategies and tactics to continue the dialogue with the oppressor student and change the environment that continues to produces students who oppress. Before the dialogue occurs, the oppressed has to love the oppressor student, which means he or she must forgive the oppressor student for his or her actions, because without love and forgiveness he or she will not be able to listen to his classmates with an open mind.

In the College Teaching course, I kept it real in a process that was partly forced on me because my professor asked me to speak about my experiences in class. First, I used class time to confront my classmates' oppressive treatment toward me. Second, I provided detailed examples of their oppressive treatment. In addition, I provided my classmates with textual examples through popular culture artifacts from the movie *Friday* and the television show *Seinfeld* to illustrate my feelings on the specific examples of their oppressive behavior. After the confrontation, I attempted to listen to my classmates both inside and outside class, although in some conversations it was difficult for me to understand their positions because they refused to admit they had done anything wrong. Third, attempts were made to resolve the problem I presented in class, but I was only able to have civil interactions with some of my classmates post-confrontation. I could have done more to organize dialogues to discuss the themes brought out during the confrontation; instead, I chose to maintain a comfortable, civil interaction and distance with these classmates. Last, it was difficult for me to forgive some of my classmates for their action because they were unwilling to admit to their oppressive actions. In hindsight, I should have forgiven them regardless of the outcome of the dialogue because not forgiving meant that I continued to internalize the pain from the situation.

Conclusion

The Chappellian Contradiction is an internal struggle that Black students endure within predominately White-dominated educational spaces. A simplistic understanding of the Chappellian Contradiction is that Black students have to choose whether they will keep it real or *not* keep it real by struggling against the oppressive treatment within a White-dominated educational space. What I offer for resolving the Chappellian Contradiction is how to keep it real while reducing the number of possible negative repercussions. For me, keeping it real entails Black students considering the risks and benefits of engaging in immediate or delayed confrontation. Once students decide to keep it real, they have to determine the appropriate setting (individual or group). In an individual setting, a student can engage in a one-on-one conversation with the person who has acted oppressively toward him or her. A group setting provides a student with an opportunity to confront his or her classmates in a classroom environment. The act of keeping it real also entails working with oppressor classmates in the development of a better educational space.

CHAPTER FOUR

Blue Collar Scholar

.•———•.

Social Class, Race, and Life as a Black Man in Academe

MARK S. GILES

This chapter represents a combination of Critical Race Theory (CRT) counter-narrative (Crenshaw, Gotanda, Peller, & Thomas, 1996; Solórzano & Yosso, 2002), educational autobiography and self-story (Denzin, 1989), and autoethnography (Ellis & Bochner, 2000; Roth, 2005). This chapter examines and highlights several critical and key events (Wolcott, 1994) from my life, including an interpretation of my social class positionality. I seek to bring authentic voice to those self-perceived experiences that intersect with the power relationships and realities of being a Black male faculty member in higher education. The themes presented in this chapter transform my story from a passive victim narrative, or deficit modeling, to a creative tale of self-agency. Shaped by my identity and role as a Black man who earned college degrees at predominately White institutions (PWIs), I share my counter-narrative (Bell, 1992; Solórzano & Yosso, 2002) standing in the so-called power spaces that can support, or hinder, students' progress. Sharing aspects of my personal journey provides insight into the complexities of racially contested spaces in educational settings.

I have intentionally maintained a strategic critical social consciousness while challenging and surviving schooling processes and navigating the tricky landscape of higher education (Shujaa, 1994). Although I feel fortunate to have gained access to advanced degree programs, I recognize that many others who are far better suited never received similar chances. This chapter theorizes dynamics of educational access, opportunity, worthiness, and privilege. Earning a PhD and entering academe as a Black faculty member takes more than luck, and remembering your authentic self requires

more than earning institutional freedom papers represented by promotion
and tenure. This chapter opens a discourse on navigating racialized educational environments and ways of living and being in academic spaces with
values that challenge master narratives of academe.

Yeah, I'm from the West End . . . So What?

bell hooks (1990) states, "Home, however fragile and tenuous . . . had a
radical dimension. Despite the brutal reality of racial apartheid, of domination, one's home-place was the site where one could freely confront the
issue of humanization, where one could resist" (p. 46). I was born into a
working-class Black family in the West End neighborhood of Cincinnati,
Ohio. The West End, adjoining the Over-the-Rhine neighborhood, is among
the oldest in the city. Both communities are within a short walk of the
central downtown business district and the Ohio River. Many industries
historically important to the economic health of Cincinnati were located
in or near that part of town. I grew up within a few miles of beer brewer-
ies, meat processing factories, steel manufacturing companies, and chemical
companies (e.g., Proctor and Gamble's Ivorydale plant and some of its sub-
sidiaries). Several of those businesses were within a 10- to 20-minute walk
from my neighborhood, including the old Crosley Field, the longtime home
of the Cincinnati Reds until 1970, when the team moved to Riverfront
Stadium. As a result, my childhood memories were shaped by the complex
smells and daily work life activities of the neighborhood.

As a child of the 1960s and a teen of the 1970s, I never questioned my
Blackness; I was proud of it. Nor did I question or reject the community to
which I belonged. I did not grow up confused as to my role within my family
or my place within the few blocks surrounding my house. I feel fortunate
to have experienced many of the best traditions of growing up in a positive
Black community without knowing just how special and fleeting those times
were. It seemed as though most folks in the West End knew each other going
back one or more generations and shared a common sense of living in a
type of mutually beneficial harmony. The West End held its own community
cultural wealth, and I benefited from it (Yosso, 2005). I learned how to listen
carefully to my elders and observe acceptable versus unacceptable behaviors.
I learned how to protect myself. I learned whom to trust among those around
me and how to cope with conflict and/or getting my feelings hurt. I did not
win at everything I did, nor did I lose at everything I attempted. I learned
not to trust strangers and not to believe everything people told me. I learned
always to apply common sense with book knowledge and to look twice both
ways before crossing the street. I was encouraged to think for myself and to
take responsibility for my actions and choices.

I proudly attended predominately Black neighborhood schools. My earliest memories about formal learning include an enjoyment of classroom activities, books, reading, and a natural curiosity about things I did not know. The pressure from schoolteachers and administrators consisted of doing the best we could every day, good citizenship among schoolmates, good behavior (following the rigid conditioning of school rules), and always trying to reach whatever potential the teachers stated they saw in us. Clearly, the variation of expectations from teachers who might like one child more than another creates obvious problems, but we did not have to deal with any talk of White versus Black student achievement gaps and that line of deficit ideology. I grew up across the street from Lafayette Bloom Jr. High School, built in 1915, and two blocks from Heberle Elementary School, built in 1929. I attended both schools, as well as St. Augustine Catholic School (grades 3–8), which was located in the block between the other two.

This safe cocoon of early educational experiences deeply grounded me in the social and cultural life of the community and provided a rich sense of belonging to the six- to seven-block area that comprised the majority of my daily travels. The weekly community rhythm consisted of school-aged students walking to or from the neighborhood schools, watching adults going to and coming from jobs; Sunday-morning parades of people dressed in their best clothing going to and returning from worship services; and folks routinely hanging out at nearby ballparks, watching little league baseball, or semi-pro baseball teams composed of workers from local factories and businesses. Local bars were often filled with workers having drinks after quitting time, many of whom only came into the neighborhood for their jobs. This left these venues free nights and weekends for residents to maintain the economic flow of beer, gin, and other activities that we children were not supposed to know about. My family believed in work, school, and rules that children must obey.

My father, who died when I was an infant, was at the time of his passing the pastor of the York Street United Methodist Church. The church was located a few blocks from our modest house built in the early twentieth century, which is another way of saying that it was an old house. Actually, immediately around the corner from our house were several buildings built from the 1860s to the 1880s, which were owned by absentee landlords who only visited the neighborhood in the first week of each month to collect rent. That was among the occasional times I saw White people in our neighborhood, which also included some business owners, the workers traveling to and from their jobs, and the few White kids who attended my schools.

My mother made sure my brother and I attended church each Sunday. Members of our church included some of my own schoolteachers, local storeowners, hairdressers, and so forth; in other words, I experienced a multilayered, reinforcing web of non-monolithic cultural contexts that helped to shape my self-pride, sense of belonging, self-identity, and my evolving understanding of my environment. My mother always stressed the importance of education, although I don't think she went beyond a high-school education. When it was time to go to church, complete chores, or engage in any other important activity, she did not tolerate any questions, complaints, or whining. She worked hard as a housekeeper at a local hospital near the University of Cincinnati, which was only a couple of miles from our house. She worked even when she was ill to make sure my brother and I had food, clothing, and shelter and that the other bills were paid. It all took a mortal toll on her, and in 1971, she died from a combination of health problems, stress and worry, and undercompensated, underappreciated, physically taxing hard work. My mother died the same month of my tenth birthday. My brother and I continued to live in the same house with my aunt (my mother's younger sister), uncle, and cousins. They had been residing on the second floor of our home since about 1966. Obviously, that was a difficult and traumatic time for me, and I am sure for the rest of the family. I found myself not wanting to talk much, although some family members kept asking me how I was feeling. How would any child feel if they lost their only parent suddenly and unexpectedly? I learned to keep many of my feelings to myself because the grown-ups never seemed able to do any problem solving for me. My aunt began removing my mother's pictures and some of the "familiar" artifacts from the living room in an attempt, I suppose, to help my brother and me "move on." Another older brother painted the interior doors and wood trim in the house black. That was strange and weird, but I helped with the painting and never asked any questions. I lived with my aunt, uncle, and cousins until 1977, when I moved to another neighborhood to stay with my maternal grandmother. I lived with her until I graduated from high school in 1979.

Within a four- or five-block radius of our house in the West End, we had several small "mom and pop" stores that sold more groceries, dry goods, and household items than beer, wine, and cigarettes. Black people owned many of these stores. Neighborhood families found most of the things they needed from these small businesses. Children went there to get the things they most wanted, like potato chips, soda pop, penny candy, and items needed for playing neighborhood games. Throughout my formative years, I witnessed Black folks in leadership and decision-making positions and never questioned whether they, or I, could accomplish certain things.

I reject attempts to use some high-minded academic theories to explain what it meant to be Black in a Black neighborhood to me; I lived it. In the late 1960s, James Brown and his big hit *I'm Black and I'm Proud* established a memorable feeling of self-agency, self-worth, and community pride that contributed to my early development and my current critical consciousness. James Brown's music exudes rhythm and soul, and I try hard to retain much of that spiritual and cultural strength for my teaching, mentoring, and scholarship so they can represent the same meaningful authenticity. Brown never tried to sing, dance, or talk like anyone but himself, a Black man from rural Georgia. What does it mean to be Black in America? Listen to some James Brown songs, and you'll start to get a sense of the pain, joy, pride, struggle, spirituality, creativity, and power that come from knowing who you are and knowing that excellence comes from all walks of life.

My autobiographical and autoethnographical intersubjectivity help to frame and make meaning of memories that shape my work as an educator-scholar (Meneley & Young, 2005; Roth, 2005). In this context, I define intersubjectivity as my attempt to balance the subjective nature of self-presentation of life experiences with an attempt at objectivity about my past to share consciously accessible information so that others might find shared meanings. Moreover, according to Margaret Eisenhart (2005), auto/biography, despite its traditional perception as unfiltered and unbiased, represents a contextualized, subjective telling of someone's life story with certain intentions at a specific moment and for a particular audience. I admit to this and say that what I share here is not a neutral, objective, or totally transparent account of events from my life; it is situationally represented, based on the purpose of this chapter. My professional role and life as a faculty member conflict with several aspects of my earlier experiences. Most obvious to me are the middle-class norms for what a college faculty member should be and do compared with how I view myself, based on the neighborhood that nurtured and shaped my identity. In one sense, I am no longer a "native" of the West End and have become an "other" to the very spaces that I once called home. That tension disturbs and disrupts my claim of authenticity as a blue-collar scholar. I wish to identify myself as a member of the "everyday people" class, but to exist honestly in the spaces of academe, I must acknowledge the complex social class transformation that educational processes imposed on me across my undergraduate and graduate journeys. I use the term *imposed* here to mean that in many instances, the social class changes due to my educational experiences were initially unconscious, and, in other cases, they were a knowing attempt to pursue education in the hopes of improving my station in life. I have long believed in the transformational power of education yet struggled to prevent that process, and end product, from altering my critical consciousness and my connections to what I believe is part of my core identity as a man from a working-class neighborhood grounded in blue-collar sensibilities.

In consideration of that explanation, what I present here is not myth. It is an accurate description of selected life experiences intended to allow readers inside aspects of my journey toward becoming a faculty member. This autoethnography thus shares selected experiences as a faculty member interpreted through my cultural identity as a Black man. Readers should understand that my selection includes certain facts, experiences, and interpretations that I feel comfortable sharing and that I hope have meaning for those my writing seeks to influence. My self-agency has been shaped by my identity and role as a heterosexual Black man in America who earned credentials at so-called "top tier" PWIs and who now exists in the White spaces that once hindered, influenced, and supported my own educational progress. My development as a Black scholar-educator was hindered by my experiences in PWIs (e.g., University of Cincinnati, Miami University, and Indiana University) due to by their dominant cultures not strongly valuing people who look like me, or those from working-class backgrounds. I had to dig deep into my own sense of self-pride and intellectual, emotional, and psychological interests in Black history to successfully navigate my way to completion. Those institutions influenced me to trust in my ability to learn, grow, and develop new skills that helped me expand my perspectives on people who were different from me and from my cultural background and knowledge areas that I found challenging but worth investigating. In addition, those institutions played a key role in supporting my pursuit of post-secondary and advanced degrees through personal and professional networking, need-based and merit-based financial aid, and for pushing me beyond my intellectual and cultural comfort zones.

My personal background has helped me make choices and navigate White academic spaces that seek to sometimes welcome me for their own benefit, of which I too benefit in various ways. These spaces have sometimes trapped me into a pseudo-reality that is antithetical to who I am, and wish to be, as a Black man connected to my working-class youth. I have worked hard to maintain a critical social consciousness while challenging and surviving schooling processes and navigating the tricky forests of higher education (Shujaa, 1994). I am proud that I survived the processes of earning those pieces of parchment that indicate high achievement in a society that still stereotypes people like me as deficient and unworthy. However, earning a doctorate degree and entering academe as a Black faculty member takes more than luck, and remembering your authentic self requires more than earning institutional freedom papers that represent the higher education promised land of promotion and tenure.

Faculty Life as Contested Ground

I believe that what we do as faculty members and how we do it demands a close but reflexive connection to who we are. Connecting the dots of one's life is never easy, yet for Black faculty in White spaces it is elemental and essential.

I earned my doctorate at Indiana University in higher education administration with a minor in 20th-century United States history. Because my main intellectual interests focused on African-American history, leadership, and spirituality, I completed my dissertation on 20th-century theologian Howard Thurman and his career in and influence on higher education (Giles, 2003). Although my first doctoral advisor and a few other "well-meaning" White faculty members at Indiana University advised me to avoid focusing on African-American history and culture because it would pigeonhole me as an educator and scholar, I consciously followed my interests and not their warnings. I neither entered nor departed that ivory-towered space thinking I would pursue a faculty career. As a late bloomer in graduate school, I carried the benefit of many years of work and life experiences that shaped my identity and worldview. The faculty thing happened quite unexpectedly.

After earning my degree from Indiana University, I worked briefly in a diversity-focused administrative leadership position in Washington, DC, at one of the national higher education advocacy organizations. Issues of race shaped that experience. Although I enjoyed that position, I had a rocky experience mostly due to a personal conflict with my direct supervisor, who had hired me. I think the problem started when I "dared" to negotiate my salary with her. She presented herself as a liberal White person, grounded in feminist and diversity credentials, and that is how I accepted her. Our initial negotiations failed, and I reluctantly declined the position. What surprised me was how she raised her voice during the phone call when I gave her my decision, saying how I was making a "big mistake" by turning down such a great opportunity.

However, I needed a livable salary, considering the cost of housing in the nation's capital. A few days later, I received a call from another top administrator, a Black woman at the same agency, and she encouraged me to reopen the job negotiations because "they" really wanted to hire me. I agreed and reached a salary agreement that was close to what I asked for, accepted the job, and relocated to DC. About two months later, a colleague—a Black doctoral student finishing her degree at the University of Maryland—pulled me aside and asked what had happened during the hiring process. I asked her what she meant, and she shared that my supervisor "does not negotiate" with anyone and had slammed down the phone on the day I initially declined the job. When I later joined the agency the gossip among the staff was that I had made an enemy—one who smiled and acted pleasantly but was not to be trusted. Within that first year, the conflict became unbearable, and I knew I had to begin looking for another opportunity. I had received a raise with the first six months and a letter of commendation from the agency's president. Was that bad experience due to racial prejudice or personality conflict or some other issue? Whatever the reason, it was an emotional setback considering it was my first job after completing my PhD.

One Saturday afternoon, while still working in DC, I received a call from a faculty member from my master's degree program at Miami University–Ohio about her last-minute need for someone to step in on short notice and teach several courses on a visiting assistant professor one-year contract. Because the job in DC had its obvious problems and limitations, I decided to pursue this teaching opportunity, which meant returning to my hometown area (Miami University is about 30–40 miles northwest from Cincinnati). After I began the job at Miami, I received an unexpected call from a "scholar-in-residence" who worked at the DC agency. He asked how I was doing and said that he personally felt bad about me leaving. He wanted to know what he could do to help, which I thought was a strange question considering I had already resigned, relocated back to Ohio, and was working in another position. That was the last time I heard from anyone at that prestigious agency focused on liberal education.

Teaching at the same institution where I had earned my master's degree felt strange and became dangerous over time. It felt strange because I had never imagined myself as a classroom educator. It represented danger because I realized that I must stay in control of my emotions at all times or else face being accused of the angry Black man syndrome. In addition, I had to learn to navigate a somewhat uncomfortable programmatic space, which felt personally constraining and intellectually debilitating. I learned to show patience when confronted with passive racism from White students who asked if I had a PhD, as if that would allow them to respect me more, and from senior colleagues who discouraged me from publishing work in journals different from those they valued. I had to show restraint when White graduate students complained of "diversity fatigue" and wanted to know why I continually focused on issues related to race and racism in higher education. These and other racial micro-aggressions are conscious and unconscious routine, subtle, verbal and nonverbal, sometimes visual insults directed toward people of color (Solórzano, Ceja, Yosso, 2000; Sue, Capodilupo, Nadal, & Torino, 2008). Learning to understand, cope with, and counter racial micro-aggressions (Solórzano, Ceja, & Yosso, 2000) became a "natural" way of existing within that academic White space. However, these subtle and not so subtle insults have cumulative effects that reinforce the oppression experienced by people of color. Because many Whites claim their racist actions and comments are unintentional or nonexistent, the injury and lasting burden of the injury rests largely with the victim. However, I realized early on that I could help students from all racial and ethnic backgrounds, both graduate and undergraduate, successfully navigate some of those allegedly colorblind, equitable waters. This realization connected to what I had hoped to do years earlier, to help college students, especially students of color and those from marginalized groups find success in college. Thus, becoming a faculty member began to close a past-present-future circle, which even now offers new interpretations on my life and calling.

When deciding to become a faculty member, I never considered all of the things I would eventually discover while navigating the faculty experience. Reflecting on my first faculty experience through the lens of a participant observer (Jorgensen, 1989), I lived that experience as an outsider (i.e., someone new to faculty life and culture) with insider knowledge (i.e., familiarity with Miami University and with extensive prior experiences with my faculty colleagues). Jorgensen (1989) states that "participant observation provides direct experiential and observational access to the insiders' world of meaning" (p. 15). With that position at Miami University, I was new to full-time teaching at a university, which made me an outsider to many of the nuances of faculty culture. My feelings of teaching at an institution where I was once a student posed interesting, self-critical, and collegial challenges. I was not only teaching at the institution where I earned my master's degree, but in the same program area with my former instructors as professional colleagues. I needed to make meaning of that environment and my experiences in it, although I never felt accepted as a full-fledged member of that culture or as if I authentically fit in with that space. In sum, I was a type of insider-outsider, a participant observer.

Although I wanted to approach the job as an "equal," I began to receive a lot of unsolicited advice couched as protective guidance, which I understood it as a type of wavering confidence in my abilities to do the job well. For example, I was told how to conduct my classes, which readings I should emphasize, and the best ways to frame the learning outcomes for the courses I taught. In other words, I was counseled to teach the way my former instructors taught to maintain what they saw as rigor and excellence. I got the message that I should follow their syllabi and continue using the readings they had selected when they taught those courses. I was there to mirror what they did. In addition, I understood some of the personalities of my colleagues from my prior experience, which provided me with some insider information that could be ignored when I tried to stay open and objective to their interactions with each other and with me. In other words, I had already peeked behind the curtain and seen the inside of the internal operations of the program and the philosophical agendas of the faculty, which I could respect, but did not necessarily agree with. One of the most glaring problems I first encountered was passive-aggressive resistance from some of the White students, who originally expressed high degrees of welcome, but quickly expected me to teach and think like my White colleagues. Those students would regularly complain and report to my White colleagues about my teaching style and offer the kind of racially biased, passive resistance to learning that many other faculty of color have often documented (Cleveland, 2004; Jackson & Johnson, 2011). I survived that first year mostly because of the comforting reconnection to home community, family, and friends that I experienced by returning to the Cincinnati area. After another year on a one-year contract, I earned a tenure track position within the same program. The fun really began with the ticking of the tenure clock with the imposition of sharper, more deeply oppressive academy norms.

One of the first pieces of master narrative "mentoring" advice I received from a well-meaning and kind White colleague was for me to be especially careful about spending too much time working with and advising students of color. Her argument suggested that because I was one of the few Black faculty members in the department, within the division, and at the university, students of color who wanted role models would seek out my help. However, she carefully cooed, I should avoid doing too much along those lines because my primary focus must be to publish, publish, publish, and earn tenure. In other words, I took her comments to mean that I was there primarily to serve the needs of the department, add to its diversity profile, and adopt the dominant ideology of individualism to secure my continued place within it. This interest convergence meant that opportunities for faculty of color are open only as long as our presence and work serve the needs and vision of the White structure; if those conditions go unchallenged, assuredly the current and future reality will not change (Bell, 1992; Taylor, Gillborn, & Ladson-Billings, 2009). Resisting the interest convergence paradigm represents a fundamental threat, which for faculty of color shows its results in unfavorable annual, third-year, and promotion and tenure reviews.

That type of advice from my well-intended colleague cuts deeply against the grain of someone who operates from a collectivistic paradigm (Bordas, 2007). Understanding this through the lens of CRT helps me shape my counter-narrative response to the dominant discourse and well-meaning advice, which carries some truth about how to succeed in the academy, but does real harm to the racial reality of being a Black man with a critical consciousness operating in a hostile system. I began to see that the dominant view of so-called successful faculty life meant submitting to an individualistic paradigm. That individualism cuts at the core of cultural difference between Eurocentric-American orientation and African-American heritage collectivist orientations. Frantz Fanon (1994) argues about the permanence of racist structures and the necessity to resist them. As a Black faculty member in a

White space, I too must constantly recognize the permanence of structural racism yet find my survival, salvation, and success through multiple forms of resistance.

William Smith (2004) examines the concept of racial battle fatigue as it relates to African-American faculty and students within White spaces. Smith defines it this way: "[R]acial battle fatigue is a response to the distressing mental/emotional conditions that result from facing racism daily . . ." (p. 180). He identifies many issues that connect directly with my own experiences, such as how most White administrators, and some Black folks in administrative positions, downplay the "race-based stress" Black faculty experience on White campuses (p. 179)—White in terms of the people, policies, and practices. Smith identifies a multitude of symptoms many Black faculty experience because of race-based stress and cites several scholars whose work document these phenomena. I too have experienced many of these symptoms over the past five years, including "tension headaches and backaches . . . rapid breathing in anticipation of a conflict . . . constant anxiety and worrying . . . inability to sleep . . . loss of confidence in oneself and one's colleagues . . . rapid mood swings . . ." (p. 181). These physiological, psychological, and emotional tolls exact a price on your ability to perform at optimal levels, yet the causes of this very real phenomenon are difficult to prove when working in a nice, White space. Whom should Black faculty trust within White spaces? How do Black faculty get respect from an environment that historically constructed obstacles for their very presence? Many early career Black faculty stumble, assuming that there is a level playing field and our racial or ethnic backgrounds no longer matter.

I think what has helped me avoid certain pitfalls as a faculty member is that I try hard to retain my critical consciousness and remind myself that the environments in which I work were not created for me, people who look like me, or people from my type of background. Perhaps my early life experiences taught me to trust myself; pay attention to patterns of human nature; maintain a healthy sense of distance, skepticism, and intellectual curiosity to investigate the claims of others; and the interpersonal skills to navigate and learn from various environments. In addition, I have developed a supportive network of colleagues who share many common perspectives grounded in shared interests, such as CRT and the importance of not allowing the negatives of any academic environments deter us from pursing our multiple understandings of a greater purpose for our work. Working in higher education does put me on alert mode most of the time, but that has proven to be a good thing. It is like having an early warning radar system actively surveying the landscape for possible attacks, yet not becoming so paranoid that I think that everything that happens or might happen is personally directed at others or me. I have learned to think more systemically rather than personally about institutional racism, which has helped me avoid some stumbles regarding self-defeating attitudes or actions. I have tried always to remember where I came from and why I am trying to make a positive difference within the space of higher education. I do not try to avoid my racial heritage or my continual process to remain sensitive to the human condition. However, race always matters, whatever the environment.

Attending PWIs for my undergraduate and graduate education began to make me question my previously unquestioned personal pride and pride in my Blackness. Teaching in a historically and predominately White institution served as a constant reminder that I must continually prove myself regardless of achievements and recognize the message that I am merely a guest in their house.

Remembering that I am a Black man in America, staying connected to my roots and questioning the social, political, and cultural complexities of race and racism in the United States and internationally keeps me reasonably sane and ready to excel within White spaces despite systemic obstacles. Working as a faculty member in academe demonstrates that Black folks earned various degrees of respect and dignity a long time ago. I stand on the shoulders of those who paved this path for me. Although I do not compare myself to legendary Black scholars and educators like W. E. B. DuBois, Anna Julia Cooper, bell hooks, Paula Giddings, Sarah Lawrence-Lightfoot, James Cone, Patricia Hill-Collins, and Derrick Bell, among many others, I try to keep their spirit, successes, and sacrifices in mind as I do this work. It is my responsibility to remember how and why I got here and what I must do to remain.

I found that not knowing who I am and where I come from could destroy any shred of self-confidence and self-worth. The system was not created for folks like me, but folks like me can enter into it, resist its most poisonous aspects, learn from the guides who point us in the best directions and hold the door of opportunity open for those who follow. This mission or calling informs my philosophy and pedagogy. I try to demonstrate my commitment in every class I teach and with each student I mentor. I did not get here alone. My sense of collective purpose and collective benefit is grounded in what I know of African and African-American cultural practice. I believe unexplained forces and influences, not of any plan I designed or anticipated, have shaped my journey. I feel duty bound to take seriously the greater purpose of this work and the responsibility I have to inspire and guide others in the best tradition of our profession.

CHAPTER FIVE

Too Black, Yet Not Black Enough

Challenging White Supremacy in U.S. Teacher Education and the Making of Two Radical Social Misfits

BRENDA G. JUÁREZ AND CLEVELAND HAYES

She's a lunatic, a Nazi against White people. She hates her own kind. Get out now.

—comment, RateYourProfessor.com, Spring 2009

I know that you are incredibly angry. Believe me—we all know that . . . I personally perceive you to be an angry Black supremacist.

—E-mail correspondence, Fall 2009

Although one of us is a White female and the other is a Black male— Brenda and Cleveland, respectively, both of us have been and continue to be regularly viewed by those around us as simultaneously being too Black, yet not Black enough within the confines of our respective personal and professional lives. We are each seen, specifically, as being too Black in a Malcolm X kind of a way—too offensive, too loud, too angry, too force- ful, too bold, too demanding, and too unapologetic in our efforts to name and denounce the profound racial disparities that are everywhere around us and so widely visible for all to see—*it might as well be written across the sky* (Baldwin, 1970).

At the same time, very importantly, both of us are also seen as being not Black enough. Two teacher educators who put Blackness at the center of our teaching—indeed, we are each seen as not Black enough because one of us comes from the (apparently) wrong (White) racial background, and the other one (in a Black body) is (apparently) wrong in continuously insisting that traditional understandings of academic excellence are not inherently at odds with being Black or from any other community of color. Neither of us finds in any way compelling the Hollywood images of Black, Latino, and other students of color in so-called urban school settings as unruly, rebellious thugs and aspiring thugs who become interested in education only when and after a teacher, preferably a White woman, helps them to see the joys of education and change their wrong-headed ways.

This image of respectively being too Black, yet not Black enough very importantly has been institutionally created and applied to us as we have struggled through our teaching, research, and interactions with colleagues, students, and others in teacher education. For both of us, our aim has been to draw on every aspect of our individual personal and professional lives to explore the possibilities of and barriers to education as a practice of social dreaming and living toward a more socially just world. Our respective identities as critical educators were forged by and emerged out of struggles each of us has had with working to help challenge and pull down U.S. teacher education's historical privileging of Whiteness. To be too Black, yet not Black enough, we learned, was to be deemed a radical misfit. "You are the radical one here for sure," one of the department administrators, a White man, told Brenda in a passing conversation in the hallway.

As the epigraph above describes, similarly, Cleveland was named an angry Black supremacist. In the teacher education programs we each worked in, the Blackness of our approaches to the preparation of future teachers was a problem for the Whiteness of teacher education. Put bluntly, our Blackness as teacher educators was a problem for U.S. teacher education's Whiteness. Accordingly, it has been out of our experiences of being respectively named as too Black, yet not Black enough that our identities as critical educators have emerged.

Whiteness, Blackness, Racial Dominance, and the Making of Critical Educators

This chapter is an account of our respective stories of becoming critical educators as we emerged from our challenges to U.S. teacher education's Whiteness racially marked as Black despite our differently raced and gendered bodies. In particular, we are concerned in this chapter with processes of White racial domination and ways that these relationships of power structure group advantages and disadvantages in U.S. society and thus fundamentally and unequally influence individuals' lives and life chances, including our own. Using autoethnographic methods, we present and compare, contrast, and critically analyze our respective pasts and journeys of learning to struggle against the systemic privileging of Whiteness while living our lives from very differently valued subject positions within historically White institutions.

Our purpose in this chapter is to draw on our personal and professional experiences to identify and critically analyze the points of intersection between the systemic privileging of Whiteness and the daily business of teacher education. Our intent, moreover, is not to blame or indict individuals or groups and their actions or choices taken out of context. Rather, we hope to highlight the moments when individuals and groups draw on the institutional power and authority available to them to make decisions, act, and interact in ways that help to sustain and protect the historical supremacy of Whites. As we have learned, the protection of U.S. teacher education's Whiteness may mean the removal or silencing of those individuals or groups that are deemed to pose sufficient threat to the stability of White supremacy.

Following Leonardo (2005), we define White supremacy as "a racialized social system that upholds, reifies and reinforces the superiority of Whites" (p. 127). By Blackness, in turn, we refer not to any specific skin tone or phenotypical features, but rather to a political stance or association strategically, explicitly, and unwaveringly taken up to stand with and become a part and direct target of the suffering and misery that afflicts *the wretched of the earth* (Fanon, 1963; West, 1993)—those individuals and groups whose humanity has systematically been violated through the last four centuries in the name of a superior God and in the service of imperialist, colonizing endeavors (Wright, 1954). Whiteness likewise refers not to a specific skin color, but instead to the historical privileging or overvaluing of characteristics, interests, values, histories, accomplishments, and values associated with White people while simultaneously devaluing all that signifies and is associated with Blackness, being Black, African-American, and other communities of color (Lipsitz, 2006). Indeed, individuals and groups are racially marked as other than White—they are named as Black, for example, as they are positioned and negatively evaluated and measured against the normative standard of Whiteness (Dyer, 1998).

Importantly, the privileging of Whiteness is produced through processes of White racial domination (Leonardo, 2005). The dominance of Whites is reflected across nearly all domains of U.S. society and by the system of White supremacy (Feagin, 2010; Gillborn, 2005). Processes of White racial domination are secured through "those acts, decisions, and policies that White subjects perpetrate on people of color" (Leonardo, 2005, p. 75). Specifically, "[d]omination is a relation of power that subjects enter into and is forged in the historical process. It does not form out of random acts of hatred, although these are condemnable, but rather out of a patterned and enduring treatment of social groups" (Leonardo, 2005, p. 77).

Because the supremacy of Whites must be continually made and remade, very significantly, we posit that it can also be unmade.

Loving Blackness to Challenge Whiteness: Considering Dangers and Possibilities

It has been our experience, pointedly, that there are serious consequences to being labeled too Black, yet not Black enough, and to being called a radical, critical educator. Nat Turner, John Brown, Malcolm X, and the Rev. Dr. King Jr. were just a few among the named and unnamed countless who have paid with their lives for their identification with Blackness. We have found that regardless of how one's body is identified—White, Black, female or male, and more, if one pushes back hard enough, there most surely will be significant, very material, very deeply felt and very personal consequences for standing "against White supremacy by choosing to value, indeed to love, Blackness" (hooks, 1992, p. 11). In contrast to the Black male body always and already inscribed as a White-invented *thing of danger* (Bennett, 1966), for example, a White female body—not immediately presumed dangerous—may, perhaps, purchase some temporary reprieve before consequences are rendered. Ultimately, however, even a White female body will not provide adequate means to escape from or remain unscathed by the militant aggression of Whiteness reserved for those who sufficiently threaten White racial dominance.

Writers of the Black Power manifesto Kwame Ture and Charles Hamilton (1967) strongly suggested, and today we know that "[j]obs will have to be sacrificed, positions of prestige and status given up, favors forfeited . . . When one forcefully challenges the racist system, one cannot, at the same time, expect that system to reward [her] or even treat [her] comfortably" (p. 15). Between us—both Brenda and Cleveland—we have experienced being fired from jobs, passed over for promotions, forced to leave places and people we call home and love; and this is not to mention the daily micro-aggressions we have been subjected to for being identified with Blackness and thus outside the realm of respectability within the contexts of our personal and professional lives.

To love Blackness, accordingly and perhaps not surprisingly, "is rarely a political stance that is reflected in daily life. When present it is deemed suspect, dangerous and threatening" (hooks, 1992, p. 10). This chapter contains the respective stories of how we each came to be named as too Black, the wrong kind of Black, yet not Black enough and thus both became critical educators despite the very different starting points we were born into within society and given the differently gendered and raced bodies in which we each live our lives.

Life Stories, White Supremacy, and the Domination Problem

How is it, then, that our stories can be used as a tool to challenge the existing racial hierarchy? Like the life story of fictional heroine Miss Jane Pittman, which carried and reflected the events and dynamics of the Reconstruction era immediately following the Civil War in the American Deep South (Gaines, 1971), our lived experiences (and those of others) are embedded within and hence also reflect the larger institutionalized story of White supremacy in the United States over time (Feagin, 2010). Our stories reflect and connect us as individuals to the patterned inequities that characterize larger society. Pointedly, without breaking down these points at which societal patterns of inequity crash into individuals' daily lives, the racial status quo remains intact and undisturbed (hooks, 1989; Picca & Feagin, 2007). That Brenda is White and Cleveland is Black, therefore, is not insignificant in terms of the racial knowledge we were raised with, taught to apply and use to interpret the world.

Racial Knowledge: Learning to Be White

Reflected in Brenda's background, indeed, the stories collectively told and passed down by Whites have typically served to justify White supremacy. Brenda was raised in the Midwest in a predominantly White community. She is the eldest of seven children from a working-class family and the first in her family to attend and graduate from college. Not uncommon among White people (Picca & Feagin, 2007), Brenda grew up with virtually no contact with people of color. For Brenda, hearing anti-Black jokes and stories was regular conversation fare at the dinner table. Yet Brenda also grew up exposed to dominant White society's liberal discourses of democracy, equality, and freedom for all [in rhetoric], albeit in practice reserved for Whites and those few *well-screened, well-scrubbed* people of color (Lomax, 1966). As is true for many Whites (Bonilla Silva, 2001), Brenda grew up inspired by the idea of equality and freedom while simultaneously learning to be [color]blind to race and racial disparities—*see no race, hear no race, speak no race* (Leonardo, 2005). She thus learned from early on in her life to filter out the fact that she and her community lived on land forcibly taken from American Indians.

Importantly, it wasn't until Brenda left her community and home state to attend a university far from where she grew up and then some years later returned home for a visit that she was able to racially "see"—the streets signs, towns, and mascots named for those who had long ago been removed from their homelands. Just before finishing her bachelor's degree in elementary education, Brenda had spent some time living in South America, where she got married. Upon returning to the United States, she had become a mother of children who could not pass for White. She also became a public schoolteacher of children, economic refugees from Mexico who were learning English. These two conditions better enabled Brenda to begin "seeing" and questioning society's deeply race-based disparities and look for a way to understand and explain them—a quest for understanding that led her to graduate school.

Racial Knowledge: Learning to Be Black

Cleveland, in turn, was born and raised in the American Deep South. He is the eldest child of three in a family of parents and grandparents who have spent their lives seeking the betterment not only of immediate family members, but also of the entire Black community through public education. Both of Cleveland's parents graduated from college and spent their professional lives as public schoolteachers working in public schools of the U.S. South. Cleveland's paternal grandmother was well known in the region as a highly effective teacher who taught for more than fifty years in her community's public schools. Given his group membership and childhood experiences within a predominantly Black community in the U.S. South, Cleveland grew up exposed to a body of racial knowledge different from that with which Brenda was raised in a nearly all-White community. Cleveland, unlike Brenda, grew up knowing a great deal about and able to clearly "see" the race-based disparities everywhere around him—these racial disparities were part of his everyday life growing up as a young Black man in the U.S. South during the 1970s. Communicated to him by the adults in his life—his paternal grandmother, his parents, and other elders in his family and community (Hayes, 2006; Hayes, Juárez, & Cross, 2012), Cleveland was raised hearing and being taught from the stories and wisdoms collectively told and passed down by African-Americans across generations in his home state and the region.

For example, that White people typically retained for themselves and passed down to their kin some of the best educational, political, economic, and other forms of social opportunities and resources by using racially exclusionary practices, sometimes changing the rules of the game and other such kinds of trickery to maintain their racial privileges, was not new news to Cleveland as he graduated from high school and entered adulthood. As Cleveland was growing up, it was not uncommon for him to be within hearing of adults around him discussing the ways that Whites often collaborated to maintain their advantages as they talked about events in the area—he could still hear the elders talking, "Of course Lily Scribner was hired. Her father has known the mayor all of his life." And sometimes the elders spoke directly to Cleveland about the kinds of racially exclusionary practices that Whites used to maintain their advantages—none of the adults around him wanted Cleveland to be crushed if he wasn't chosen for the award over a White child despite his clear ability to perform well. It was widely known that Whites would choose one of their own even when it wasn't merited. Moreover, Cleveland was not blind to the world around him. He could clearly see everywhere around him that Whites were the ones in positions of power across the region despite the high percentage of African-Americans in his home state, for example. As he looked around his hometown, Cleveland could see that Whites tended to have the better jobs, the better homes, the better schools, and other types of social advantages.

Not for a moment did Cleveland or anyone in his community make the mistake of thinking that Whites had all of that social advantage simply because they supposedly worked harder and were smarter and more culturally astute than people of color. People from Cleveland's community knew that Whites believed that story of White hard work and that they also wanted Blacks to believe that story of White hard work, but they also knew that one would be hard-pressed to find any Black person who actually did believe that story of White hard work. Seeing the world through the racial knowledge of his community's collective wisdoms, Cleveland had learned early in his childhood not to unquestioningly accept the assumptions of Whites' supposedly rightful place as rulers and owners of the world and more put forth by Whites to justify their race-based supremacy in the United States. There was a reason that Whites retained supremacy in U.S. society, and it wasn't just because of their hard work and effort.

Those group-based racial stories and collective wisdoms, like those of other communities of color in the United States, have typically served as an important tool used by African-Americans collectively and individually over time to resist and challenge or counter, rather than sustain and rationalize, the readily visible supremacy of Whites within U.S. society. This racial knowledge was passed down to Cleveland in the form of counter-stories recounted by Big Mama, his paternal grandmother, and other elders within the African-American community in his hometown. This group-based racial knowledge was conveyed to Cleveland as a means to protect him as he grew up in a world hostile to Blackness by providing him (and other children) with alternative understandings and interpretations of the surrounding world not dependent on assumptions of White superiority and Black inferiority. These alternative interpretations were conveyed to the rising generation by the elders through counter-stories about life and how to make sense of being Black in a hostile White world. Reflective of the experiences and conditions of communities of color as defined by themselves, counter-stories provide spaces for challenging, dismantling, and reinterpreting dominant White notions of African-Americans and other people of color as morally and culturally deficient.

Take Your Racial Knowledge Inheritance and Do with It What You Will

Raised in very different regions of the United States, we were each socialized to view the world through very different forms of racial knowledge. Yet—and we cannot overemphasize the importance of this point—while the racial groups into which we were each born do indeed strongly influence us and the ways we approach and make sense of the surrounding world, the racial knowledge we were each raised with *does not determine* the racial knowledge we now make use of to guide our lives (Leonardo, 2005). It simply means that each of us is likely to be more familiar with, draw on, and make use of one rather than another form of race-based knowledge given our different racial group memberships.

For this reason—because racial knowledge is not definitely determined by group membership—we posit that it is possible for Brenda (and other White people) to learn to draw on and apply the collective wisdoms of communities of color despite not being a person of color. At the same time, significantly, we recognize that there are and have been very few Whites who have learned to and do draw on the racial knowledge of communities of color. Rather, most White people continue to draw on and pass on understandings of the world that justify White supremacy (Feagin, 2012). Moreover, we also recognize that no matter how well Brenda or other Whites learn to see and act in the world through a Black perspective, they cannot themselves directly tap into the existential experience of Blackness. Perhaps more importantly, as White people, they are the benefactors of the continually renewed and accumulated/ing privileging of Whiteness even when they prefer not to be (Lipstiz, 2006).

Regarding people of color and racial knowledge, in turn, we also recognize that although Cleveland is a Black man raised with the counter-knowledge of the African-American community, he very well could embody White racial knowledge in ways that collude with and support the ongoing dominance of Whites; again, one's group membership influences but does not determine one's racial understandings. To be very clear, then, Cleveland does not *have* to draw on the counter-stories or racial knowledge of the African-American community even though he is Black. Indeed, as a young man just out of high school and starting college, Cleveland remembers feeling that the key to his success in life was for him to become as White-like as possible and thus as un-Black as possible—that it was he, not society, who needed to change. Specifically, to achieve some level of success in his life, Cleveland felt that he needed to change his mannerisms, ways of talking, and dialect, all of which identified him as a Southern-born and -raised Black man. Seeking conformity (to Whiteness) as a way to achieve, Cleveland likewise felt some personal responsibility for helping to erase the many negative stereotypes that he knew most Whites and others continue to carry about Blacks, especially young Black men. Always conscious of his group membership, Cleveland took pains not to act in ways that would reflect badly on Blacks or help to give credence to the many assumptions of Black cultural and moral inferiority.

Later, as a public schoolteacher, Cleveland also sought to help his students of color work to overcome this perceived Black and Latino *lack* by becoming as White-like as possible. Over time, however, Cleveland learned the hard way a lesson that many people of color also learn—that, for Whites in general, he would always be too Black and never really White-like enough no matter how hard he worked or how carefully and exactly he played by the dominant society's rules. Cleveland felt that both he and his students somehow always seemed to come up short when measured by and against White standards.

It wasn't until he entered graduate school and started working on a master's degree, moreover, that Cleveland, like Brenda, began to learn about and acquire the language and skills that enabled him to examine more carefully the Whiteness of society and to further challenge the idea of moral and cultural deficiencies ascribed to him and communities of color. No language of critique or transcendence—ironically? we think not—was made available to either of us in our schooling prior to our graduate education. Far too many of us, for far too many generations, have received too much schooling and not enough education (Shujaa, 1994).

From Teachers to Teacher Educators: Dreams of Multicultural Teacher Preparation

Interestingly, although we—Brenda and Cleveland—taught in the same school district for several years, it was not until we were both enrolled in the same class in the same doctoral program that we happened to meet each other. Our respective public school experiences of teaching in classrooms made up predominantly of students of color led each of us to enter graduate school with the same misgivings. We were concerned with what we had seen acted out daily at work—that most teachers enter the classroom unprepared to teach all students effectively (Juárez & Hayes, 2010; Ladson-Billings, 2000). Both of us became teacher educators because we were committed to public schools and knew that all teachers must be prepared to teach all students effectively if race-based disparities in education are to be successfully interrupted (Juárez & Hayes, 2012).

Right after we each finished graduate school, then, Brenda became part of a teacher education faculty that officially promoted democratic education for all students. Cleveland, in turn, became part of a teacher education faculty that officially pronounced its commitment to social justice education. However, neither of us was aware at that time that when teacher preparation programs make official pronouncements that they are committed to democratic education and social justice in education, they are referring to education that is democratic and socially just for White people (Juárez, Smith, & Hayes, 2008).

We Are Not What We Seem:[1]
Whiteness, Blackness, and Racial Identities

Conflicts over competing understandings of multicultural teacher education emerged for each of us when we failed to conform to the institution's racialized expectations of us. From the looks of us—one White and female and one Black and male—those around us, including teacher educators, expect us to act in racially specific and gendered ways. Those expectations function as mechanisms of control to contain and direct our activities, interactions, and even our speech (especially about race and racism) within the formal settings of teacher education. Brenda is expected to act and speak according to the norms of a "well-behaved" White woman who does not see, hear, or speak of race and racism. Cleveland, in turn, is expected to act and speak according to the norms of a "well-behaved" Black man. He is supposed to speak and act as if race and racism do not matter, because he is just like us (White people)—"well-mannered," never angry, never loud—except in an always-compliant Black body.

This racial identity–based control mechanism is exercised by individuals and groups who have and are authorized to use institutional power to sanction or reward us according to the alignment of our behavior with institutional (White) norms; the more aligned with the normative standards and values of Whiteness our behavior is, the more our behavior is considered respectable and worthy of social reward and acknowledgement by the institutional representatives. The more we speak and act like the "well-behaved" White woman and Black man we are expected to be, then the more we are deemed respectable and rewarded by the institution. Unfortunately, neither of us—Brenda or Cleveland—has acted or spoken in ways that closely align with the institution's race-based expectations of us, especially in matters of race and racism.

In the words of Richard Wright (1941), *we are not what we seem*. There is a big disparity between people's expectations of us and their actual experiences in their interactions with us, and we have been sanctioned materially for this race-based disparity. Thus, we become alarmed when others have the power to act on and sanction us for their disapproval and dislike of our speech and activity. Indeed, we don't mind when others think poorly of us unless they have the authority and ability to act on their negative perceptions of us—which often has been the case for us in our professional lives.

Within a society that privileges Whiteness in part by negatively stereotyping people of color, as a Black man, Cleveland is more likely to be immediately and already seen as a troublemaker than Brenda is as a White woman. Of medium height and build, with blue eyes and long, blond hair, for example, Brenda is known for going to class wearing black jeans, black boots, a silver-studded black belt, and a black, short-sleeved T-shirt that doesn't hide the Malcolm X tattoo on her upper left arm. Identified and identifiable as a White woman, Brenda's attire for class is often judged by others as "eccentric" but not necessarily as bad or disrespectful. On the other hand, Cleveland—a tall, gifted football player, and beautifully not able to pass for White, if we may say so—prefers and realizes that it is important for him to dress up for class. Donning slacks, a white shirt, and perhaps a bow tie, Cleveland dresses for campus with a professional look in mind as he prepares to teach a class, attend a meeting, and more. For Cleveland, jeans and a T-shirt are out of the question. As a Black man, Cleveland is continually required to establish and reestablish his credibility and authority on campus to counter the already inscribed White racial understandings of him as an interloper who doesn't belong or fit in such a professional setting.

Given our race-based and gendered appearances, many people take Brenda as being warm, friendly, quiet to the point of being shy, not dangerous at all, and certainly no threat to anyone verbally or physically. One of Brenda's students once said of her, "She is kindergarten sweet, with her feminine, high-pitched voice, and it takes you a minute to register in your head that this sweet lady just called you a racist." This is not to suggest that Brenda isn't warm, friendly, and sweet (in personality); it's more the case that she is not afraid to speak out against Whiteness. The reverberations of society's expectations for White women as ideally fragile, quiet, docile, not terribly smart, passive, nonthreatening, and not taking up much space is encapsulated in the idea of Brenda as sweet.

By comparison, with his height and physical build, Blackness, and maleness, when Cleveland enters a predominantly White space, he is rarely taken as already approachable, warm, and friendly—and certainly not as sweet. Indeed, Cleveland knows that each time he enters a predominantly

White space, especially one where he is not already known and White women are present, he is immediately seen as a threat who must prove himself otherwise. On course evaluations, students have often described Cleveland as "unapproachable," "arrogant," and "not warm."

Despite these negative ascriptions, Cleveland has received many positive course evaluations from students. These positive evaluations include such things as "This was the best class I ever took" or "I learned more in this class than any other." However, the negative evaluations, used in concert with other official practices, have been used by the institution to label him as deficient in his abilities to relate to and interact with others in the classroom and as part of an academic department and teacher education program.

The ways we are each seen within the institution have real, material consequences for us; these institutional ascriptions are used as mechanisms of social control, providing a rationale for sanctions against us. Pointedly, in contrast to Cleveland, Brenda is given some leeway with her deviations from the institution's expectations for professors viewed as "weird" but not necessarily dangerous or threatening as a benefit of the historical privileging of Whiteness. Like Cleveland, Brenda has received her share of student evaluations that describe her as "crazy," and "prejudiced against White people" as well as others that suggest she is an outstanding teacher. These negative student evaluations, however, were not immediately seized by the institution to negatively sanction Brenda, as in Cleveland's case. As illustrated by subsequent descriptions of her classroom experiences, it was only after Brenda continued to push up against Whiteness that negative student evaluations were used by the institution as one tool among others to sanction her and ultimately to physically remove her.

Brenda's insistence on naming the Whiteness of teacher education located her as too Black when evaluated against and compared to the Whiteness of the institution. At the same time, however, Brenda was not Black enough given her physically White body and skin color. Because of the Whiteness of her physical body, Brenda is initially given some leeway by the institution—she is seen as odd or strange by other Whites. She is able to push the boundaries of Whiteness in ways that Cleveland is not allowed to because of her physically White body and skin color.

Yet Brenda is still White—assuming that she can be controlled (by Whiteness), Brenda will never be Black (enough) in her physical appearance and skin color to be useful to the institution as a window-dressing form of tamed, unthreatening (to Whiteness) racial diversity. Because Brenda will not ever be or become the form of Blackness useful to the institution (this window-dressing, tamed form of racial diversity), she therefore is expected to conform to and allow herself to be policed back into Whiteness. She is expected to behave like a good White person, and good White people do not challenge Whiteness. Ultimately, when Brenda refuses to return to the fold of Whites and view the world through White racial knowledge, she is literally physically expelled. The privileging of Whiteness extended to White bodies is elastic and therefore able to stretch the boundaries of White standards—but only to a point when refusal to return to Whiteness is redefined as the enemy challenging Whites' collective interests.

Named by Whiteness as Too Black:
Processes of White Racial Domination Enacted

To be considered strange or arrogant by students has differently weighted consequences depending on whom the targeted individual is—more specifically, what he or she looks like. It has been our experience that it is far more acceptable for Brenda, a White female, compared to Cleveland, a Black male, to be considered strange and arrogant as the professor in the classroom. Yet being named as strange and arrogant by the institution did not carry enough weight on its own to silence or sanction Cleveland. It was only when this institutional naming of Cleveland as deviant and deficient was combined with other institutional practices that serious harm resulted.

As multiple institutional practices combine and reinforce the naming of the individual as deficient, serious repercussions begin to emerge. A web of social meaning ascribed to and locking in the targeted individual is produced as an outcome of multiple practices enacted by the institution. For Brenda and Cleveland, the institutional practice of annual faculty reviews was made concrete in the form of official letters that articulated the institution's assessment of their performance as defined by administrators. The convergence of formal and informal institutional practices—in our cases, student evaluations, faculty reviews, and interactions with administrators and others in meetings officially and unofficially in hallway conversations—combined to produce a fairly durable, stable, and authoritative definition of us as deficient against the hidden referent of Whiteness.

In the following excerpted official letter of evaluation from Brenda's annual faculty review in 2010, the authority of the institution is drawn on and enacted through the power-laden practice of annual evaluations to officially name her as outside respectability and therefore illegitimate in the academy:

> She knows a lot about cultural diversity and is very outspoken . . .
> She receives some of the best student evaluations in the department and college and some of the worst. Consistent with past evaluations, students often couch a negative comment within an

otherwise positive comment saying that the workload is heavy
and that she uses "shock and awe" techniques which include
the use of profanity . . . She has been advised to continue to
evaluate the effectiveness of her teaching practices to ensure she
meets the needs of and reaches all of her students. (Third Year
Review Department Report, Spring 2010)

Representatives of the university, using their more powerful positioning,
draw on the institution's authority to name Brenda as "knowledgeable" and
"very outspoken"; this is an act of power. Brenda may or may not agree with
this assessment. However, her self-definition does not carry the power of the
institution's definition because she does not have access to the institution's
authority for self-naming or the means to reward or sanction herself on the
basis of that naming.

Carried in this excerpted official evaluation, moreover, are assumptions of Whiteness, and Brenda's violations of these implied normative
standards are reflected in the descriptors applied to her and her teaching. These descriptors reflect a hidden assumption that Brenda has crossed
the line of respectability—to be very outspoken is to have violated and
crossed the boundaries of accepted standards of how to speak; the word
"very" means that Brenda has not gone just a little over the boundaries of
acceptability but far beyond them. The implied expectation is that Brenda
should constrain her speaking about cultural diversity (a euphemism for
race and racism) to a level that does not move to "very" or beyond what
is acceptable speaking.

From the institution's White perspective, Brenda needs to speak in
a quieter, gentler tone; she is too Black in her ways of speaking. Similarly,
the description of Brenda's course evaluations as some of the best and worst
of the department and college and her use of "shock and awe techniques,"
including the use of profanity, again define her as outside what the institution implicitly considers reasonable, appropriate, and respectable. The official letter makes note of the pattern of deviance in Brenda's teaching with
reference to past evaluations.

As the following excerpted documents suggest, the institution also
defines Cleveland's way of presenting himself and communicating with others as problematic (for the institution and its representatives); like Brenda,
Cleveland is too Black. That Cleveland is too Black becomes visible when
representatives of the institution respond by organizing a helping committee
to "help" him learn to communicate more effectively—that is to say, in a
way that is more acceptable to Whites. Addressed to senior faculty members,
an official letter in Cleveland's personnel file describes the purpose of the
helping committee organized by institutional administrators.

This letter reads:

> Thank you for volunteering to work with Cleveland through a helping committee. The area of greatest concern that the faculty has perceived is Cleveland's passion for social justice as being too confrontational or impatient with others' development in ability to understand these social justice issues.

Within this letter, Cleveland is officially defined as "too confrontational" and too "impatient" with others (White people), and his passion for social justice is officially named as a problem (for the mostly White faculty). It might be said here, as has been suggested to us (and we agree), that in this official letter, Cleveland is being named as too uppity. Being called too confrontational, too impatient, and always needing to be right seems to be the new way of telling Black people that they have not stayed in their place, and they have become too uppity for Whites' taste.

The practice of drawing on institutional authority to organize a helping committee is an act of power that formally locates Cleveland outside the institution's standards. It also is punitive, as it coerces him into attending humiliating meetings with helpers, which also take time away from his academic duties. Like Brenda, Cleveland has crossed an implied line of respectability in terms of what he may speak about and how he may speak. Cleveland is expected to be less confrontational, more patient, and therefore softer and gentler in his approach to social justice with those around him if he is to remain within implicit interactional boundaries of the institution. Interestingly, despite the institution's pronounced commitment to social justice, the greatest concern conveyed through the letter is not realizing social justice but Cleveland's apparent inability to relate to others (White people) in a way that they deem palatable.

Despite the efforts of the helping committee to help him speak about social justice in ways more tolerable to and for Whites, Cleveland is defined by the institution as falling short and thus still crossing boundaries it sets for appropriateness in behavior and conversation. Cleveland's failure to conform to the rules of Whiteness in his ways of speaking and communicating about social justice are conveyed in a follow-up letter that also remains in his personnel file:

> Cleveland's colleagues have noted some growth, but there needs to be significantly more growth. His passion about his social justice agenda often presents itself as inflexibility and as a lack of ability to consider others' perspectives. Cleveland comes across as arrogant and as if he always needs to be right.

Once again, Cleveland's passion for social justice is named by the institution as a problem (for White people). Defining Cleveland as having made "some growth" toward speaking in more White-accepted ways but still falling short of the normative standard is an act of power. The institution assigns negative characteristics to Cleveland's personality and character, that is to say, "arrogant," "uncaring," "inflexible," and "too passionate" in his annual evaluation letter. This letter acts as a control mechanism to shift attention away from the institution's hidden referent of Whiteness and toward Cleveland and his apparent inability to get along with others, particularly his colleagues. The Whiteness remains undisturbed and thus protected, with the focus shifted to Cleveland and his perceived personality deficiencies, the solution to which is a committee designated to help him get along better with others.

Hence, the Whiteness of the institution is (re)secured as representatives of the institution draw on their authority to enact power through formal evaluation practices, discrediting us and thereby sanctioning us for our ongoing critiques of the Whiteness in teacher education. By naming each of us as deviant, not able to get along with others, and outside respectability, the problems are located within us—we are each too Black. For both of us, official documents defining us as outside of reasonable have been used against us to sanction us by jeopardizing our continued employment and job security.

Not Black Enough: Not the Right Kind of Black— the Desired and Desirable Kind of Black

In our experience, the dominance of Whiteness is not always visually and officially secured through direct power, such as in faculty evaluations and "helping" committees. Informal and formal interactions with others have also played a significant, albeit less explicit role. Through informal interactions, each of us has been marked as the wrong kind of Black and thus inappropriate for teacher education. For us, the higher education classroom has been a site where the normative standards of Whiteness police our respective actions, interactions, and speech as individuals and teachers. These interactions, although not officially documented, operate just as effectively as formal evaluation methods to protect the supremacy of Whites. Indeed, they support and reinforce official ascriptions of us as deficient. To illustrate how Whiteness serves as the hidden referent that polices interactions and helps to name each of us as the wrong kind of Black, we share representative class discussions that have occurred within each of our mostly White female classrooms.

First Graders and Bad Words on the School Bus

The first discussion we share took place in Brenda's classroom:

White female future teacher sharing about her school site visit with the class: "I was waiting in the front office of the school today when I overhead this seven-year-old African-American boy getting suspended. The principal was calling the boy's grandma. His mom is in jail. She had been driving on a suspended license. She had been trying to get her son to school when she was pulled over. He's a first grader. He had been having trouble on the [school] bus. The bus driver was there. He is White. The teacher is White. The principal is White. Almost everyone in the school is White. The driver had told this kid that if he gets in trouble one more time on the bus, he would be suspended.

This morning he said the "F" word on the bus."

[*There is an audible, collective gasp of disapproval that emerges from this class of future teachers that includes 20 White younger women, one older Black woman, and one White younger man.*]

Brenda: "Ahhh . . . So you think this child is a bad boy from a bad home who deserves to be punished, correct? We've been talking all semester long about the overrepresentation of Black and Latino students, especially boys, and racial disparities in school discipline practices . . . but none of you see any red flags here, right? What about the racial disparities in the court system and arrest rates? Nobody thought about any of that with regard to why his mother might be in jail for a suspended driver's license? No red flags here for anybody?

Hmm . . . Well, I will tell you something—I admit it, sometimes I do get angry and yes . . . sometimes I do say fuck, too, when I'm angry. But you are trying to tell me that you never say bad words—ever, correct? Because you are good people, correct? And those of us who do say fuck when we are angry, we are bad people, right?

[*A second audible, collective gasp of offended disapproval emerges from the group of future teachers.*]

I'm disappointed. Not one of us here even wondered what drove that child to say "fuck" on the bus?—was he being teased every day on the bus? Called the "N" word? We don't know. Yet we are all here on our moral high horse ready to suspend a child that already has trouble getting to school because he said "fuck" on the bus. And, of course [sarcastically], wwe-eee-ee [strong emphasis and elongation of the word 'we'] NEVER [with self-righteous tone] say "fuck," good people that we are. And even though we know that Black males in particular are over-represented in school discipline patterns in schools, right, we are ready to suspend this child." [*No one speaks or moves for a long, uncomfortable moment. Brenda breaks the silence; she assigns the homework and excuses the class. There is nothing more to say. Students leave quietly.*]

In this classroom interaction, Brenda's aim was to challenge the students' implied assumptions about the moral goodness of Whites and the moral deficiencies of Blacks and other communities of color. The hidden referent of Whiteness becomes visible through these implied assumptions of the moral goodness of Whites and the moral deficiencies of Blacks conveyed through the future teachers' expressed shock at the use of profanity by the child in the story and then Brenda's own use of profanity in the classroom. Held by many White people, including these future teachers, this act of a Black child using profanity on the school bus fits and confirms for them the stereotype of Black people as morally and culturally deficient and Black parents and families in particular as criminal and delinquent in raising well-behaved, appropriately speaking Black children; profanity falls outside of the realms of respectable, appropriate speech.

That White people and White children in particular do not use the word "fuck" and that only Black people and Black children do use it is clearly a faulty assumption. Yet this assumption does expose this group of future teachers' belief in White people's moral goodness. Brenda's aim was to expose the implicit assumptions of White moral goodness and Black moral badness carried within the students' reactions and conversations. Brenda's intent was to help her students learn how to question the racial knowledge they used to make sense of social situations—in this case, involving African-Americans—as a way to help them learn to interrupt rather than buttress racial disparities in education, especially as future teachers.

In using profanity herself, Brenda is seeking to make visible how Whiteness structures the lives of individuals, privileging Whites and oppressing people of color through assumptions of White goodness and Black badness. Significantly, Brenda's use of profanity was taken out of context in the official evaluations of her teaching and used to define her as a deviant teacher. She is too Black because she uses profanity, which is considered inappropriate and bad, and bad is associated with Blacks. This naming of Brenda as a deviant teacher is informal at first but is later translated into an official evaluative document.

The informal naming of Brenda as deviant carries significance because it is the basis on which her professional reputation is built and circulated throughout the institution and the community. Eventually, Brenda learned that some faculty were openly advising students not to take her class, although they had never attended one of her classes or communicated with her in any way about her teaching perspectives and practices. Had Brenda failed to challenge the hidden assumptions of White goodness in this scenario, however, she would have left unchallenged the Whiteness of the institutional structures that negatively influence people of color on a daily basis—the patterns of interacting between individuals and groups based on their relationship to Whiteness and the ability of that group to impose their perspectives as normative standards. Although Brenda is not Black in terms of her own racial identity, she is nevertheless not Black enough. Given her stance in the classroom, she has aligned herself with Blackness although she is a White person and thus has become the wrong kind of Black, a target of processes of White racial domination.

Cleveland is likewise informally defined as not Black enough through interactions in the classroom. In the following classroom scenario, Cleveland challenges the assumptions circulating in the conversation that take as a given that people of color are morally, culturally, and educationally deficient. His challenge to Whiteness is then used against him to reinforce the institution's formal and thus official definition of him as deficient and illegitimate in the academy.

Making Accommodations for Race, Class, and Poverty: Cleveland's Question

Cleveland is sitting in on a colleague's multicultural education class for future teachers. The students in this class, as well as the professor, are White and female with the exception of two White males. The class has been discussing Ruby Payne's (1998) book A Framework for Understanding Poverty as a springboard for a discussion on lesson planning and issues of poverty in teaching, learning, and curriculum design.

Cleveland inserts himself into the class's discussion: "I have been sitting here listening to this conversation about students from economically poor backgrounds. I am sorry, but I have to ask this—why is there a modification for poverty on the lesson plan form? My fear is that with this modification expectation on the lesson plan, teachers will lower their expectations for students who come from other than middle class backgrounds."

Professor teaching the class and leading the discussion (She is a tenured full professor): "That will not happen."

Cleveland: "Well, I'm not sure. There has been some research to suggest that it does. Moreover, it is often the kids of color that are com-

ing from poor backgrounds, and teachers often have lower expectations for
them."

Professor (She appears to be angry and defensive and speaks in a sharp
tone): "Race is not the factor here, it is poverty. I grew up poor, and I know
that [lowering of expectations] is not going to happen."

At this point in the class discussion, Cleveland decided to say no more. He
remained silent for the duration of this class meeting. The next day, this professor came to Cleveland's office to talk to him about the previous evening:

Professor: "We need to talk about what happened last night in my class.
What you did was completely inappropriate."

Cleveland: "I was simply trying to ask a question that would spark dialogue
about the role of poverty and teacher expectations. Students need to hear
and be engaged in these kinds of discussions."

Professor: "No, they do not. I do not want you to come to any more of
my classes. You are no longer welcome."

After her exit, Cleveland correctly guessed that this conversation was
not going to be the last he heard of the incident in her classroom. A few
weeks later, having no prior notification or knowledge of what had happened, Cleveland was called into the administration's office and told that
a letter of reprimand had been placed in his personnel file. Having been
given no opportunity to respond, Cleveland was aware that representatives
of the institution were drawing on their official authority to sanction him
for his challenges to Whiteness. As in Brenda's classroom scenario, Whiteness is the hidden referent operating to silence Cleveland's ability to pose
questions about the appropriateness of teaching approaches designated for
students identified as economically poor, although imposed by his colleague
rather than students. Cleveland's colleague used her position of authority as
the senior colleague and professor of the class he was visiting to silence his
questioning of the intersection between race and class in classrooms—as we
have seen, Whiteness insists that we *see no race, hear no race, and speak no
race*. Cleveland is institutionally defined as not Black enough because of his
refusal to take as given the implied assumption that economically poor (or
Black) students will not successfully engage the curriculum and therefore
must have specific poverty-related accommodations in teachers' lesson plans.
As we have learned, moreover, processes of White racial domination target
those who become constant irritations and threats to White supremacy.
Representatives of the institution will not hesitate to draw on their official

authority to sanction behavior that questions and thus threatens White supremacy.

On the Radar of Whiteness: Some Consequences of Challenging White Dominance

Over time, depending on the degree and consistency of their challenges, those who push long and hard enough will eventually register on the radar of White supremacy as enough of a problem to require sanctions. For Brenda, the institution moved to eliminate her as a threat to Whiteness by removing her completely from the context; White women who can speak about multicultural issues in ways that are much less threatening, and much more mild-mannered and tame, are indeed quite plentiful—a dime a dozen. As illustrated, Brenda could be and easily was replaced with someone deemed more respectable, someone who would pose less of a challenge to Whiteness:

White male college administrator standing with a department administrator who is also White and male: "Some bad news." [Holds out an official document on university letterhead that states employment contract will not be renewed] "University policy doesn't allow us to discuss the reasons why."

Brenda has just arrived at the administrator's office foyer, standing just inside the doorway: [Skims letter and looks up. Long, awkward pause of silence] "Okay. Thank you for your time." [She turns to go]

White male department administrator: "I would normally ask if you have any questions. But I can't."

The continuous challenges Brenda posed to the dominance of Whiteness in this context accumulated to the point that she was considered enough of a threat to have to be physically removed from the context. The representatives of the institution drew on their institutional authority to use official means to remove her from the context. Brenda's contract of employment was terminated in an act of domination to (re)secure Whiteness.

Processes of domination were likewise used to silence Cleveland, albeit in a different way. Cleveland, unlike Brenda, has some usefulness as a man in a Black body. As long as he is tamed and controlled, he can be used by the institution as multicultural diversity window dressing. He need only act like one of us (White people) who happens to be in a Black body. The helping committee, importantly, was designed to assist him in learning how to speak and interact appropriately White and thus in a way that would no longer alienate and offend Whites. That Cleveland was not compliant enough in modifying his behavior and speech in ways that would be considered appropriate to Whites around him became apparent a few weeks after the questioning incident in his colleague's classroom. Action to minimize or eliminate his continued challenges to Whiteness was taken by the representative of the institution, as suggested in the following excerpted official document summarizing a complaint against him placed in his personnel file. It reads:

> Given the reports I have received from a number of sources including faculty whose judgment and observations I trust, and students regarding your performance to date, it seems apparent that the process is not working for you. You have been reported as both casual in your attitude and presence. You have interrupted class to argue with the instructor regarding instructional resources and pedagogy. Comments from students include indifferent, rude, and hostile.

Based on this negative evaluation of Cleveland's perceived unwillingness to comply with the normative standards of Whiteness in his speech and interactions, actions were taken by representatives of the institution to move his office to a more centrally located area of the department. This new office location meant that Cleveland was more readily visible and under the surveillance of the institution's representatives. The space Cleveland would have to move about and levy challenges to Whiteness could be much more closely controlled with his proximity to the administration's center of control. The rationale given for the change of office location, like that for the helping committee, was to assist Cleveland in his growth and development toward communicating better with others (Whites).

Cleveland's Black body had some usefulness to the institution in terms of representing racial diversity, but only in a tamed and controlled form; for Whiteness to remain secure, Cleveland was required to be Black in ways determined as acceptable to Whites. Accordingly, processes of domination used to silence Cleveland differed from the processes of domination used to silence Brenda. Very importantly, however, both of us, Brenda and Cleveland, were effectively sanctioned by processes of White racial domination—at least in the short term and for the moment. Of course, no reason was given for the nonrenewal of Brenda's contract of employment; it just happened to be that as the last one hired, she was the first one fired—again, she is too Black, yet not Black enough.

Cleveland, in turn, remembered Big Mama's advice that there are times when silence is golden. He now uses his silence strategically to help ensure his survival in the academy. Ironically, now that Cleveland has less to say to his colleagues, his colleagues often freely congratulate themselves on the success of their efforts to help him learn to speak in a way that they consider more appropriate—never realizing, apparently, that Cleveland has simply chosen to stop speaking to them.

Discussion and Conclusions:
The Struggle toward Freedom Must Continually Expand

To date, it is unnerving to relive the events we have recounted here among others; it is truly frightening to be targeted by the militant aggressiveness of Whiteness. We nevertheless take comfort in the fact that, to paraphrase Malcolm X, if we weren't posing a very serious threat to Whiteness, we would never have been so seriously threatened (and sanctioned) by Whiteness because we probably weren't saying much anyway. Whiteness only and most strongly responds to threats deemed serious enough to seriously destabilize its dominance.

However, we recognize that our individual efforts toward freedom and our freedom dreams realized are small and insufficient, albeit our best and important to us. We also posit that it will not be until there are many and more systemic, collaborative challenges to Whiteness that the ideals of freedom and democracy will have the full potential be realized (West, 1993). For us, there has been a great deal of pain and sacrifice, some that we knew was coming and much that we didn't, in response to our challenges to Whiteness. While we do not seek out pain and suffering for its own sake—we are determined, not crazy, as some would suggest—we nevertheless feel that we have come too far and endured too much to be turned back now in our struggles toward freedom dreams.

We feel that our experiences in challenging Whiteness, as painful and difficult as they have been, have also been beneficial to us—we have learned things that are important to us. For both of us, we feel that we have together and individually gleaned important experiences and knowledge from our encounters with confronting and head-on challenging Whiteness head-on—for instance, we have gained a deep and sincere appreciation of the time commitment and systematic collaboration that is required to begin to seriously destabilize and ultimately dismantle White supremacy. We do not expect to see this task realized in our lifetimes or perhaps in the lifetimes of our children, although we are never without hope.

We also appreciate and value on a level we have not known before the ways that our experiences of confronting White supremacy, again, as painful and difficult as they have been, have shaped us into the educators we are today. It is our hope that we have become better, more critical educators because of what we have learned in our experiences of challenging Whiteness. We have gained a newer and deeper appreciation for the humanity of others, even and perhaps especially including the humanity of those with whom we have long disagreed and those who we have often felt sought to evict us from particular institutional spaces we shared. We have come out of our experiences in challenging Whiteness with a renewed and expanded commitment to spend our lifetimes and all of our talents, resources, and strength working with others to push forward social justice for all and dismantle White supremacy. Finally, we are aware that freedom is never voluntarily given; it must always be taken (King, 1964). Malcolm X once said that if you aren't willing to die for freedom, you should take it out of your vocabulary. We feel that we have moved a little closer to understanding what it was that Malcolm X was hoping to convey to all of us in making his statement about freedom. We hope that our stories and the lessons we have learned from our experiences in challenging Whiteness help to push forward this ongoing struggle to take freedom for all.

Note

1. This is Richard Wright's phrase from his book *Twelve Million Black Voices*.

Chapter Six

Unbecoming . . . Responding to Colorblindness

·◆———◆·

An Autoethnography

Joy Howard

We need to undress Whites' claims of color blindness before a huge mirror. That mirror must reflect the myriad facts of contemporary Whiteness, such as Whites living in White neighborhoods, sending their kids to White schools, associating primarily with Whites, and having all their primary relationships with Whites . . . Researchers also need to turn the analytical lenses on White segregation and isolation from minorities and begin documenting how this isolation affects Whites' views, emotions, and cognitions about themselves and about minorities.

—Bonilla-Silva, 2003, pp. 183–184

My story, this story, is a mirror reflecting my enculturation into colorblindness and my reeducation about race in American society. Initially, I embarked on this research journey as a reflexive practice to better understand myself, my pedagogy, and my students. However, in my review of the literature on critical Whiteness and White allies, it became apparent to me that there is a voice missing. That is the voice of those of us who find ourselves concurrently between, among, and outside Black and White social worlds. This study captures moments that demonstrate my (author's/research subject's) racial identity performances, how this identity has changed over time, and lessons that I have learned along the way. Analyzing my racialized identity construction as a White person who was formerly "colorblind" adds to scholarly conversations about the tension between the colorblind discourse and discourses that recognize race as a social construction that oppresses groups and individuals within racialized groups.

I am a White, bilingual (Spanish/English), California-born, middle-class woman married to a Southern Black man, mother of three biracial sons, and currently living in South Carolina. My identity construction is what Ngo (2008), borrowing from Hall (1996), describes as a "double movement." Ngo (2008) explains an understanding of identity and discourse as

> a double movement, where we are identified by a history of discourse—ideas and images of who we are—and identify ourselves by responding to the representations that have already identified us. The ways we respond may repeat, resist, or contradict how we have been identified. (Ngo, 2008, p. 6)

In a sense, this double movement in my life has been a deconstruction of the colorblind discourse that explained race—my own and others'—as something not to be acknowledged or discussed aloud. This colorblind discourse remained constant for my formative years, but failed to capture my lived experiences when the colorblind monologue narrating my life was interrupted.

Colorblindness, which I discuss in more depth in the following section, is the idea that racial justice has been achieved (Winant, 2000). It can be motivated by guilt, ambivalence, and/or confusion about race and racism (Blaisdell, 2005; Bonilla-Silva, 2003; Lensmire, 2008). Teacher educators have expressed a profound and enduring challenge in working toward *racial literacy* (Guinier, 2004) when their students claim colorblindness (Howard, 1999; King, 1991; Milner, 2008; Pennington, 2007; Tatum, 1994). Succinctly, racial literacy can be described as resources, patterns of practice, conceptual tools, and vocabularies that help to describe, interpret, explain, and act on practices that comprise racism and anti-racism (Rogers & Mosley, 2008). In response to the personal and professional quandaries that I have encountered as a colleague, student, teacher, researcher, friend, wife, and mother with respect to racial literacy, I decided to interrogate my own experiences when I was limited by the colorblind discourse. Thus, this critical autoethnography asks: *What are some of the syllogisms in the colorblind ideology? How are these messages learned, and can they be unlearned?*

This longitudinal study creates a platform for critical pedagogy[1] and provides both a resource and model for examining the confounding myths of colorblindness. Therefore, the goals of this study are twofold: to introduce a unique voice into the literature on race and to demonstrate tools for deconstructing the colorblind discourse to work toward racial literacy. In what follows, I begin by explaining my theoretical frame for this study. Next, I clearly identify the notion of colorblind D/discourse. Then I discuss how I used the method of autoethnography and my process for collecting and analyzing data. After that, I present short vignettes that represent themes from my data, followed by my analysis of the individual vignettes. Finally, I present a dialogue poem that captures the more emotional side of this work and an analysis of the poem, which introduces the concept of unbecoming. I conclude with examples and a discussion about the ways in which engagement with critical social theories and this autoethnographic project have profoundly impacted my teaching and research holistically.

Conceptual Frame

This study is guided by principles from three interrelated critical social theories. In this section, I briefly describe those theories and explain specifically how each is used. I conclude this section by applying this theoretical frame to the notion of colorblindness, which undergirds the study as a whole.

Critical Race Theory (CRT)

There are five basic tenets that form the basis of CRT: 1) the centrality and intersectionality of race and racism; 2) the challenge to dominant ideology; 3) the commitment to social justice; 4) the centrality of experiential knowledge; and 5) the use of an interdisciplinary perspective (DeCuir & Dixson, 2004; Ladson-Billings, 2004; Solorzano, 1997; Yosso, 2002). Particularly pertinent to the present study is how CRT confronts the notions of meritocracy and colorblindness and the value it places on experiential knowledge. Counter-narratives, based on experiential knowledge, pose challenges to the dominant discourse about race (Solorzano, 1997). I use the tools of CRT to inform my approach toward deconstructing colorblindness. Specifically, I use counter-narratives, my own and others', to interrupt the colorblind discourse.

Critical Geography

Critical geography analyzes the complex geographies of everyday life in globalized spaces (Helfenbein & Taylor, 2009; Taylor & Helfenbein, 2009). In particular, I found the notion of the *socio-spatial dialectic* (Soja, 2010) useful for understanding and analyzing my experiences. Edward Soja (2010) explains the concept of the socio-spatial dialectic—how space is social and how the social works to shape space. This lens analyzes the spatiality of subjects that are "viewed as shaping social relations and social development just as much as social processes configure and give meaning to the human geographies or spatialities in which we live" (p. 4). Specifically, I used this lens to examine how my geographic locations gave meaning to my racialized experiences and how locations were racialized in turn (e.g., my experiences in California with a discourse about "illegal aliens" amid the strong presence of Mexican Americans and Mexican immigrants and my exposure to clear examples of racism from White peers and authorities toward African-Americans in South Carolina when, for example, a group of Black peers and I were told to leave a restaurant by a policeman who said, "You've had a nice time. It's time for you to leave.").

Feminist Theory

I borrowed ideas from feminist standpoint theories to interrogate the ways that race and gender identities work to create and maintain material inequalities (Anzaldúa, 2003; Collins, 2002; hooks, 1990; Mohanty, 2003; Sandoval, 2004). Through this project, I hope to unveil some of the ways that I was offered material privileges and how I learned to define woman in terms of my own (White) experience (Lorde, 1984). This study also builds on the work of Judith Butler (2003). Butler argues that identity is socially constructed and performed and is not something that is chosen independent of society; rather, it is inextricably linked to the social forces that inform and restrict the possibilities of identities. In this way, gender performances are publicly regulated, and performing one's gender against the norm will result in a set of punishments (Butler, 2003; Noble, 2006). Using this framework, I analyzed how both my racial and gender performances are called into question by social norms that mark me as "socially Black" (Collins, 2009) and therefore performing my role as a White woman incorrectly.

Colorblind D/discourse

Using these diverse but interrelated critical social theories, I examined the colorblind discourse. In my review of the literature, *colorblindness* (Blaisdell, 2005; Bonilla-Silva, 2003/2009; Lensmire, 2008; Marx, 2006) and *White talk* are veiled and strategic discursive tools that are used to avoid, interrupt, and dismiss counter-arguments; to collude with other White actors to create a culture of niceness and minimize or redefine racism to include reverse racism; and to declare commitment or act paternalistically toward racial others (Frankenberg, 1993; McIntyre, 1997; Nash, 2012). Bonilla-Silva (2009) identifies four central frames that advance colorblind discourse used by White people. Those frames are

(a) Abstract liberalism—the discourse that attempts to rationalize racial unfairness with notions of equality, meritocracy, opportunity, and choice;

(b) Naturalization—the discourse that advances the idea that racism is just the way some people are;

(c) Cultural racism—the discourse that advances racism as the result of cultural deficiencies and the fault of people of color; and

(d) Minimization—the discourse that draws on the argument that racism is not prevalent anymore in American society. (pp. 30–45)

Marx (2006) adds an important layer for understanding colorblindness by explaining that colorblind discourse often includes a discrimination against heritage languages, or languages other than English. I have been a witness to and a part of all of these forms of colorblind discourse in my life experience.

To say that colorblindness is a discourse is, for me, insufficient without a clear definition of the notion of discourse. Discourse involves ways of interacting, representing, and being (Fairclough, 1995; Gee, 1996; Rogers, 2002). Discourse in this sense requires an understanding of the inextricable link between the use of language as a cultural tool and its connection with the social realities that language is used to describe. In this way, the idea of discourse signifies that language informs culture and culture informs language. James Gee (1996; 1999) adds to this definition by explaining the difference between big "D" discourse and little "d" discourse. For Gee, Discourse involves the ways of believing, representing, acting, performing, and valuing that support a person's ability to be a competent user of languages. On the other hand, discourse is how people actually use language to make meanings with each other as they interact in social situations. Though there is a wide body of literature on this topic (see, e.g., Fairclough, 1995; Rogers, 2002), the distinction between Discourse as ideological and discourse as the units of language used to represent thoughts and ideas is sufficient for this particular discussion of colorblindness.

Identifying Discourse and discourse in this way adds an extra layer of understanding how the colorblind D/discourse operates. I now define colorblind Discourse and colorblind discourse, respectively. These definitions are based on both scholarly literature as well as the experiences presented in the present study. Colorblindness Discourse upholds a firm belief in the reality of meritocracy, a hegemonic viewpoint that claims both the fairness and universality of social norms as interpreted by White culture. This representation of the United States as a race-neutral society results in a denial of both historical and contemporary racism with respect to how they inform everyday social life in the present time. It has also resulted in a failure to acknowledge the expertise, experiences, or knowledge of people who have been racially marginalized as well as the systemic racism that normalizes Whiteness. Colorblind discourse, in my experience and research (e.g., Howard, 2012) as well as my review of literature on colorblindness (e.g., Lewis, 2001; 2003; Pollock, 2005), involves the use of language that denies racism and race as a social construct. Colorblind discourse includes the omission of racial signifiers or discussions about the topic of race in speech (e.g., referring to a man and avoiding a racial description of him; justifying racist remarks by avoiding talk about race, saying something like, "She was probably just having a bad day"); making statements to downplay race as significant (e.g., "I don't care what color you are, Black, White or purple"), claiming innocence (e.g., "I would never judge anyone because of the color of their skin"), or making the idea of race into a joke to downplay the gravity of the effects of the construction of race (e.g., using a name that signifies an ethnic group other than Whiteness to self-identify, e.g., "Laquisha" or "Paco").

With this understanding of colorblind D/discourse, I analyzed stories as they were told to me and retold by me. I deconstructed these stories based on both experiential and academic knowledge. Specifically, I analyzed how my spatial, racial, and gender locations were created and performed within colorblindness (Blaisdell, 2005; Bonilla-Silva, 2003; Lensmire, 2008; Pollock, 2005), and I identified specific and implicit messages about race that became explicit when I viewed them through a critical lens.

Using autoethnography to unpack the Discourse of colorblindness is particularly powerful because the connections between Discourse and discourse are often very difficult, if not impossible, to determine. There are always questions of reliability and accuracy of analysis to determine participants' meanings as interpreted by a researcher with limited insight into another person's life or mind-set. While autoethnography certainly has a number of limitations, including decisions on reporting and in one's ability to objectively analyze oneself, a strength of autoethnography lies in its unique ability to connect ideology with discursive markers (e.g., speech, writing). Thus, I argue that autoethnography is an appropriate method for adding to the literature on colorblindness by connecting colorblind Discourse to colorblind discourse.

Methods

In this study, I posit that the construction of race (Apple, 2003; McLaren, 2006; Omi & Winant, 1986) is learned over the course of a lifetime and can be changed and challenged; therefore, it is important for researchers to look at longitudinal data and leave room for diversions and contradictions to a phenomenon that is not static. To explore the shifting phenomenon of my *racialized* identity, or my location within a system that creates divisions of disparate interests based on race (Bonilla Silva, 2003), I chose autoethnography as my method of inquiry.

Autoethnography is the study of self (auto) in connection to one's sociocultural world (ethno) with the application of the research process (graphy) (Wall, 2008). Autoethnographies are "highly personalized accounts that draw upon the experience of the author/researcher for the purposes of extending sociological understanding" (Sparkes, 2000 p. 21). An advantage of this method is that it opens up space for wider audiences to access academic work; encourages witnessing, empathy, and connection; and contributes to social understanding in ways that are self-luminous (Smith & Sparkes, 2008). This method provides rich data and multiple layers of analysis that are extensive enough to provide substantive material to enhance the scholarly discussion about colorblindness and serve as a model for others seeking to do similar projects. I am aware that using this method of inquiry has been questioned in terms of its validity, so in the section that follows I discuss how I addressed this concern through data selection and analysis.

Data Collection and Analysis

To answer the questions "What are some of the syllogisms in colorblind ideology?" and "How are these messages learned, and can they be unlearned?," I carefully selected written data. I collected the following written documents: 1) five notebook-sized personal journals written by myself since late adolescence through early adulthood (a twelve-year period); 2) documents that include a formal philosophy statement and three course assignments about my race, class, and gender identity; 3) self-authored sections of a dialogue journal (written with a colleague) that was recorded digitally; and 4) three high school yearbooks, including pictures, captions, and copious notes from peers.

Data analyzed were originally written and saved without the intention of publication or formal scrutiny. As such, I put forth that these data represent one White female's racial reality[2] in its truest sense, because data did not have the bias of being consciously abridged or edited for an audience. Data represented in this study are based on textual data; I did not include memories that did not have strong representation through the material texts.

Data were analyzed in two ways. First, I used *narrative analysis* (Clandinin & Connely, 1994), which relies "on stories as a way of knowing [and is] framed and rendered through an analytical process that is artistic as well as rigorous" (Coulter & Smith, 2009, p. 577). Narrative analysis was used to organize the data into themes. Major themes that emerged from the data were White entitlement (nine clear examples), learned e-racing (nine clear examples), fear (nine clear examples), and geographical separation (eleven clear examples). Data themes were renamed to fit the vignettes that represent an example of each theme. White entitlement became "White is right," fear and geographical separation were combined into "borders," and geographical separation and learned e-racing became "racism."

I extracted racial stories from the data that best represented these themes and then organized them into vignettes. These vignettes illuminate my lived experience as a (colorblind) White, middle-class female growing up in California, whose racial ideology was transformed through experiences and relationships that disrupted the colorblind discourse. I examined each theme, demonstrated here through vignettes, for *syllogisms*—an argument with a major premise, minor premise, and a conclusion—and *enthymemes*— incomplete or careless logical inferences (Feldman et al., 2004) about the concept of race.

To more fully address the performative (Butler, 2003) nature of identity and contestation of ideologies, I also used poetic analysis to "find, experience, and express the desire, passion, ambivalence, powerlessness, uncertainty, shame, love, fear and other emotions that are hidden in our relationships and our cultural discourses" (Oikarinen-Jabai, 2003, p. 578). Poetic analysis is a way that "researchers can enhance their abilities to listen and notice in the field during data collection, creatively play with metaphor and image during analysis, and communicate with more liveliness and accuracy when representing data to larger audiences" (Cahnmann, 2003, p. 32). In this study, I used poetic analysis to capture metaphors and images that serve to extend the analysis of stories. With the creation of a dialogue poem, I was more able to represent ideological conflicts that can best be represented through the affective. In the following two sections, I present vignettes that represent themes from the data and my analysis of each.

Colorblind Vignettes

WHITE IS RIGHT

My respected private school was about 95 percent White and disproportionately wealthy for the area. I never quite felt like I fit in; Nicky didn't, either. Nicky was always with "us." He was adopted as a baby from Korea by White parents and was the only person of color in my class until middle school. In high school, while chatting with a group of my (White) friends, I remember saying, "I guess there are not a whole lot of different races at our school. Well, there's Nicky, but really he's White." Everyone nodded as if in agreement, and I was sure I was paying Nicky a compliment.

BORDERS

I grew up in a nice, quiet suburb in California called La Caja.[3] Racism just was not part of my daily consciousness. Almost all of my friends, family, and neighbors looked like me, talked like me, and aided in my ability to remain relatively ambivalent about race. Until I was in college, it did not occur to me it was not an accident that my community and school were overwhelmingly White. Throughout my childhood and adolescence, I went on school-sponsored mission trips to Mexico. We (my White elders and peers) wanted to help, so we gave them materials to build with and food to eat for a day or two. We didn't know much Spanish, so we relied on gesture and smiles. Tucked away in the back of our minds was always a silent warning that we must be on guard at all times, because crossing the border was a dangerous mission. We always breathed a sigh of relief when we returned to our homeland, leaving danger behind.

RACISM?

In fourth grade, I watched *Mississippi Burning* (Colesbery et al., 1988). My mom reminded me that I cried for days afterward at the injustice of slavery. I felt guilty because people whose skin looked like mine had done something so horrific. What I don't remember is any critical dialogue with my elders about the causes and effects of slavery. I concluded that the South is where the racists live and thanked God that I didn't live in that backward place!

Years later, I was recruited to play softball at a university in South Carolina. Though I never planned to stay in the South long-term, in the fall semester of my sophomore year I fell in love with the man I was sure that I would marry. I was devastated when, shortly after we returned for classes in the spring, he brought something to my attention that I had never seriously considered. He was Black and I was White, and our world said we couldn't be together. "It didn't matter, it's 1999," I thought. In my diary I wrote, "Why can't he just get over this whole race issue!" Around Valentine's Day, he walked out of my life and left me with only one explanation: "We live in a racist society." I resolved to go home to La Caja, a place free from racism.

Narrative Analysis

Each section below is an analysis of the vignettes presented above. Each theme includes a syllogism (an argument with a major premise, a minor premise, and a conclusion). Explicit statements that were articulated to me as I learned the syllogism are in all capital letters; implicit sentiments are

italicized. Enthymemes (incorrect or careless inferences) are then deconstructed based on experiential and theoretical counter-narratives.

WHITE IS RIGHT

Interruptions to the master narrative in my school were rare. Becoming
White was part of my upbringing, or my racial socialization. By high school,
I had internalized the discourse of colorblindness to the degree that I was
able to make the comment that "Nicky was White." In truth, I saw his
distinctly Korean phenotype, but when I said he was White, I was trying
to say that he was a good person. Through 16 years of White conservative
cultural apprenticeship, I had learned the syllogism *Whiteness is a marker of
moral goodness and purity* (Dyer, 1997). *I viewed Nicky as good, so* NICKY
WAS WHITE. The fault in this reasoning, I have learned mostly through
interactions and relationships with people who are not White. That is, not
all people whom I would consider morally good are White, and not all
White people are morally good.

BORDERS

In this vignette, the syllogism was THE UNITED STATES IS GOOD.
Mexico is bad/dangerous. (e.g., Policastro, 2010). *Americans who go to Mexico
bring good, while Mexicans who come to the United States bring bad.* There are
a number of major flaws in this way of thinking, which could constitute an
entire book; however, I concentrate here on one portion of the enthymeme.
That is the faulty logic in labeling racialized others (Bonilla-Silva, 2003)
based on geographical location.

Many years after my first mission trip, I went to Mexico for work on
my master's thesis. My friends and family had repeatedly warned me about
the dangers of crossing the border before, during, and after my study. However, as I waited for the trolley in San Diego that would take me down
to the U.S./Mexican border, there was a gang fight at the trolley station.
Men, U.S. citizens, with guns and bats were arrested, while trolley custom-
ers cowered behind the benches. The irony in the "danger" narrative was
that immediately after the U.S. gang fight, I boarded the trolley and sat
next to a Mexican man, and we talked about my project for the 30-minute
trolley ride. Then he escorted me over the border, ensured that I got into
a taxi safely, gave the driver directions to the school that I was visiting,
and wished me luck on my project. Then, in Mexico, the teachers at the
school invited me to lunch. After school, one of the teachers invited me
into her home, served me dinner, and took a great deal of time to answer

all my questions. Afterward, she drove me back to the border so I could avoid any confusion at the late-night hour.

Through this experience, and many more, Mexican people became fellow "I's" (Freire, 1970/2000), or subjects and not objects. These people and these experiences forced me to question the discourse that creates political and social borders that divide humans into categories of good or bad based on geographical locations. As Gomez-Peña (1996) has pointed out, when people travel from the Northern to the Southern hemisphere, they are viewed as "tourists," while, conversely, when people travel from southern to northern regions, they are marked as "aliens." I am deeply disturbed by the popular discourse which names Mexicans "aliens" when they cross the U.S. border. This way of thinking allows "tourists" to *eat the other*, to use the words of bell hooks. Hooks (2003) explains that White people often treat the racial "other" as if they are a product to be consumed, a spirit that might be transferred. In many ways, I am culpable of tourist consumption of Mexican culture. At the same time, traversing borders also made room for my racial imaginary to expand and to see some of the costs that racialized others pay for White privilege.

RACISM?

There were two syllogisms that can be read in this narrative. By the time I left for college, I had learned to be "colorblind," which is why, in my journal entries, I never referenced my *first love's*[4] racial identity as Black until he brought it up in the spring. The syllogism here was RACISM AND RACIAL DIFFERENCE NO LONGER EXIST. *Everyone in my racially integrated school arrived based on meritocracy.* INTEGRATION *proves that racism no longer exists.* The fault in this logic, the enthymeme, was presented to me by my *first love* when he left me with the parting idea that not seeing racism does not constitute the absence of racism.

As a result, I wanted to flee to a place I had come to think of as "free from racism": La Caja, California. The syllogism I understood at this point through my racial education was *Racism in America is located in the southeastern region because of slavery.* THE LOCALITY (Massey, 1994) OF LA CAJA, AND CALIFORNIA IN GENERAL, IS GEOGRAPHICALLY REMOVED FROM THE LEGACY OF SLAVERY. LA CAJA WAS INNOCENT OF RACISM. However, the error in this claim is twofold. First, the dominant group in California (Whites) treated Mexican people as second-class humans (McLaren, 1999), which is demonstrated in immigration raids (Gallegos, 2007) and unfair policies in education (e.g., Alvarez v. Board of Trustees of Lemon Grove School District). In reviewing my high school yearbooks, ironically titled "Painting the picture, Where everybody knows your name, and Lasting impressions," there were no overt comments about the race of the few Black students, but there were a number of comments that explicitly named and referenced Mexican students and jokingly took on Mexican identities, such as "Ofelia" or "chica." Though I was ambivalently blind to it at the time, some of the Mexican students who attended our school took on or were given nicknames like "the Big Mexican Dude" or "Mexican homi." None of us was blind to race, but we remained silent about race and especially racism. Primarily through *colormute* responses (Pollock, 2005), we collectively denied that race mattered.

The second problem of the racially innocent California syllogism is that racism anywhere infects people everywhere. Disengagement from dialogue is a powerful tool in the racial education of colorblindness. The pattern of disproportionately White suburbs and disproportionately White schools is a tool of disengagement in dialogue and strengthens the colorblind discourse. Geographic separation allows for an uninvolved ambivalence on the part of young White apprentices. Ambivalence and denial of "race" and racism (Lensmire, 2008) in my case was reinterpreted through geographic dislocation when I moved to the South and lived in close proximity to Black people who challenged my denial and ambivalence toward racism in America.

Poetic Analysis

Because of the performative (Butler, 2003) nature of identity and the emotional and persuasive nature of colorblind ideologies (Trainor, 2005), I found narrative analysis to be an important but incomplete method of analysis. It was insufficient to capture the emotional and liminal process of deconstructing colorblindness and the subsequent process of reconstructing a new ideology about race. As a result, I used the themes, syllogisms, and enthymemes to craft a poem that more fully completes my analysis and portrayal of my responses to the inferences within colorblind discourse.

The dialogue poem should be read in a call-and-response fashion to an audience. This poem is a counter-narrative to colorblind ideologies. The words in italics represent what I have learned as the colorblind discourse has been interrupted in my life; the underlined portions represent messages that I have heard from individuals affirming colorblindness; and the bold words represent the overwhelming collective message of the colorblind discourse. The italicized words should be read by one person (a witness, representing my internal dialogue as colorblind discourse is interrupted); the underlined words should by another person (the prosecuting attorney, representing messages I receive/d about race from colorblind individuals); and the bold words should be read in tandem by a group (the judge and jury, representing messages I receive/d about race from the dominant colorblind discourse).

> My particular shade of White draws from rivers of tears
> Not mine alone, but those which I have caused.
> Rivers of tears that have passed over the dam . . .
> of disparity from which my cup overflows
> Quiet! You are delusional.
> What's passed is past, you are not responsible.
> **Erase that from your memory.**
> ¿quién eres chica? Who do you think you are!
> This land that you think you own, was stolen.
> Try to learn.
> Listen for whispers of stories untold.
> Quiet! False witness.
> Strike the testimony from the record.
> **Erase that from your memory.**
> I am a witness to truths,
> Even when they ain't sound right at firs'.
> Truths wrapped in mysteries,
> based on histories of greatness wider than the Atlantic
> on which they traveled to these shores.
> Quiet! Impermissible evidence.
> Evidence did not pass protocol.
> **Erase that from your memory.**
> I'm taking off the blindfold,
> I won't wear it anymore,
> I want to see who is speaking to me.
> I want to face the trauma.
> Quiet! Order!
> Erase that from your memory.
> **Erase! Erace! E-race!!**
> No!
> I will not repeat your lies.
> I choose a new way,
> Justice—and liberty—for all.
> I choose . . . unbecoming.
> Unbecoming the entitlement my skin promised.
> Unbecoming my incessant need to speak.
> Unbecoming my temptation to hide in silence.
> Unbecoming as I listen.

Unbecoming these stains on my soul.
Unbecoming so that my children,
our children,
might be,
free—
at last.
Unbecoming . . .

To unpack some of the content of this poem, I begin with a quote from Homi Bhaba (1986), who offers that social "remembering is never a quiet act of introspection or retrospection. It is a painful remembering, a putting together of the dismembered past to make sense of the trauma of the present" (p. xxiii). Indeed social remembering, for either the oppressor or the oppressed, is neither a simple nor easy task when it involves inhumane accounts of injustice. I have learned this at a personal level as well as professionally as a teacher and educational researcher. However, though the colorblind discourse may seem to be a benign way of knowing the world (Rains, 2000), it dims out uncomfortable and tragic injustices of our past and present, so that people are not asked to endure working through these racist traumas in an articulatory process (LaCapra, 2001). In the end, the colorblind discourse demands that people forget the past and ultimately requires aporia, or continual confusion, about race. The result is that there is a psychosis with regard to historical or contemporary racism.

The poem, set in a courtroom, seeks to testify against this aporia. As I wrote it and read it, I thought about Lady Justice, or Justitia, who appears in courtrooms across the country. Lady Justice is blindfolded and therefore is colorblind. However, no one in the United States has ever truly been blind to color. By maintaining a colorblind discourse, we fail to see past the blindfold, and we make wrong judgments about the pain of others and the trauma on which White privilege is built. The fabricated blindfold of colorblindness must be removed to work past aporia and toward social justice. For White people who, like me, struggle with the gaps in colorblind logic, I propose what I call unbecoming.

Patricia Hill Collins' (2009) term for White people like me who are in interracial relationships as "socially Black" does not fully capture the constant process and double movement of my identity (Ngo, 2008). Additionally, the term "White Ally," or someone who engages in antiracist activities on behalf of or with people of color, does not entirely capture the identity that I claim and embody as a White woman married to a Black man and the mother of biracial children. Thus, I want to introduce the term *unbecoming . . .* as a double entendre. I mean to say that unbecoming . . . is a process of unlearning the privileges and colorblindness of a

White dominant cultural upbringing. At the same time, I acknowledge that the unbecoming . . . way of being and seeing the world is offensive to the White majority's social imaginary.

Unbecoming . . . is an interrogation of unjust privileges based on the oppression of racialized groups and a process of unraveling harmful epistemologies that sustain these privileges. It is never static. It is fluid. It is about moving beyond individual guilt in order to problematize the confines of racial divisions. Unbecoming . . . moves toward agency that makes possible material and interrelational action that always seeks justice, for all of humanity. Importantly, it requires the rejection of the now intrinsic and naturalized White domination over other races (Dyer, 1997). Therefore, the second definition of unbecoming (unflattering, not right or proper) is necessary.

Clearly, the notion of unbecoming . . . is not fully developed in theory or social reality, because America is still a racially stratified nation. This hybrid identity (Blaisdell, 2005; Gomez-Peña, 1996) puts notions of race on the defense stand and continually asks why racial divisions remain, leaving no room for lies within silencing statements about race and White privilege. Unbecoming . . . as a fluid process, requires action and constant (re) development of identity. In the next section, I discuss some of the ways that this process has materialized in my life's work.

Applications to Teaching and Research

My explicit study of race has profoundly affected the ways in which I interact with students and my research methodologies and practices. As a teacher, it has impacted both my curriculum and pedagogy. For example, one day I was reading a book with a small group of second graders. All of the characters in the book were Black. A Mexican-American student asked, "Where are all the White people?" Part of me wanted to quickly move past the question, as the colorblind discourse would suggest. Instead, I chose to engage the difficult conversation, not knowing where it would lead.

It did not take long for another student to state his opinion that "Black people are bad" and the Mexican-American student to declare, "I am White." The group engaged in a dialogue where students tested their understanding of race and I problematized some of their racially biased conceptions. The result of this short conversation was a disruption of the notion that White is necessarily good and Black is necessarily bad. If I had silenced the comment, as I was trained to do by the colorblind discourse, these children's horizontal[5] and internalized racist thinking would have gone uninterrupted (Speight, 2007; Tamale, 1996).

Engaging in autoethnography has advanced my understanding of critical theory and critical pedagogy. As an educational researcher, this deeper level of understanding of my own racial identity and discourse has deepened my conceptualization, and abilities, for interviewing people about the concept of race. I now more openly dialogue about race with those who are racially different from me and acknowledge the limitations of my own White racial experiences. I also value and understand the need for the art of listening to racial narratives, which is not possible in colorblind discourse. Finally, I now engage in dialogue with people who are perplexed and uncomfortable discussing the topic of race. For example, because I understood the difficulty of discussing race, when I conducted a focus group with White teachers I decided to utilize a storybox[6] (Hamera, 2005) to advance the conversation to explicitly respond to race and racism. Not only did the storybox create a forum for a dialogue about race, but afterward each of the teachers also expressed gratitude for a nonthreatening environment in which to engage in a discussion about race and share ideas for addressing racism. If I had examined my own experiences and colorblind discourse through a critical lens, I would not have understood which questions needed to be asked or how to ask them.

Conclusion

In a sense, this autoethnographic mirror served as critical pedagogy for me. I now talk to and understand a wider group of people, decoding racial signifiers that are not explicitly named race (e.g., geographical identities). I hope this study also promotes a wider discussion about the emotional and ideological complexities of the colorblind discourse that is so often invisible and silent for those of us who were brought up seeing and reading the world in this way. This study adds to our understanding of the diverse and contradictory epistemologies that are embedded and embodied within colorblindness. This study can serve as a useful text and model for teachers, teacher educators, and researchers who are faced with the challenge of deconstructing colorblindness and working toward racial literacy (Guinier, 2004).

Asking teachers, future teachers, and ourselves, no matter what our positions in education or research, to examine the discourses and ideologies about race by explicitly writing out syllogisms and enthymemes through narrative analysis (Clandinin & Connelly, 1994) or incorporating the craft, practice, and possibilities of poetry (Cahnmann, 2003) are useful tools in advancing difficult conversations about race and reducing the aporia about race. Additionally, exploring the notion of unbecoming . . . what it means and could mean in different contexts and in different embodiments would be a fruitful line of research and educational practice. Questions are plentiful and might include "Who can fit into this category?" "What motivates people to choose to engage in culturally ostracizing ways of being?" Finally, critical research studies could explore the limitations and definitions of this idea, such as, "Without intimate connection to marginalized communities, is unbecoming . . . possible or even desirable?"

I conclude by acknowledging that any wisdom I shared through this project is largely built on the shoulders of knowledge that unfortunately remains separate from traditional White canons of knowledge. As I seek to encourage a healthy dialogue that necessitates voices from various and divergent paradigms, I borrow these words from James Baldwin (1985): "If you are not afraid to look at the past, nothing you are facing can frighten you" (p. xx).

Notes

1. Critical pedagogy, as a pedagogy of struggle with and for the oppressed, has a wide range of definitions. Peter McLaren (1999) explains that critical pedagogy has no blueprint, but it is always opposed to narrow thinking.

2. To be clear, I do not mean to imply that I could possibly speak for all White women.

3. All names of people and places are pseudonyms.

4. My first love is now my husband of eight years.

5. Horizontal racism is the intergroup racial prejudice from one racial minority group toward another racial minority group (e.g., Latino Americans toward African-Americans) that is situated within a larger structural racism that stratifies and stereotypes racial groups.

6. The way that I used a storybox in my research was by creating a PowerPoint presentation that encompassed a collection of pictures, teaching scenarios, documents, and transcripts clearly demonstrating racialized themes. For example, one slide included a scene that I had observed at the school site earlier in the research project where a third-grade White student told a third-grade Black student that he could not be on his kickball team because it was "White only." The White teachers were then asked to discuss how they would respond to this scenario.

Critical Feminist Autoethnographic Case Studies

Critical Feminisms

◦•────•◦

Gendered Experiences of Oppression and Resistance

FELECIA M. BRISCOE

The autoethnographies in Section III are feminist critiques, as they focus on women's experiences and the colonizing forces that operate around gender. The term *critical feminism* is somewhat redundant, as feminist theory has always been concerned with oppression—especially, but not only, women's oppression—as one of its foundational principles is to critique in order to create equitable practices and power relations. Feminist theory is closely associated with the woman's movement, but unlike the name might suggest to some, it encompasses far more and "intersects with other socio-cultural agendas" (Muller & O'Callaghan, 2013). However, there are many debates within the field (Muller & O'Callaghan, 2013), as it is profoundly inter-disciplinary and intentionally crosses boundaries internally and externally:

> In the realm of feminism, 2011 was undoubtedly a year in which the unstable and artificial distinctions often drawn between feminist theory, practice and activism were shaken by women taking to the streets in attempts to claim their rights as humans, citizens, and political, sexual and intellectual agents. (Acklesburg, 2013, p. 23)

Given the wide range of feminist theory, it is difficult to briefly introduce this theoretical field. Therefore, I simply provide a suggestion of some of the contributions of feminist theory, focusing on feminist narratives, as they are most relevant to Section IV.

Feminist theory has contributed to or originated the following scholarly fields: intersectional theory (e.g., Collins, 1990); different ways of knowing (e.g., Gilligan, 1982); horizontal rather than vertical organizational structures (Strathern, 1987); the relationship between oppression of people and environments/ecologies (e.g., Merchant, 1980); the relationship between patriarchy and capitalism (e.g., Cud & Holmstrom, 2011); the performance and/or construction of gender (e.g., Butler, 1988); agency as a political aspect of identity (e.g., Irigaray, 1985, Eng. trans. 2002); the importance of narratives—vis-à-vis the personal is political (e.g., Anzaldúa, 2007); and many more.

Many feminists point out the importance of feminist narrative inquiry. Gillman (2013), a feminist, notes, "The emergence of subaltern struggles in the last half of the twentieth century has generated the rise of resistance narratives on a global scale" (p. 646). She asserts that these resistance narratives provide an alternative epistemology and worldview to that which has traditionally guided knowledge production, which continually reproduces oppressive understandings.

> Against the view that the physical sciences should be the privileged source of reliable knowledge within the academy in general . . . [narrative inquiry helps to] form the basis of a revised naturalized epistemology that is more accountable to a socially engaged inquiry. This revised naturalism shifts orientation from the idealized setting of the laboratory and its a priori conditions for knowledge to localized settings, where knowledge emerges out of diverse contextualized interpretations of the natural and social world that interlocutors produce as they dialogue with one another. (Gillman, 2013, p. 646)

The two chapters in Section III are examples of feminist narrative inquiry, as they engage readers in a dialogue about a resistance to the colonizing forces of sexism that occur in both overt and subtle forms. These forces act on the identities and thus subjectivities of both women and men. These subjectivities induce actions of men, women, and other genders that limit the possibilities for fulfillment of all genders. Likewise, the two autoethnographies encompass the above foundational principles of feminism, as they describe the gendered experiences of two women.

They also exemplify many of the foci of current feminisms: (1) the diversity of women's experiences of oppression across the globe and their resistance to that oppression and (2) increased (and often gendered) economic inequalities and classed politics in the context of neoliberalism (Walby, 2011). Likewise, they help to actualize Hemmings's suggestion that feminist theory ought to avoid oversimplifying and thus essentializing women's diverse experiences while maintaining a political and theoretical edge, which requires noticing commonalities. These two autoethnographies, which describe women's experiences of oppression, acquiescence, and resistance on two different continents, share an unusual commonality in that both are set in polygamous contexts. In Chapter 7, Felecia Briscoe traces the conflicting truths about women that she learned in school/society and at home in a polygamous community. Her tracing includes an examination of her experiences in graduate school and as a professor in higher education. Dr. Briscoe delineates how these early conflicting truths about women have become part of people's subjectivities. These subjectivities enact an ever-more-subtle power relation—the double-bind—which continue to oppress women within higher education and covertly enacts a glass ceiling for women in higher education.

In Chapter 8, Damaris Choti describes the oppressive situations surrounding the lives of girls and women in most societies in the world. Arguing against female subordination, she investigates gender socialization patterns that oppress women and girls in the Gusii community of Kenya. Dr. Choti examines the role of colonialism, culture (e.g., patriarchy, family, and marriage), religion, educational institutions, and social hierarchy in the suppression of women among the Gusii. Her narrative explores her personal experiences and those of other females in her community. She concludes with an analysis of how those experiences have influenced her to become a critical researcher.

CHAPTER SEVEN

From Fundamentalist Mormon to the Academy

·◆———◆·

A "Plyg" Girl's Experiences with the Evolving Sexist Double-Bind

FELECIA M. BRISCOE

In 1832, the founder and first president of the Mormon Church, Joseph Smith, my great-great-great-uncle and a practicing polygamist, was tarred and feathered by a mob and then, in 1844, killed in Carthage Illinois. The church then fled to the Rocky Mountains and founded Zion, what is now known as Salt Lake City, Utah. There, they were safe from persecution until 1882, when the United States passed a law, stating any man "guilty of polygamy . . . shall be punished by a fine of not more than $500 and by imprisonment for a term of not more than five years" (*The Waukesha Freeman*, 1882, para. 1). Federal agents began invading Utah homes and imprisoning Mormon men who practiced polygamy. Eight years later, Mormon Church President Woodruff claimed a revelation from God that Mormons were no longer to practice polygamy; instead, they were to "believe God's standard of marriage is monogamy, or marriage between one man and one woman" (Church of Jesus Christ of Latter Day Saints, 2013, para. 1). Some Mormons resisted, protesting that this was no revelation but a matter of political expediency. They splintered off into various polygamous groups (e.g., Short Creekers) known as Mormon Fundamentalists or Plygs. I grew up in one of these Plyg communities.

I trace the ongoing development of my awareness of oppressive power/knowledge relations circulating around women. I do not write merely to titillate people by exposing the obvious and overt oppression of women in Plyg communities—that would be no counter-narrative. Rather, I show how these relations covertly manifest in higher education. Thus, my autoethnography demonstrates a multiply layered and shifting power/knowledge strategy—the *double-bind*, which acts in multiple public and private spaces to marginalize women and creates a glass ceiling in higher education. Autoethnography is particularly appropriate for this research, as "[f]eminist scholars have advocated using personal narratives in examining women's experiences as primary centers of knowledge and interrogating the intersections of race, gender, and class in shaping women's identities" (Young, 2009, p. 130). This narrative charts my growing consciousness as a critical scholar in one realm only: my growing awareness of the oppression of women.

Before beginning my narrative, I briefly describe the Foucauldian conceptual framework that I use to analyze my experiences. I then contextualize my critical narrative with a description of my early childhood, focusing on the oppressive "truths" that I learned about women at home and in school. My counter-narrative describes my experiences in learning conflicting truths about being a woman and my emerging awareness and changing negotiation of the double-bind—where there are no good choices. In different forms, I encountered and negotiated this double-bind as a student, socially, and professionally. My story demonstrates how this double-bind shapes men's and women's subjectivities so as to marginalize women in both social and professional worlds. My counter-narrative includes moments of both acquiescence and resistance. The double-bind marginalizes women in the enlightened spaces of higher education by shaping the subjectivities of women and the institutional gatekeepers in higher education.

Foucault's Power/Knowledge As an Analytical Frame

Science historians (e.g., Kuhn, 1962) and philosophers (e.g., Hume, 1888) have challenged the truth-producing authority of empirical science. But Foucault unequivocally declared the death of "Truth" and debunked Truth as a linear product of logical rational processes (*Power/Knowledge*, 1980a; and *The History of Sexuality: Volume I*, 1980b). Rather, for Foucault (1980a; 1980b), the understandings that supported by dominant power relations are the dominant discourse and are accepted as truth; whereas understandings that conflict with this dominant discourse are subordinated truths or counter discourses. Thus, "truths" are part of complex power relations and as such both influence and are influenced by other power relations.

For Foucault, power relations are the practices/truths that influence/coerce the actions of individuals and groups. However, "[o]ne doesn't have here a power which is totally in the hands of one person who can exercise it alone and totally over the others" (Foucault, 1980a, p. 156). Furthermore, people cannot be neatly divided into oppressors and the oppressed, but rather in general we are oppressed in some ways, while we are oppressors in other ways. Likewise, individuals "are not inert or consenting target; they are always also the elements of its articulation. In other words, individuals are the vehicles of power, not its points of application" (Foucault, 1980a, p. 98). The coercive effects of power do not operate the same way on everyone. As Foucault (1980a) indicates, "[c]ertainly everyone doesn't occupy the same position: certain positions preponderate and permit an effect of supremacy to be produced" (p. 156). In other words, some people are positioned subordinately within power relations—or oppressed. Nonetheless, according to Foucault (1980a, 1980b), even the most subordinate of us can resist. But the consequences of resistance for those positioned more subordinately are much more severe than for others. While Foucault fails to analyze resistance, I understand resistance as the power relations enacted by practices and discourses that act against oppressive power relations.[1]

One of the ways that power acts to influence our actions is by inducing people to develop particular subjectivities based on their positioning. Subjectivities are desires, expectations, values, attitudes, and *understandings*. As power relations are fluid and dynamic, so too are our understandings. But at the same time, our actions are conduits of power, whether resistant or in accordance with dominant power relations, and therefore also act on our own and others' understandings. Further, power relations are never static but rather dynamic and always acting (Foucault, 1980b). For Foucault, power acts both positively and negatively on all individuals and groups—there are no margins of freedom in which to frolic (Foucault, 1980b).[2] Power acts positively when it coerces us to some actions and negatively when it inhibits us from performing other actions. For Foucault (1980a), power relations are enacted through everyday micropractices. Gendered micropractices include such things as who washes the dishes, who plays with dolls, language conventions (God gendered as a male), our clothing, prayer, and so on. According to Foucault, these everyday practices enact the truths and norms from which gendered macroeconomic, social, discursive, and cultural practices of society emerge.

Finally, power acts where there is conflict or potential conflict (Foucault 1980b). In other words, power relations develop around resistance or potential resistance. Habermas (1968) similarly points out that one can pinpoint oppression by noting the distortions or contradiction in what we understand as truths. Thus, by tracing sites of gendered conflict and/or resistance, one can discern the contour of power/knowledge relationships with regard to gender. I trace my negotiations of conflicts with regard to women. These tracings focus on the power/knowledge (truth) relations taught to me and emerging from everyday practices (including conversations); the subjectivities that are shaped by those various practices; and how those subjectivities and practices act to marginalize women. This tracing provides a counter-narrative and helps to resist oppressive practices and understandings about of women.

My Community and Home Context

I was my father's third child in what eventually came to be more than 33 children. Like Jesus, as he often remarked, my father was a carpenter. My mother was his second wife and I was the first of her four children. My mother and Auntie (my father's first sister wife) have lived together in the same house since my earliest memories. During my elementary school years we lived in the desert on the outskirts of Las Vegas, Nevada. My father had other wives, but they did not live in the same house with us. Therefore, when I refer to my brothers and sisters, I am writing about the 11 children my two mothers raised together. My parents were working-class. As might be imagined with so many children, we were always on the brink of—and at times slipped into—poverty. For example, when I was in sixth grade, my mother told me to make chili for dinner. I asked where the meat was; she said we had none. I asked about the green peppers and seasoning; she said we only had salt. Finally, in frustration I cried out, "It's not chili; its just beans again!" She laughed, saying, "Yeah, I guess you're right." One impoverished summer, my parents invented a new type of salad. We went to a nearby hayfield; cut off the tips of alfalfa, and brought them home to eat as a salad.

Fundamentalist Truths about Women

While we were monetarily poor, we were rich in religious dogma about women. Much of this dogma is antiquated and echoes earlier historical "truths" about women in Western society. I learned my parents' truths about women by explicit lessons and implicitly through storytelling and by watching their actions. I focus on three types of conflicts regarding these truths about women: 1) truths that conflicted with the person I wanted to be; 2) conflicting alternative truths that I learned about women; and 3) truths that contradicted my lived conditions.

MEN WERE MORE HOLY AND THEREFORE THE DECIDERS

My parents taught us, "As God is to man, so is man to woman." We prayed to "our father in heaven," not "our mother in heaven." Much like Catholic dogma, only men could hold the priesthood. Further, in a marriage, while a woman could discuss issues with her husband, he had the right to tell her to "be quiet" and ultimately made the decisions. Sons were valued more than daughters, and the oldest son most of all. Women were irrational, childish, prone to sinning, and, as daughters of Eve, were cursed. Nonetheless, all women were not the same; some were better than others.

Some Women Are Better than Others

Within polygamous families, complex power relations are played out between husband and wives. Within these fundamentalist communities, the first wife (Auntie) has authority over the other wives, who are often treated more like concubines. In other words, their relationships are structured similarly to Abraham, his wife Rachel and her handmaiden, Hagar, in the Christian Bible. Thus, my father and Auntie treated my mother more like a servant than an equal. This treatment was exacerbated by the fact that my mother came from "inferior" bloodlines and lacked a high school degree.[3] My mother was expected to follow both my father's and Auntie's instruction and correction on a variety of matters: child rearing, diet, manner of dress, and so on. My mother's children were likewise accorded a status secondary to Auntie's children.

While Auntie and Dad went out and worked every day, my mother had the housekeeping and childcare duties; she made sure that dinner was prepared when they came home from work and then served them. Often my father would yell for my mother and, pointing to a spot on his drinking glass or spoon or improperly (according to his definition) cooked food, demanding that she rectify the situation immediately. My mother would scurry from the kitchen out to where they sat with their TV trays with a new glass of ice water or whatever was demanded. Every time I saw these little scenarios, as her child, I felt both angry and demeaned. However, as a child and teenager, I blamed her. Why did she let them treat her that way? Alternatively, what was wrong with her, and by extension me, such that she deserved to be treated this way? Why did she have to be so inferior, and so, too, me? I wanted desperately not to be her daughter.

A Woman's Positioning Is Fluid and Dynamic, But Men Are Always Better

However, God also valued intelligence, especially the development of whatever intelligence we had been given. So despite our negative proclivities, each of us—woman, child, and man—was to strive to develop our intelligence as much as possible. By developing their intelligence, women could better themselves. Another way a woman could better herself was to learn to be tough—like Mormon pioneer women, who pushed carts across the mountains and desert to Zion. We children thoroughly embraced the notion that to be tougher was to be better. For example, every summer we children competed to see how quickly we could adjust to running barefoot over the sharp desert pavement without flinching.[1] We ridiculed those who were slow in achieving this ability. It was a matter of pride to be tough enough to do it sooner rather than later. Also, when we children were disciplined by being spanked with an extension cord,[2] we'd compare our looping bruises to see whose legs were most vividly marked. We also made fun of whoever had cried the loudest and/or longest when they were whipped. Nevertheless, no matter how hard a woman strove to be tougher or smarter, men would ultimately be better.

THE DWINDLING INTELLECT OF GIRLS BECOMING WOMEN

I had an ongoing battle with my older brother, the oldest son. He, as Auntie's child, would always make fun of me for being a "dirty Briscoe." However, his grades were not so great compared with mine. Knowing that intelligence made you better, I would reply, "Well, at least I am smarter than you are!" One time, after a few rounds of this argument, Auntie pulled us aside and explained, "Sometimes girls are smarter than boys when they are young, but somewhere around high school boys get smarter and girls get dumber." So I was always on the lookout for signs that I was becoming dumber. As a sophomore in high school, when I had a temperature higher than 102 degrees, I was afraid my fever was accelerating the progress of my stupidity. So I got out my algebra book and made sure I could still understand and solve the problems. This was just one of the insecurities I developed as a woman. These insecurities were induced by all of my parents.

WOMEN AS TEACHERS ARE A SPECIAL CATEGORY

As a preschooler, I watched wistfully from the sidelines as my father played with my younger half-sister, affectionately calling her his "little toady" while ignoring me. He only noticed me after being informed by a teacher that I was "near genius"; then he recognized me as his daughter. He saw little, if any, value in me until he was informed of my "intelligence" by a school authority figure. But afterward he developed a new story—I had been blessed because I was the first polygamous child in the family. This was the first time I had seen him change his story and actions because of something a "woman" said, but the woman was a teacher.[3] Maybe women who were teachers had more power than ordinary women.

In sum, I had learned that men were better (smarter, more rational, more moral, and so on) than women. Thus, it made sense in that world that women were to be subservient and deferential to men. I also learned that some women were better than others, and if you were not one of the better women, you had to be deferential to the better women. But your position was somewhat fluid—you could improve yourself by becoming smarter and/or tougher.

Public School Lessons about Women

As a student in the public schools, I learned further "truths" about women, some of which supported truths I had learned in my home community and others that conflicted and offered alternative ways of understanding the nature of women. Because I graduated from high school in the mid-1970s, these are the truths that were dominant during that time period. The truths I learned in school came from my teachers as well as from reading both the school and public library books. After I learned to read, I became enthralled with reading and read whenever I possibly could. Auntie worried about my "antisocial tendencies" and forbade me to read anything except school assignments. Instead of ceasing to read, I learned to be sneaky—or strategically subversive. I found places where I could read without being caught. I would sneak a flashlight into my bed and read when I was supposed to be going to sleep; hide in the backyard; or go into the bathroom, lock the door, and read until someone knocked on the door.

On Being Rational and Logical

One of the truths promulgated at home and at school was that most women did not think as rationally and logically as men. This "truth" caused me to question whether I would even be able to recognize whether my thinking was illogical or irrational, as I was by nature not suited to logic or rationality. How could I become logical and rational if I was incapable of distinguishing the difference between logical and illogical or rational and irrational thoughts? Even as I tried to reason something out, my reasoning itself might be flawed. These questions haunted me even into graduate school and influenced my path in the arts and in the sciences. As a master's-graduate student in experimental cognitive psychology, I sought to answers to just how it was that people thought and how the thinking of women and men differed.[4] And as a doctoral graduate student, I focused on epistemology: How exactly does one determine whether something is rational, logical, and/or true?

The Deciders: Making History and Other Adventures

The home/society/school truth that men were more rational and logical thinkers meant that they were the natural deciders. This was aptly illustrated by former President George W. Bush's statement, "I am the decider, and I decide what is best" (cited in Meyer, 2006, para. 2). Thus, in all my worlds it made sense that men, not women, were the deciders. They made history—another truth promulgated at home/school/society. When I was in grade school, I loved historical lessons about "Indians" and the ways they lived. As someone with Mohawk ancestry, I wanted to learn everything I could about the Indians—especially if the Indians were romanticized rather than denigrated.

However, in high school I learned to hate history and civics, both of which were taught by a White male teacher to supplement his football coaching duties. History and civics became boring lists of facts, names, and dates that seemed irrelevant to me as a woman—I learned that women never did anything but sew flags or weep for the men who had gone to war or on some other adventure. Borman and O'Reilly's (1989) examination of history textbooks supports my learning of women's role in history. They found that women were rarely included in history books (on average fewer than 5 pages of 200–300 pages). And when they were included, it was often in descriptions of fashion (the Gibson girl) or sewing (Betsy Ross and the flag). The roles women played in history books were not interesting to me—I wanted to be an artist or a scientist.

A similar hard truth supported at school/society was that men did things, such as having adventures, many of which included saving a woman, but the reverse was not true. I attended elementary school during the 1960s, and I read, and heard only one tale (*A Wrinkle in Time*) in which a female rescued a male. But the cliché of a male rescuing a female persisted—think of Nell rescued by Dudley Do-Right or Princess Lea and Han Solo.

Why Can't Women Do Both?

Another mutually supported truth was that men had careers (or adventures) *and* families but women had families *or* careers. I was angry that I had to make a choice and that boys did not. I questioned why I and other women *had* to make such a choice, while men could naturally have both. But I took it for granted that I would have to make the choice. I also remember George Steiner in *Bluebeard's Castle* saying that men were more creative than women because women had children, and that satisfied their creative drive. Men never had to choose either careers and creativity or children. But women did.

Who's Your Daddy (Husband)?

Another difficult truth is that a woman's status is largely determined by her father's and/or husband's status. In public high school, my siblings and

I were often ridiculed for our clothes, lack of home amenities, and so forth by other students because my father and therefore our family was so poor. Twenty years later in a different community at my son's graduation, a woman promptly and proudly introduced herself as Margaret Snyder,[5] Dr. Snyder's wife. Without a blink, I replied, "Hi, I am Dr. Felecia Briscoe, Eric's mother." She looked startled and, after a quick hello, walked away. I had failed to conform to the gender norms of this small Latter Day Saint community. Even in the 1990s, at my first higher education position, the college president sent out invitations to the faculty that addressed women as "Miss" or "Mrs." and men as "Dr."

Who Is the Fairest of Us All?

Yet another difficult school/society truth for me was that beauty is far more important for women than for men. Many of the stories I read described women who were beautiful (and White). The size of their eyes, their hair, their slenderness, and so on were described in great detail. While men were sometimes described as handsome, their looks were never integral to who they were; nor was their appearance ever described in such exhaustive detail. Women who did not fit the White stereotype of beauty were consigned to being ignored or evil. Think of Cinderella and her ugly stepsisters, or witches. Snow White's stepmother was bested mostly by Snow White's beauty: When making a wish for Snow White, her mother even wishes for her to have beauty (e.g., rose-red lips, skin as White as snow) rather than intelligence or kindheartedness. The message over and over again is that a woman's most important asset is the degree to which her physical appearance fits the socially constructed (White) version of beauty. When I was in the fourth grade, I looked at myself in the mirror and decided that I would never be beautiful; therefore, I had better concentrate on being smart. After all, my father had noticed me when the school IQ tests revealed my heretofore unsuspected intelligence. While being smart was not as good as being pretty, it still meant something.

Strong Women Are Undesirable

Even worse, one of the truths I learned at school conflicted with those that I had learned at home but painted a dismal picture of what it meant to be a woman. That conflicting truth was that weak, vulnerable women are more desirable than strong, tough women, as in "The Princess and the Pea." I remember being both angry and confused that the woman who was incapacitated by the bruising caused by sleeping on a pea 20 mattresses beneath her was more desirable than the women who slept soundly without noticing the pea. I had to reread it make sure I wasn't misunderstanding the story. The desirable woman in this story was very different from those in the stories I had learned at home. I was not alone in learning this dismal lesson. Almost 30 years later as an assistant professor, I worked on a gender and class study with a White middle-class woman. She told me she wanted to be soft and vulnerable; she resisted and feared becoming tough or strong, as it would make her unfeminine and undesirable.

Alternative Worlds

Books, albeit much less frequently, also opened up new worlds of possibilities for me as a woman. In grade school, two female characters, Pippi Longstocking and Meg in A Wrinkle in Time, stand out for me. They were the only two female central figures in adventure tales that I learned about while in elementary school. I did find library books about real women in history who did not have to choose between being a wife/mother and having a career, although they were much more rare than those about men.[6] I remember being excited by the story of Madame Curie, who discovered radium but then died from exposure to radiation. Then there was Amelia Earhart, who flew planes, but she also disappeared when trying to fly around the world— are you sensing a theme here? Women who live like men come to a bad end. On my own, I learned about Sacajawea, the guide for Lewis and Clark who brought her child with her during the trip. How cool. Of course, she was an "Indian," not a White woman, but then I was part Indian, too.[7]

Fifth grade was an instrumental year in situating alternative worlds into my own developing epistemology, and it induced me to develop a lasting goal of attending college. My school started a program for the gifted and talented, and I was selected to be a member of the first cohort in this program. The other thing that happened is that my fifth grade teacher told me it would be a shame if I didn't go to college. Together, those two experiences, along with the Mormon imperative to develop our intelligence, induced me to develop a firm goal of going to college. However, I was sad, because this meant that I probably would not get married or have children. But I wanted to be creative and have adventures, despite these sacrifices—anyway, I was no beauty, so unlikely to marry well. Based on the truths that I had learned, I figured that if I wanted to stay smart enough to go to college, I would have to learn to think like a man. So, except for reading required by my classes, I began reading only books written by men. I wanted to learn how to think rationally and logically. However, in reading science fiction, such as that written by Andre Norton (whom at that time I thought was a man), I learned about an alternative world—a world where women were respected and treated as equals by men *and did not have to choose between being a wife/mother and having a career.* I was determined to join or help cre-ate that world. My reading had convinced me that the path to that world entailed that I become educated and get a "professional" job.

My First Negotiation of the Enduring Double-Bind

Three things happened around high school that affected the way that I pursued my college goal: We moved to a small town 70 miles north of Las Vegas; my father left to go to chiropractic school; and an equally important goal impressed itself on me. I wanted romance, to find love, but it seemed that you had to date to find love. I had learned at school and at home that men (and high school boys) shied away from women who were more intel-ligent, athletic, creative, tougher, or who made more money than they did. Men's egos were much more fragile than women's; women had to protect their fragile egos. Even then it seemed strange that men's egos would be so fragile, when they were theoretically so superior to women in other ways. Thus, the discourse of truths about women and men contained within itself a distortion or conflict. From a Foucauldian perspective, power was operating around a conflict or potential conflict. The point of conflict was that women and men were equally intelligent and capable. Power/knowledge relations in my high school acted to induce particular actions (become desirable) and discourage others (don't become learned). Habermas (1968) claimed that such self-contradictory truths were a distortion of knowledge and thus an indicator of oppression.

The following story illustrates one way in which these knowledge/pow-er relations acted upon me to shape my subjectivities, actions, and expecta-tions, as well as my moments of resistance and acquiescence. Throughout my childhood, I played chess, raced, and otherwise played competitive games with my brothers and sisters. One of my younger brothers and I were talk-ing about a handball game we had played in high school that day. I had won this particular game, and we were arguing about who was the better player. My mother overheard us and chastised me. "Felecia, you have to let your brothers win more; think of their egos." I was sort of surprised by her remark, because we children had always played and competed with one another, and this was my *younger* brother after all. My brother spoke up, "I think Felecia has an ego, too." Either I took this lesson to heart or I was moved by sympathy. Because four years later, I behaved differently when my older brother and I engaged in one of our competitions. We often ran races against each other as children. My older brother always won these races up until I reached the age of 16. We were racing and for the first time, I was winning. He was still getting bad grades in school, and as we neared the finish line, it flashed through my mind how he might feel if I got better grades than he did *and* could run faster. So I slowed down. Yet I think if things had been reversed, he would not have been concerned for my ego. Rather, he *and I* would have seen it as ordinary.

The need for women to be deferential to men was also supported by a host of other gendered truths that I had learned in home and school/ society: 1) women were not as smart, rational, logical, or moral as men; 2) men were the deciders; 3) men had adventures and women were rescued by them or waited for them to come home; 4) women had to choose between a family and a career; 5) men had made history, not women; 6) beauty was a woman's most important asset; 7) strong, tough, and competent women are romantically undesirable; and 8) girls' intelligence was temporary. Together, these truths about women in my home community, in the public schools, and later as a professional created a recurring conflict.

By the time I reached high school, I had learned well the need for women to defer to men. However, because of my entrenched goal of going to college, I had already earned a reputation as a brain in our small high school of 119 students. I was known for getting the highest grades, and my work was often held up as an example to others. I was even approached by students in grades higher than mine for help writing their papers. So what was I to do? I wanted to be smart enough to go to college, but I also wanted a boyfriend and eventually a husband. It became completely clear to me that women had to walk a very fine line. In the world of romance, like the "Princess and the Pea," attributes that were strengths in a man and made him more desirable were defects for women and made her less desirable. But if a woman did not develop these strengths, she would be marginalized in the public portion of the world. This double-bind strategy of power/knowledge affected my actions and subjectivities. My negotiation of it had elements of resistance and of acquiescence

I decided I would keep getting high grades, as I still wanted to enter that better world—a world in which I could be smart, tough, and equal to a man and be respected for that self. However, I would stop raising my hand in class and would give the wrong answer sometimes. Most importantly, whenever I talked to a guy I was interested in dating, I would consciously use smaller words, giggle a lot, and make sure the conversation was focused on the guy. This was my first conscious negotiation of women's enduring double-bind: to be respected and treated as an equal to men, you had to be as smart, skillful, and otherwise as accomplished as a man. However, as a heterosexual woman, if you wanted to be romantically desired by a man, you needed to perform as if you were inferior. This double-bind shaped my actions—no longer would I publicly display my learning or intelligence. My negotiation of this power/knowledge relation divided me in two, splitting in my subjectivities. My secret self worked to learn as much as possible in order to go to college, but my outer performative self was silly, giggly, deferential to any romantic interest, and focused on building a man's ego.

Fractures in—and a Counter-narrative to— the Dominant Discourse about Women

When I was 16, my father left my mother and Auntie with 11 children to finish bringing up on their own. He showed up sporadically for family celebrations and kept claiming that he was going to come back one day, but he never did. My father's abandonment of my mother, who had never been anything but meek and deferential, had fractured the story that men would desire you if you were deferential and kowtowed to them. When I was 18, my father married me to a fundamentalist man. While we were never legally married, we had three children. In addition, contrary to my advice to him, my husband continued to make very bad financial decisions—but then, that was his prerogative as a man and as my husband. Finally, I could stand it no more, and at the age of 24, with three sons under the age of five, I left my husband and the polygamous community in which I had matured. I became very outspoken, letting everyone know in no uncertain terms that women were equal to men and that I expected to be treated that way. This sparked a huge scene during one of my father's sporadic visits.

My father was ensconced in the center of a room crowded with family members and a Christmas tree. He was saying something about the need for wives to defer to their husbands.

I immediately responded, "Wives shouldn't have to defer to their husbands. They should decide things together and treat each other as equals. Men aren't better than women, nor are men naturally the boss of women."

My father's face turned red; the veins popped out on his face and neck. He stood up and began a tirade, denouncing me in a loud voice: "You are one of those women who will be in sack cloth and ashes at the end of times. No man will want you. You will be down on your knees begging a man to take you. You are going to end up old and alone."

I retorted, "You mean like my mother and Auntie, whom you abandoned and left to raise 11 kids?"

He looked taken aback and then waded in again, "I gave them 20 good years of my life, and then I had to leave them because they were no longer obedient to me!"

I countered, "You mean you took the 20 best years of their lives and then abandoned them." At this point, everyone in the room looked uneasy. So I left the room, not wanting to spoil Christmas for everyone. However, not long after that scene, two of my married sisters told their recently married husbands that they were not going to live polygamy and if their husbands took another wife, my sisters would leave them. Their husbands never did take a second wife.

I had resisted the knowledge/power relation concerning the desirability of deferential women by articulating the unspoken story of my mothers' lives, which was a counter-narrative to the sexist tales. Women who gave up their career options, got married, and were deferential to men could be abandoned and left to live and raise their children on their own. Thus, why be deferential? Why give up your career options? You could very well end up alone and with no means to support yourself. I looked forward to abandoning my explicitly sexist home community. No longer would my accomplished and smart self have to be kept an inner secret, and I could do away with my dumb and deferential postures. But to what degree had my posturing stopped being a performance and become my identity? Many scholars contend that our performance of gender is indeed part of our identity (Butler, 1999). And later on I struggled with some of the subjectivities developed by my outer performing self in my formative years.

You've Come a Long Way, Baby (Really?)

As a single woman with three children, I eventually earned an undergraduate degree in education and a master's degree in psychology. I taught for four years as a middle school science teacher and then earned a doctorate in the social foundations of education. I was subsequently hired as an assistant professor in a small town in West Virginia. I worked there until I got tenure and promotion. The year after that, upon being hired at the University of Texas at San Antonio, I moved to Texas, where I again got tenure and promotion. After leaving the fundamentalist community, I fully expected mainstream society to be largely nonsexist, especially in the professional world. By leaving my small community with its antiquated notions of women, I thought I had largely escaped the sexist double-bind. After all, the Virginia Slims commercials claimed, "You've come a long way, baby."

It took me a long time to perceive sexism in this larger, more professional world. During my first 10 years in higher education, I scoffed at women who talked about sexism limiting their success in schools, society, and even higher education. To my mind, they were simply making excuses. Compared with my home community, there seemed to be little, maybe no sexism. I refused to see the new form of sexism. I kept dismissing evidence to the contrary, and it took me some time to discern the systematic oppression of women, which was far more subtle and covert than what I had previously experienced. Unknowingly, I was complicit in a knowledge/power relation that invisibilized sexism in the public sphere of society. However, I eventually became aware that the double-bind continued to constrain women even in higher education; while men overtly claimed to be women's equal, their patterns of communication and other social practices often said otherwise.

When I was teaching in a small college in West Virginia, a slightly older, married, White male assistant professor explained a situation to me that was to become all too familiar. He explained that I would probably remain single, as the available single men would not be interested in a woman who was more educated than they were, or even who was *as* educated as they were. It seemed in West Virginia that the warnings of my mothers about the fragility of men's egos were true; seemingly unaccomplished women were still more desirable than accomplished women—especially women who were more accomplished than men.[8] However, southern West Virginia has a very distinct and somewhat antiquated Appalachian culture; perhaps this unique culture explained the fact that society outside my community seemed to be just as sexist as my community when it came to the double-bind. Thus, I was delighted at my first opportunity to meet up with some of my friends from graduate school. I was in for a shock.

Tread Carefully

I had been very close with a number of students in my doctoral cohort. We had challenged each other to think, write better, and in other numerous other ways help each other through the doctoral process. A number of us, now assistant professors, met at a professional conference. It was exciting to see all my friends, whom I had not seen since earning my doctorate. We decided to meet for dinner and catch up on each other's lives. Six of us, three women and three men, showed up for dinner. At dinner we all sat eating and chatting; I gradually noticed that the men were doing almost all of the talking. As these former student colleagues had claimed to be focused on helping to create greater equity, I decided to bring up the matter. I thought we could discuss it intellectually and determine why it was happening even with us. I was thinking that it was both the women's and men's fault. The women, including me, were at fault for failing to speak up, and the men were at fault for failing to invite or at least leave space for the women's participation. I thought we could talk about it in light of all the social theory we all knew. So I spoke up. "Have you all noticed that the men are doing almost all of the talking?" The reaction was not at all what I expected from this group of "progressive thinkers."

I was shocked when one of the men, who claimed to be an ardent feminist, scowled and then spit out, "Felecia, stop trying to grab the moral high ground!" I was stunned and confused: What moral high ground was he talking about? Then I realized he must have felt guilty about what I had said, though I didn't think it was just the men's fault. I tried to explain this, but the conversation spiraled out of control into an argument, with the man getting angrier and angrier, as a silence settled over the rest of the table. I guess his ego was indeed fragile.

I was shocked to be scolded by one of my "progressive" friends for bringing up the lack of gender equity being played out in our social situation. I didn't say anything further. Notably, neither did any of the other men or women. It seemed that the topic was simply too hot for any of them to say anything. In resisting the power/knowledge relations of double-bind in this situation, I acted by confronting the group and pointing out whose voice was silent. But when the conflict escalated in this social situation, I too was silenced. I was dispirited by the continuing prospect of this social double-bind. However, I thought maybe it was a White male (even when they were progressive) thing and only applied to social situations. Maybe men of color, who too had undergone discrimination, would be more sensitive and not enact this double-bind in social situations. I left West Virginia and moved to San Antonio, Texas.

Down in Texas

I expected the folks in the eighth-largest city in the United States to have less provincial and less traditional sexism perspectives. But in my department all of my female colleagues, regardless of their ethnicity and age, were single, while all of my male colleagues, regardless of their ethnicity and age, were married—many of them to former students. I asked a slightly younger, single, Black and Latino male colleague who claimed to be nonsexist why this might be the case. He candidly told me that he would never publicly date a woman who was more successful than he was, as he wanted to be "the one people saw, rather than the one in the shadow." I guess that means the woman needs to be in the shadow so as to highlight the man.

Here are the lessons learned through my various conflicts with gendered power/knowledge relations. These power/knowledge relations have engendered (no pun intended) particular subjectivities in both men and women. While gendered truths may be rejected, the gendered norms and behavioral expectations based on those truths are much harder to identify and reject for both men and women. Furthermore, as patriarchy has been a part of Western culture for more than 2,000 years, these gendered subjectivities have permeated institutional cultures. As these patriarchal behavioral norms and expectations privilege men, men are less likely to become aware of their sexist nature, according to Collins (2000). The men who have been most privileged and thus are most likely to see such privileging as natural are older White men. (This is not to say that younger men, men of color, or even women may not adopt the same gendered norms, as institutional cultures have already integrated those patriarchal norms.) Thus, even highly educated men who claim to be progressive thinkers and opposed to sexism are unlikely to question norms or expectations that position women as deferential. I find that I as a woman have had to consciously watch myself to ensure that I do not enact patriarchal norms when in the company of men—to be silent and listen to them, extol their accomplishments, and be modest about my own accomplishments. Friedan (1963) was correct: The personal is political, or in this case professional.

The Double-Bind as Manifested in Professional Situations

I had expected to act and be treated as an equal in higher education. However, this expectation proved to be wrong. When women fail to act deferentially toward men who still unquestioningly retain these old subjectivities, men will perceive their behavior as rude and inappropriate. And when those men are gatekeepers, women may be punished by slower or no promotions. When I failed to reproduce patriarchal power relations by responding deferentially to the patronizing attitude of White male full professors, my professional advancement was jeopardized. Yet he may claim, and even believe, that he has gone out of his way to be helpful and encouraging to me, but that I rebuffed him.

Creating Distance

When I was up for my third-year review, an older White full professor explained to me, "You have such a nice smile; we want to keep you around." I do not think he realized how inappropriate his patronizing comment was, because he said it in front of the dean. This full professor also had difficulty interacting appropriately with others who have historically been oppressed. For example, he confided to a newly hired assistant professor who was an African-American, "I never see color; I just see the person." Perhaps he meant his comments to be encouraging. However, such comments have exactly the opposite effect; they induce women and racialized people to distance their selves as much as possible from the person making such statements. Such distancing exacts a price when such men are the gatekeepers to advancement. Later, when I was going up for tenure, this same older White male professor came into my office and placed a hand on my shoulder. He helpfully offered, "I will be glad to assist you in writing your self-statement or in other ways help you prepare your application for tenure and promotion."

Because of my past history with him and because his disciplinary area and focus of research were entirely different than mine, my reaction was immediate, visceral, and distancing. I icily replied, "That will not be necessary. I have other people who are mentoring me." While I did not act deferential or grateful, I was not rude. He may genuinely have been offering to help. However, based on my earlier interaction with him and what I felt was inappropriate touching,[9] I wanted nothing more than to be as far from him as possible. I think that he was irritated by my rebuff. He was one of the three men and the only full professor assigned to my departmental review committee (DRC)—there were no women on the DRC. While I do not know the types of considerations and discussions that took place during that meeting, I know that the DRC reviewed my application and voted unanimously against my tenure and promotion.

I was ultimately deemed worthy of tenure and promotion because, aside from the DRC, each of the five other reviewing bodies disagreed with the DRC's decision.

The Soft Sexism: I'm So Sorry That You Are Not Good Enough . . .

Now, as I begin the process for applying to become a full professor, he has gotten an administrative position and is now a more powerful gatekeeper on my path to promotion. Thus, his decision carries even more weight in determining whether or not I am promoted to full professor. His responses thus far have been so continually and illogically negative that I have become exhausted. Further, my sense of futility has become so strong that I have to fight off an impulse to withdraw my application for full professor.

As a courtesy, I e-mailed him that I would be going up for full professor in the spring. He asked for a copy of my vita and then demanded that we meet in person as soon as possible to discuss my prospects for advancement, ostensibly in order for him to help me. He admitted that I have a good teaching, service, and research record, but he was worried about the "sustained" nature of my research, because there were two years, 2007 and 2009, when I did not publish anything. The fact that in the subsequent academic years I published more than usual was immaterial to him. I tried to be positive and said, "Well, at least, looking at my record no one will think that I suddenly started publishing just for this promotion."

He looked at me and then replied, "But that is *just* what it looks like to me."

I was surprised, wondering how he could say that, when in 2009, I had my greatest number of publications and it was now 2012. He had reviewed my vita but had failed to note this pattern. So I said to him, "Although my effort toward research is sustained, it isn't going to yield a machinelike regularity in publication due to a number of factors. For example, one journal accepted one of my articles as I submitted it in 2008, but the journal took two and a half years to publish it because the journal changed editors during that time and lost the manuscript."

He was quiet a moment and then said, "Why don't you meet with other people who will be on your DRC and see what they think?" He completely failed to address the point that I had made. (When I showed my vita to a woman in my department who was a full professor, she thought I had a great publication record.)

Then I optimistically pointed out that I was first of three authors of a published book and would have a completed draft of an edited book under contract when I went up for full professor. He said depreciatingly, "Books don't count for much."

I was appalled and said, "In the college of liberal and fine arts, a published book is considered to be the equivalent of three published articles."

With some ire, he replied, "Well, you are in the college of education, not the college of liberal and fine arts." I thought about pointing out to him that people from the college of liberal and fine arts would be on the university level of review. However, at that point, I realized, nothing I could say would move him from his position, as he continued on, "Furthermore, you have only shown outstanding leadership at the university and not in the professional arena."

However, I persevered with regard to my service record and said that I did not have to show outstanding leadership in both arenas, just one. I showed him what it said in the *Handbook of Operating Procedures*. He then showed me a white paper the provost had recently sent to him. He pointed to where the white paper said you had to show leadership in both arenas to go up for full professor. I then pointed out that in the white paper it said that you had to be outstanding in one of the three arenas—teaching, research, or service—but not in all three. He said that he knew that. But he had been talking as if I had to be outstanding in all three arenas. He then looked sad and said, "I am sorry, I would like to support you, but I just can't see that you qualify to be full professor." No matter my record in any of the three areas or what I said, it was clear that he was again going to try to block my promotion.

By his past and current actions, this White male full professor discouraged rather than encouraged my application for advancement. Such behaviors by relevant gatekeepers create a chilly environment for women's advancement (Meyer & Firestone, 2005) and may help account for the fact that fewer full professors are women, and women take on average more than three years longer to advance from associate professor to full professor (Misra, Lundquist, Holmes, & Agiomavritis, 2011). Furthermore, qualified women are more likely than qualified men to be passed over in promotions (Joy, 1998). In the face of his discouraging responses, it took time and energy to recover from his negativity and keep going. Both time and energy could have been better spent on actual academic work. However, if I succumb to his discouragement, I will be one less woman who is a full professor.

When women fail to be deferential to some older White male full professors, these males create a discouraging environment for those women and thereby help maintain the disproportionate number of male full professors. And when women who are not deferential fail to be discouraged, these men use their positioning to block their advancement. The above incidents may simply seem to be isolated, to pertain to only one White male gatekeeper, or to be merely a self-serving interpretation. However, the disproportionate number of White male full professors suggests that this kind of treatment of women or some variant is common. Misra et al. (2011) find that

> [w]omen are less likely ever to be promoted to full professor than men, and their promotions take longer . . . women [take] from one to three and a half years longer than men to advance to full professorships, with women at doctoral universities lagging farthest behind. Men still hold more than three-quarters of full professorships in the United States. (para. 2)

The demographics at my college and university (which is a doctoral university) reflect research such as the above showing the lack of advancement by women. In 2013, based on the listings of the faculty on the college Web site (COEHD, n.d.), 21.8% of the women were full professors compared with 35.1% of the men; the racialized ratio of full professors was 17 Whites to 10 people of color. Thus, older White men were disproportionately full professors in my college and disproportionately represented in gatekeeper positions. Older White men developed their subjectivities under more patriarchal knowledge/power relations than their younger counterparts. These men tend to see women's deference to them as "natural" and the lack of such deference as inappropriate and rude. Thus, older White men are likely to react negatively to women who do not automatically assume a deferential posture. However, older White men can be reflective and begin to question their own reactions and those of their colleagues. And some do. Nevertheless, given their preponderance in gatekeeping roles in higher education, such patriarchal subjectivities result in a glass ceiling for the advancement of women in higher education. As Jackson and O'Callaghan (2009) note,

> [t]he negative effects on career prospects, stemming from being female, increase over the course of a career. That is, the effects of gender stratification are additive in nature and disproportionately affect women the longer they persist in their careers. In other

words, glass ceiling effects operates throughout a woman's career, and may get worse as her career grows. (p. 473).

It makes sense that as I begin the process for advancing to full professor, I should receive the greatest degree of discouragement thus far in higher education. Further, even when women overcome such covert hostility and advance to full professors, they still suffer from the institutionalized patriarchy. For example, in my university, full professors who are women on average make $12,100 less than those who are men (Almanac of Higher Education, 2012). Through discouragement and blocking decisions, the gender status quo is maintained, as women are marginalized to the lower ranks of academia.

There is still another way in which the double-bind negatively affects women's advancement. After years of negotiating patriarchal knowledge/power relations, being deferential to men became almost automatic for me. My earlier split half that sought to highlight men's accomplishments while hiding my own never did disappear. It is not so easy for women to eliminate or ignore these gendered subjectivities shaped by patriarchal knowledge/power relations. This could help account for the fact that women have more difficulty advancing in the academic and business world. We learn to hide our own accomplishments. When I write my self-statements, I often have to remind myself not to be modest, but to self-praise. But every time I proofread my self-statement, subjectively I feel that I am being inappropriately boastful, and I am tempted to soften my accomplishments. Thus, advancement is difficult for women, as one is supposed to praise oneself.

In higher education, a woman is punished if she is not deferential in behavior toward predominantly older White male gatekeepers. However, even if a woman is deferential and modest, she may still be punished if she fails to praise herself sufficiently in her applications for promotion. In sum, to be promoted, a woman must simultaneously be both deferential and self-aggrandizing—a double-bind that is difficult or impossible to achieve.

Some Lessons Concerning the "Truths" about Women

This narrative represents my critical consciousness as it exists in this moment. If the past tells me anything, it is that my critical consciousness will not remain the same, but will continue to grow and develop in different directions and produce further understandings. However, there are some resistant knowledge/power formations that I have developed through my experiences:

First, when oppression goes from being overt and explicit to covert and subtle (as in my experiences with the double-bind), it may take some time for the person experiencing the more covert sexism to become aware of it (and perhaps even for those who are enacting the covert oppression). I hope that this narrative helps both women and men to become conscious of the ways that power/knowledge relations of their youth have shaped our subjectivities. Despite our opposing conscious understandings, these subjectivities may influence our interpretation of the behaviors of those who have been oppressed and privileged. Our behaviors based on those interpretations may unwittingly act to maintain that oppression/privilege.

Second, oppressive truths that occur in multiple contexts are harder to discern than those truths that occur in only one context. It was harder for me to question and discern oppressive truths about women when those truths were supported in most of my experiences at both home and school.

Third, women as well as men produce patriarchal truths, as seen in the behavior of Auntie and, during grad school, my own interpretation of women who complained of sexism.

Fourth, sexism as constituted in the double-bind of knowledge/power relations continues to act even in the professional realm, often framed as inappropriate rudeness. However, I hope my narrative is not interpreted by men, especially older White men, to mean that they should not offer help. Rather, that it be interpreted that they should offer help focused on a woman's professional work, not on her smile or other physical attributes.

Fifth, in the professional context of higher education, a woman's double-bind is that no matter which course (deferential and modest vs. not deferential and touting her accomplishments) she takes in her professional life, she may be punished professionally. Hopefully, this narrative sheds some light on how the subjectivities of men and women formed under patriarchal power/knowledge relations may even, without anyone's conscious intention, serve to keep the glass ceiling in place.

Notes

1. While Foucault never explicitly refers to oppressive or emancipatory power relations, he clearly indicates that the dominant power relations are oppressive (Fraser, 1989).

2. In some of his later work (e.g., *Hermeneutics of the Self*), Foucault distinguishes between constructed truths that control and truths that help *free* the self.

3. My mother's bloodlines included Mohawk ancestry as well as White. While my mother's Mohawk ancestry was discernable in her visage, we, her children, all have a White appearance. Nevertheless, among the Plygs, our bloodlines were viewed as inferior. However, I do not address my experiences in regard to race and ethnicity in this paper, as I have previously addressed these complex issues in another article (Briscoe, 2012).

4. With few monetary resources, it was taken for granted that we would go barefoot in the warm summers.

5. Because of their tendency to sin, women and children needed discipline and at times to be physically disciplined by their fathers or husbands. For to "spare the rod, was to spoil the child" or woman.

6. As an adult, I wondered if this was just a childish perception motivated by normal sibling rivalry. However, without prompting from me, as an adult, my sister told me that she had always resented me for stealing our father's affection from her by being so smart.

7. My master's program in cognitive psychology supported my Auntie's assertion to a certain extent. Quantitative studies indicate that after puberty, boys progressively have higher achievement, especially in math, than girls.

8. Except for my own name, all other names used in this chapter are pseudonyms.

9. Women and men who stay home and take care of a family are engaged in real work—real work that is some of the most important work in our society, even though it often unacknowledged by society or their partners.

10. Later, perhaps inspired by her story, I was to follow Sacajawea's path—at the age of 30, I packed all my worldly goods and took my three young sons with me as I drove across the United States to enter a doctoral program at the University of Cincinnati.

11. There is much literature that indicates that strong women are also more desirable than weak women in other marginalized cultures, such as in some African-American and Native American cultures.

12. This is not to say that I feel that a hand on my shoulder from a male colleague who is a friend would be inappropriate. However, from someone whom I did not regard as a friend and who was my superior in terms of rank, I felt that his behavior was out of bounds.

CHAPTER EIGHT

Where Did the Girls Go?

.•⎯⎯•·

The Role of Socialization and Institutions in Silencing Female Voices

DAMARIS MORAA CHOTI

In many societies around the world, women are disadvantaged in various ways, including educational achievement, access to employment opportunities, and the pay scale (Kim, 2000). In spite of that, the economic development of most countries depends on women (Dollar & Gatti, 1999). This trend can be attributed to various factors, but as some scholars have observed, gender-based socialization across the various institutions and levels of the social structure plays a key role in determining the underprivileged position of women in society, particularly in developing countries (Corcoran & Courant, 1985). Gender socialization "starts at birth and it is a process of learning cultural roles according to one's sex. Right from the beginning, boys and girls are treated differently by the members of their own environment, and learn the differences between boys and girls, women and men" (UNICEF, 2007). Gender socialization continues through adulthood and may be effected through a range of socializing agents, such as parents and other family members, other adults, religious and educational institutions, and the mass media. Writing about gender socialization among the Gusii community of Kenya, Silberschmidt (1999, p. 56) reports that "Gusii boys and girls are socialized into different patterns of roles and behavior starting in their early childhood and underpinning their different 'place' and status in the society as well as norms and values." Therefore, children in this community learn gender appropriate behavior through their parents, other family members, and other adults in their immediate environment, ranging from the family level up to school and church settings. Embodied in various institutions, gender socialization has impacted my life in notable ways.

By "institution," I mean the structures and mechanisms that socialize and regulate the behavior of a people as a nation, ethnic community, school, university, or church.

In this autoethnography, I focus on my experiences growing up in the Gusii community. Specifically, I examine the gender socialization practices that I and other girls experienced as well as the historical and colonial genesis of these socialization practices. In this examination, I ask in what ways my experiences were similar to and different from the Gusii subordination of girls in general. I also ask what supports I experienced that enabled me to see and reject this oppression, and what mechanisms kept other women from being able to reject their oppression. Finally, I ask how these experiences have influenced my development as a critical researcher.

My own experience as a girl growing up in the Gusii community informed me of gender-based socialization patterns embodied in institutions skewed against females. In my community, our roles as girls typically confine us to the domestic sphere. We are trained to become "good" future wives and therefore must learn skills related to cooking, collecting firewood and water, childrearing, housecleaning, and farming. Gender-based socialization among the Gusii is not limited to the family environment. Gendered behavior is well developed and reinforced in educational, religious, and other institutions through a system of well-defined gender roles for boys and girls and positions that males and females may hold in these institutions. Consequently, there is a clear pattern of behavioral norms for males and females in my community; this pattern is clearly replicated in the public domain. This situation may explain the persistent prejudice targeted at Gusii women pursuing leadership positions in the public domain.

In this chapter, I tell my personal story, bringing together my experiences from my childhood, growing up, schooling, and through marriage to show how socialization and major institutions (e.g., culture, schools, religion, colonialism) can combine to shape the experiences and status of women and girls in Kenya and/or Africa. I examine my experiences to expose the extent to which these factors shaped my journey and destination. In recounting my past, I critically examine the roles that culture, religion, class, institutional factors, and colonialism played in my life. Thus, my story includes both observed and lived experiences from childhood through my present position as a researcher in K-12 educational administration. I begin with an examination of how colonialism has entrenched more firmly male domination into my Kenyan community.

Colonialism and Patriarchy

Colonialism in Kenya played a big role in reinforcing the patriarchal system among Kenyan communities, including the Gusii. Kenya was induced to become a capitalistic state during the colonial period. During the colonial era, Kenyan men were recruited into low-wage labor while women remained at home to be in charge of domestic roles and subsistence agriculture (Shadle, 2006, Silberschmidt, 1999). In the pre-colonial period, the main preoccupation of Kenyan men was mostly herding cattle. Cattle villages were collections of small huts that were built away from the homesteads where men lived while taking care of their cattle. The area around the cattle camps comprised fresh grazing fields. The older boys accompanied men to the cattle camps to be trained in herding and fighting skills. Because the Gusii were initially not receptive to the colonial administration, the cattle camps became a threat to the colonialists. They feared that the men and boys at the cattle camps would scheme to attack them. Colonial administrators therefore abolished the cattle villages, leaving men with only a subsidiary role in agriculture, which forced them to leave their traditional work of cattle herding and migrate outside Gusii to work and raise money for the taxes demanded by the colonial masters (Silberschmidt, 1999). While Gusii men got wage jobs in cities, women were excluded from this "prestigious" job market. Instead, women remained in the villages, where they practiced subsistence farming to provide food for the large families, a core characteristic of the Gusii. In addition, seeking jobs outside Gusii separated men from their wives and children. This situation encouraged the men to establish extramarital relations in cities. Back in the villages, the women starved sexually and had to wait long periods for their husbands to return to the village. This trend survived and continued even after the colonialists had left.

The "patriarchal ideology also solidified during the colonial era, as the colonialists relied on the Victorian ideology of the woman as good/responsible housewife/lady while providing jobs to male loyalists" (Omwoyo, 2008, p. 158). To establish colonial rule, the support of men was sought, as they were the most influential members of the community during the pre-colonial era. The colonial masters, for instance, demanded that men (not women) pay household taxes as a strategy to convince men that the colonial rule still recognized their higher status in society. Omwoyo (2008) notes that during the colonial period, the male heads of the household were responsible for paying the hut and poll taxes (flat-rate taxes that were charged for inhabited huts), most of which benefited the colonial government in the early 1900s. The colonial administrators also demanded "an 'educated' White collar labor force" (Mutua, 1978, p. 161), but only selected boys to train for these jobs. However, young girls only received an education that prepared them to be good future wives. Thus, women and girls were restricted to domestic chores, while men and boys were introduced to jobs oriented to the public domain. The increased subordination of women through their exclusion from paid labor disempowered them socially and even politically.

The aftermath of the colonial era continues to afflict Kenyan women in different ways. Though I was born 13 years after Kenya gained independence from Britain, I experienced some of the cultural detritus of the deplorable colonial era. Gusii men still retain the "head of household" title, even those who depend on their wives to provide for the household; school education and wage employment were still considered to be primarily for men and boys; even today, subsistence farming among the Gusii is a woman's preoccupation.

The Status of Gusii Women as Embodied in the Institutions of Family and Marriage

Today, the Gusii culture is openly biased against women in multiple ways. To begin with, the Gusii community and families continue to be mainly patriarchal. In this community, men have authority over women and children, and the male parent is the head of the family regardless of whether he is a responsible father and/or husband. This is one aspect of my community's culture that has bothered me ever since I was a child. During my childhood, I noticed that many men in my neighborhood would demand a meal from their wives even when these men did not contribute anything to their family food supplies. Instead of working hard to provide for their families, most of the men spent long hours either drinking traditional brews or playing games and chatting at the shopping centers. This they did from morning to evening. In the evening, they returned home drunk and demanded a meal from their wives.

In my village, many married women dreaded the evenings, as this was the time when wife battering happened (and still does even today). Not only did most men come home drunk but also ready to "discipline" their wives at any slight provocation. At one time or another, most of the women were beaten up ruthlessly and driven out of the family house together with their children. These scenes were so frequent that hardly a single evening passed without hearing cries of battered women and children in distress running for safety. As most of these incidences occurred at dinnertime, the victims were hungry throughout the night. In most cases, the victims sought refuge in their friends' houses or spent the night outside. Sometimes the battered wife would go back to her parents' house for a few days and then return to her matrimonial home only to face the same suffering. Several women in my village were trapped in this cycle of brutality for their entire lives.

I never fathomed why a woman could be beaten almost every night and run away only to return to the same cruelty. It was not until I overheard one of my mother's close friends confide her dilemma that I understood: "Every time I seek intervention from my parents, my mother tells me to go back to my husband," explained my mother's friend. "She tells me to look around the village and count the number of women who are never been battered by their husbands. She tells me all husbands are the same and have to be respected no matter what." I could not help but shudder at this revelation. She continued, "So because I cannot stay with my parents for long with my kids and since I have nowhere else to go, I have to come back to my husband and persevere. Besides, my brothers won't let me stay at my parents' house any longer." Through this explanation, I also learned that in my community a married woman is prohibited from living at her parents' house. Under no circumstances can she abandon her matrimonial home for her parents'. This situation is reinforced by the fact that Gusii men pay a bride price. Silberschmidt (1999) concluded that the basis for most Gusii women's acceptance of their prejudiced status in society stems from the dilemma that battered wives face. Thus, Gusii women are forced to live within the confinement of restraining social norms to be socially accepted. Gusii men take advantage of their higher social status and mistreat their wives. They abuse their wives not because they are drunk or their wives have necessarily disrespected them, but simply to exercise and affirm their power and authority over women in marriage. The men want to reassure themselves that they are the ones in charge of their households and that women must submit to them at all times.

This need for reassurance originates mainly in the setup of the family structure during both the pre-colonial and colonial periods in Gusii, when men were respected as the head of household and expected to acquire wealth in form of land, cattle, many wives, and children to maintain their manliness (Silberschmidt, 1992). According to Silberschmidt, most of the men were able to perform their expected roles. However, the increase in the Gusii population has jeopardized the men's ability to perform their expected roles. The population of the Gusii has increased rather rapidly. In 1948, the population was 255,000 (Whiteley, 1960). By 2010, the population had reached 1,152, 282 (Kenya Decides, 2013). This population growth represents an increase of 71%, leading to increased unemployment. Thus, the men's ability to earn and control household income has been undermined because women have become "invaluable contributors to the needs of the household. Not because they have attempted to take over male roles, but because men have not . . . been able to live up to their (prescribed and expected) role as head of household" (Silberschmidt, 2001, p. 5). With the loss of economic power over their households, some men revert to violence and aggression as an avenue for reclaiming their lost power of control over women (Silberschmidt, 2001). I count myself lucky to have never witnessed such brutality meted out on my mother. Not even once did I see my parents even argue.

The other disturbing trend I observed in my community as I grew up was that, in general, women provided for family needs, such as food and clothing, yet the man was the "head" of the household. Today, the situation has changed only slightly; Gusii "men are [still] branded the "breadwinners," while women are seen as mere recipients together with other members of the family" (Omwoyo, 2008, p. 158). A typical day for Gusii women is rather crowded with daily chores. They get up early in the morning to prepare breakfast, prepare children for school, and feed livestock and flocks. Then they have to work on the family farm in land preparation, planting, weeding, or harvesting. The Gusii people are hardworking mixed farmers, but, sadly, it is only the women who perform most of the farming activities, with help from the children. The Gusii believe in large families, and children are a vital source of farm labor.

The societal status based on sons and expectations of large families among the Gusii caused my parents unnecessary strain. Both of my parents worked hard to provide for our needs. My father was a church minister until his retirement, whereas my mother was a subsistence farmer. However, raising seven children—two boys and five girls—was a daunting task for my parents. We did not always have enough food to eat, and the meals were not nutritionally balanced. In most cases, our breakfast consisted of porridge. We ate boiled potatoes or banana for lunch and *ugali* (cooked cornmeal balls) with vegetables, milk, or beans/meat stew for dinner.

In addition to insufficient food, housing, and clothing, it became increasingly difficult for my parents to raise our school fees. The situation worsened when three of us (my older sister, my brother, and I) joined high school. In Kenya, high school students are required to pay tuition. Our tuition and other school related expenses became unbearable to our parents because all three of us attended boarding high schools, which are more expensive than day schools. My father sacrificed to enroll us in local boarding schools instead of day schools because they offered more educational opportunities than the day schools. In Kenya, the boarding school environment affords students more time to concentrate on their schoolwork and to interact closely with teachers because most teachers reside within or near the school. In the evenings, students in boarding schools also get extra time for homework or private study, while most day scholars have to complete a lot of chores before and after school and during weekends. Besides, day-school students who live far away find commuting to be exhaustive and time-consuming. It was against that background that my parents decided to send us to boarding schools even though our family income was insufficient. In order to cope, we had to forgo some school necessities, such as pocket money, sports gear, snacks, and academic or/and religious or club trips. We envied some of our school friends from well-off families who were able to meet these needs. At some point, my family's financial situation deteriorated to the extent that we had to stay away from school because of unpaid tuition bills. This situation lowered our grades. The situation would have been different with a smaller family size.

The marital bond is another dimension of the Gusii culture that denigrates women. In marriage, the Gusii woman is treated as a "property" of the man, a fact reinforced through bride price and an entrenched patriarchal system (Ayanga, 1996; Wangila, 2007). Among the Gusii, for a marriage to be recognized, the man has to pay a bride price to the woman's family. If a man lives with a woman without paying a bride price, the relationship is considered cohabitation. In the case of cohabitation, if the man, woman, or man's parents die, a bride price must be paid before the burial ceremonies can be conducted. Bride price may be in the form of cows or money. Once the bride price has been paid, the woman no longer belongs to her parents; she belongs to her husband and his family. The woman's father may use the cows or money obtained from the bride price to acquire another wife. Alternatively, the woman's brothers can use the cows to pay the bride price for their own wives. The significance of daughters in a Gusii family revolves around the wealth the family gets for their bride price. In this respect, the Gusii girl is valued for the role she plays as a source of wealth to her family. Underlying this role as a source of wealth is the undeniable truth that the practice of bride price objectifies Gusii girls.

Objectification of Gusii women in marriage is enacted through a variety of practices. After marriage, the woman becomes the husband's property, "not only [for] sexual companionship, but [also for] agricultural labor, reproduction, and the completion of burdensome daily household chores" (Shadle, 2003, p. 250). Even career women are not spared, as their job responsibilities have to be harmonized with household chores. In marriage, the husband usually makes financial decisions even when he does not contribute to the household income. In addition, the husband has the power to determine where and when the wife may work. For instance, if a woman is offered a promotion or transfer, the husband has to approve it. Women, who decide to exercise their freedom within marriage by objecting to their husbands' decisions are in most cases abused by their husbands or end up divorcing. Yet divorce is associated with a social stigma against women, though not for men. This gender-based stigmatization forces most women to live with abusive husbands to retain the married title and avoid exclusion in their communities. In a community where many families are on the edge of survival, exclusion is a very serious matter. By contrast, if a man gets a promotion or transfer, the woman has to follow him. The woman's career ranks lower than her husband's. Gusii women are also objectified by the frequent use of the term *omorugi* (cook) by men to refer to their wives.

Polygamy is a culturally accepted practice among the Gusii. Fathers can use the bride price from their first daughter to pay the bride price for another wife. However, nowadays fathers do not necessarily use their oldest daughters' bride price to marry a second wife. They mostly claim it for personal use, as polygamy is waning. Formerly, sons might use their sisters' bride price to marry. However, today a timely dowry from their sisters is not guaranteed. This is because, unlike in the past when dowry had to be paid before marriage, people now often decide to live as husband and wife for a long time before the man pays the bride price for his wife. Therefore, sons may be forced to raise their own cows or money for bride price. Furthermore, some families only have sons, with no daughters from whom to get a bride price. In the past, families without daughters were considered poor because, ultimately, neighbors or relatives had to raise bride price for them to get married. Children born to these sons were considered the neighbor's or the relative's. This situation also forced some men to remain bachelors because the bride price was quite unaffordable for them (Shadle, 2003). However, today, not only can the bride price be delayed, but it is also relatively more affordable than in the past.

The higher status that Gusii give to boys over girls further undermines the position of females in this community. Among the Gusii, only boys can inherit ancestral land and family wealth. Moreover, the line of descent is traced through men in the family because it is male children who pass down the family name. As a result, couples who have only girls are considered to be a dead end and therefore are despised in society. If a woman gives birth to only female children, she may be disowned by the husband, but not vice versa. Eventually, she may be sent away from her marital home so that the husband can marry a second wife who may bear him sons. Whenever a couple does not have a boy child, the woman is blamed.

Another way in which the higher status of boys is manifested is that in most families, boys are given educational priority over girls. Because of high levels of poverty, many families are forced to decide whom among their children to educate, and sons are given precedence. Girl children tend to be overlooked and neglected because they will one day, upon getting married, belong to another family. In spite of the higher value my parents put on boys, I appreciate the fact that my father valued education and educated all of us regardless of our gender.

I come from a family of seven: five girls and two boys. The first- and lastborn in my family are boys. Seemingly, my parents were not satisfied with only one son, given the Gusii expectation of large families and many boys. In their attempt to have many sons, they continued to have children until the birth of their second son. This resulted in a family of nine and the burden of raising a big family. Furthermore, the ancestral land that my father inherited from his father is too small to divide between the two sons. My father's case is not unusual in our community. There are numerous families in my village who have 10 or more children in their attempts to have sons. Given the increase in population, the arable land, once enough to be shared among many sons, is not sufficient anymore. Against this background, it appears rather unreasonable for the Gusii to insist on having many sons. The lower status of girl children continues as they become older and get married.

My own experience in marriage does not fully reflect the characteristics of a typical Gusii marriage that I previously described. There are some cultural requirements I have not met for two major reasons. First, I was married away from home, and I have not spent my married life in my country, or community. I am therefore not under close scrutiny by my community members, which gives me greater freedom to disregard some cultural practices. For example, my husband and I have two daughters but no son, and I am not planning to "work hard" to have a son(s); neither my husband nor I approves of the idea of valuing sons over daughters. Moreover, because we live outside our community, we do not experience the pressure to have sons. In addition, my husband and I share household chores, such as looking after the children, cooking, dishwashing, and laundry without either of us worrying about the reaction of neighbors or family members. Our situation would be different if we lived among our people in our community. I would not let my husband perform such "feminine" duties, as this would make me a disgrace to the community and/or be thought of as having bewitched my husband. Besides, my husband would not accept doing household chores if we lived among our people. The second reason why I think my marriage is not a typical Gusii marriage is that my husband prioritizes human dignity over cultural principles. He believes in dialogue in that we make decisions based on contributions from both of us. However, my husband did pay a bride price to my parents to fulfill this strong cultural requirement. Nevertheless, I do not feel objectified in any way because of the immense support I get from my husband.

Another significant cultural practice that disadvantages girls and women in the Gusii community is clitoridectomy (i.e., the surgical removal of the clitoris), a form of initiation into womanhood. It is sometimes referred to as *female circumcision* or *female genital mutilation*. Kenya has about 42 ethnic communities, but female genital mutilation is most rampant among the Gusii, Somali, and Maasai ethnic communities (Njue & Askew, 2004). A number of factors have contributed to the entrenchment of clitoridectomy among the Gusii people. First, the Gusii believe that clitoridectomy is one of the identifying cultural symbols of the community and that if the practice is discarded, there will be cultural discontinuity. Second, clitoridectomy is intended to lower women's sexual urges so as to prevent premarital and adulterous sexual relations, particularly in polygamous marriages (Njue & Askew, 2004; Oloo, Wanjiru, & Newell-Jones, 2011). Among the Gusii, it is acceptable for men to marry more than one wife but an abomination for a woman to have more than one husband or to take a lover. Clitoridectomy is devastating to women because it limits their sexual pleasure and exposes them to health-related risks in addition to subjecting them to excruciating pain, given the sensitivity of the area. Some people have argued that the clitoris is not the only sexually stimulating organ in the woman's body, and therefore excising it is not a big deal. Such arguments have no basis, because biologically the clitoris has no other known function in the woman's body other than arousing her sexually (Creighton, 2006). Therefore, chopping it off or incising part of it denies women their right to sexual pleasure.

It is worth noting that, despite the prominence of clitoridectomy among the Gusii, not all girls or women value the practice for what it is supposed to symbolize. Some girls choose to undergo clitoridectomy out of the fear of the stigma attached to forgoing it. Njue and Askew's (2004) research established that, "for younger girls, the cut is something they have to do and not something they want or understand" (p. 9). In other words, girls have been socialized to believe that clitoridectomy is part of the process of becoming good future wives. Furthermore, to be marriageable, girls must undergo clitoridectomy, because very few men will marry an uncircumcised woman. However, in the past 10 or 20 years, with the persistence of activist campaigns, religious teachings, and government policies against clitoridec-tomy, the practice has been reduced drastically as more and more parents have started to abandon it. Thus, Njue and Askew (2004, p. 15) found that "several respondents believed that whether a woman is circumcised or uncircumcised is becoming less of a criterion for marriageability." In this study, some young men indicated that they had no problem marrying an uncircumcised girl. However, older and conservative Gusii women cannot just let go of this most "cherished" aspect of the community's culture. They pass down the cultural belief by discouraging their own sons from marrying uncircumcised girls. Such women are also convinced and seek to convince their daughters that they will not find husbands unless they are circumcised.

My own experience of clitoridectomy is quite complex. It is complex in the sense that I underwent it with an unwilling inner self but a willing outer self. During my childhood, clitoridectomy was almost universal in my community. Forgoing this rite of passage was a rare occurrence, and it only happened to girls whose parents were educated. Most lived and worked away from the community, particularly in cities. Therefore, local uninitiated girls were rare. Girls who had reached initiation age but had not yet undergone clitoridectomy had to conceal their status so as to avoid ridicule from their peers and other members of the community. I was born and raised in the village. My parents are devoted Christians of the Seventh-day Adventist Church. So I grew up within a Christian environment. Neither of my parents supported clitoridectomy. Every evening, we all gathered in the living room for worship. We sang hymns, read texts from the Bible, and prayed. In the mornings, we also had devotion time before we left for school. It was during such worship sessions that my parents spoke against clitoridectomy and other cultural practices not sanctioned by the Bible.

However, the pressure to get circumcised to belong to the community weighed heavily on my older sister and me. The conflict between culture and Christianity was so great that we felt its devastating impact. We were convinced that the Bible-based teachings were right, but it was hard to live by the teachings alone because very few people in our community shared our position. We became outcasts in our own village. The powerful influence that culture and religion had on our lives deprived us of our freedom to do what we thought was right. To date, I do not understand why it was so hard to practice Christianity within my culture. Religion of all types and culture can coexist only if people in any particular culture believe in freedom of expression. In our case, pressure to undergo clitoridectomy to fit in in the community was all around us, particularly at school.

At the beginning of every school term in January, my friends told us stories about their initiation experiences. They told us about the fun during seclusion (a period of healing when the initiates were separated from the rest of the community). The initiation ceremonies took place during the December holidays. Each year I had at least one friend or classmate who underwent clitoridectomy. And once a girl was initiated, she earned a higher status and graduated to become a member of the "mature" girls in the class. Those of us who had not been initiated felt the urge to undergo clitoridectomy to belong to the higher-status, mature group of girls. Before I underwent clitoridectomy, I was excluded from participating games in which initiated girls played. I was an outsider, a member of the out-group. I could not argue with a circumcised girl, because I was immature. I could not argue with initiated girls for fear of being called *egesagane* (i.e., uninitiated girl). Not even being at the top of my class could make up for my uncircumcised status. This situation caused me mental turmoil, just as it did my older sister, who attended the same school.

We experienced a lot of ridicule, but we were determined to uphold our father's teachings. We were bullied almost every single day of school. We sometimes went back home and complained to our parents about our situation. Our parents told us to ignore the insults, because we would emerge as victors in the long run. The messages we received at home and church collided with those we received at school. The tension was so high that we sometimes wished to stay at home and never go to school at all. With the passage of each year, the tension multiplied. At one point I contemplated running away from home to get circumcised and bring to a stop our endless humiliation and suffering. But the love and respect I had for my parents held me back. However, when my older sister and I turned 12 and 10, respectively, the unexpected happened.

Around this time, my sister and I used to sleep at Grandma's house. Despite the fact that Grandma was a Christian, she never supported the religious position on clitoridectomy. One evening, she invited my older sister and me to sit with her by the fireplace. We often sat by the fireplace for bedtime stories, but Grandma used this particular evening to reveal to us her scheme to have us secretly undergo clitoridectomy the next morning. Some of our village friends who were younger than we were were to be initiated the following morning. The plan was for us to join them. Grandma bombarded us with persuasive questions: "If you miss tomorrow's chance, who will be your friends? Who will you visit? Who will marry you? Do you think you are going to live with your parents forever?" Her words were loud and clear. Our dad was not home around this time. He had traveled to another district to conduct a religious seminar for one week. His absence gave Grandma the best opportunity to implement her plans. Though Grandma put us in bed to sleep that night, we did not sleep a wink. She woke us up at 5 a.m., escorted us to our friends' house, and left us there. She did not accompany us to the traditional surgeon's house. In the company of our friends, we got so excited that we forgot about what awaited us. By 8 a.m., we had undergone the surgery, a very painful operation—the specific details of which are too painful to me to relive.

There were six of us who were initiated. Initiation ceremonies were always a joyous occasion. A group of women accompanied us to the initiation scene. There was a lot of singing, dancing, and ululating as we were escorted back home. The morning was chilly, and we were all wrapped up in traditional clothes called *shuka*. I bled and shivered in the cold morning. I became sad when it dawned on me that my parents were not aware of our new state. My heart was broken, and the singing and dancing around me were now irritating. My sister and I were the first initiates to be escorted home. We were led into Grandma's house. Tradition had it that girl initiates spend their seclusion period in their grandmother's house. The other girls were then escorted to their homes. While there was feasting and merrymaking in their homes, in our home an atmosphere of quietness and emptiness reigned. Although Grandma had prepared some delicious food to celebrate the occasion, I never ate, as I gradually got covered by a blanket of sadness, guilt, and betrayal. I did not see my mom for three days. She was disheartened, as she could not understand why we decided to undergo clitoridectomy. She finally came to see us at Grandma's house, though she remained speechless. She looked so disturbed, and this made me sad. A week passed without her paying us another visit. I think she needed time to overcome the pain we had caused in her heart. In the weeks that followed, she started bringing us meals and spending some time with us at Grandma's house.

My dad came back home after one week but we did not get to talk to him or know about his first reaction. He could not see us until the seclusion period was over. I knew I was not going to see him for about a month. Thinking about how I was going to face him was not easy for me. It was the worst feeling of my life. Our seclusion period ended after four weeks. There was always feasting on the day marking the end of seclusion. The candidates received all sorts of gifts from family, relatives, and friends. In our case, this did not happen. Our initiation had not been planned, and our parents were still recovering from the confusion we had caused. Our older cousins took us to the river and gave us a thorough bath, because for the whole seclusion period we never bathed in conformity with tradition. After bathing, we nervously walked back home to meet our parents. On meeting us, our father hugged us warmly. He appeared calm and forgiving.

In retrospect, I find clitoridectomy to be a meaningless and barbaric cultural practice. It not only mutilates girls' genitalia, but it also subjects innocent girls to excessive pain and health-related risks. I do not see any sense in cutting off the clitoris, an organ vital for women's sexual pleasure. I feel that the rites of passage for girls can be implemented without making the mutilation of female genitalia part of the initiation. The cutting of the clitoris as part of the initiation is unnecessary. In addition to serving as a cultural symbol, this rite of passage is meant to provide a special time for older women to teach the initiates the dynamics of womanhood. Despite the general practice of clitoridectomy among the Gusii, cases of school-aged girls becoming pregnant are rampant (Silberschmidt, 1999), which contradicts the idea that clitoridectomy curtails premarital sex. Also, my own initiation experience did not include the instruction initiates are supposed to get from older women during seclusion. I was never taught about womanhood during seclusion. Sadly, the only effect of clitoridectomy I have to live with permanently is the mutilation of my genitalia and its related effects.

How the Institution of Religion Influenced Me

Religion played a central role in my socialization and schooling. My parents are devoted Christians, and my father worked as a church minister until he retired. My parents introduced all my siblings and me into their faith early in our childhood. They also used our church teachings to strongly oppose some of the Gusii cultural practices, such as female circumcision and polygamy.

The church teachings we received on Saturdays reinforced the instruction we received at home from our parents. Our church upholds high moral standards by promoting abstinence as the best protection against premarital sex. Our church also emphasizes the importance of education for both boys and girls and promotes instruction that embraces the mental, physical, social, and spiritual growth of all individuals. Our church teachings emphasize the idea that God is the source of knowledge and wisdom. God requires us to love other people and above all respect our own bodies by not indulging in acts of immorality such as drug abuse and sexual promiscuity. In addition, our church teaches obedience to God and parents, and respectful relations between husband and wife.

Our religious beliefs put our family on a collision course with our community at large. Some of the villagers perceived my family as radicals. Most of the people, especially those who were nonreligious, did not understand why my dad struggled to educate his daughters. Unlike most families in our village, my parents did not discriminate against girls, as they treated us equally. Also, while my church socializes men to love their wives and wives to submit to their husbands, my culture socializes women to submit to their husbands at all times, even in abusive marriages. I cherished my church teachings because of the emphasis it puts on education for all, mutual love in marriage, and the idea that all men are equal before God.

My church's teachings inculcated in me the positive perception that I hold toward schooling and the morals I previously articulated. From my church, I learned early in life the need to avoid negative cultural influences, such as the subjugation of women among the Gusii. I was also able to avoid intimate relationships with men during my teenage years. Of course I knew that one day I would like to be married, but I did not want to marry before I completed my undergraduate education. I also realized that men in my community do not encourage long courtship periods. In most cases, men anticipated to marry after a few months of courting, which means high school relationships generally result in early marriages or pregnancies. Such relationships lead girls to drop out of school to get married. I embraced our church teachings against premarital sex and its emphasis on education and equality among sexes, and I steered clear of relationships with men while I was in high school. At the college level, I was old enough to make sound decisions regarding my future life. I met my lovely husband while I was a sophomore in college, and we wedded four years later while I was pursuing a master's degree. I loved and still love him for his liberal thinking. He is the kind of man who sees a future in women. He believes and loves education for all and does not expect any less from me. He is and has been my emotional anchor and has cheered me on throughout my studies. Throughout my graduate studies, I have faced acute financial challenges. In my master's program, my sponsor was unexpectedly unable to support me financially. Being a new student in a new environment, I was devastated. My efforts to find another source of funding were fruitless. Throughout this time, my husband kept reminding me that the worst enemy in life is losing hope, and that if we didn't keep hoping for a better tomorrow, we would not have come this far. I lived by my husband's words of encouragement through my final year in the doctoral program. His willingness to do household chores has also eased my duties a great deal.

The Impact of Socioeconomic Hierarchy on My Life

Kenya is a classed society with discernible hierarchical groupings based on social, economic, and educational status. These classes are evident across the several ethnic communities in the country, including the Gusii. My parents did not attend college, though my father worked as an untrained teacher before he became a church minister. My mother is a homemaker who spent most of her time raising her seven children. Thus, I was raised in a working-class family with modest housing, food, and clothing. As our family was large and had limited resources, we attended poorly equipped schools. After my primary school examinations, I was selected to join a national girls' secondary school. However, because it was expensive and far from home, I was forced to attend a relatively less expensive, local, mixed-sex secondary school with limited resources. Some of my primary school classmates from well-off families attended well-resourced schools with abundant privileges, including greater learning opportunities for students. The Kenyan government allocates more funding to national and provincial schools, which are already well resourced, when such funds would have been designated for district schools where the neediest students get enrolled. Also, given that most families value educating sons more than daughters, the government should set aside funds to offer scholarships for girls as an incentive to encourage more girls to get an education.

After high school, I intended to join a medical training college, but unfortunately the admissions process was highly corrupt; influential people took most of the vacancies. Because my parents believe in fairness and did not engage in corrupt practices, I did not gain admission into a medical college. After applying year after year without any success, I gave up. Then my father decided to enroll me in a university established by our church, where I met my husband, who later facilitated my admission to the K-12 administration program at Michigan State University because he was already a graduate student there.

Because of financial constraints in my family, some of my siblings dropped out of college, and I took longer than average to complete my degree. I had to take time off to work to pay my tuition fees. Because the work-study opportunities in the college one of my sisters was attending were reduced, she had to spend a lot of time out of school trying to raise her school fees, but this was in vain. She found marriage to be her best option at that moment and ended up getting married before finishing her first year in college. When faced with school-related financial difficulties, most girls opt to marry rather than lose both a husband and an education. Girls have been brought up to believe that marriage is a necessity and that Gusii men prefer marrying women who are younger and less educated than they are. Therefore, most girls find it hard to hang in there when they lack financial support for their education.

How Educational Institutions Influenced My Life

My life in primary school (grades one to eight) was characterized by gendered patterns similar to those found in the wider community. The gender-based chores that boys and girls performed at home were replicated at school. These tasks included cooking for teachers, cleaning the classroom and teachers' houses, fetching water, taking maize to the power mill for grinding, and going to buy vegetables from the market. Most of these duties were carried out by older girls in grades six, seven, and eight. However, even when I reached these upper primary school classes, I did not participate in most of these errands because I was the youngest girl in my class. I did take part in cleaning the classroom and fetching water for teachers. Some of these chores were performed even when lessons were in progress and some during recess. Schoolboys did some repairs around the school, erected fences, and cut the grass. A typical school day ended at 4:30 p.m. Between 3:00 p.m. and 4:30 p.m., students participated in various recreational games and sports. However, during this time, girls had to fetch water for the teachers who lived on the school property. Because there was no tap water in my village, we had to make several trips to the stream to get water.

In addition to running errands for teachers, schoolgirls plastered classrooms walls and floors. The walls of our school buildings were made from mud. The floors were covered with layers of clayey soil, so the muddy walls and dusty floors needed frequent plastering. We plastered classroom walls and floors twice a month using a mixture of clay and cow dung. Both boys and girls fetched the clayey soil, cow dung, and water, but it was the girls who did the plastering. My family did not own cows, so I had to go and beg for cow dung from my aunt's yard. We carried the cow dung in 2-kg tins and the clay in larger containers.

I totally disliked the idea of using my playtime at school to do chores. I also hated the idea that teachers' kids never participated in any of the duties. They were given special treatment because in those days teachers were highly regarded, and their families enjoyed this status. I always wished I were a teacher's kid so that I could be exempted from doing chores. I wondered why female children had to sacrifice their study time to run errands for teachers. The teachers knew very well that the chores deprived girls of their valuable time but still assigned them these duties. Instead of teachers creating extra time for girls to complete their assignments, the teachers overburdened girls with extra chores. Because boys had fewer chores at both school and home, they had much more time to focus on their studies.

Life in high school was slightly better than life in primary school. In high school, we did not do chores for our teachers. I attended a mixed-sex boarding school established and run by our church. In this school, gender-based chores were not common. The students were drawn from many different communities other than Gusii, providing a good mix of cultures. The infrastructure of the school was better that of my primary school. There were no mud structures in my high school, and because it was a boarding school, students were never asked to bring materials to school as in primary school. Occasionally we fetched water from the streams for our personal use when our taps ran dry. The major drawback I experienced during my high school days was my father's inability to pay my tuition fees in time. This meant that I had to spend some time out of school until I cleared the fee balance. These absences affected my performance in class.

Furthermore, for a number of reasons girls in my high school were laid back when it came to the sciences. We did not have enough laboratory equipment, and during laboratory lessons, we shared equipment such as light microscopes. In most of the lab sessions, boys took the lead in operating the equipment and performing the experiments because they believed they knew better. Some of the girls copied results of experiments from the boys. Moreover, most girls did not want to compete with boys in the sciences. All of my high school science teachers were male, and few encouraged female students to participate in laboratory experiments. This trend translated into girls relying on boys for results of experiments and getting lower and lower grades in the sciences. By contrast, I developed a strong liking for biology in high school. My 10th grade biology teacher was a very skilled teacher and ensured that students understood what he taught. His excellent teaching skills and encouragement made me love biology and believe in myself. My excitement about biology was ignited when I understood how the *nephon* works in the kidneys. Within a short time I became top in my biology class, and our biology teacher recognized my special interest in biology. I ended up selecting biology as my undergraduate major. If all male teachers treated all students equally, like my tenth grade biology teacher did, perhaps many girls would end up performing better in their studies.

Generally, girls performed poorly in school compared with boys. In addition, the number of girls attending school was much lower than that of boys. Some girls dropped out of school as a result of household chores, early marriages, and poverty. However, the main cause of fewer girls enrolling in schools was the escalating percentage of girls dropping out of school because of unexpected pregnancies (Brockman, 2009; Ministry of education, 2009; Chang'ach 2012). When a girl got pregnant, even if the responsible boy was in the same school, only the girl got expelled from school. In my high school, some girls confessed to being impregnated by boys in our school, but only the girls were expelled. The boys remained in school and continued with their studies. Schoolgirls suffer doubly by becoming pregnant and getting expelled from school. The government makes no effort to protect girls or penalize the men who make schoolgirls pregnant.

When I was in high school, we had pregnancy tests at the beginning and end of each semester. Any girl found to be pregnant was expelled from school. The school did not accept them back after delivery, and the stigma associated with such pregnancy discouraged them from returning to the same school. Some of the girls were so determined to continue with their education that they enrolled in different schools. However, most ended up getting married because they would not have had any support in taking care of the baby if they had decided to return to school. Some parents took advantage and married off their daughters who had dropped out of school because of pregnancy. My society blamed the girls who got pregnant but ignored the part played by the men in the pregnancy. I was not a victim of unexpected pregnancy, but my colleagues who became pregnant exposed the prejudice that Gusii females face in the community and schools. Ironically, girls are expected to be competitive and excel in their studies. Clearly, Gusii girls face multiple challenges that hinder their success in their studies. Boys face fewer such challenges. One of the outcomes of this discrepancy is the general underrepresentation of women in employment and leadership.

Summary and Conclusion

In this chapter, I have examined my life experiences, specifically the influence that gender-based socialization within various institutions has had on my life. The core institutions examined include colonialism and patriarchy, family and marriage, religion, educational institutions, and social hierarchy. It emerges that my life experience is a product of the interaction between these factors, among others. The negative and positive effects of these factors on my life have taught me the need to critically examine the role that social structures and institutions play in promoting the objectification of women and girls on the one hand and the glorification of men and boys on the other. Indeed, a people's culture is important in establishing their own identity through shared symbols, values, and norms. However, I detest the oppressive aspects of many cultures. Meaningful cultural practices and beliefs should treat all members with utmost fairness. My community's culture treats women and girls as second-class citizens and leaves their needs and desires under the control of men. The Gusii culture has silenced female voices through patriarchal practices such as bride-price, clitoridectomy, wife-battering, and polygamy. I believe in marriage, but bride-price and polygamy denigrate women. Wife-battering, child marriages, female genital mutilation, polygamy, and forced marriages ought to be outlawed. My life experience with religion shows that religion can be liberating and rewarding to women. I believe that my father's religious principles led him to value education for his daughters despite the opposition he faced from the community. The teachings I received from church helped me to value myself and education as well as uphold high moral standards. My church also preaches mutual respect and love in marriage, virtues that I observed in my parents' marriage and now experience in my own marriage, as my husband and I share the same faith.

The socioeconomic hierarchy of Kenya determines people's access to resources and opportunities. It dictates the kind of neighborhood one lives in, the school one attends, one's employment prospects and income levels, and so on. By virtue of my low socioeconomic class, I missed the opportunity to attend a national high school and had to forgo school-related privileges in the ill-equipped local schools that I attended. My friends from a higher social class attended well-equipped schools and enjoyed all the attendant privileges. Socioeconomic stratification may be an inevitable characteristic of capitalistic societies; however, it need not deny some people their rights and apportion undue privileges to others. I believe fairness can still prevail in a class-based society. Governments should make deliberate effort to give financial support to poverty-stricken schools so that girls in poor families may have more opportunities for education, because their families tend to prioritize boys' education. In addition, access to college and employment should be based on qualifications and not social networks. Colonialism also introduced and perpetuated gender-based biases against women in Gusii.

Finally, educational institutions played a big role in my life and the lives of girls in my community. Educational institutions are supposed to make society better through the knowledge and skills that students acquire from them. A closer examination of my schooling experience reveals patterns of behavior that disadvantaged girls at school as they did at home. Instead of being a liberating agent for girls, school enhanced gender-based socialization that objectified females. We spent valuable time running errands for teachers. We could have invested this time to better our grades. Schoolgirls who were expelled from school for getting pregnant ought to have been readmitted. Moreover, the boys who made these girls pregnant ought to have been equally penalized. One may argue that the immediate culture influences school culture; however, I believe schools have a much greater capability to establish equal opportunities for both girls and boys. For instance, instead of assigning girls chores such as fetching water for teachers, schools should involve both girls and boys or devise alternate ways that will not not affect girls' class time and playtime. Also, it makes a big difference when teachers recognize and nurture the potential in the girl child, who is mostly neglected in Gusii and other societies. Some of my high school teachers made me believe that a supporting and caring teacher can make one's school experience more meaningful. Simply put, girls' performance at school depends mainly on the kind of orientation they get both at home and school. If they cannot get a positive orientation at home, at least the school should provide it. However, when institutional socialization patterns are biased against females, female voices will never be heard.

Critical Intersectional Autoethnographic Case Studies

Intersecting Dimensions of Identity, Oppression, and Resistance

.•◆————◆•.

FELECIA M. BRISCOE

This introduction briefly describes critical intersectional theory and relates this theoretical approach to the four chapters comprising section IV. "The concept of intersectionality was coined in Critical Race Feminist legal scholarship to address how some of these dimensions differentially affect life opportunities" (Núñez, 2014, p. 85). One of the earliest scholars to explore this concept was Patricia Hill Collins (1990), who noted that race and gender interact differently depending on one's race and gender. In other words, the oppression experienced by Black women and their consequential forms of resistance are different from that experienced and enacted by White women or Black men. Núñez (2014) notes that scholars have identified more than 12 other intersecting dimensions of identity, including class, sexual orientation, religion, nationality, language, phenotype, and so on. As Collins (2000) notes, given the different possible intersections of these dimensions of identity, most of us are oppressed in some ways and privileged in others.

The autoethnographies in Section IV focus on the intersection of at least two dimensions, describing how their experiences of oppression related to their intersecting dimensions of identity. Likewise, their resistance, understandings, and eventual critical identities were shaped by the kinds of oppression they experienced. The first autoethnography, by Elizabeth de la Portilla, uses Chicana critical theory to focus on gender and ethnicity as she experienced them. The second one, by Muhammad A. Khalifa, focuses on the criminalizing forces of the White imaginative, acting on Black men. The third autoethnography, by Aisha El-Amin, B. Genise Henry, and Crystal T. Laura, critiques three Black women's experiences in integrating the hyphen into their research. The final one, by Miguel de Oliver, looks at multiple ascriptions of identity to him and the loss of any specific academic identity in an increasingly neoliberal university. Following are brief descriptions of the intersectional autoethnographies as written by their authors.

In Chapter 9, Dr. de la Portilla reflexively analyzes vignettes from her early life and from experiences as a doctoral student. She examines the often tacit agreements we enter into with the institutions we attend as people of color and/or women. She used the strategies she learned in her childhood—reinforced by the writings of Chicana Feminist theorists—to navigate the politics and prejudices of the university. Dr. de la Portilla also describes the ways we become commodities and our "self," that becomes an object of exchange. These exchanges are lopsided, rather than one-sided; although the institution determines the parameters for acceptance and advancement, she describes some latitude in the degree to which we acquiesce.

In Chapter 10, Dr. Khalifa explores one Black man's contestations, as Black men continue to be oppressed in ways unique and dynamic to them. He utilizes, yet pushes beyond, Critical Race Theory (CRT). CRT was useful for understanding his challenges to Whiteness and his ubiquitous experiences of oppression, but less useful for understanding Dr. Khalifa's experience of being Black and *male*. Black male statistics of oppression include the highest rates of incarcerations, school failures, school suspensions, pushout/dropouts, arrests, murder and homicide, drug use, and new HIV infections. They also have the most rapidly growing suicide rate and the most negative image media. His narrative explores the polarities and contradictions in the lives of Black men, accentuating both their promise and demise.

In Chapter 11, Drs. El-Amin, Henry, and Laura explore pivotal moments in their journeys as critical-Black-female-scholars who have deliberately connected their personal and professional lives through research. The authors found that fully engaging their hyphenated personal and professional identities, in many ways, challenges the socialization processes established for becoming a PhD in academia. Highlighting the saliency of their hyphenated identities, they invite readers to witness their experiences of negotiating those identities in higher education. They conclude by arguing for a rearticulation of socialization processes within the academy as one way to increase the startling low numbers for Black-female PhDs in the United States.

In Chapter 12, Dr. Miguel de Oliver examines the increasing and problematic encroachment of materialist aesthetics on the academic profession. Dr. de Oliver's experiences as a person of ambiguous racial/ethnic identification ironically proved advantageous with respect to his becoming aware of the growing alienation that many academics are experiencing regardless of race, ethnicity, gender, class, or lifestyle—an alienation from the Enlightenment aesthetic that has heretofore been central to the academy.

He focuses on his experiences with the systemic compromising of the "university scholar" as a coherent identity amid the consumerist milieu within which the academy has become embedded.

CHAPTER NINE

"You Look Like a Wetback; You Shouldn't Have any Trouble"

Deals We Make with the Devil on the Road Less Traveled

ELIZABETH DE LA PORTILLA

Late in the 1990s, in preparation for my doctoral fieldwork, I sought out the help of a biology faculty member at the university I was attending. One of my objectives was to collect plant samples in the Mexico border region for comparison to plants on the U.S side. It was not just the plant material itself I was interested in, but also how people describe them, name, and use them. Ethnography is my stock in trade, and drawing information out from people is something I do well. My goal on that early spring day in Michigan was to get the necessary paperwork and a letter of introduction from a professor outside my program in order to conduct my research without problems from either nation's bureaucracies. In academe, as in society and its institutions, access to resources is often a matter of whom you know. Gatekeepers are what we call them in anthropology. I needed this man's help, and I got it. He helped me understand the tangle of regulations and paperwork of the USDA and learn what to anticipate from customs. He gave me a letter of introduction acknowledging his support of my work and the ties the university had to a research institution in Mexico. He was gracious, generous, and very senior. We walked out of his office and into the afternoon sunlight, talking of fieldwork and the stumbling blocks you can sometimes encounter when trying to elicit information from individuals. "It can be difficult," he said, "especially if you aren't from the area, but you look like a wetback; you shouldn't have any trouble." He laughed at his witty remark. I was stunned, but apparently it didn't show because he kept talking in a friendly manner until our paths diverged. He wished me well and sent a hello to my advisor, another very senior fellow who held an endowed chair.

It's odd what you remember of events that upon reflection you recognize as pivotal moments in your life. The saucer magnolias were in flower—they smell like candy to me. There was no rain that day, and a distinguished researcher had called me a wetback. What do you say to something like that? I said nothing, laughed at little as if I agreed. What did I feel? Was it shame, anger, indignation, humiliation, resignation, disappointment? A sick hole in my gut opened up, but I had learned to keep these kinds of things to myself. I pushed the emerging thoughts and feelings down deep before I could think too hard about them. Walking home, I felt very lucky to get this professor's help and thought that it was a wonderful thing that such a distinguished scholar had taken so much time to listen to me. Until the writing of this paper, I had never told anyone. It was what the Latina Feminist Group (2001) called my *papelito guardado*, and now this little slip of memory is laid out in front of those who read my story.

My time in Ann Arbor was more than an academic enterprise; I learned many lessons in how power and prestige are used and negotiated. Show me an "acknowledged" genius, and I'll show you a pedigree worth millions. For some of us though—women, gays, lesbians, and people of color, "the others" in academic terms—a postsecondary education of any kind requires entering into at least one deal with the devil. The catch is that you do not always know what the payment ultimately will be for his, her, or its help.

Methods and Theory

To examine my own *testimonios* and those of others, I use theories that focus on the objectification of a person and the commoditization of the object that the person becomes (Simmel in Appadurai, 1996). What we are willing to become in the pursuit of our goal(s) or what we are willing to do are the deals we make with the devil to be successful in our ventures. Power is the shiny glass ball the devil holds in front of us. Power, in and of itself, like most tools, is neither good nor evil. The action, which puts power into motion, its effects, and how those effects will be understood are what we come to understand as good or evil (Foucault in Abu-Lughod, 1990). Are we as minority scholars due to always remain either on the margins or on the fringes of academic legitimacy because of the way we are perceived or how we apply what we learn? We are often perceived as less rigorous, and we frequently choose to apply our learning in fashions not sanctioned by the institution. Are Faustian deals our only recourse if we wish to escape from the margins? What types of deals are we willing to make in order to obtain our heart's desire? The same question can be asked of those who are on the upside of power relationships: "What are you willing to do to maintain the status quo?"

What I experienced by being called a wetback is representative of the type of domination and subordination to which I was exposed as a child and young adult. It is why my father on his deathbed told my younger brother, "Don't trust White people. They'll hurt you." My narrative exemplifies a minor deal with the devil: Say nothing when insulted if you are not equal to in status (social, economic, racial, professional) to the person delivering the insult. Play the grateful student but tuck away the lessons learned from this kind of experience to use when needed in the future and to pass along to others. The stories and anecdotes I have chosen for this essay are those that stand out for me as markers on the way to gaining my doctorate. They were part of my education as much as any seminar in phenomenology or poetics. I have attempted to align them in chronological order from my entering the anthropology program in 1995 until the time I left Michigan for my fieldwork site late in 1999.

Though I was in my thirties when I entered the graduate program, I was extremely naive about how academia works. I had grown up in a tough neighborhood; surviving difficulties was not an issue, but I was woefully unprepared for the scholastic and political rigors of a graduate program at a tier-one school. While no two individuals can have the same life, many of the structures and authority figures we must contend with see us (people of color, women, gays, and lesbians) with the marginalizing same eyes, if they see us at all. As such, this chapter is also a call for others to share their narratives in a reflexive manner. The other people's stories support the narratives I've chosen to tell, as they share common themes. One of these themes is that some of us come to a conscious decision in willingly accommodating the dictates and expectations that are placed before us by the institutions we are a part of. At the same time, I grew to understand that I could manipulate some aspects of the power structure to gain my desired goal, a doctorate from one of the best universities in the country. If the epistemologies we are inculcated with as graduate students demand validation, let our words be that validation. I share these narratives as cautionary tales, but they are also tales of triumph, trickster tales, and soul loss.

I also reference Chicana Feminist Theory (CFT), which constructs a holistic worldview in which spirituality and empiricism are not separate from one another. I have come to believe that understanding the world from a holistic perspective enables people to assess situations quickly and shift identities in order to precipitate successful outcomes. It is a different way of knowing the world than the prevailing "objective" Western tradition, which pretends to keep these two realms separate and, by doing so, privileges the current hierarchical social structure. Knowledge may be power, but it is foremost a commodity in the current dominant worldview. In CFT, the use of personal narratives has a long tradition. The knowledge gained from a woman's lived experience—whether the experiences take place in the sphere of home, public life, or in her occupation—is equal in worth to knowledge constructed by traditional positivist methodologies (Hurtado, 1996). CFT differs from White women's feminism because it brings in issues of race and class as overlays to gender. There is a body of work about institutional resistance to validating the use of autoethnography as an analytical tool (Holt, Denzin, & Lincoln, 1994; Sparkes, 2000). Anything that may lead to a change in hegemonic ideology can have a domino effect, becoming a threat to gatekeepers of other institutions. But understanding the quiet power of *testimonio*, its foundation and utility, benefits both out-groups and in-groups by building cultural understanding and strategies. These understandings of—and respect for—cultural differences that arise help both in-groups and out-groups realize that sharing power does not mean *loss* of power. In the end, though, our stories are markers along the road, choices in direction, and reminders to other travelers that they are not alone.

The Story Begins and the Stories That Shape Us

I am a first-generation Mexican-American college graduate born to parents who had little education and whose income never rose above the national poverty level. Yet there were things that I learned in that milieu from my parents. The following two vignettes not only illustrate lessons I learned from my mother that helped me later in my doctoral program, but is also a counter-story, as it shows the work and responsibility we Chicana children began assuming at a young age and the courage and dignity of Chicana domestic workers.

In the afternoons, my mother and her sisters, who were all maids in the households of middle-class and upper middle-class families, would get together for a cup of coffee. In their White maids' uniforms and nurse's shoes, they would sit and relax before going home to make dinner. On these occasions, the daughters would serve their mothers. In our house, my younger sister, Diana, and I would arrange the furniture in a circle, bringing chairs from the kitchen to the living room so none would have to hunt for a place to sit. I would run to the bakery and order a dollar's worth of *pan dulce*. The baker always tossed in an extra piece as a *pilón*, "*Pa ti niña.*" It amused him that a little girl barely able to see over the counter would take the job of picking out sweet bread so seriously. In the kitchen we arranged the bread on a plate, licking the sugar off our fingers when finished. The coffee percolating, my aunts talking and laughing in the living room, Diana and I would hurriedly drag a chair to the kitchen counter to reach the overhead cupboards. Out came the cups and saucers, the ones saved for visitors, followed by a creamer and sugar bowl. We would walk into the living room slowly one cup and saucer in each hand. First our mom and then each woman in turn accepted our offering. "Aye mija, thank you. Mira que linda es Lisa."

During these visits, my sister and I would sit on the floor or stand behind our mom and listen to the talk of women. Husbands and employers were a regular topic; Tia Lupe had a way of mimicking the cadence of White women, which would send her sisters into peals of laughter. She could draw the word "shit" when accenting her defiant attitude in response to the unfair treatment she sometimes received. The faults and stinginess of each woman for whom they cleaned houses were scrutinized at length. To their face, my mom and aunts called them "ma'am," but at home they were known collectively as las viejas (old women).

In these afternoon coffee talks, my aunts and mother collectively shared stories about their workplace and together came up with ways to deal with the problems they faced there. At the same time, through their storytelling they were able to release some of their anger and frustration that built up within them because of the humiliations they often faced in their places of employment. In releasing this anger, they also developed alternative ways of understanding who they were—people of dignity and worth. For example, I remember my mother telling a story about boundary setting when one of the las viejas went too far.

Las viejas on occasion made my mother's life a misery. They wanted her to be available at their whim. They expected her, tired or not, to come to the telephone when they called; to take care of their children at a moment's notice; and to be grateful for the cans of tuna fish and Fresca they left her as a lunch, because if my mom left for lunch and then went back to finish cleaning their houses, they would have to pay her for a full as opposed to a half-day. Once she was called on short notice to clean a regular client's home and promises were made of extra pay. Though she had to rearrange her schedule, she took on the job. In the end, the woman's husband pressed an additional dollar in her hand as "the extra" pay. My mother looked down at the single dollar bill in her palm, wadded it up, and threw it in the man's face. "This is what I think of your dollar and don't ever call me again because I won't come." True to her word, she never took their calls again, and never you mind the apologies.

Over the years, I heard just about every story that could be told, of love and children; of men and women; success and failure. The work they had to do did not define who they were as people. Their personal value was not in scrubbing floors or washing the bottoms of other people's children. It was in what they thought of themselves as they worked. Romero explains: "The nature of housework is not intrinsically degrading or demeaning, nor is it intrinsically sexist. Accounts given by household workers indicate that conflict exists when employers attempt to structure the work to include demeaning and degrading aspects" (Romero, 2002, p. 163).

Romero's (1992) interviews of domestic workers and their employers demonstrate the persistence of racial biases by the perpetuation of "structures that support cultural systems of gender, class, and racial domination" (p. 163). Romero explains that domestic workers who are White or men are not subject to the same demeaning treatment that women of color experience. The Chicana domestic workers she interviewed understood and described the complexities of domestic service: the trade-offs they had to make in their personal lives and the importance of social relationships in finding work and negotiating the conditions of their work (Romero, 2002).

I am also a product of the Civil Rights era: the first generation of minority children who directly benefited from affirmative action and early childhood development. I am a true Head Start baby, part of the first cohort of children enrolled in the program. I belong to that transitional group of individuals who at birth were part of a racially segregated social system but came of age during a time period of dynamic political and cultural change in the United States. In terms of beating the odds—not becoming the stereotype ascribed by dominant society to women born poor and of color—I am a success. The mythology of U.S. culture tells us that anyone can move upwardly across social and economic lines; people can obtain whatever they dream of if they just work hard enough. But gated communities, the right zip code, and social networks built by attending "good" schools tell a different story.

Academia is also full of narratives that are passed from one generation to the next within disciplines. Cautionary tales of professorial habits and behaviors are told from one cohort of graduate students to the succeeding one. What we learn *informally* (re: socially) has worth—in this case, how to navigate one's department successfully and prudently. This is often known as the hidden curriculum (e.g., Margolis & Romero, 1998). Culture is both overtly and tacitly taught and learned. In this country, whether the institutional culture under examination is business, religion, education, or politics, it reflects a common ideology set in motion more than 400 years ago. There are dictates, codes, norms, and behaviors that are embedded within, enforced, and replicated by its participants, particularly privileged participants. There are categories of belonging in which not all of us have participated; when called to do so, the results can undermine the individual emotionally and psychologically, further reinforcing a sense of marginalization.

These results are illustrated in Robert Granfield's (2010) interviews of working-class students who attend a prestigious law schools:

I had a real problem my first year because law and legal education are based on upper-middle class values. The class debates had to do with profit maximization, laws, and economics, all predicated upon atomistic individualism. I remember in class we were talking about landlords' responsibility to maintain decent housing in rental apartments. Some people were saying that there were good reasons not to do this. Well, I think that's bullshit because I grew up with people who lived in apartments with rats, leaks, and roaches, I feel really different because I didn't grow up in suburbia. (pp. 126–127)

The students Granfield interviewed all expressed similar sentiments and reported higher levels of stress during their first year than their more privileged classmates. They quickly learned what was expected of them, in appearance and behavior, and began to compromise their cultural identities on the advice of professional career counselors. They did what I did to survive and succeed. But at what cost to the individual?

"I" as an Object, Deals in Selling Our "Self"

One cost is that we agree to our own commoditization when seeking and accepting entrance into institutions, which have been defined by the dominant power structure. This is not a case of blaming the victim; there are no victims, only volunteers. The more prestigious the place to which a person seeks entrance, the more there is at stake for both the gatekeeper(s) and the individual. A person's status and worth are determined not just by three little letters one receives after his or her name. A person's pedigree. meaning the university that confers the degree, who mentored him or her, and who was on the dissertation committee, also determines intellectual value and how much investment an institution is willing to make, as set by the academic marketplace. In *The Social Life of Things* (1996), Appadurai uses the work of Georg Simmel to discuss the worth of objects. For Simmel, value is not inherent to the object, "but is a judgment made about them by subjects" (p. 3, Appardurai, 1996). Appadurai (1996) explains further that the "economic object does not have an absolute value as a result of the demand for it, but the demand, as the basis of a real or imagined exchange, endows the object with value. It is the *exchange* that sets the parameters of utility and scarcity rather than the other way round . . . exchange is not a by-product of the mutual valuation of objects, but its source" (p. 4). An object (or thing) therefore reflects values of different parties as it changes hands. This is just one aspect; we are conditioned to see the worth of objects or things only through the meaning "that human transactions, attributions, and motivations endow them with . . . [But] we have to follow the things themselves, for their meanings are inscribed in their forms, their uses, their trajectories. It is only through the analysis of these trajectories that we can interpret the human transactions and calculations that enliven things" (Appadurai, 1996, p. 5).

In applying this idea to pedigreed minority scholars, we are objects of worth. How much we are worth is determined not just by the institution and our own efforts, but also by forces that have shaped and continue to influence *what* we are as well as *what* we are thought to be at any particular time. The transaction we enter into with our institutions cannot be divorced from the social, political, and economic history that have shaped our academic context. When we decided on a life in academia, knowingly or not we became objects of scrutiny—all graduate students are, but even more so for a working-class woman of color (Gandara, 1995). Clearly, Granfield's example above indicates that many of us who come from working-class/minority backgrounds were not ready for the experience. The institution decides to take a gamble on us. We apply for fellowships and hope for the best as our background is reviewed and our potential assessed. But what is each side willing to put on the table to make things happen? Of what value is the *exchange*? For students like us, is a degree worth compromising our identity, values, and sense of self? Granfield reported that students were often overwhelmed by feelings of ambivalence. Many began law school with the intention to practice in the arena of social justice, but the pull of big law firms induced them to second-guess their original plans. As one student reported, his brother would ask him if he "had become republican yet" (Granfield, 2010, p. 131).

For the institutions, there is the outward appearance of readdressing past inequalities by instituting affirmative action programs or hiring practices that are to "assist" meritorious members of an out-group; being eligible for, and the recipient of, federal funds helps also. But what do institutions do with these individuals once they have them? How do they protect their investment? In this sense, the hierarchies among colleges and universities are no different from the American Kennel Club (AKC). High-ranking institutions are invested in turning out scholars who reflect the same intellectual values (purebreds) and will be accepted into domains of equal worth (bloodlines); we are tacitly charged to engage in constant competition with other graduate students in order to meet certain standards. Even competition in gaining the attention of and aligning yourself with a patron, a senior scholar (pedigrees), your work is reviewed and your progress recorded (registered). The effort to be officially recognized as part of the "club" is arduous and fortitude is often tested, as there can be multiple setbacks.

A professor in my department once told me that I had to focus and work hard because out in the job market I "had to be better than any White man applying for the same job." At the end of my second year, I met with the fellowship director at the graduate school. He glanced over my work and faculty review and said, "You were one of the students we had high hopes for." In my socialized position as a traditional Mexican-American female, I felt a deep sense of guilt and shame at having let these two men down. I blamed myself for not being "Michigan" material. It did not matter that I had merited a National Science Foundation Fellowship and a three-year fellowship from the University of Michigan; what mattered was that I was proving to be a "bad" investment. In keeping with the AKC analogy, I wasn't up to standards.

Making the Victim

Dr. Mary Romero came to Ann Arbor in 1997 as a speaker at a graduate student conference. I was familiar with her work and mentioned to her afterward that my mother had been a maid. I had read her book *Maid in America* and because of my family background found it easy to relate to the themes she laid out. She asked to interview me on my experience as a graduate student at UM. It was a cathartic experience to be able to speak to someone about the doubts I had about myself and how difficult it was to relate to other students and to the faculty. There had been an incident early in my time there that had quickly disabused me of any romantic notions I had of academia as a place less concerned with hierarchy than the corporation in which I had worked for sixteen years. All new graduate students were expected to apply for funding from well-known sources, like the Ford Foundation and the National Science Foundation. Applications were dropped into our mail folders to make sure the point was well made.

I was sitting with several members of a new cohort as they discussed where they would apply and the chances of being awarded. One young woman of African-American background asked a friend of ours, a White male in his thirties, if he was going to apply. He said that his chances were not as good as hers because he had to apply under "that" category, pointing with his finger to the NSF Predoctoral Fellowship program instead of the NSF's program for minority graduate students. We "colored" folk had a better chance, in his view, of obtaining funding. Remarks like these, which were meant to be ironic or humorous, were not new to me. I had experienced this kind of thing most of my life, but I was saddened to come across such ignorance in a place where knowledge is to be lauded.

Sometime later, Dr. Romero sent me a copy of an article she had co-written with Eric Margolis (1998) titled "'The Department Is Very Male,

Very White, Very Old, and Very Conservative': The Functioning of the Hidden Curriculum in Graduate Sociology Departments." By this time, I was entering my third year as a graduate student. Drs. Margolis and Romero's article helped me understand what I was experiencing in the department: a sense of not belonging, which was not an uncommon occurrence for women of color seeking graduate degrees. My first two years as a graduate student were difficult. I was playing catch-up in terms of theory and anthropological writings with which other students in my cohort were already familiar when we began, as well as staying abreast of current work on an everyday basis. When I read this article, things came to a head for me. I was constantly blaming myself for the way things stood; for my inadequacies. At the time, it would have been unthinkable for me to believe that the academic culture in which I was participating had as much of a cultural deficit as I thought I had. In their article, Margolis and Romero (1998) write, "Blaming the victim refers to social interactions that socialize students to define themselves as the problem, rather than exploring the structural causes for their experiences within the institutions" (p. 13).

In my cohort, I was the only Mexican-American; I cannot remember another person of color being admitted in 1995. There were students from other countries, but aside from me, no other U.S. minority students and very few with a working-class background. In the two years immediately after my arrival, three minority women were admitted. The department described in the article Dr. Romero sent me looked and behaved very much like mine. The irony for me is that my department housed a discipline that was supposed to study and understand the whole of human experience. Yet all of us regardless of background were supposed to perform in a uniformly prescribed fashion.

Survival Strategies

In speaking with my advisor, Richard (Dick) Ford, about the incident with the graduate school administrator, I learned that part of the problem was that I had come into the program with academic deficits. My undergraduate studies in anthropology were traditional, not a "post-mo" in sight. The fault was not my own but due to a lack of these course offerings in my undergraduate institution. There was no way I could have come in with the same scholastic background as others in my cohort. He said that if I felt overwhelmed, I could transfer to the University of Texas at Austin and be closer to my family and home. The problem was not that I missed my family but the academic deficit I had come in with, and I would have the same problem in Austin. Besides, I had my NSF for funding at Michigan. I understand now that this is part of the "cooling out" process Romero describes in her article (2008). My response was a strong "no." I made it clear that my coming to Michigan had meant letting go of my old life. This was my Faustian moment. My then husband and I had sold our home, quit our jobs, and left our families so I could pursue a graduate degree. I told Dick I had nothing to go back to and that I wasn't giving up, so what did I need to do to get through the process? My advisor was everything a senior faculty member should be, and his advice was to be proactive in my efforts. He told me whom I should get to know and to visit him during office hours and not avoid him if I fell behind in my work. I became his Thursday regular at office hours, whether I needed to see him or not. I asked him questions about everything related to anthropology, and I learned about the usefulness of having a strong faculty member as a patron.

Aida Hurtado (1996) argues that women of color learn survival skills early in childhood. Sometimes they act as translators for their families out in the public sphere (as I was for my parents). Learning how to access networks and getting people to listen to me was something I had to do. I had to get people to listen to me in order to care for my younger sister and brother, because our parents both worked and old women in the neighborhood only sporadically provided childcare. The lessons I learned at the age of five, before I could even speak English, came back to me as I sat with my advisor that afternoon. I did as he suggested, and I began to drop in on my other professors, too, during their office hours. Even so, contentious issues continued to arise.

Understanding and agreeing to what was expected of me as a graduate student necessitated a shift in my identity. I purposely took on the role modeled by other graduate students. But I could not have survived those early years at Michigan without making friends outside the department. I became friends with women in the Department of Education and in the American Studies program. These friendships gave me distance from my department and a clearer picture of what was in play—the same games of male privilege and class biases seen in every strata and institution across our society. What made it different for us (as female academicians) were the expectation and presumption that we would willingly duplicate the same configurations even as these structures were under examination in our studies.

I had learned early on the value of female friendship, and the dinners I often hosted took on the feeling of the afternoons spent long ago with my mother and her sisters. The opportunity to unwind and talk about the bosses without fear of reprisals—the safe space(s) Rosaldo (1993) describes in his introduction to *Culture & Truth: The Remaking of Social Analysis* that are needed by minority students in institutions like Michigan. I realize now those were some of the "flashes" Gramsci (1971) refers to. The women I became friends with are my friends still, nearly 20 years later. We were each other's support system then, and it is the same today. Each of us went on to gain advanced degrees, all but one of them doctorates.

As I advanced to candidacy, Ruth Behar agreed to co-chair my dissertation committee with Dick Ford. It was from Dr. Behar that the writings in borderland studies came to me. Another student of hers, Alicia Enciso, also took up borderland studies. She and I would joke that we were a program of two. We read Gloria Anzaldúa, Norma Cantu, Sandra Cisneros, Ana Castillo, and Sonia Saldivar-Hull. Through Ruth's instruction and the writings of borderland feminists, Alicia and I could see that a critical mass was building—a critical mass for changing how research is conducted among disenfranchised communities. Reading these works told me I wasn't alone in how I thought and behaved. I also got angry, which is something else Hurtado and other Chicana feminist write about. Anger can be constructive and is a powerful form of resistance if channeled correctly. It can hold you together, your psyche, your intentions—the trick is to keep it shadowed.

> Women of color in America have grown up within a symphony of anger, at being silenced, at being unchosen, at knowing that when we survive, it is in spite of a world that takes for granted our lack of humanness, and which hates our very existence outside of its service. And I say symphony rather than cacophony because we have had to learn to orchestrate those furies so that they do not tear us apart. We have had to learn to move through them and use them for strength and force and insight within our daily lives. Those of us who did not learn this difficult lesson did not survive. And part of my anger is always libation for my fallen sisters. (Lorde, 1984, p. 119 in Huratado, 1996, p. 21)

My anger came from being made to feel as if I were a foreigner in my own country. That because I chose to study my own people, somehow my work was not as "rigorous" as that of my peers. In a conference, after I delivered a paper on my fieldwork among *curanderas* in San Antonio, a young woman remarked that it seemed I was too close to my subject to be objective. Yet if I had been a White woman or man studying with a traditional healer, that remark would have been closer to a compliment than a slight. In an article, Monica Russel y Rodriguez (1998) writes:

> "The normative practice and the theory of anthropology contradict each other. Its practice demands an ethnographer Native informer dyad, placing the ethnographer as the knower while only valuing the knowledge of the Native. Its theory values Native knowledge and exalts a diversity vis-à-vis cultural relativism.

Opposing either theory or practice underscores the paradox. As a Chicana anthropologist, I experience a tricky conflation of these competing agendas, agendas that leave me little space to stand." (p. 15)

In two lines, she sums up what I had been feeling: "I cannot find my place among anthropologists. For I have experienced myself among anthropologists not with a position but absent, voiceless, nearly invisible" (p. 15). Russel y Rodriguez (1998) brought home for me the paradox of how we embrace our roles as anthropologists with the understanding that the legitimacy of being a native anthropologist will always label our research just a little bit questionable or, if you are a traditionalist (i.e., one of the old guard), very questionable. She, Behar, Kirin Narayan, Virginia Dominguez, and others study our own communities, often with the intent of using what we learn to benefit our people.

This again counters the intent of anthropology, which for the most part means for the separation between ethnographer and informant to be unbreachable. Anthropologists never expected the native to talk back. Russel y Rodriguez, as well as other Latina anthropologists whom I read and know personally, do more than talk back; they have created a different way of approaching and doing research, thereby undercutting sources of power within the academy by bridging disciplines. For many of us, the liminal space, *Nepantla*, described by Gloria Anzaldúa, provides a way for us to conceptualize our identities as bridging from one another; our shifting selves accommodate the scholar and the poet, the ivory tower and the wage laborer. I may never have to clean another person's toilet for money but neither will I forget that I, my mother, and my aunts once did.

So What Did All This Learning Get Me?

By the time the incident with the biology professor occurred, I was dismayed but not surprised. I was well armed by my mother and aunts and the women I had come to know personally or through their work. I didn't know the man's intent, but after thinking about it for a bit, I decided those particular words held no power over me. This "wetback" story is not part of the hero's journey that we embrace as part of our cultural heritage; at least not until the end of act one. My story is not the old "I pulled myself up by the bootstraps" type of American story. I have had plenty of help through the stories told by my mother and aunts, by the female organizers of the Civil Rights movement, and by the second-wave feminists. The stories, theories, and praxis—developed and told by these women of color and reflecting their position in society—deeply ingrained in me that the personal truly is political and our experiences, especially the writing and telling of them, serve as *testimonios* for others who find themselves strangers in their own homeland (Chicana Feminisms, 2003).

Testimonios (personal accounts) teach lessons and/or validate outcomes (DeLeon, 2010; Saldivar-Hull, 2000). Our lives are the results of hypotheses testing. Significant life events become the narrative of our *testimonio* and these in turn become the history of our efforts—theory and practice bound together. The common themes in many of these narratives rise up effortlessly in examination; oppression, resignation, resistance, negotiation, plasticity, success, and failure (Saldivar-Hull, 2000). Through it all Latinas collectively support one another. This does not mean there are not divisions, subterfuge or betrayals but in my experience there is tangible network of support, which is both personal and professional in that we understand our lives are not compartmentalized but holistic.

My negative experiences in graduate school became realms of analysis for me. Using CFT, borderland studies, and reflexive anthropology gave me ways to understand both the uniqueness and commonality of my life as a graduate student during the first difficult years at Michigan. I gained an understanding of power through experiences and reflections on those experiences, such as the biology professor's "joke." I learned how power works to bring people into conformity or silence. But the writings of Chicana feminists gave me the tools and language to deal with these issues. I learned to use the language of the academy to claim space.

I began to question whether the theory I was learning in my courses could be of benefit to my community when I returned home. I wanted to put to use what I had learned. One professor said in seminar that we are in the business of constructing theory; the knowledge we acquire is in and of itself enough. But I had spent part of my late adolescence and young adulthood working with community organizers. In this work, I found that knowledge has to have utility; sometimes it can mean the difference in whether or not someone you know eats that day or if that person's child gets vaccinated in time for the first day of school. I learned the real meaning of the phrase "The personal is political" because, on the surface, these may seem like everyday problems that can be easily solved by obtaining the appropriate information, but they are not that simple. These issues speak to the access of resources—who controls them and who is allowed to access them—who the decision makers are in this scenario; in sum, who is positioned more powerfully?

After I went home to San Antonio, women in academia reached out to me first; they included me in their company and gave me the lay of the land. Some women I knew by their work, others were new to me. A few I knew from living in San Antonio. Antonia Castañeda, a Chicana feminist historian, once said to several Chicanas, none of us tenured at the time, to remember when we get up in the morning that we change our disciplines simply by being in them. This is something I, as a graduate student, never thought I would hear. Dr. Castaneda, now retired from St. Mary's University, is acknowledged as an expert in women and gender in borderland history. Her road has been more difficult than my generation of scholars. Knowing her and other women academic-activists in my community of Antonia's generation, including Dr. Ellen Riojas-Clark, Rosie Castro, and María Antonietta Berriozábal, has reinforced the belief I hold dear: that a life of service is a life worth living. Somehow I don't think this is what the anthropology department from which I received my degree expected from its students.

One Last Story

When I submitted my completed PhD dissertation, one of my professors asked if I had received any help in its writing. I had run several drafts by my chair, but aside from that, what I turned in was my work.

"Why?" I asked.

"Several of the faculty believe that you couldn't have written it yourself," was her response. I felt as if someone had punched me in the stomach, and then I got angry. I stood there in disbelief, not really knowing what to say. I told her Dick had read every draft I had written and that no one had helped me with the writing. It was all original work.

I also learned a valuable lesson: Having a senior person in your corner is worth more than gold. Richard I. Ford, now professor emeritus, believed in me from the very start, and for that I'll always be grateful. He'd seen and commented on every draft I wrote. I then learned something else about graduate school. Sometimes you're just used by one faculty member to score a point in an ongoing fight with another. There was a bit of a power struggle among the ethnology faculty. I don't know if it was because Dick is an archaeologist and certain members took umbrage, thinking that because I was studying cultural anthropology, I shouldn't have been under his purview. However, he was also an ethnobotanist, and I was studying the field under his guidance. My work was cross-disciplinary. My sense of it was that some of the faculty with whom I took classes early on could not believe I was capable of the intellectual growth necessary to get past preliminary exams and develop my dissertation proposal. I also learned that outwardly progressive and liberal individuals can be as bigoted as the little old lady who locks her car door as you walk by. Nothing is said, but the implications are clear.

When I asked a sympathetic professor why the ethnology faculty would believe such a thing about me, she explained it this way: There is a type of student that the faculty in this program is used to seeing. Heretofore, the students had predominantly been White, middle-class men. The students with whom the faculty was familiar learned and gained knowledge at a regular and steady rate. She moved her hand upward at an angle as if going up the side of a hill; you did this and she held her hand out level and then raised it upward, still level and stopped. She was signaling that I had made leaps in my learning and comprehension. I would stay in a period of stasis and then make another leap. My progress was akin to Gould's theory of Punctuated Equilibrium or more to the point, as Anzaldúa has described her experiences in the academy. My type of student was not typical to the program, and my work was suspect because of their ignorance of different patterns of learning. This brings the discussion back to why it would help those in power at institutions like the University of Michigan to consider other ways of viewing the world.

Conclusion

"The personal is political" may seem to be a mere cliché, but for many people it is an everyday reality, though for those positioned advantageously it may seem farfetched. Our stories, whether you call them *papelitos guardados*, *testimonios*, autoethnography, or narrative, are in many ways problematic for academicians who see our efforts as navel-gazing exercises or an arbitrary refusal to conform to academic norms. Holt (2003) writes, "Whereas those who produce autoethnography are at risk of being overly narcissistic and self-indulgent, there does seem to be a place for research that links the personal with the cultural. Autoethnography can encourage empathy and connection beyond the self of the author and contribute to sociological understandings." He continues, "Researchers would be well advised to be persistent in their autoethnographic intentions, and be prepared to face rejection and critiques of their chosen genre. Resilience and conviction are required to pursue this methodology" (Holt, 2003, p. 26).

While his intentions may be well meaning and revelatory to him, to minority scholars this is nothing new. Juxtapose his musings to those from Anzaldúa's autoethnography *Borderlands/La Frontera*:

> The work of the mestiza consciousness is to break down the subject-object duality that keeps her a prisoner and to show in the flesh and through the images in her work how duality is transcended. The answer to the problem between the White race and colored, between males and females, lies in healing the split that originates in the very foundation of our lives, our culture, our languages, our thoughts. (Anzaldúa, 1999, p. 102)

Throughout her book, Anzaldúa weaves together personal reflection, poetry, indigenous spirituality, and philosophy to outline a theory and praxis based on Mestisaje. A Mestiza is a woman who is a racial/ethnic mix of Spanish and Native American. Of mixed blood, mixed heritage, to be mestiza or mestizo is to have a foot planted on either side of the border—we belong neither here nor there. But Anzaldúa taught us to see the benefit of not belonging, we can make our own space which reflects the many aspects of our lives, whether they are positive ones, trials, or challenges. The essence of Mestisaje is to recognize that there is no pure anything, whether language, blood, pedigrees, ideology, religion, or culture; we carry both the colonized and colonizer within us. Our duality enables us to more than sense what is behind the actions of gatekeepers because in some past incarnation we have also been gatekeepers, we have been the oppressor.

In 2004 Huntington's essay "The Hispanic Challenge" argued that the "creed" written by Thomas Jefferson and included in the Declaration of Independence is what defines America. Huntington further argues that this creed has been endorsed by statesmen and the public into the present period. The creed Huntington (2004) describes refers to

> the distinct Anglo-Protestant culture of the founding settlers. Key elements of that culture include the English language; Christianity; religious commitment; English concepts of the rule of law, including the responsibility of rulers and the rights of individuals; and dissenting Protestant values of individualism, the work ethic, and the belief that humans have the ability and the duty to try to create a heaven on earth, a "city on a hill." (p. 1)

For nearly sixteen pages, Huntington paints a xenophobic portrait of a people who threaten White America by refusing to assimilate into American culture. Holding on to our culture and language is a contemptuous act he believes to this country. My first reaction when I read this paper was to think, "I wonder what he's saying behind our backs?" But he lays out what many "gatekeepers" are thinking: that maybe we won't assimilate (whatever that means), that the more successful of us will lead some type of rebellion, that if too much power moves from the WASP patriarchs to people like me, they'll have to learn Spanish or, heaven forbid, I'll move into their neighborhood and walk in through people's front doors, not the back ones. Is it this type of thinking which led some professors to refuse my dissertation proposal? But the writings of those like Anzaldúa and others don't advocate a take-over of any kind, or a "reconquesta" of our traditional homelands. We call for a dialogue, a discussion of possibly seeing the world in a different way, not one in which the production of knowledge has to follow the parameters of a 400-year-old ideology, but one that recognizes and understands that societies change. As an anthropologist, I know that if a culture doesn't change, it will die out. Right now, in academe, we are in a struggle to fight erasure and invisibility by using our voices in ways the Devil did not expect or, I'm sure, appreciate.

The Faustian deals don't always turn out as expected. A generation ago, women began to approach higher education in a different way than what patriarchal tradition dictated the personal and political are woven together. Through our methods, *testimonios* being one of them, we are bringing about change. The small flashes Gramsci (1971) wrote about are all that is needed for the coalescence of individual instances of resistance to morph together. When this happens, "the group is acting as an organic totality" (Gramsci, 1971, p. 632) and the outcome is social change. Those of us, who speak out, understand that what is beneficial to those closest to us, benefits everyone in the end. My stories are largely of things I wish had not happened but they serve a purpose. When I advise students, we don't just talk about schools and programs but also departmental politics and what they may encounter. My experiences, though painful, taught me that the skills I learned as a borderlander work just as well in the halls of the University of Michigan as they do in San Antonio's toughest part of town.

Chapter Ten

A Critical Autoethnography of a
Black Man from Detroit

.•——•.

Resisting the White Imaginative's Criminalization of Black Men

Muhammad A. Khalifa

My life experiences and opportunities as a Black man in America are dynamically complex. I hold a PhD in education and a faculty position at a prestigious university department. But for a period of years, I was also my parents' only free (nonimprisoned) son. The complex lives of Black American males expose them to an ordering reality that no other people have been made to endure; from slavery to Jim Crow, then to ghettoization and mass incarceration, Black men have been made to endure incisive realities. Yet, in all of this, there is a role of resistance and self-reform. In this essay, I use, yet push beyond, Critical Race Theory (CRT) as I attempt to make sense of my own contested experiences. CRT is useful in helping me to understand my challenges to Whiteness and ubiquitous experiences of oppression. But it was less useful in helping me to understand me being Black, and *male*, and *Muslim*, for example.

Indeed, many minoritized groups have endured unimaginable forms of U.S. aggression and oppression. Black women, for example, have at times in the past been forced to carry the White man's burden, literally—that is, birthing his children, only to have their mixed-race children sold to another slaveholder. Since then, they have been discursively objectified, seen as loud, mischaracterized from resilient to "aggressive," and even blamed for being single parents. We are also all quite familiar with the oppressive circumstances that Latinos face, as they are often asked: "What are you, and where are your parents from?" Such oppressive questions dehistoricize and denationalize Whites while casting Latinos as *other* and forcing them to explain that their indigeneity predates the colonizing settlers who would later be simply known as White. Likewise, the First Nation Peoples (Indigenous Americans) have and continue to face intractable forms of oppression in society and school.

While I recognize these oppressions, in this autoethnography I focus on Black male contestations and argue that they continue to be oppressed in ways unique and dynamic to them. Their statistics of oppression foreshadow others': the highest incarceration rate, highest school failure rate, highest school suspension rate, highest pushout/dropout rate, highest arrest rate, highest murder and homicide rate, most negative media image, highest drug use rate, highest rate of new HIV infections, most rapidly growing suicide rate, and most likely to be recidivist. Yet the president is a Black man. Such factual contrasts show the extreme polarities and contradictions in the lives of Black men and accentuate both their promise and demise.

Critical Race Theory (CRT) and Lived Experiences

Of the tenets laid out by CRT scholars, I find the pervasiveness, normality, invisibility, and acceptedness of racism most useful in my plight as a young Black male. Though unaware of this during my formative years, I came to learn that racism is not merely individualized acts of discrimination, but rather systems of racial oppression that imbue every aspect of U.S. society (Delgado & Stefancic, 2001). CRT helped me to explain to questioners who inquired: "How did you end up so differently than your own brothers?"

In ways so embedded that they are rarely apparent, the set of assumptions, privileges, and benefits that accompany the status of being White have become a valuable asset that Whites actively protect. Whites have come to expect, advocate for, and rely on these benefits, and over time these expectations have been affirmed, legitimated, and protected by the law (Lipsitz, 2006). Among other minoritized peoples, Black men have also—often unacknowledged—sought these same privileges for themselves, but have frequently been denied. CRT is derived from Critical Legal Studies, which demonstrates ways that U.S. laws have been systemically biased against some groups while privileging other groups. Though the law is neither uniform nor explicit in all instances, in protecting settled expectations based on White privileges, American law has recognized a property interest in Whiteness that, although unacknowledged, now forms the background against which legal disputes are framed, argued, and adjudicated (Haris, 1992).

Contexts like my hometown of Detroit, therefore, can and *only should* be understood in the backdrop of the United States' racial past (Sugrue, 2005). In this regard, my story highlights how many Black Detroiters—who endured violations of legal (i.e., criminalization of African-American behaviors and disparities in criminal prosecutions), educational (i.e., racialized differences in school funding based on property values; racialized disparities in school discipline, quality of education, resources, and achievement), civil (i.e., racialized differences in unemployment, job accessibility, and income), residential (i.e., the result of years of racial covenants), and electoral (i.e., voting rights act and recent redistricting of political maps of minoritized voting areas that tilt election outcomes in favor of republican candidates)— came to be in their current situation and how they continue to face similar regimes of oppression.

Methodology and Presentation of Data

Methodology. I argue that Black male contestations can only be explained by Black males. I also acknowledge that they are not unique, and that we are a diverse group. There are, however, some peculiarities that we all share. Autoethnography is useful for me in telling the story of my personal experiences as a Black male for a number of reasons. For one, I recognize that all research has bias and subjectivity. Yet I agree with Alan Peshkin (1988), who states that "acknowledgments and assertions are not sufficient. Beginning with the premise that subjectivity is inevitable, . . . researchers should systematically seek out their subjectivity, not retrospectively when the data have been collected and the analysis is complete, but while their research is actively in progress." By powerful self-monitoring, Peshkin (1988) argues, we are able to discover and uncover our own personal researcher subjectivities. Oddly, this process for me was iterative, but without an end goal in mind. Because of societal and research exoticizations of urban people of color in the past—including stereotypes that we people of color often have about ourselves—I never strove or wanted to reach a point where I was able to say, "I have found and declared all of my subjectivities." Rather, in much the same way that Sherick Hughes (2008) used autoethnography to "involve a transformative caring agent to disrupt oppressive experiences and narratives of race," I sought to continuously interrogate my own subjectivities, but in ways that respond to the constantly changing and morphing contexts of oppression that confront Black men.

Though our lives constantly change, currently, I am all of the following at once: Black male, Muslim, father of three sons; attended the same universities as my parents; either lived in or visited more than 25 countries; and am now a college professor. As a Detroiter and thus cultural insider, my interpretations of lived reality in Detroit are unique and likely will differ from those of other researchers. Yet my ontological realities may be useful to those who prepare themselves, their students, or their loved ones to serve or conduct research in areas like urban Detroit. My autoethnographic approach agrees with Spry (2001),[2] who writes that "autoethnographic performance is the convergence of the 'autobiographic impulse' and the 'ethnographic moment' represented through movement and critical self-reflexive discourse in performance, articulating the intersections of peoples and culture through inner sanctions of the always migratory identity." My experiences as a Black male were often so conflicting that I swung between feeling severely oppressed to deeply blessed to be a Black male. Much of what happened to me caused me to often think, "Why me and not them?" But the "critical self-reflective discourse" that Spry mentions led me to iteratively return to the same positionality of resistance and build my own criticalities.

Black Male Identity at Romulus High School: Theorizing beyond CRT

In many ways, the socially acceptable Black male identities in my high school culture were to either be a hypersexual, Black-male gangster or to become a professional-bound athlete. This was unique, although other minoritized and gendered students already had their own unique contestations around identity. Black male scholars or academics were not even a remote possibility for Black males. My Black female classmates were pressured to focus on their appearances rather than their intellects, to objectify their own bodies, and to be aggressive with other students. I was delighted to see many of my Black female classmates resist these pressures and go on to engage their intellects, attend college, and engage otherwise productive lives. Yet the pressure to conform to the more nihilistic modalities was also powerful and destructive, and too many Black female students made poor decisions. We Black students did not understand how we came to be confronted with such identities that were often not coterminous with our home or neighborhood lives. Nor did we understand that many of the decisions that we made at that time—which, again, were associated with very specific and often destructive behaviors—would impact us for the remainder of our lives. The popular American imaginative and popularized narratives of Black girl behaviors may have only been entertainment for White girls, but they left an indelible impact on the woman of color in my school. None of us students of color understood that by subscribing to these invented yet costly identities, we were participating in our own marginalization, accepting our status as "other," and reconfirming the pejorative comparisons of ourselves as inferior to the "normal" White standard. Indeed, CRT is explanatory in our understanding of how marginalization of African-Americans occurs, as Bell (1995) explains:

> The problem is that not all positioned perspectives are equally valued, equally heard, or equally included. From the perspective

of critical race theory, some positions have historically been oppressed, distorted, ignored, silenced, destroyed, appropriated, commodified, and marginalized—and all of this, not accidentally. Conversely, the law simultaneously and systematically privileges subjects who are White. (p. 901)

Whereas Whiteness has multiple, "positive" forms of existence in high school, and White students had access to White multiple identities from which to choose—some of which were even "Black" identities, Black female students had access to only a limited number of identities, and fewer yet with which they felt comfortable in school and would not be accused of cultural apostasy (Chambers, 2009; Fordham & Ogbu, 1986; Khalifa, 2012, 2011). Interestingly, in my high school, it was acceptable—if not mildly encouraged—that Black female students could choose to perform well in school. But it was *not* socially acceptable for Black males to do so. This nuance highlights that while CRT explains some Black male contestations, it does not explain all. Unique to a Black *male* experience, I found myself boasting far more about how I was a great athlete or how I was in contact with some of my gangster relatives than about my academic successes. Indeed, Black women deal with double (or even multiple) oppressions. Similarly, Black men face their own unique set of challenges that no other subgroup faces. America's racist past normalized, and thus privileged, White men, but this was antithetically done, as Black men were represented as their polar opposite: aggressive, criminal, unintelligent, hypersexual (especially toward White women), untamed, lazy, uncommitted, exotic, and beastly. But, perhaps more than anything, *threatening*—something, again, that may differ from Black women and most other marginalized groups. Those unacknowledged privileges that are often conferred on Whites are openly identified by Bell (1995):

> Decontextualization, in our view, too often masks unregulated—even unrecognized—power. We insist, for example, that abstraction, put forth as "rational" or "objective" truth, smuggles the privileged choice of the privileged to depersonify their claims and then pass them off as the universal authority and the universal good. (p. 901)

These unacknowledged White privileges and White positionalities are not described as neo-European or even postcolonial, but rather are passed off as normal and universal. As a result, the Black male proclivities and behaviors are first inscribed and then othered, and in the case of school, criminalized. The results for Black males are particularly bleak in U.S. schools and society.

In this chapter, I share a number of authoethnographic moments that illustrate the oppressive confrontations that many Black boys endure in school.

By describing and then theorizing about my own life experiences and those of other Black men around me, I attempt to understand how the intersection of our Blackness and maleness has situated us in our unique position in school and society. The socially constructed school pressures we faced offered a narrow range of identities we felt comfortable assuming, and many were often nihilistic. For example, not even one-tenth of one percentage point of the athletes will go on to play with a professional sports program (fewer than .01%), and even fewer aspiring hip-hop artists will actually go on to become entertainers, yet such lifestyles were equally glamorized and discursively promoted to us Black males. Surely, my brothers and other Black males in my high school made mistakes in their lives. But this discursive context normalized and glamorized the lifestyle, such that even I—a Black kid from a middle-class family, with a high GPA and collegiate aspirations—sought to fit in. I was one of only two Black male students in my high school to attend college immediately after high school graduation.

White Supremacy and the Criminalization of Black Men

White privilege and Whiteness were constructed, guarded, and conferred with privileged meanings in the United States from very early moments in American history (Roediger, 2005). The relationship between actions, and the meanings associated with these actions, explain my usage of discursiveness and has much to do with how I view identities as being co-constructed and formed. Though ethnicities such as the Irish, Italians, and Jews were eventually able to ascend into Whiteness, Blacks, poorer and browner Latinos, and Indigenous Native Americans were not. And because of that, they were not afforded the same power, meaning, and ultimately statuses and resources. This is why the work of earlier CRT scholars is so paramount in understanding contexts like Detroit. Eventually, such representations became law, which, as Derrick Bell (1995) explains, "systematically privileges subjects who are White" (p. 901).

These discursive privileges and advantages constantly played out throughout my schooling years, and I was pushed to embrace what the system had already characterized about my kind. In one moment in my senior year, I was starkly reminded of the expectation of me to embrace a gangster nature. This involved a trailer for the movie *Boyz N the Hood*, which aired during a morning newscast in my chemistry class. The movie, set in a gang-ridden, violent neighborhood in South Central Los Angeles, involved dichotomized and stereotypical representations of Black male gangster life and success among Black teenage boys. There was a successful

Black male representation in the movie, but he was portrayed as weak and out of place. Not only did he cry uncontrollably throughout the movie, but he also was not able to dance well, often could not successfully obtain dates with women, displayed cowardice for not partaking in a retaliatory killing, and was depicted as being dishonest about his personal to life to his father. While its representations of Black women were also very problematic—for example, in its portrayal of single Black women as incapable of successfully raising children—the real draw to this movie, as indicated by the title, was the representations—indeed, glorifications—of a gangster, nihilistic lifestyle. The movie trailer was replete with shootings, killings, animosities that invariably resulted in fights, and gang life.

Given that my parents were highly educated professionals who had attended a university routinely ranked as one of the top-ten universities in the world and that I was not being raised an environment similar to the movie's exoticized representations, I was as shocked as anyone else by the trailer. After all, it had been decades since the Blaxploitation films of the 1970s were released, so this was new to me. But what happened next took me by surprise: the entire class, including the White female teacher, all, as if on cue, turned their gazes and bodies toward me and remained elicitingly silent. Of course, given this pressure, I needed to respond. As they attentively listened and as I was being othered and placed into this gangster category, I cleared my throat to respond, "Yup, it's gonna be good," though there had not been an explicit question. This example actually highlights my complicity in the powerful processes by which my identity was co-constructed—my confirmation, acceptance, appropriation, and even enhancement of the powerful stereotypes that the popular White imaginative has of Black males.

Perduring Marginalization: Cost of a Single Error

Eventually I began to invest in my own representations by exuding one of my high school's accepted Black male modalities. Indeed, my body was ordered (Foucault, 1980a). In fact, Foucault (1980a) makes it clear that it was not so much that I had freely chosen an identity as that I had chosen one of the two identities that the hegemonic White imaginative had made accessible to me. The protest that the Black community had once known had been dismantled by a move toward liberal consumerism and individuality. Unlike the post–Jim Crow era, success was no longer defined by unity and Black liberation from White oppression, but rather by whether *individuals* had money and accessibility to middle-class trappings. In my community, it was unimportant how this financial ascendency was attained, even in cases where the Black community may have been harmed (e.g., drug selling or corrupt religious leaders). Thus, the Black community began to lose the means to resist the types of identities I found in my high school. So because I was not a great athlete, I made moderate investments into my gangster identity. Though I was very well behaved, maintained above-average grades, and had solid plans to go to college, I took solace in the fact that, although I was not a gangster, I was related to gangsters—one of my uncles had been to prison for murder. The details were even more legitimizing given that my uncle had stabbed the man, a flashy Black man from a neighboring town, through his heart with a cane. It was also reported that my grandfather was a murderer and had killed two White men who sexually harassed my Black grandmother. Yet my father was a regal, educated Black man with whom I lived and on whom I also modeled myself. Though there were some glimpses of agency, the identities and ordering of bodies that were discursively ordered in my school typically didn't allow for much else.

Two moments demonstrate my contestations of this gangster identity quite well. The first is the story of my cousin Troy. Troy is a distant cousin on my father's side of my family and was a well-known drug dealer in our area. His image had all of trappings of being a "big-time roller" or successful, affluent drug dealer—the swag, the gold chains and rings, the willingness to fight at the drop of a dime, the new jeeps with loud music and flashy tire rims, and the respect of other aspirant gangsters. I got good traction from mentioning that Troy was my cousin. Troy's entrance into school was always dramatic; he was only 5-foot-1, but people feared him. On the first day of school, he would show up and walk through the hallways draped in jewelry and new clothes. There would always be a fan club of sorts following him around. During my sophomore year, I was looking to be accepted by my peers; mentioning my affiliation with my cousins was particularly useful in one class conversation I had. I had broken my foot during the summer, which required me to wear a cast on my foot for several weeks. I had a job at a local Little Caesar's pizza and had saved my money. I bought a few expensive clothes with my earnings, and with the few dollars my parents would give me for school clothes. In this particular conversation, I was accused of selling drugs. "That nigga Moe is rolling," one of my classmates charged. I responded, "Well, you don't need to worry about that!" But I said this in a way as to almost confirm that I was indeed selling drugs. I continued, "Yeah, I was just with Troy the other night, so don't ask about things you don't really know about." Well, I didn't know much about it, either, but the discursive rewards were generous when I accepted this particular ordering of the Black male identity. Today, Troy is wheelchair bound, addicted to the very same highly lethal drugs that he once sold, and is not able to work or even physically take care of himself. One of his siblings has since died of AIDS, believed to have been contracted through intravenous drug usage. The same holds true for many of the gangsters in his circle who were from our "hood." Yet in my school environment, Black male gangsters are heroicized because they are the only powerful masculine identities offered in movies and White imaginative discourses.

The complexity and danger of having gangster identities would not be finished with me yet, nor would it be confined to my school life. Indeed, these identities were present in larger society, and they were exoticized in society's larger White imaginative. This was not only present in, for example, the largely White-produced Blaxploitation films of the 1970s, but also in the largely White-produced gangster hip-hop music and movies in the 1990s and beyond. Thus, America has been induced to accept the belief that Whites and immigrants make decisions to go to college and get ahead in society while Blacks, Latinos, and Native Americans *choose* not to do so. Likewise, Whites largely choose to abstain from committing crimes while those same minoritized bodies choose to partake in crime. Both of these beliefs benefit Whites at the expense of other ethnicities. A more difficult articulation to find, however, is the notion that official policies and practices have and continue to create a context within which minoritized bodies are fashioned to be gangsta.

For example, these co-constructions are also manifested in the expectations individuals have of Black males. During the last semester of my senior year, I was preparing to begin my post-secondary education at the University of Michigan. At the time, the university was so prestigious that it was ranked number 11 worldwide. I was one of two Black men in my entire high school graduating class (though there were a total of roughly 50 Black male students) who had been accepted to college and had solid plans to attend. But I was still traversing two worlds—one gangster and one college bound. In the spring of that year, just before I was to graduate from high school, I decided to purchase an illegal gun—a large (6-inch barrel), chrome-plated, .44 caliber Smith & Wesson revolver. White fears of Blacks having guns, I presume, led to a great number of Black films in which Blacks acquiring guns was glamorized and became centerpieces to the narrative. This is the case in much earlier movies such as *Superfly* (1972), through the 1990s in *New Jack City* (1991) and *Menace II Society* (1993), to the current era, in *Django Unchained* (2012). Though offering vastly different but rich story-lines, these movies all have focal scenes where the main character somehow obtains a gun and things drastically change, often for the better. This was my second illegal gun. The first was a .22 caliber, and I quickly got rid of it because, for one, the cousin from whom I bought it was begging me to sell it back to him, and, secondly, it was not strong enough for the protection that I convinced myself I needed. Actually, I felt I needed it to conform to this hegemonic identity, but also *just in case* I needed to protect myself. I purchased the gun from a sibling and one of his accomplices. I would later find out that the gun had been recently used in a spate of local robberies.

However, the event that would have permanently changed my destiny involved me putting the gun under the driver's seat in my car and going to visit my friend Richard, who was the valedictorian of a nearby high school and also recently admitted to the University of Michigan. After I flashed the gun to him, we decided to go up to a local megaplex shopping center not far away. As we were nearing the shopping mall in a racist district—Dearborn, Michigan—we noticed a police cruiser behind us, "running" the license plate of my car. We froze, our hearts fell through the car floor, and we panicked, for we knew that a gun charge in Michigan carried a mandatory two- to five-year year prison sentence. Moreover, we didn't know the history of the gun—the robberies, or even worse, that someone might have been earlier killed with the gun. I quickly switched lanes and was able to lose the police officer.

Had the officer tailed us more quickly and been able to stop us, my life—or both of our lives—would have been changed forever. We, or at least I, not only would have gone to prison, but also would have been permanently barred from attending the University of Michigan and most other universities, from my later career in teaching and thus being a professor and being able to write this very essay, and from living any type of dignified life. As scholars like Michelle Alexander (2012) and Khalil Gibran Muhammad (2010) have shown, Black males with a criminal background are relegated to lives of blocked challenges and second-class citizenry. Voting rights, many occupational opportunities, housing opportunities, mobility and travel restrictions, higher education opportunities, and a permanent stigma all lead to a very restricted and challenging existence. God, as Richard went on to recently retrospectively reflect, had different plans for us. Frighteningly, we were of the "*good*" Black males. I can only imagine what life must be like for, well, my brothers, and countless other Black men who more stringently subscribed to the gangster lifestyle. They are now likely to be within the third of Black men who are permanent subjects of the state, permanently disabled and disadvantaged.

My Agency and Developing Criticality

As I finished high school and entered college, I still was not aware of how the identities available to me as a young Black man had been constructed and ordered. I thought each of our decisions to be personal. Yet this ordering was complex, and there were glimpses of agency throughout my high school. As I described, I had relatively high marks in school and had solid plans to go to college. But I had seen my parents go to college, so it was to an extent demystified to me. My Black male classmates did not have this resource, however. Thus, the typical heroic gangster identity was no doubt even more compelling for them. The milieu in which young Black men grew up was complex. Another example of this complexity was that another classmate of mine and I started the Black Student Union at our school. Its impact was largely ceremonial, as the pinnacle of our activities consisted of showing the movie *Glory* (1989) after school and giving speeches at the Black History Month Assembly.

These experiences indicated some of the complexities of young Black male life in the United States. This was also visible in Black popular media and culture. Hip-hop artists such as Public Enemy (PE), Eric B. & Rakim, Paris, KRS-One, and Queen Latifah all had organically positive messages in their music that often confronted the nihilistic messages found in the West coast gangster music. But even these gangster rappers had positive tracks, as in NWA's song "Express Yourself." I focus on hip-hop music because, as PE rapper Chuck D once explained, "Rap is CNN for Black people (Interview, *Mother Jones*, Sept./Oct. 2004)." This form of music, despite the fact that it was ultimately and increasingly informed by the White imaginative, was most impactful on me in how I saw my positionality and myself in society. For my Black male classmates—many of whom did not have their fathers or other positive Black male imagery in the home like we did—I only surmise that the music and media imagery were that much more powerful. As hip-hop music was co-opted by corporate greed and the powerful White imaginative, so too were the lives of so many of my Black male classmates.

My own complex and often contradictory response to this discursive context came to the fray once when my father, who was on spring break in the school district where he worked, served as substitute teacher in my school. He saw me in the hall, jumped up in what I thought was a very goofy manner, and called me by my nickname: "Hey Moe!" And waved. I believe I turned and went in the other direction but may have passed him by, barely giving eye contact or a response. Whatever the case, I was highly embarrassed and did not want to be in any way associated with what was actually an upright representation of a Black man. My embarrassment of him, because of such an impregnable tapestry of Black male identities indicates my rejection of his societally positive identities, which, conversely for me in this context, was a negative identity. Certainly my high school education was based on the notion of individualism and was not amenable to any types of community-based schooling that emphasize overlap of school and family/community. But my embarrassment was neither chimerical nor whimsical; the expectations that my teachers had for me and other Black men were so low that we began to embody or at least exude these identities. Researchers have since shown that the types of academic expectations that teachers have for us directly impact our performance and academic success (Khalifa, 2011; Ream, 2003). But perhaps even more alarming, the deficit stereotypes and *cultural* expectations in a school can have a huge negative impact on the academic achievement of students.

It seemed to me that my commitment to at least trying find a voice of Black protest was encouraged by some of the staff at my school. I can remember being asked to "control" the Black kids after the Rodney King Riots. The school counselor and principal were worried that Black students would revolt because of the acquittal of four White police officers who beat an unarmed Black motorist so badly that he nearly died. The beating was secretly videotaped, and when the four officers were exonerated of all charges, parts of Los Angeles (and a few other cities around the country) erupted into riots. I was surprised—and in retrospect realize that it is both likely related to this protest identity *and* a hegemonic posture on the part of the school principal and counselor to believe that it is okay to suppress the voice of students—that they would be asking this of me. Strangely, despite the fact I was being used for oppression and "control," I was also honored that they would ask. I was happy to see that they trusted me and cared enough about the issue. It didn't enter my mind that they might have agreed with the court's decision to exonerate the officers. So moving on the momentum of our strong relationship and the fact that I knew they liked me, I was far more comfortable asking the counselor for the letter of recommendation for my college application that I needed from him to be admitted to the university.

I asked him, and he replied, "U of M, you sure? That's a tough school to get into!" Upon seeing my eyebrows protrude and visual perplexity set in, he said "Sure, c'mon by the office." I must have gone by his office four or five times, and he kept putting me off, saying for me to come by later. I finally one day cornered him and said, "My application is due in two days, and I will drive it to U of M campus, but I just need your letter of recommendation." Without saying anything, he took my application and wrote his recommendation directly on the U of M application: three to four sentences, across the page slanted and diagonally, and in writing that I could barely read. I thought that high school counselor's handwritten note in my college application for the U of M was strange; I felt discouraged. And his reaction was one of gloom when I was admitted in February of my senior year in high school. When I informed him I had been admitted, he was silent, did not congratulate me, and had a look of bother or annoyance on his face.

I had begun learning that the structural racism that Black men faced was indeed unique. I question whether my school counselor (and other staff) responded to me this way out of any sort of conscious discrimination or deliberate racism. Rather, I surmise that it was based on the fears that

American society has always had of Black men, and the staff was acting in concert. That Black men were seen as lazy, subhuman, out to rape White women, and as criminals still seems to be impacting the White imaginative in U.S. society and popular culture, and now in my high school. In other words, while U.S. law and school policy prevented de jure types of discrimination in cases such as *Brown v. Board of Education*, informal types of discrimination were allowed if not endorsed, as Harris (1992) illustrates:

> In failing to clearly expose the real inequalities produced by segregation, the status quo of substantive disadvantage was ratified as an accepted and acceptable base line—a neutral state operating to the disadvantage of Blacks long after de jure segregation had ceased to do so. (p. 1753)

I knew something was terribly wrong in my high school. I couldn't understand why we were targeted in classes for disciplinary action, why so many of my Black male classmates were failing and deciding to enact a machismo gangster reality, and why so many were discursively encouraged to aspire for the National Basketball Association (NBA) but not college. Despite my good grades in school, I cannot recall a single teacher in my high school encouraging me to go to college. When some of my teachers found out that I was attending the U of M, some seemed surprised and even angry. The ways that we were treated in my school were not really different from how society as a whole treated Black men. My post-secondary experiences only confirmed my high school realities. These constructed Black male identities in high school were so deleterious for us that I wonder why more was not done. Yet Harris (1992) again notes, "White privilege accorded as a legal right was rejected, but de facto White privilege not mandated by law remained unaddressed" (p. 1753). It all began to make sense to me now—no matter how confusing and appalling to me, this was how Black men were to be permanently treated in this country.

Always a "Boy": The Enduring Nature of Black Male Marginalization

As I left high school and entered college and professional life, many of the same White imaginative identities awaited me. I had begun to be the spook who sat by the classroom door; I felt like a token Negro, a Black male who was accepted into this thriving intellectual community only to find the same hostilities I'd encountered before. On a couple of occasions, I was questioned by police for no reason. I had applied for a job as a security officer at the U of M hospital, which oddly required an IQ test. I scored extremely high, but then came the psychological examination interview. The White woman, who immediately identified herself as Jewish, began to ask questions with a perplexing look and tone. I can recall her asking me if I ever got "stressed out." I responded with a question, "Sure, doesn't everybody?" She went on to rate me as highly intelligent but not psychologically fit for this job because of its highly stressful nature. I found this laughable but consistent with the stereotypical and imaginative discourses that I'd encountered in high school.

After languishing as a pre-med student for a number of years, I switched my major to science education. During my senior year at the University of Michigan and after becoming a certified science teacher, I learned that a number of my White high school classmates who had also become teach-ers were going to apply for jobs in Romulus Community Schools, our high school home district. I became very enthusiastic about the idea, too, and reasoned with myself, "Finally, a chance to give back!" This was my opportu-nity to help so many of the Black and White working-class students virtually identical to the ones with whom I had attended school. Surely they knew me, as I had volunteered to tutor Romulus elementary schoolchildren for years, had been given awards, and had started the Black Student Union at my school. I was even more hopeful because the head of human resources at Romulus Community Schools was also a Black man. Moreover, unlike some of my White classmates who had attended other universities, the College of Education had one of the best reputations in the world, and my grades were good. After we applied for jobs, each one of my White female classmates was called in for a job and hired. I never received a call. I spoke to the African-American head of human resources a number of times, and he was first evasive and then dismissive. I came to learn not only that all African-Americans in the district were weary of him and that they viewed him as being distant if not abrasive toward other Blacks, but also that Romulus Community Schools had specifically sought this type of administrator out.

This White supremacist and post-colonial tactic, however, is nothing new. Whites, both here in the United States as well as in oppressive colo-nial nations, have for years sought out puppet administrations that would do the bidding of the White power structure. In retrospect, I suppose that is why I was asked to control the potential Black local anger after the Rodney King verdict. I found that Romulus was no exception. Though it had a Black face, indeed the White power structure had yet again, years after my graduation, found a way to extend its culturally exclusionary reach. Meanwhile, all of those hired by the district were young White teachers, primarily women. Needless to say, they had a demonstrably poor, if not deleterious, impact on young Black boys in school, and the Black male achievement and suspension gaps endure. When I spoke to my classmates who were hired, they said of the Black HR director things like, "Yeah, you should call him, he loves people from Michigan" and "He's such a great guy, and he loves Romulus alumni." Some years later, I spoke to a Black and a White administrator in the district, and they both acknowledged that they knew that the Black HR director was very unlikely to hire African-American teachers, especially Black men. In retrospect, I couldn't be more thankful that I eventually got a job in much larger and more urban Detroit. But I was also horrified, because I now knew that the Romulus environment that was so hostile toward Black men—apparently at every level—was being reproduced; today, I have more than 15 Black male family members who attend Romulus Community Schools.

Still a Black Boy in Academe:
Quad-Consciousness and the Continued Struggle

One ever feels his twoness—an American, a Negro; two souls, two thoughts, two unreconciled strivings; two warring ideals in one dark body, whose dogged strength alone keeps it from being torn asunder. (Du Bois, 2008, p. 12)

I write this critical autoethnography about my experiences as a Black male and theorize about what first led me to become a critical teacher and researcher. My experiences transcend the Black and White double consciousness that Du Bois discussed, however. Like most other Black folks, I see this double consciousness in my own life, but, as I have discussed in this chapter, being Black and *male* means something even more distinct. Black males exist as criminals in the White imaginative, and I was thus co-opted, feared, and criminalized in school. And the comfortable identities (e.g., gangster or athlete) that I could have assumed in my high school or post-secondary contexts were inextricably linked to the minstrel caricatures that have *always* existed in the broader White supremacist society. I fared okay, but my brothers, cousins, and countless friends did not. Thus, in my experience, the "Blackness" that Black males face is as unique as an intersectionality that is not well understood.

Yet I am also a *Muslim* and my name is an *Islamic* name, and I exist in a deeply xenophobic and Islamophobic context. Ultimately, I have come to understand that these experiences in our schools, universities, and professional circles are reflective of a broader fearful White imaginative. The race of the person is both important yet inconsequential, as the support of White supremacy takes precedence. As Lipsitz (2006) explains:

White supremacy is an equal opportunity employer; nonwhite people can become active agents of white supremacy as well as passive participants in its hierarchies and rewards. One way of becoming an insider is by participating in the exclusion of other outsiders. An individual might even secure a seat on the Supreme Court on this basis. On the other hand, if not every white supremacist is white, it follows that not all white people have to become complicit with white supremacy—there is an element of choice in all of this. White people always have the option of becoming antiracist, although not enough have done so. (p. viii)

In my high school, university, and professional experiences, I have come to learn to navigate the White imaginative expectations held for Black males. At times I have embraced these identities and at other times resisted. But I certainly did not invent them, and I have found them in all my contexts, waiting, as a piece of clothing, to be tried on, worn, and exhibited. Indeed, like all people, we Black folk have strength, transcendence, agency, and the ability to imagine our own destiny. But, given the 500-plus years of colonization, it is unlikely that any identity we Black Americans ourselves construct will be free from the influence of the White imaginative. Even in our identities of protest and resistance, we are still resisting the imaginative and its oppressions.

Even though I was a faculty member at a major institution, having earned a PhD from a top-ranked program and published in the top journals in my field, one colleague remarked to another Black male colleague about me: "He seems so lazy!" My Black male colleague responded to the White female, "Are you sure you want to use *that* term to describe Black people?" She responded, "Well, glib." This challenge was indeed appropriate, given that one of the most abusive historical representations of Black slaves was of being "shiftless" and "lazy." These discourses were also in step with the hegemonically oppressive White imaginative. White slaveholders worked their Black slaves from dawn to dusk under the hot Southern sun and then, without a qualm and in complete disregard of their own lack of industriousness, referred to the enslaved Blacks as lazy. The minstrel and infamous blackface images were also conveyed as overly religious and subversive, if not nefarious, toward the rule of law and good, respectable White folks (Peffley & Hurwitz, 1988). In recent years, such representations have been confirmed to the White imaginative through representations of Black welfare mothers and Black men who shiftlessly commit to a life of selling drugs. I was initially shocked that I would be described in this way but went on to understand the events in light of how earlier Whites had viewed and oppressed me.

In another incident, I had a White female colleague convey the fearful White imaginative: "Sarah [a pseudonym] is afraid of you, Muhammad!"

She was referring to a White female student who was in an *online* diversity graduate class who was consistently avoiding the topic of race in her writings. Given that there is no face-to-face contact in our online courses, I wrote to a student asking her to come and visit me during my office hours. The student was indeed scared of me, but given that it was an online class, I couldn't understand why. I asked my colleague why but then recognized a familiar fear in her face. The exchange was confusing to me because I actually try very hard to be kind and welcoming to students. I had never been told by anyone, colleague or student—or person—that he or she was afraid of me. I often wonder where the fear actually came from—displaced fears from my colleague, or from the student, or perhaps both. But once again, I was consoled that their fear was not caused by my behavior, but rather was informed by the White imaginative fears of the Black male—criminal, lazy, and lusting to rape White women.

Final Reflections: Black Male Hybridity between Protean White Imaginatives

I have written about multiple instances in which the White Imaginative has impacted me, as a Black male, and about how I have been viewed by White supremacist thinking and stereotypical affirmations—something that I refer to in this paper as the *White imaginative*. Indeed, many Blacks and people of other races also enact this imaginative and even contribute to its oppressive continued development. These oppressive representations of Black males have been embraced and operationalized by both Whites and Blacks in my spaces, as White supremacy is more about discursive *words* and *actions* than racist *people*. I have also written about the tensions and contestations around my embracing these identities, even when I was aware that they may not truly represent me or may even be nihilistic. Moreover, my experiences also conveyed the perduring nature of the representations. They are deep in nature and were largely invented first to justify Black chattel slavery and then to continue Black oppression. But now this history has largely been invisiblized, yet the stereotypical representations of Blacks persist. We found these identities when we arrived at the first day of school, not in our homes. With this invisiblized history, my brothers and I, and countless other Black males, would go on to accept, embrace, and even celebrate these identity constructions—identity constructions that oppressed us.

How would I interpret my high school teachers who, when learning that I was admitted to school, said things like: "*You?* Got into the *University of Michigan?*" in disbelief? I was being molded at every turn—by administrators, teachers, other Black males, and my professors and professorial colleagues—to acquiesce to the hegemonic White imaginative. I mentioned that I was always asked why I was successful and so different from my brothers, both of whom chose the gangster lifestyle and spent time in prison. Though the question itself is problematic, I am not altogether sure that I *am* much different from them at all. In much the same way that a higher power (or a twist of fate, whichever you prefer) would allow a particular sperm to make it into my mother's egg in her womb forming me, the same power was more generous with my gangster indiscretions in my earlier years. In fact, had I actually been stopped by that police car with a gun under my seat, our lives would likely look identical. Prominent CRT scholar Derrick Bell (1995) posits, "All of our institutions of education and information—political and civic, religious and creative—either knowingly or unknowingly provide the public rationale to justify, explain, legitimize or tolerate racism" (p. 399). This reverberates in my own experiences, as each system and level of education that I encountered imbued the same racially oppressive imaginative, its everyday presence invisiblized and enshrined in all echelons of society. I surmise that the perpetrators of these White supremacist imaginatives did not notice how they were being racist or even that they were racist. But that is exactly what CRT theorists argue: that racism is so endemic, systemic, and normalized in U.S. society that it goes unnoticed and often unchallenged.

Learning from My Criticality:
Advice for Urban Educators and Administrators

If racism were merely isolated, unrelated, individual acts, we would expect to see at least a few examples of educational excellence and equity together in the nation's public schools. Instead, those places where African-Americans do experience educational success tend to be outside of the public schools. While some might argue that poor children, regardless of race, do worse in school, and that the high proportion of African-American poor contributes to their dismal school performance, we argue that the cause of their poverty in conjunction with the condition of their schools and schooling is institutional and structural racism. (Ladson-Billings & Tate, 1995, p. 55)

My Black male experiences are relevant for other minoritized students, be they Black females, Latinas, Indigenous, Muslims and other religious minorities, language minorities, or even poor White students. Though their experiences will be unique, they, too, are undoubtedly responding to the oppressive White male imaginative. As the above quote indicates, this chapter is situated in the reality that racism is indeed ubiquitous throughout public schooling at every level. My experiences show that it is such a profound part of the U.S. narrative that it impacts each person in unique and adaptive ways, yet some patterns exist, and some of these patterns relate to being a Black man. It is my hope that schoolteachers and administrators begin to recognize how their school policies and practices are deeply connected to the metanarratives in White society. Given that racism is normalized and endemic, they must be actively anti-racist; there can be no neutrality in this matter.

Because of the precarious position of Black males, this is even more true. In the case of education, it is now widely acknowledged that Black boys are more likely to be forcibly removed from and failed out of schools (Gregory, Skiba, & Noguera, 2010; Noguera, 2003). But they are also more likely to encounter identity expectations—some which are harmful—that hegemonically encourage a connection to the White imaginative (Chambers, 2009; Fordham & Ogbu, 1986; Khalifa, 2012). This places school officials in a unique position; I argue that they must do three things:

- Develop written and measurable anti-racist and anti-oppressive educational policy;

- Develop classroom and school cultures that reaffirm other positive identities that Black boys already have; and

- Create classroom and school cultures that allow for the merging of identities that children have chosen (e.g., athlete or gangster identities) and identities of high achievement

If my experiences and those of other Black men who have been a part of my life and my story can help in this regard, then I am able to acknowledge that all has not been lost in my struggle.

Chapter Eleven

Working the Hyphens

·◆——◆·

Ethnographic Snapshots in Becoming Critical-Female-Black-Scholars

Aisha El-Amin, B. Genise Henry, and Crystal T. Laura

The Ph.D. cohort, source of the nation's college and university faculty, is not changing quickly enough to reflect the diversity of the nation. The next generation of college students will include dramatically more students of color, but their teachers will remain overwhelmingly White, because a White student is three times as likely as a student of color to earn the doctorate.

—Weisbuch, 2005, p. 7

The PhD cohort, source of the nation's college and university faculty, is not changing quickly enough to reflect the diversity of the nation. With only 1.9% of all PhDs in the United States belonging to African-American women (Dowdy 2008), it is imperative that those promoting diversity, as well as those matriculating in the academy, enhance understandings of what contributes to the success of diverse groups. In response to these startling statistics, African-American feminists have offered valuable insights to help understand, negotiate, and deconstruct the academy while empowering and edifying African-American women (Boykin, 1998; Collins, 1991/2000). As hooks (1994) reveals in her seminal work, African-American female educators may "develop important strategies for survival and resistance that need to be shared . . ." (p.118). While several scholars have discussed the socialization experiences of doctoral students, most have not paid particular attention to Black females or rates of attrition (e.g., Gardner, 2007; Gonzalez, 2006; Mendoza, 2007; Weidman & Stein, 2003). In addition, strategies for surviving as Black women at the doctoral level have recently been explored by some scholars (e.g., Barnes, 2009; Fries-Britt & Kelly, 2005; Lee, 2009). Nevertheless, most of these studies have grouped Black women together as one uniform group. Yet the other aspects of Black women's identity can significantly impact their negotiations of academia.

Realizing the power of storytelling (e.g., Dowdy, 2008; Guajardo & Guajardo, 2002; Ruder, 2010) and disheartened by the statistics on Black female PhDs, this chapter documents the experiences of three Black female doctoral students. Using autoethnography, we examine the moments in our journeys to become critical-Black-female-scholars when we deliberately connected our personal and professional lives through research—risky moves that we attribute to envisioning and realizing successful completion of our PhDs. Aisha, a Black-Muslim-mother, found a way to make her research personally and politically relevant by investigating Black Muslim parents and school choice in a post 9/11 Islamophobic era. Likewise, Genise, a spirit-filled scholar, conducted research that was attentive to her desire to incorporate spirituality in her work as an educational leader. Finally, Crystal, a justice-seeking sister, struggled to investigate her own brother's tragic journey through systems of education and criminal justice, bringing the scholarly metaphor "school-to-prison pipeline" close to home.

In 1915, Theodore Roosevelt stated, "There is no room in this country for hyphenated Americanism." We emphatically disagree. Moreover, we define our hyphenated identities as salient labels that should not be reduced into to a single referent because their distinct natures—politically, personally, and historically rooted—are worthy of pause (Haman & England, 2011; Lomawaima & McCarty, 2006). By embracing the personal, political, and historical complexities of our identity, we "work the hyphens" of understanding the "other" in relationship to the "self" (Fine, 1994). The three autoethnographies presented here expose how our socialization process pushed us to "unpack the notions of scientific neutrality, universal truths, and researcher dispassion" (Fine, 1994, p. 131). Adopting the scholarship of Michelle Fine (1994), we understand "working the hyphen" as a way to "probe who we are in relation with the context we study and with our informants, understanding that we are all multiple in those relationships" (p.135). In doing so, we critically question whose story is being told, why, by whom, with what interpretation, and with what consequences (Fine, 1994; Woodrow Wilson National Fellowship Foundation, 2005). Reminiscent of President Roosevelt's statement, we heard, in both explicit and implicit ways, that there is no room for *real* PhDs to take seriously scholarship that is politically, historically, and personally rooted in multiple identities. In this chapter, we discuss our resistance to this assertion, positing that the ability to *work the hyphens* enriched our journeys making our research more relevant, our analysis more keenly critical, and our successful completion feasible.

To make sense of our doctoral experiences, we use a socialization framework borrowed from Bragg (1976), which allows us to examine the process by which we learned, often subconsciously, to adopt the values, skills, attitudes, and norms needed to join the academic ranks (Austin, 2002; Gardner, 2007; Turner & Thompson, 1993). Bragg (1976) argues that socialization occurs through three layers of interactions: 1) interactions of students within the educational structures; 2) interactions among students in the same discipline or department; and 3) interactions between students and faculty members. Our autoethnographies encompass reflections on each form of interaction but focus poignantly on our experiences grappling with educational structures, including program goals, the spaces for learning and practicing values (e.g., coursework, internships, or examinations), the isolation of students of color from their cultural communities, and the provisions for positive and negative sanctions as feedback for students (Gardner, 2007). We give special attention to our socialization in relation to the educational setting because educational settings "affect or facilitate the change in a student's attitudes and values, because they reflect the attitudes and values of the profession itself" (Bragg, 1976, p. 14). More specifically, as students we focus on the university's attitudes toward the interconnections of our identity with our scholarship, how the negative and/or positive attitudes related to our research choices, and the impact of those attitudes on our commitment to successfully complete the doctoral program.

Our work is also grounded in Dillard's (2000) *endarkened feminist epistemology*, which assists in our articulation of "a distinguishable difference in cultural standpoint located in the intersection/overlap of the culturally constructed socializations of race, gender and other identities and the historical and contemporary contexts of oppressions and resistance of African-American women" (p. 662). In other words, endarkened feminist epistemology demands that we embrace our hyphenated identities as a source of strength and resilience. Through these understandings, we explore the intellectual and spiritual development of our research agendas. Additionally, endarkened feminists understand the necessity of binding individuals to community context and the use of dialogue to help those individuals grow and evolve (Dillard, 2000). Using this epistemology, we hope that our collective autoethnographies emerge as part of the building blocks for a community of successful Black female PhDs.

Aisha's Story—Research: A Personal and Political Act

I am a newly minted PhD. However, the road of my life has not been a straight one; quite the contrary, it has been fraught with unexpected curves, roughly paved roads, and countless blind spots. There are points in my life, that, when I share them with others, cause listeners to quickly accuse me of giving a recount of their favorite daytime soap opera. Case in point: At 18 years of age, I caught my then live-in boyfriend cheating on me. I promptly gathered my things, headed directly to a military recruitment office, and asked the recruiter to "get me on the first thing smokin' out of town." Two weeks later, I began a five-year stint oversees as a military police officer.

THE ROAD CURVES

At the age of 23, I was introduced to a handsome Muslim brotha' who was part of a cipher held at a Chicago South Side Masjid (or place of worship). On the first day we met, our group performed a community service together. We found ourselves paired up. We began talking, and the more we talked the more I realized that an unforeseen curve had been thrown in my path; I really liked this guy. We talked on the phone every free moment we could find in the days to come. We married the following week and are enjoying our 13th year of wedded bliss.

I am adventurous, and my faith has no limits. When I say "faith," I'm speaking about that deep-seated, innate, and inherent part of myself that knows "nothing happens without the will of Allah (God) and he is my guide." That faith allowed me to make life-altering decisions in just a few short weeks. As a matter of fact, when it comes to my decision making, this is "just the way I roll." When I am pulled, or sometimes pushed, toward something, I don't resist. During these times, I rely on that deep-seated faith, which often outdistances my own understanding, and allow it to carry me. Now let's talk about the exception to this—my extended journey to embracing scholarship that expresses the full essence of who I am: an African-American-Muslim woman and mother.

I began my doctoral studies in policy studies of urban education, on a clear straight road, knowing I wanted to conduct research on the Black experience and use this knowledge to help advance my people. With my emergence from a low-income family and as the first ever in my family to attend graduate school, I recognized the privilege of this space. I came in understanding education as a political act, as would be the research I engaged in, whom I selected to be part of my committee, and the classes I elected. When afforded the opportunity, I eagerly enrolled in classes like Critical Race Theory, Neoliberalism in Education, and Understanding Paulo Freire. These courses fed my intellectually starved mind.

Although I was intellectually engaged, personally I was in turmoil over my ongoing struggle to find my three daughters a *good* school. I had transferred my daughters four times to four different schools in five years. Every transfer strengthened my resolve to find the right fit—the ever-elusive *good* school. Through this iterative process, I realized that a *good* school for me is a space that is academically sound, grounded in a social justice philosophy, and welcoming to my children's Black *and* Muslim self, in practice and policy.

AN UNEXPECTED TURN

I started talking to other African-American-Muslim parents, asking them questions that were close to my heart. I asked about the schools they had selected, why they had selected them, and their experiences in them. I needed some insight, advice, and a sense of solidarity. Countless African-American-Muslim parents shared with me their struggles, triumphs, and tidbits about how they "worked the system." I recycled their stories to replenish others as they had replenished me in self-therapeutic reciprocal relationships. Unintentionally, I found personal and intellectual fulfillment in a dual space where my skills and knowledge as a researcher were working in concert with my identity in, and service to, the African-American-Muslim community.

My *official* research avoided religious identifiers and focused on racial inequalities. This research fit neatly into the normed socializing forces of my doctoral program. I found comfort and ease in discussing race in academia, while I felt anxious, even fearful, about discussing a religiously focused research agenda. My fear was fed by the socialization processes in academia predicated on the historical view in the social sciences that the observer has the potential to taint or contaminate research and therefore should be neutralized or controlled. Behar (1996) describes this phenomenon, contending that we as researchers usually "ask for revelations from others, but we reveal little to nothing of ourselves; we make others vulnerable while we remain invulnerable" (p. 273). Being Black and conducting research on Blacks was in essence my way of revealing little about myself. However, adding the hyphen and conducting research on African-American-Muslims left me vulnerable. So, in a fearful, bifurcated manner, I pushed against my intuitive nature. I successfully kept my two worlds separated for almost a year.

During this year, my critical perspective sharpened. My socialization in academia required me to learn about research design, qualitative data collection, and historical foundations of education. However, beyond the required, I began asking who is being legitimated or disqualified by the course offerings and selected readings and whether my scholarship will perpetuate or dismantle this phenomenon. The work of asking, sorting out, and answering these questions is the process of becoming critical (Cannella & Lincoln, 2009). I was being socialized in a doctoral program highly regarded for its critical perspectives on racial inequalities and its discussions of marginalized populations. Yet Muslims post-9/11 were never part of our dialogue. This part of my identity was not legitimated in this space.

Because I intimately understood and sympathized with the educational encounters and experiences of my African-American-Muslim daughters, I began questioning my path to and reason for becoming a PhD. This process of becoming critical, or asking piercing questions both of myself and to others, was a bit out of my comfort zone. Please don't forget, I am the one who met and married my husband in two weeks and joined the military without asking anything but "When does my plane leave?"

Exhausted with my bifurcated life, I joined my two worlds. I found the collective will of my being—my spirit, my hyphenated identities and my intellect—deafening and undeniable. I read everything I could get my hands on about Muslims and education. Although this literature is scarce, its mere existence assured me that I was not alone. My personally relevant research and my official research did not have to be maintained in silos. Others were doing this type of work. This research satisfied my spirit and intellect and was liberating, self-affirming, and empowering. I met with a trusted faculty member for advice. She had been a valued source of encouragement, support, and a willing critical ear and therefore was the only person I could bring myself to be vulnerable and exposed to. Nevertheless, she also represented the academy and all the judgment I feared. I approached her hesitantly but was unwavering in my stance. With my fist clenched so tight that the imprints of my nails were left once I released it, I pithily declared, "I'm going to change my research topic. I have to do what fulfills me. I'm going to look at school choice for African-American Muslims." These words whisked from my mouth and immediately crowded the room with a sense of discomfort and query. I heard myself saying these words. I realized that I had wrapped them in a cloth of fear and relegated them to the recesses of my mind and heart. I needed to hear these words. I needed to claim a true scholarly identity—and I did. A sense of peace overcame me. Her reply was inconsequential and muted by my internal jubilation. The courage to simply offer these words put me on a new path—a clear straight path.

We spent the next two hours discussing my new research agenda, my new scholarly identity, and of course what school my daughters were attending. This faculty member later became my academic advisor and dissertation chair. She understood, as Smith (1999) argues, that research is a way of "talking back" and is a form of "recovery of ourselves . . . and a struggle for self determination" (p. 7). I forged ahead with my research, appreciative of this journey. It has led (or I might even say pushed) me to a coterminous space with my identity as an African-American-Muslim and my scholarly endeavors concerning the African-American-Muslim experience. Still situated in the social justice framework in which I began my studies, I had truly begun to embrace the three R's of social justice as described by Ayers, Quinn, and Stovall (2009) of "Relevant, Rigorous and Revolutionary" (p. xiv).

My history and membership in the African-American Muslim community has and will continue to affect how I understand and experience the world. I align myself with a body of literature that contends that membership in the group you are researching is valuable and worthy (Brannick & Coghlan, 2001). I am now able to *work the hyphens* in my identity. I understand social research as both a process and a product (Wolcott, 1990). I entered into my research topic in a rather maladroit manner. However, discovering that I was not alone in seeking personally relevant research has helped me *carve out* a space of belonging in my journey to obtaining a PhD. As an African-American-Muslim woman, I contend that this *carving out* was a distinct contributor to my successful completion.

Genise's Story—Resurgence of the Spirit: A Scholar's Journey

There is a popular Christian song that is sung to describe the light of God that shines within people. The song begins with the chorus repeating "This little light of mine/I'm going to let it shine" and then continues to describe all of the places where the light will shine. As a child, I loved this song, as I truly felt that there was a light that shone within me. I imagined this light gleaming from inside me and lighting a path toward a future filled with purpose. My imagination as a child led to an adult understanding of what I now describe as a calling—a calling to purposeful living and being of service to the world. This calling led me to the field of education as a teacher and educational leader. Seeking greater fulfillment toward purposeful living, I determined that there was untapped potential within the public educational system that could provide better opportunities for students, teachers, and other stakeholders within the system. In 2007, I enrolled in a doctoral program, eagerly prepared to engage more deeply in the process of learning, unlike prior experiences of formal learning. I wanted to unlearn the behaviors that previous years of formal schooling had taught me, which I found to be an acceptance of knowledge as it was presented and disengagement of self in the process of learning. Rather, I wanted to embrace "a paradigm surrounding research and teaching that is consciously engaged toward freedom of body, mind, and spirit of all involved" (Dillard, 2006, pp. 68–69). However, I soon found myself lost within the fold of the academy, struggling to maintain my desire to engage more deeply as a learner while dealing with expectations that seemed to be fundamentally different from what I imagined coming into the doctoral program. I began changing the way I thought about myself as a whole person. I changed my habits of eating, thinking, and being. These changes led to a shedding of thirty pounds and a focus on physical and emotional health and well-being. I held myself accountable to goals beyond the educational and professional. I believed that taking care of self in the process of thinking about the university's goals that speak to the need of creating socially just environments of learning for all students regardless of race, gender, or class required this change.

While the goals of the university are aligned with my goals as an educator-practitioner, I recognized a need for personal relevancy within the curriculum that extends the work beyond both the university setting and basic cognitive reasoning. Despite the well-intentioned effort on behalf of professors, who seem to desire purposeful and relevant learning for all students, theoretical instruction is often privileged in universities (Caboni & Proper, 2009). Overwhelmingly western European philosophies infiltrate the curriculum, discourse, and programming, creating a challenge toward deepening the levels of engagement. It is also considerably challenging that many students enroll in the doctoral program solely for the purpose of obtaining a PhD to increase job opportunities, with little consideration toward personal growth and self-development as an educational leader.

During my first few years in the doctoral program, I harbored feelings of discontent due to the superficial depth of classroom discourse. Many students were either not prepared or disinterested in the deeper levels of engagement that I sought. Although the cohort of students who entered the program with me were touted as the most diverse cohort the doctoral program had seen, it did not change the fact that the culture and curriculum remained largely unchanged and that the majority of students were still White and middle class. For the most part, higher education continues to be a male-dominated institution that reflects the experiences and culture of older White men (Gardner, 2008). I am recognizably the minority—a Black female with a desire to move beyond the traditional norms of formal schooling. While the traditional norms reflect classroom hierarchies, limited faculty of color, and a sole focus on cognitive that excluded social and emotional development (Ayers, Wheeler, Fracasso, Galupo, Rabin, & Slater, 1999; Turner, Gonzalez, & Wood, 2008), my grounded sense of self begged an alternative academic experience. Solorzano, Ceja, and Yosso (2000) "assert that a positive collegiate racial climate can facilitate and lead to important, positive academic outcomes for African-American students" (p. 63). Unfortunately, during the first class meeting, one of the two White professors announced that the admission standards had been lowered to admit such a diverse cohort of students. This announcement created a racial climate that invited a number of other racial micro-aggressions that followed.

One particular classroom discussion led to a White male student pointing a finger at the few Black students around the room, saying, "I'm tired of trying to figure out what to call you all. Can we just go around the room and you tell us what we should call you?" In addition to these subtle and sometimes not-so-subtle insults, or racial micro-aggressions, class after class offered theoretical literature from a predominately White male perspective and subsequent classroom discourse that focused on Eurocentric values. I began feeling more and more out of place in this terrain, where I was notably recognized as "the other" symbolized by Collins (1991/2002) as "the oppositional difference of mind/body and culture/nature" distinguished from everyone else (p. 72). For me, the doctoral program, like our P-20 public educational system, has the potential to move beyond what the curriculum currently offers and to reach for more than three letters. My doctoral education is a calling of the human spirit. I purposefully pursue this endeavor in order to make an impact within the educational system, which I believe has the potential to better serve me and others like me.

My immense feelings of displacement surfaced on a particular evening when our class watched the film *Savage Inequalities*. This film exposed the ugly truth that many of our schools are faced with students who struggle to learn by rote from behind barbed-wired fences and teachers who stand lifelessly behind walled-off spaces. They are both physically and mentally removed from the daily community activities outside that space. All the while, seemingly helpless, parents struggle to attain more for their children amid an often unwelcoming school environment. These images pierced my heart as I thought about my journey through the doctoral program in educational leadership. I understood the film to represent the removal of humanness within educational institutions. The scenes presented in the film were all too familiar. They mirrored my own educational journey in many ways. As I watched, my educational life experience seemed to flash before me.

That evening, I saw myself in the leading roles of student, teacher, parent, and educational leader. When the film came to an end, I raced from the room toward the elevator. I was nearly gasping for air as I tried to make sense of the experience. I caught my breath as I entered the elevator. My professor entered behind me and stood beside me. As my face warmed, my eyes welled and I burst into tears. She turned to me, placed her hand on my shoulder, and asked, "Are you okay?" I searched blindly for words to describe how I had felt during and after the film. At that moment, it was though I could only explain it as a spiritual surge, or a resurgence of my spirit, which caused me to experience something beyond the normal limits of body and mind, connecting to aspects of the external world that I value, to others and to a higher being (Mackeracher, 2004). The film allowed me to recognize that throughout much of my educational journey, like the individuals in the film, my spirit had been missing. My spirit is culturally situated and permeated with a desire for myself and for others to be free from oppression (Stewart, 1999). Surmounting emotions encircled me that evening in class and called me towards the release of my full human potential through an engagement of my spirit. As Dillard (2006) suggests "Engaging one's spirit . . . is key to the creation and transformation of one's inner and outer life." (p.42). Engagement allows us to connect relationally with others. An engagement of the human spirit takes us a step further, allowing us to connect with others as we grapple with our own intentions in our interactions while addressing today's social challenges (Dillard, 2006). Similar to that little light shining within me, begging to show the way, my spirit begged to be released within this environment. While I recognize the presence of my spirit in my personal life, I have not fully allowed it to emerge within the academic environment, as I felt it unwelcomed. Even though my spirit drew me toward a career in education and towards the pursuit of a doctoral degree, I was not allowing it to influence how I engaged as a scholar. Similar to the little light within, a metaphor representative of my spirit, I did not allow my spirit to shine.

Later, hearkening the call of my spirit, I understood that I would be remiss if I did not fully engage the human spirit in the process of my scholarly educational journey. This became my mission as my response to conversations and assignments surrounding my academic pursuit began to change. Desiring more from the curriculum and classroom, I gained the courage to question and seek more. For example, when given a list of several White males and asked to choose the "expert" on whom I would base a presentation, I approached my professor and asked for another list—one that contained *experts* who were women of color. Scrambling for words, the professor left the room only to return with one name. This experience, collectively with other experiences along the doctoral journey, raised my consciousness toward the need to seek beyond the curriculum, question beyond the system, and courageously add the hyphen of critical as I continue the journey as a Black-female-scholar. Thus, I have approached writing my dissertation by considering the ways that I would represent this newfound courage more critically and expressively in my scholarly work in order to engage the fullness of myself in the process. Embracing the hyphenated identity, as a critical-Black-female-scholar, I consider and imagine the possibilities inherent within all that I do. I also recognize this consideration and imagining as a process, not an immediate singular step.

The emotional distress and feelings of misplacement that I experienced at the beginning of the doctoral program and during the evening of class when I witnessed the film turned into what Sanders (2009) calls soul unrest, "a general malaise (depression) that infiltrates all areas of life" (p. 18). I began the inward search for answers about my journey in education while pondering my potential to do the work that my spirit called me to do within the academy. I exercised my mind and body, seeking solace in the belief that a focus on my spirit was exactly the reinvigorating and sustaining force that I needed within the academy. These reflections and experiences led to a "life change" moment characterized by the altering of my normal routine and a change in my perceptions (Muller & Dennis, 2007). These reflective decisions about the direction of my work were encouraged and motivated by people outside of my academic program, my family, friends, and professors—all of whom believed and imagined greater possibilities in our educational system. These sources of motivation took root in my life and served as the fuel I needed to bring all of myself into my doctoral journey, regardless of the curriculum or other dissuading forces. The shift in my thinking allows me to recognize the potential in exploring the spiritual dimensions of education by refocusing my attention inwardly and contextually toward understanding the contribution of spirituality in the preparation of educational leaders like myself. As I move forward educationally, I must invite wholeness of self and an engagement of the human spirit in my work without settling for anything less. I am determined that my work will represent the metaphor Dillard (2006) puts forth as the way our research should be seen, which is that of a responsibility.

Research speaks to the significant role that spirituality plays in Black women's lives (Wheeler, Ampadu, & Wangari, 2002; Dantley, 2003; Mattis, 2000). Although there tends to be guardedness within the academy toward issues of spirituality (Becker, 2009), focusing on my spirituality provides me with the sustaining force that I need within the academy. As a critical-Black-female-scholar, I am met with oppression at the intersection of race, class, and gender (Collins, 1998; hooks, 2005). Such oppressive experiences are often explored in the context of higher education (Collins, 1998; Cozart, 2010; Dillard, 2006). Although the notion of the strong Black woman has been critiqued (Beauboeuf-Lafontant, 2009), there is a documented history of Black women drawing on our spirituality for strength in many of the hardships we face. Thus, I embrace my hyphenated identity and my calling to move forward with courage. I act responsibility by engaging deeply by incorporating spirituality in my scholarly work.

Crystal's Story—Beginnings of Home/Work: An Intimate Methodology

Three years ago, when my then 15-year-old brother, Chris, began flirting with the idea of dropping out of school, I was finishing a pilot study of student discipline policies in one of Chicago's public high schools. I spent most of my days immersed in recent research on the ways in which "common sense" discourses, school practices, and educational policies work in concert to facilitate the movement of poor youth and youth of color from schools to alternative educational placements, the streets, and ultimately prisons. Because I desperately wanted Chris to stay and do well in school,

I began to draw on these literatures and perspectives for insight into his lived world. I revisited each scholarly piece to search for explanations of his past social and academic experiences, prophecies about what laid ahead for him, and indications of what I could do in that moment to change the educational course of his life. I looked at programs that could assist him, talked to people, and read more material. In November 2007, I practically moved back into my parents' home to be near my teenage brother in the midst of his decision-making process as it unfolded. Almost intuitively, the researcher in me began documenting much of what occurred in my family home: talking with my kin casually and sometimes more formally about how they made sense of my brother's social and academic lives and retrieving and analyzing many of his personal artifacts to contextualize what I observed and heard.

In the meantime, our parents sought professional support—from psychologists, medical doctors, social workers, and teachers—to help Chris and themselves. I ran across and eventually recommended to my mother Helen Featherstone's A Difference in the Family: Life with a Disabled Child (1980), a book about families who love, live with, and share the impact of a child's "difference." In this text, Featherstone describes some of the advantages and limitations that such professionals generally bring to the tasks of advising parents and describing their experiences. As for the strengths, she writes,

> many of these professionals have received some training in thinking about feelings and human behavior and in evaluating evidence; most have also worked extensively with parents and children and thus may have learned to see common themes and to set individual responses in some larger perspective. . . . [On the other hand,] a professional sees each family from a certain distance, and his or her understanding is in some sense theoretical; lacking an insider's view, neutral credentialed parties watch, listen, and make inferences, focusing so intensively on parents' vulnerability that they [may] miss their strengths [or worse, blame parents for all family problems]. (Featherstone, 1980, p. 7)

While, as far as I know, my parents never felt compelled to admit culpability under the care of their professional advisors, Mom and Dad inevitably pointed their fingers inward. They held themselves accountable for Chris's problems because they led busy working lives. They mined their memories for inconsistencies and delays in applying discipline, for relying on different and sometimes competing approaches to child rearing, for providing Chris with what he wanted as much as what he needed, and for failing or being unable to respond to their son's complaints about uncomfortable experiences in school. Then, all of a sudden, they would move from self-reproach to blaming Chris, and the burden of responsibility would shift to his shoulders. His flunking grades were blamed on attributes such as his presumed laziness, "bad" attitude, spoiled identity, active nature, and the naughtiness of his gender. His impatience with teachers was associated with his attention deficit hyperactivity disorder. His growing disciplinary record was connected to his dire need to fit in at all costs with kids of his own age who came from backgrounds vastly different from the comfortable, middle-class suburban lifestyle that he was afforded. At times my sister and I were caught in the middle and at others along the periphery, and somewhere in the midst of all this was Chris. The tension at home was so thick that I could taste it.

Against this backdrop, in January and March 2008 we endured the loss of both maternal grandparents and a close cousin. These sudden tragedies seemed to amplify the frequency and intensity of Chris's academic and behavior troubles at home, at school, in our surrounding community, and with the law. By now, these problems had lingered unabated for nearly six years. To cope with the grief of our kinfolk's deaths and to track the issues raised during my recurrent visits, I kept a journal and catalogued the details of critical incidents, the settings in which they took place, the conversations that occurred within and/or about them, and my own reflections on it all. With no histories of usage to ground academic work so close to home, it took me nearly one year "in the field" to begin publicly articulating the questions that I developed about my little brother's life pathway and, with their permission, to frame certain aspects of my family members' personal lives as researchable educational problems.

Unfortunately, my intervention proved to be too little and too late. As a final prerequisite for enrollment in the U.S. Department of Labor's Job Corps, his educational alternative of choice, Chris withdrew from high school altogether in October 2008. He was sixteen.

While most researchers appear to select their research projects—melding personal interests and skills to select a particular topic of research, which, in turn, appears to guide the research methods employed in its service (Stacey, 1991)—I began with the end in mind. I knew that I wanted to study the school-leaving experiences of Black middle class youth because I needed to work with, learn more about, and create useful knowledge for my own immediate family. Born in the heat of a furnace and thrust into action on the basis of urgency and conviction rather than cosseted reflection on research question and design, my intimate scholarly endeavor *chose me*.

The most obvious reason for calling my methodological approach "intimate" is that it reveals my positionality—who I am in connection with the people under study—and the nature of our affiliation. In a brief and concise way, it emphasizes, as dictionary definitions of the term do, a familiar and significant relationship that would exist even if the research did not. In another sense, this term announces the way that I see the world and how I believe that we come to know others and ourselves within it. Nobody schooled in autoethnography will be amazed to learn that I think people, especially young people, are active thinkers, movers, and shakers of the world. Further, each of us has the capacity to make sense of our experiences and to claim expertise in our own lives. "Intimate" inquiry is grounded in the idea that the fastest way to the get to the "truth"—that is, the reality that a person constructs—is to delve close to the source of the quandary. It entails asking the simplest questions and paying scrupulous attention while the individual describes what he or she is up to—and in light of the person's social surroundings, interpreting (to the best of our ability) what these descriptions tell us. At the same time, "intimate" refers to the personal and emotional aspects of life on the "inside." Not to be confused with the distant and voyeuristic cliché about "self as instrument" of research, here "intimate" signifies the concern, passion, and individual will that drive critical, engaged, and political work.

Academics have a hard time talking about the place of intimacy in educational studies, and the lack of a working definition for its meaning only partly explains our difficulty. The more substantial barrier is our tendency to think about "research" not as a careful exploration of specific social, intellectual, or methodological problems that bear on the lives of real people, but as the product of observable and replicable processes, of "objective" science. Love, many would argue, has nothing to do with this.

Case in point: In my third year of graduate school, as I was nearing doctoral candidacy, I enrolled in a research design seminar led by a senior scholar at a large university in the Midwest to facilitate the trudge toward a rough draft of my dissertation proposal. We began one particular class meeting by soliciting feedback on oral sketches of each student's project. These exchanges often focused on underscoring the significance of research questions or clarifying justifications of methodological choices. When it was my turn to describe the study of school-leaving experiences that I had crafted around my own family members' everyday lives, I read key passages of my problem statement and summarized other important elements of the study's design. Following what I perceived to be an awkward moment of reflective silence, my professor asked, "How will this project move beyond navel-gazing? I mean," he went on, "no one will base policy decisions on your brother."

I had some anxiety concerning my colleagues' and professors' reaction to my naming my little brother as the subject of a dissertation project about high school dropouts among the Black middle class. I expected cautionary tales about the personal and professional costs of vulnerability in academic scholarship, advice on navigating the complexities of ethics and intimacy in fieldwork, and passing references to the ongoing debate about validity in qualitative research. In retrospect, I too wondered about some of the problems that maneuvering the lines between each of my identities might pose, especially at such an early juncture in my academic career. My worries at the time, though, focused squarely on how to move back and forth between a provocative familial story and its broader contexts—in my writing and lived experiences—not on the suitability of my methods, the worth of my study, or the legitimacy of my status as a researcher.

Emergent, yes, but my research design lacked neither historical nor structural perspective. Of course, my family stood to benefit most from our work together. By mapping the ebb and flow of our emotions while we discovered more about what was going on with Chris (and us), we could have immediately approached transformation in ways that created healthier and happier spaces to learn and dwell. However, rendering my brother visible, documenting his marginality, and transforming his story into accessible texts (Gluck, 1991) served to fulfill a purpose beyond my family: to directly shape how he and other Black youth are perceived and treated in societal and intellectual contexts.

Still, as firmly as I believe in the significance of my work, I second-guessed my judgment and went back to the drawing board to devise two variations of the original research design because of my fear that my teacher's prediction that my project would bear strange fruit. Each of the three versions of my dissertation was rooted in an intimate perspective, and each raised questions about the necessity of new methodological and academic interventions in real lives and grappled with the politics of "personal" work within the academy. What differentiated the studies were the methods and ethics that I attended to, the kinds of dilemmas and possibilities that each version implied, and the progression with which I repositioned my brother at the forefront. Together, they raised concerns about the constructed nature of authenticity and point to normalizing assumptions of legitimate research that some scholars are forced to negotiate.

Most scholars are taught to confine their research to the norms of academic protocol and to maintain separation of academic knowledge from the actual people whose lives bolster our professional livelihood (Luke & Gore, 1992). While my doctoral training was no exception, it was not until a senior professor called me out on attempts to connect prior research, abstract theories, and perspectives to a single youth's real-world experiences that I felt the pressure of these standards. In the course of (re)framing my dissertation to accommodate such norms, I not only became fully cognizant of the professional costs of breaking the rules, but also attended more to the intellectual and spiritual integrity of our texts. My brother's experiences and the process of coming to know his story makes us smarter about the lives of the young people we claim to be educating. However, their alarming rates of school leaving and risk of being consumed by an ever-present prison industrial complex prove otherwise. When I reflect on the purposes of my place in—and the audience for—my work, I only regret that I did not begin sooner, not that I used my time and resources first to try to help my own.

Conclusion

This chapter highlights our experiences as three Black females seeking the PhD and exposes our struggles with the socialization processes in academia. The kind of work in which we are engaged, highlighted in our stories, is by necessity messy, moving, publicly affirming, personally empowering, humanizing, and unabashedly interventionist, precisely because it is governed by a different set of values. Aligned with endarkened feminist understandings, we work under the assumption that the process and product of our scholarship have real consequences for the lives of three-dimensional human beings (the researcher included), not for imagined "others" somewhere out there.

Even though we were drawn to careers in education and toward the pursuit of a doctoral degree as spiritual, raced, and familial beings, we each realized that, feeling it was despised, we had not allowed full expressions of self in our research. The socialization process in relation to the educational setting, or the curriculum and classes within our doctoral programs, at the two universities represented in our autoethnographies in many ways seemed to fit the traditional mold of higher learning that succumbs to Western ways of thinking. Having experienced many of the traditional models of formal schooling based on a Western perspective, at different points we were ready for something more from a doctoral program of study and from ourselves. However, we recognize that the power structure of the institution perpetuated this mold. In order for us to choose the path less traveled while articulating what we deemed as "success" for ourselves while aiming to complete our respective programs of study, it was necessary that we conjure up the courage needed to question self, the literature, the curriculum, the focus of our work, and the academy writ large.

Fleming's (1984) research suggests that African-American women, including those at the doctoral level, are generally the most isolated group of students at predominantly White institutions of higher learning. We argue for a rearticulation of the socialization processes in institutions of higher education that result in feelings of isolation and startling low numbers of Black female PhDs. Our socialization process in academia leaned on the interconnected nature of our hyphenated identities as part of a tool kit to pull from in negotiating the world of academicians (Becker, 1990). We accessed these multiple identities to provide a resolution to the problem of determining whether we were *this* (scholars and PhD worthy) or *that* (Muslim, spiritual, familial beings), replacing it with *both*—in our working of the hyphen (Hamann & England, 2011). Connecting our scholarly endeavors with our identity work allowed us to avoid the feeling of isolation that may cause some Black women to abandon their journey to becoming PhDs. As Hamann & England (2011) unapologetically argue,

> sometimes the work of a newcomer in relation to the larger host society can be accomplished within the existing semiotic schemas and other times the most compelling action available to an individual can be to contest the classificatory schema to which they are subject. (p. 209)

We contend that our successful journeys toward becoming PhDs required us to engage in research that embraces our histories and our identities. We are convinced that this type of engagement, and counter-socialization, is a necessity to increase the number of Black women who earn doctorates. As Boykin (1985, 1994) asserts, the multiple dimensions of African-American culture suggest a need for expanded research frameworks that fully capture the wide range of African-Americans experiences. When spaces in academia squelch this need, PhD hopefuls either resist or find a space where such expanded frameworks are welcomed. We stand in solidarity with those who resist.

CHAPTER TWELVE

We're All Half-Breeds Now . . .
in a Not so Ivory Tower

·•———·•·

MIGUEL DE OLIVER

"I am not a [Fill in the blank]."

I have never heard this statement aloud. But I have seen it. I have increasingly seen it in the form of a quiet enunciation in the faces of the professoriate of the academy during unguarded moments.

Pierre Bourdieu (1986) described cultural capital as the codes, signs, and affectations associated with an elite subset of a larger society that facilitates the negotiation of power and confers status.[1] Prominent among the components of cultural capital is education. To be sure, a good measure of the prestige of the academy stems from its central role as the agent of the Enlightenment ideal of progress and moral development through the individual's application of reason. But, however less acknowledged, a good measure of the prestige of the academy stems from its historical association with the elite stratum of society. As opposed to the daily toil of less wealthy classes, privilege distanced the elite from the toil of daily survival, allowing for the sponsorship, practice, and development of abstract cultural forms and scientific endeavors for their own sake. Even though the vast membership of the academy is not presently part of the upper crust, there is a substantial measure of prestige enjoyed by the professoriate in light of its facility and identification with cultural capital that is not generally available to co-citizens of equivalent income (see Apple, 1989; Bourdieu, 1984, 1988). But the current trajectory of the academy is premised on a "currency change," where cultural capital that was once valued is increasingly voided. The slow transformation of the academic workplace by commercial culture is at the core of this process. It is psychic resistance to the informal redefining of the

225

institutional scholar in contemporary society that elicits the intuitive rebuke "I am not a [Fill in the blank]." There is an ironic but valuable perspective that I find myself in possession of with respect to this resistance—perspective that was instrumental in my becoming a member of the academy.

Just prior to the completion of this chapter, I was driving on Interstate 10 in an open-topped old red jeep. I was just east of El Paso, Texas, cruising at the vehicle's paltry maximum speed of 65 miles per hour. Among the political theatrics of the day was heightened rhetoric concerning illegal aliens of Latin American origin—especially those whose motivations were presumed to exceed the acquisition of menial employment. Texas state troopers overtook me and signaled me to the side of the freeway. Polite and compliant as a rule, I stopped and was ordered to step out of the vehicle. And before the inquisitive gaze of mainstream America zipping by in their vehicles, I was directed to keep my hands out of my pockets. I began what outwardly appeared to be an easygoing conversation with one trooper as the other checked out my credentials in his cruiser.

"Yeah," I said. "That's my name. Its origins are a mystery to me. Look, if a valid license isn't working for you and you want to match name to face another way, my job—being what it is—you can call the university or . . . probably . . . get a photo of some sort on the web. Easily done."

Gesturing with his hand to my disheveled hair and general untidiness, the trooper asked, "So. . . . is this your . . . style . . . or something?"

He seemed to consider his inquiry to be founded on some implicit propriety.

"Style? It's not a style but rather a convenience."

The statement was not meant to be cryptic, but it was perceived as such. Silence prevailed as I peered downward into the stock dark sunglasses and wide-brimmed hat of the short trooper.

"I don't understand you," he stated.

The rubbernecking scrutiny of Middle America driving by, separated by glass, comforted by air conditioning, and spontaneously treated to the theatrical exercise of institutional power was unnerving, but the experience was not novel.

Smiling affably, I responded: "Considerations of coiffure while traveling in an open air jeep are sheer folly, officer. The wind imposes its own couture."

Another silence emerged—as I meant there to be.

"Why don't you cut your hair?" he said.

"Why foreshorten what breaks quite readily?"

And so it would be. Being second nature to my profession, minutes later as I drove away I could not help but cite Bourdieu's notion of "cultural capital." For I had long realized that the only means of preserving some measure of dignity when accosted by the armed minions of institutional ignorance is the modest pleasure to be had by inducing a congenial confusion. Being so close to the border, the imperatives of this space exceeded the readily deducible and had imposed a new actionable identity.

I am not a *foreigner*.

Years earlier, in an underprivileged neighborhood in San Antonio, the imposition of space on identification had taken an interesting turn when I received a ticket for a seat belt violation. The policeman's classification was wholly based on my spatial location. The area was overwhelmingly Latino dominant.

I am not a foreigner.

I am not a *Latino*.

In this particular instance, the peremptory presumption affirmed by space was distilled through an institution, the US Census Bureau, which at that time classified Latinos as a subset of the "White" category. In the box designated for the recipient's race, the policeman had written "White."

I am not a foreigner.

I am not a Latino.

I am not a *"White."*

The use of spatial location to ascribe identity is usually not so vague— and often not so problematic. For example, while passing through the Navajo reservation, like so many other travelers, I stopped for refreshment at a roadside stand. When a charter bus pulled up full of Japanese tourists, I was soon asked in broken English by a pair of intrepid women if I minded stepping back close to a nearby automobile with Colorado license plates so that some photographs might be taken. Given the difficulty in communicating the numerous errors of their presumptions, I smiled and complied; for the effort required to clarify my identity far exceeded the necessity to do so. Soon a crowd of Japanese tourists were snapping away, memorializing their trip to this space. As for me, I had been impressed with a new identity.

I am not a foreigner.

I am not a Latino.

I am not a "White."

I am not *Navajo*.

Introduction to Limbo 101

A metanarrative is an informal "story" believed by a group, which contextualizes the group's history and purpose.[2] A metanarrative need not be coherent, logical, or reflect reality, for these are not central to its function. Its function is to totalize all knowledge and experience into a singular framework of "truth" and thereby provide an ideational nucleus around which some are able to secure "legitimate" privilege. Prime examples of grand metanarratives include "Manifest Destiny" of the United States, the Christian notion of a fall from grace and immortality through redemption, or Marxist interpretation of history as the ongoing struggle between capital and labor. These constructions provide foundations for informal popular agendas that were/are central to the forging of group identities. The lack of any specific set of behaviors associated with such broad narratives of development ultimately legitimizes an extensive array of partisan practices that enhance one group's privilege over others. The simultaneously oppressive and privileging presumptions of metanarratives have been central to my experience in a variety of spaces that have conferred variable identities on me.

The most relevant singular description of my "racial" and/or ethnic affiliation is "non-White"—any other singular category being a distinctive misfit. The term "non-White" is befitting as opposed to a carnival of co-equal identities shaped by environmental contexts. For the variety of presumptions made concerning my race/ethnicity differ only in their branding. These presumptions wholly conform to the nature-culture hierarchy articulated by Carolyn Merchant (1980) with respect to minorities and women. Within the metanarratives of race in Western society, non-Whites have been stigmatized, characterized, and stationed within the social hierarchy based on their perceived degree of culture (alienation from nature). Non-White racial groups, constructed as nonindustrious, emotional, with an emphasis on their physical traits, were thought to be closer to nature (underdeveloped), while White racial groups, constructed as objective, rational, and industrious, were thought to transcend nature (developed). Historical stereotypes of racial groups directly reflect this nature-culture hierarchy (see Balibar, 1990; Banton, 1987, pp. 1–27). Whatever specific race or ethnicity, the mainstream almost always constructs me as decidedly "non-White." Thus, "non-White" comprises the pejorative end of a multicultural spectrum with which I am most familiar. Yet the group identity of "non-White," just like the group identity of "minority," does not generate an intimate community; for it implies no implicit group reciprocation, affirmation, or tribal integration from which a truly personal sense of identity might be forged. Accordingly, a "non-White" identity does not afford one the subordinate form of cultural capital described by Hall (1992) and Lamont and Lareau (1988)—that being the representational signs of identity (i.e., artistic, linguistic, stylistic) as part of an out-group required for affirmation among specific minority populations. Thus, when among any particular racial or ethnic minority group, my racially ambiguous appearance coupled with my lack of subordinate cultural capital seems to generate the same presumption of "otherness" from minorities that I've experienced from the mainstream. For the racially ambiguous, such as me, space, therefore, becomes key to presumptions of identity. It is quite ironic that these conceptions of spatially contingent identity and placelessness were given conventional shape when they passed through the "intellectual space" of 20th-century existentialism. For me, Martin Heidegger's (2008) contention that "inauthenticity" is our native state was more than the philosophical rationale for persistent feelings of alienation. Heidegger's contention that the human condition was a perpetual act of "coming into being" was my lived reality, largely induced by geography. Having an acute consciousness of the patchwork of identity-ascribing spaces through which one could be transformed was a comforting affirmation of Jean-Paul Sartre's contention that "existence precedes essence" (1958, p. 568). A familiarity with being contingent and nebulous is an experience that is proving increasingly relevant to the academic.

My introduction to the university as an identity-ascribing space was neither as student nor professor—yet it would be the scholastic dimension of university space that would prevail. I first encountered it while being a scholarship football player at a Division I-A institution. As a tight end, blocking much larger defensive ends was an unpleasant responsibility. On this particular day, the task was aggravated by the bare earth, which had been stripped of grass by a multitude of cleats over repeated practice sessions. Spring rains converted it into a pan of mud. My failed attempt to dislodge a defensive end provoked a theatrical tirade by the line coach, accented by the traditional array of verbal hysterics that is common to the daily culture of contact sports.

The coach concluded his frantic harangue by furiously thrusting his foot behind him and yelling, "*Dig! Dig! Dig! You muthaf$#%@!!!*"

"It's a morass!" I responded.

"*Whadiya-call-me?!*"

At that very moment vocabulary was not the immediate problem—*explaining* the misunderstanding of terms *would be*. For, in this particular space, doing so would violate the presumptions of comportment that demanded reflexive compliance and an enthusiastic violence undiluted by reason. As I ran stadium steps as a consequence for my insolence, I could not help but feel that the identity of the non-White football player was growing increasingly constraining. The very same traits and affectations that were celebrated in specific places of athletic competition transformed into a source of consternation immediately outside them. But it was only this small portion of the university where the identity of the non-White football player—overwhelmingly coded as "Black"—prevailed.

I am not a foreigner.

I am not a Latino.

I am not a "White."

I am not Navajo.

I am not a "<u>Black athlete</u>."

The remainder of my time at the university as an "athlete-student" was a novel experience for me. For, at its core, the collective university is a humanitarian institution. With its multiple disciplines that span both commercial and abstract humanitarian endeavors, the collective mission of the academy would seem to prioritize the development of the individual. For those with ambiguous ethnicity, this is particularly refreshing. Whether one was student or athlete, being in university space conveyed a prestige unlike the vast patchwork of identity-ascribing spaces that I was familiar with off campus. If space was so transformative, and the ethnographic landscape that harmonized with my multiple ancestries simply did not exist, then academia was perhaps a substitute place that focused instead on my truly defining trait—a consuming curiosity about the world we make for ourselves. And thus the very act of inhabiting university space provided, in effect, momentary access to cultural capital, intriguing in its novelty. Therefore, while an "athlete-student" I resolved to pursue a place in the academy that would sponsor the examination and comprehension of the utility of space in confirming identity and negotiating power.

Years later I received my PhD in geography.

While the larger humanitarian and philosophical dimensions of the academic profession were appealing facets of "university space," for me they were not the primary appeal of the academy. The idea of an interpersonal network (community) free of conventional markers of tribe *was*—in this case, a community of curiosity-"saters" (so to speak) within which the casual rituals and practices that construct "group" might develop. It was an appealing conception. But my entry into academia and its Enlightenment mystique coincided with the full emergence of late capitalist culture sometimes referred to as "postmodernism." And a principal feature of the postmodern era is an "incredulity towards metanarratives" (Lyotard, 1984, p. xxiv), of which the Enlightenment project was a prominent example. Amid an increasingly postmodern culture, scholarly identity affixed in "Enlightenment space" grows progressively obsolete.

Enlightenment, Inc.

As Jacques Derrida (in Group Mu, 1978, pp. 34–35) put it, the postmodern form represents "a signification which could be neither univocal nor stable"—a form that negates the preference of any singular perspective in favor of transient and multiple *I*'s. In spatial terms, the immense geography of racialized spaces—each conceived within some grand narrative of historical propriety—is increasingly obsolete in the postmodern era. The fragmentation of the prevailing architecture of racial and ethnic identities (among others) should be a fortuitous development for someone like me, whose otherness is applicable across the ethno-racial spectrum of identity.

Or so it would seem.

The problematic linkage of large-scale imperatives of international capitalism to noncommercial "community spaces"—and ultimately group identity—is an instructive one. There is a growing body of scholarship with respect to the encroachment of commercial imperatives in the academy (e.g., Fitzsimons, 2002; Giroux, 2002; Levidow, 2002). The Enlightenment ideals of academia are among numerous organizational principles of progress that have recently been replaced (e.g., "Melting Pot" by multiculturalism, urbanism by suburbanism, nuclear family by single-parent family, nationalism by supranationalism, apartheid by multiracialism, work ethic by investment capitalism) from their hegemonic status as implicit components of advancement. The point of this section is not to review the literature on the material imperatives encroaching on academia but to ensure that my personal experiences that follow are seen as neither excessively exotic nor simply anecdotal by framing them within a systemic context.

The diminishing growth rates at the end of the post-WWII "Golden Era of Capitalism" (1945–70) required new markets to forestall systemic economic stagnation. The response to diminished profitability emphasized the need for new markets and greater leeway (lack of regulation) for private interests (Harvey, 2005). With the markets of the underdeveloped world fully subordinated to neocolonial economics, the most lucrative potential markets were the public sectors of the international state system—principally those of the developed world, which are the most expansive. The expansion of electronic mass media coupled with diminishing transportation costs at this time enabled an expansion of "globalization." The result has been the contemporary era of neoliberal economics. Neoliberal economics defines progress explicitly by material means, which is to be achieved by minimal restrictions on market participants and the shrinking of regulation/intervention in the economy by the territorial governments of the international state system. The curtailment of restrictions that inhibit accumulation is not limited to administrative constraints on capital by state governments or the privatization of the public sector; the removal of constraints to accumulation includes particularizing aesthetics (i.e., the metanarratives of modernity) that inhibit market expansion. The intense scrambling of aesthetical models available to individuals (considered "consumers") challenged the grand narratives of history and the fixed social forms that they fostered with a decidedly commercial ethic of "choice." In effect, the neoliberal period of capitalist development has been a particularly acute phase of industrial evolution where the social bonds of society are increasingly splintered, partitioned, and conveyed "over-the-counter" (Nystrom, 1929, p. 469). "Postmodernism" is the cultural expression of this economic orientation. As a conveyor of "knowledge" and the principal expression of the Enlightenment metanarrative, the university has not been exempt from the infiltration of neoliberalism.

As Jean François Lyotard (1984, pp. 37–47) asserts, the delegitimation of grand narratives in the postmodern period has resulted in an emphasis on the "performativity" of knowledge—that is, knowledge that is no longer the end product of emancipating narratives with humanitarian ends but rather knowledge that is primarily legitimized by its ability to provide "proof" in the form of manifest change. The ethic of "Anything Goes" that produces measurable results "is the realism of money: in the absence of aesthetic criteria it is still possible and useful to measure . . . value . . . by the profits they realize" (Lyotard, 1993, p. 8). While debates about the material instrumentality of the university are long-standing, material instrumentality as a functioning aesthetic in the general experience of the university has reached unprecedented heights. The objective of the remainder of this section is to demonstrate the personal experience of a "community identity" under siege. For it is not the ideological or humanitarian principles of the institution that galvanizes some semblance of personal "community"; it is the broad spectrum of the individual's personal experience of place and others (via gossip, work, courtesy, humor, posture, cooperation, dining, inquiry) where cultural capital resonates and engenders fibers of extrafamilial mutuality. For personal interaction still provides an emotional dimension of affirmation that professional societies and cyber-mediated clubs do not (see Smith & Kollock, 2000, p. 17; Wilbur, 1997). Georg Simmel's (2004, p. 186) assertion is still true: "the interaction between individuals is the starting point of all social formations."

As the remainder of the class slowly drifted to the door, the student pointed to the principal text listed in the syllabus. "Do I need this book for class?"

"Absolutely," I responded.

The question was peculiar but understandable in light of the rapidly increasing prices of textbooks. Students of modest economic means often appreciated my putting the book on reserve in the library. But some asked this question with a $4 cup of coffee in one hand and a touch-screen cell phone in the other. And increasingly disturbing was the fact that the latter occasionally had the economic status of the former.

Another female student who had been standing patiently nearby interjected. "Amazon.com has it used for a fraction of that price."

"That'll work," I said, perturbed about the considerable markup of the campus bookstore. "And for next Wednesday I need you to have read the two articles of mine on some relevant dynamics of local urban renewal that you see in the syllabus."

"And where do we get those?"

"They are on the class Web site."

"And how much do you charge for those?"

I looked away with a broad smile in affirmation of her sarcasm. But her inquisitive expression had not altered when my gaze returned to her.

"On the house, ma'am. *Gratis* . . . free."

"So are they necessary then?"

However vulgar the supposition behind it, the student's inquiry was not without resonance on campus; examples were the attachment of extra-tuition "fees" to an ever lengthening spectrum of university life, the venality of parking policy, the increasing references to the student body as a "market," propositions to "liberate" the tuition structure from a flat rate per student to differential pricing based on discipline, and the specter of "mission differentia-tion"—that being the process whereby academic institutions actively prune programs and promote institutional specialization so as to save operational costs and qualify institutional success by the marketability of the student as "product" (in Bastedo and Gumport, 2003, p. 341).

In my office later that semester, a male student remained standing across the desk from me as I reviewed his scores on my Excel spreadsheet. "You've missed two of three tests so far and you scored a 44% on the test you *have* taken. Can there really be any doubt where this is heading?"

Somewhat perplexed, the student took to searching in his backpack and soon pulled out a printout. He passed it to me with a declarative air.

"What's this?"

"My receipt. Tuition and fees for this semester," he said. "All of it. Fully paid."

I peered momentarily at the student, wondering who exactly he per-ceived me to be. In recent years I had been feeling a new identity being impressed on me—an entirely alien one. Nowhere else did I sense this identity. Only here.

I am not a foreigner.

I am not a Latino.

I am not a "White."

I am not Navajo.

I am not a "Black athlete."

I am not a merchant.

Trying to suppress the pain from a throbbing tooth, I found myself in one of the larger cubicles in the university's Office of Human Resources. I needed to know why my long paid-for dental coverage was no longer in effect.

"I see you are not on Medco premiere.[3] Your program does not include dental," said the administrator.

"Since I had dental coverage last year and have made no changes, you must be in error."

"No. Your plan was switched in June of last year."

"Well, switch it back and I'll be on my way."

"We sent out a general notice to all employees in May stating that we had a new array of health care products in addition to the old and that it was necessary to make your selections known."

"Shift me over to the same 'product' in the new options . . . or keep the same 'product' I have now . . . whatever."

"Can't do that. You've missed the window to make such changes. We switched you to Medco basic."

I peered at the man clasping onto his procedural decree like a proud budgie on a stick. Glancing around the room, I stated, "Sir, you seem to have a fine array of university insignia cheerfully accessorized with an impressive array of slogans here. I commend you. I therefore presume we are both in the same tribe here. But we mustn't forget exactly where we are in 'philosophical space.' What you have just told me is absurd. The only question is if you know it is absurd. Firstly, it is somewhat more than a rumor that the university is on a semester system, and has been since its establishment. That means that much of the professoriate disappears at the beginning of summer either on vacation . . . or to pursue their research agenda . . . or what have you. It is no coincidence that the vast body of students simultaneously vacates. Choosing that chronological point as the window of response to your query from professors for a critical matter like the safeguarding of their health is absurd."

"But there is time before the end of —"

"—of semester? Sir, that is the time that professors are burdened with grading tests, reading papers, and indulging itinerant students on the lip of failure. No worse time exists for what you propose. If we are to presume that this policy of Human Resources is not simply a giddy celebration of ignorance, we must conclude that your policy is consistent with the agenda of some interest external to this university which profits from this configuration of investment of our personnel's contributions."

My tooth was pounding. The pain was eroding my composure. Nevertheless, for a brief moment I felt a rush of misplaced pride. So obscure had my economic footprint been in the world up to this point that there was a reflexive sense of gratification from acknowledging the fact that I now comprised a small part of a large collective body whose combined wealth merited being harvested by prestigious corporate entities. Having no health care coverage, a notable percentage of the country did not receive such recognition.

The sentiment vanished as quickly as it had appeared.

"Secondly, when statistically assessing a population's characteristics or democratically serving a constituency, the best results reflect the manifest input of the constituency as to preferences. Remember, you do not 'govern' the constituency but rather represent its collective health interests. In light of this, it is inappropriate to decree that there will be an automatic change from a constituent's expressed preferences to 'X' if the constituent doesn't speak up on an annual basis. As opposed to changing the preferences of those who request it, changing coverages by default means that you are shifting people to unwanted alternatives. Hoping that your 'guess' is superior to their actual needs is pure folly—especially when you have an equivalent new coverage option that matches the old. And thirdly, why is the specific coverage dropped in the fashion that it was? Surely you understand that someone who receives dialysis but fails to respond to your clarion call is really not asking you by default to pull the plug? And why would there be the presumption by this unit of the university that the coverage that is so commonly utilized by its population—such as dental—be dropped? The absurdity is titanic, especially when considering you are embedded in an educational institution ostensibly committed to dispersing such cretinism wherever it gathers. To be sure, academics are a flawed lot, but they are not your ordinary troupe of simpletons; you cannot intellectually constipate them with that hogwash. This absurdity is consistent with a prioritization of a health care corporation's business plan. Clearly, there are many other people like myself that your 'default' advocacy on our behalf has left stripped naked in the wilderness."

"No. There actually haven't been a lot of complaints."

"For a health product like this, what is the acceptable casualty rate?"

Silence prevailed as a pugnacious discomfort fell over the man's face. I had seen that expression two days prior while buying the office staff's coffee at the campus Starbucks. ". . . and add in two iced lattes, please. One 'decaffed'—the other 'caffed.' Large on the 'decaffed,'" I had said.

"Venti," she stated, waiting for confirmation.

"As large as you have, ma'am."

"That would be a 'venti.'" She stared expectantly.

I pointed to a cup behind her. "Like that, ma'am. Big as you have."

I refused to jump through a linguistic hoop by using the prescribed lingo frivolously conceived by a committee of product marketers to frame this transaction with a stamp of Italian elegance; its very use implied a repugnant servility to absurd pretense. But the cashier seemed insistent that I respond accordingly, as she had during previous visits over the past two months.

She petulantly did not look back to the large cup to which I was pointing.

"The big honkin' cup, ma'am."

"And the caffeinated latte?" she asked.

"Super-size me, please."

As she had on previous occasions, her finger poked the keys with some irritation as she entered the order. Purposefully disregarding the need for my name, she had consigned my prestigious cup of name-brand coffee to anonymity.

Such a spontaneous endorsement of corporate doctrine was an expression of the cultural hegemony articulated by Antonio Gramsci (1971) in the 1930s, which.he saw as a partisan conception of the world that is accepted by diverse groups as "common sense" and thus is not perceived (when perceived at all) as anything but an expression of the natural order of things to which scrutiny is never popularly applied. Berger and Luckmann (1966, p. 89) describe how this popular power is alienated from the consciousness of its producers and is perceived as a discrete feature of objective reality. As if derived from some transcendent ether, this form of cultural power is an unregimented form of authority. The metanarrative is thematic and provides for a chronological construction of what are presumed to be such "natural facts"—and the "natural facts" at present were that commercial aesthetics are historical norms at the center of not only behavioral propriety, but also cultural identity itself. While the commercial institution of the market is comprised of currency to be acquired through transaction, that money need be in the hands of individuals only by happenstance. Yet the popular error is to construe the market itself as a collection of individuals. The market takes on the democratic legitimacy of individual consent and, in so doing, slowly prints a new form of cultural capital for mainstream society.

With respect to my visit to the Office of Human Resources, it was patently clear that failure to give reflexive consent to the peremptory virtue of market culture was what had irritated the administrator. This irritation, when accessorized with a smile, conveyed the notion "Yes . . . *The customer is always right*—but not always correct." To such faces, the Enlightenment principles of academia was no refuge—a posture increasingly affirmed by the very university they worked for, whose new mission statement called for the embracing of "multicultural traditions and [to serve] . . . as a center for intellectual and creative resources as well as a catalyst for socioeconomic development and the **commercialization** [emphasis added] of intellectual property" (UTSA 2012).

Standing up to leave the man's cubicle in Human Resources, I stated, "Look, given that I'm not angling for an extended leave or for y'all to detail my car or something, can you just put things right and set my health coverage up like it was?"

"You will have to comply like all the rest of the—"

"—rest of the *what?*"

As I walked out of the Human Resources building fingering the gum around my tooth, the pain was momentary eclipsed by the realization of a new identity that this specific place had so effectively impressed upon me.

I am not a foreigner.

I am not a Latino.

I am not a "White."

I am not Navajo.

I am not a "Black athlete."

I am not a merchant.

I am not an institutional "wage earner."

"A penny for your thoughts"

"And what 'book-length' projects do you foresee completing in the near future should you join the department?" asked a dapper senior professor of the job candidate.

I had not seen this interview question on the list of questions we had previously agreed to ask. Given the fact that each job candidate must be asked the same interview questions and that all questions were to be preapproved by each member of the committee, a great surge of indignation came over me. But I kept my expression neutral even though this "impromptu" question clearly served particular interests.

It would be improper to portray the encroaching forces on the Enlightenment ideals of the academy as coming entirely from the periphery of the professoriate. Five decades have passed since the full blossoming of neoliberal policies in the developed world—plenty of time for the systemic rewards of vulgar materialism to dress themselves in scholarly vestments. The historical inability to apply effective metrics to abstract Enlightenment ideals was in dire contrast to postmodernity's techniques of quantification—techniques that are increasingly recognized as the only valid indicator of those historic ideals. Market share being the principal confirming agent of success, the result has been the mathematical objective to secure an ever-larger quantity of consumers of university services. As opposed to the instruction of students, who represent an "internal" market to the academy, the emphasis on marketable books by the professoriate is overwhelmingly designed for an "external" market. This means an increasing emphasis on general-appeal books over articles in scholarly journals. In general, popular-appeal books boast a standard of writing that is less dense and necessarily tend to convey less complex ideas. A commitment to addressing a more general audience is a noble and fundamental element of the academic mission—a commitment demonstrated each time the professor steps into

a classroom of undergraduates. But the translation of this ethic to academic "output" is problematic, driving an intellectual and material wedge
within the professoriate. Thus, standards have been altered, whereby, in
various departments, books—regardless of content—often earn a professor
automatic, multiple-year, top-tier rating when merit pay is determined. A
greater mass-market profile means a greater likelihood of ultimately gaining
external grant funding for the institution. In such a circumstance, descrip-
tive research is increasingly recognized, prioritized, and rewarded over theory
and interpretation. Increasingly common in the academy is the production
of books in which the principal idea is articulated in the first third of the
work, leaving the remainder tangential and repetitive. As I stated in a
protest letter with respect to the relative devaluation of scholarly articles,
"With this qualification of academic output, supporters of such conceptions
would roundly dismiss Einstein's three seminal papers in 1905 or those of
Mackinder, Freud, et cetera as irrelevant to their conception of academic
quality and confirmation that the authors should be dismissed as candidates
for our professional interaction."

During the Medieval era of Western Europe, cloistered monks labored
away in obscurity, re-recording script with decorative flourishes.

I am not a foreigner.
I am not a Latino.
I am not a "White."
I am not Navajo.
I am not a "Black athlete."
I am not a merchant.
I am not an institutional "wage earner."
I am not a _scribe_.

～

The imposition of problematic identities within "university space" continues
unabated, making it increasingly difficult to separate "university space" from
"conventional space."

"Who won the Super Bowl last year?" asked the customs official.

It wasn't the first time that I had been plucked from a broad line of
travelers reentering the United States. But now, standing alone in a large
room with extensive tables for a more in-depth examination of luggage,
the imposing force of irrational presumption was particularly evident. The
9/11 attacks and the subsequent wars in Iraq and Afghanistan made the
airport a place where the import of identity—both formally documented
and informally inferred—was a particularly intense space. The particular
official in front of me presumed that ignorance of the annual iconic finale

of the national pastime by a male US citizen might be overlooked by an ill-intentioned impostor.

I shrugged my shoulders, for I had lost touch with this dimension of the culture long ago.

With a routine air as he peered at his computer screen, the official inquired, "Race?"

"What have you got?" I responded, purposively mimicking the line from Marlon Brando's *The Wild One* while being sure to give no hint of sarcasm, anger, or distress.

This particular off-campus episode harmonized with various episodes in previous years that had taken place on campus.

For example, I was visiting the new faculty computing center, which had some data retrieval programs not yet available to office computers. I proceeded to one of the terminals and was quickly approached by a woman wearing a dress with a floral print and a doily around the neck.

"Can I help you?" asked the woman.

"Ahhhhh . . . I don't know. I heard some good things about some of the resources you have here, and, well . . . I was passing by."

"And you are?"

"Ever the inquiring soul, ma'am."

"Well . . . these facilities are restricted for faculty?"

"How thoughtful." I sat down at the machine.

I could feel the woman's dismay as she stood in silence behind me. She relented and sat down at my side.

Gesturing to the screen, I said, "You put the search parameters here?"

"What are you looking for?"

The bombing of the Murrah Federal Building in Oklahoma City had just occurred, and the students had been asking questions. A cursory search on my office computer did not provide reliable data on what had been reported as an unusually strong concentration of Muslims in the city. Additionally, with respect to another research endeavor, I was having trouble finding data on the national distribution of violent incidences at abortion clinic demonstrations.

"I'm not sure," I said. "First, let's try . . . uhhhh . . . 'Oklahoma City' . . . 'Muslims' . . . uhh . . . 'terror.'"

The woman's eyes snapped to mine but stayed there only for a moment before drifting over my features. Rarely had I ever so closely witnessed the intuitive tailoring of my appearance into the theatrical costume that the moment was thought to require.

Visibly discomfited, the woman left to confer with her supervisor.

With respect to the casual experience of the university, this reaction was unusual. University budget cuts and paltry wages stemming from diminished public support had caused the hiring of more and more staff lacking sufficient familiarity with the exploratory character of the university or with its manifest "diversity." The woman undoubtedly thought herself patriotically prudent, but in "university-space," common sense was a poor substitute for reason; it provided an entrée for actionable identities to pour into fresh territory.

Upon returning from a consultation with her superior, the woman resolutely queried, "What department are you with?"

Fatigued and without bothering to look up, I inaudibly mumbled, "What-have-you-got?"

I am not a foreigner.

I am not a Latino.

I am not a "White."

I am not Navajo.

I am not a "Black athlete."

I am not a merchant.

I am not an institutional "wage earner."

I am not a scribe.

I am not of <u>Middle Eastern origin</u>.

I am not a <u>cyber-illiterate bomb maker</u>.

I am not a [<u>Fill in blank</u>].

Back into the wilderness

The incremental consolidation of a materialist aesthetic in the routine functioning of the university is broadly familiar to the professoriate regardless of race, ethnicity, gender, class, lifestyle, or age. But for the vast majority of the professoriate, the subsequent loss of a measure of personal identity stemming from the devaluation of the profession's cultural capital would seem to be largely unfamiliar. Perhaps this is to be expected when considering that what still persists is the disproportionately White coloration of academia, the broad and routine tracing of institutional and humanitarian evolution through Western cultural models, and the consequential disciplinary and informal formation of 'like-experienced' cliques. The casual experience of "academic space" for faculty of majority cultural identification still harmonizes with the cultural capital it has always represented. Thus, for faculty of mainstream ethnic identification, the broad and private declaration of "I am not _____" that is quietly emerging may be unfamiliar psychic territory. For those professors of minority ethnic identification who have proceeded from a strong sense of self that is embedded in a somewhat coherent oppositional identity, the materialist evolution of the academy is also distressing. Various studies have shown higher discontentment among minority faculty oriented to administrative workloads, research marginalization, advancement, and collegiality (e.g., Aguirre, Martinez, & Hernandez, 1993; Martinez, 2011; Olsen, 1991). But embedded within this dissatisfaction is the local conversion of the academic from intellectual to service provider that is a poor substitute for a coherent oppositional identity with interpersonal dimensions. With respect to the dogged advance of fragmented and situational identification for both majority and minority professors, I reluctantly attest, "Been there—'dun' that." The ostensible incongruity of the *I-am-not* negations repeatedly listed in this chapter that freely juxtapose race, occupation, ethnicity, livelihood, and so forth is not happenstance. The conjunction of these negations is not an expression of emancipation from constrictive forms, but rather the standardization of alienation irrespective of whether that identity is odious or altruistic, biological or behavioral, real or imagined. For the individual in general, and the academic in particular, the consolidation of materialist aesthetics compels a strange inversion of René Descartes's (1637, part IV) dictum with respect to the affirmation of self: "I think, therefore I am" has transformed into "I think, therefore I am *not* . . . [Fill in the blank]."

Amid the commercial aesthetics that beset it, the university remains as a singular place with a philanthropic imperative. But the institution's current trajectory is slowly likening that singularity to that of a genteel anchor store in an expansive strip mall. And as such, the university slowly comes to represent one of many connected places where no singular sense of personal or philanthropic community exists, leaving geography to transform the evanescent self—one that is overwhelmingly individuated in terms of the consumption context of one's location. The dizzying array of identity negations increasingly sensed by the institutional scholar means, in short, "We are all half-breeds now . . . in a not so ivory tower."

Notes

1. Bourdieu's "cultural capital" joins "economic capital" and "social capital" as part of a triad of power. While "economic capital" might be defined as traditional material economic wealth, "social capital" comes from social networks and group memberships (Bourdieu, 1986). The cultural knowledge and skills that comprise "cultural capital" can be further subdivided into "embodied" (inherited and acquired), "linguistic," and "objectified" (possessed objects and credentials) (Bourdieu, 1991, p. 14).

2. As a more populist articulation of "history," Keith Jenkins (1999, p. 1) refers to the metanarrative as "upper case" history. Its alternative form is "lower case" history, which is produced by scholars and is generated by a "disinterested" study of the past. It is often perceived therefore as "non-ideological" or "proper" history.

3. The term "Medco" is fictitious in light of my inability to recall the specific names and plans of health care coverage.

Advances in Rhizomatic Understanding

CHAPTER THIRTEEN

Autoethnographic Sensemaking

.•————•.

What Does Our Criticality Mean? Patterns and Divergences

MUHAMMAD A. KHALIFA AND FELECIA M. BRISCOE

The collective autoethnographic stories in this book provide powerful examples of processes by which researchers and teachers developed criticality in their lives—personally, professionally, and civically. This chapter draws from these collective stories and identifies patterns, differences, recurrent themes, and common ground(s) among the contributions of scholars highlighted in this book. An examination of the trends across these stories allows for *sensemaking* (Evans, 2007; Weick, 1994).

Some of us grew up in a critical environment (e.g., Hayes); others were not initially critical in our lives and work and only later learned to understand our journeys of criticality (e.g., Briscoe); and still others of us, because of oppressive circumstances we experienced in our lives, encountered critical language, theory, and discourses later in life that allowed us to articulate many of these experiences (e.g., Giles). Some of us focused on a crucial event in our lives in the development of our criticality (e.g., Khalifa), while others took more of an overview of the developmental process (e.g., Choti). Given the size limitations of one chapter, all of us focused on a few (sometimes only one) instances of our developing criticality. What is common among all of them is that our development in criticality is a continuing process, not a onetime event.

The stories contained in the 11 critical autoethnographies examine the dynamics through which educators and researchers made sense of, and negotiated, oppressive power relations (Collins, 2005; Foucault, 1980) in which they found themselves. The rhizomatic multiplicity (Deleuze & Guattari, 1984) allowed us to follow the very unique and divergent expressions of the development of our criticality, yet identify broad patterns in this work. In our sensemaking (Evans, 2007; Weick, 1994) of the ethnographies, we focus on the collective critical experiences of the authors in this book. Evans (2007) explains the sensemaking process:

> Sensemaking is generally understood to be the cognitive act of taking in information, framing it, and using it to determine actions and behaviors in a way that manages meaning for individuals. (p. 161)

Using the autoethnographers' own critical framing, we identify collective patterns for our readers as we look for similarities and differences in the autoethnographies. In this regard, we initially focus on six themes that were explicitly described by some or all of the ethnographies.

The first three themes correspond to the development of critical epistemologies—oppression, questioning and/or self-doubt, and awareness/articulation of oppression. The next two themes concern the relation of critical epistemologies to the enactment of transformative power/knowledge relations: confronting power and the consequences of those confrontations. The final theme, resources used, is related to both the development of critical epistemologies and responses to power. We briefly discuss each of these emergent patterns in the following section of this chapter. However, we also acknowledge that the ways in which the processes of becoming critical are unique to each person and context. This is not so much to say that one of us wrote about race, gender, or sexual orientation and others did not. Rather, we acknowledge that there are general ways that we are not only similar, but also different.

For example, most or all of the critical autoethnographies were unique at the time of the authors' lives in which they began to embrace criticality. For Briscoe, Choti, and Jennings, their early formative experiences were focused on as crucial periods in the development of their criticality; Khalifa, on the other hand, focuses on his later teen and early adult years. El-Amin, Henry, and Laura as well as El-Griffin, de Oliver, and de la Portilla all focus on their university student experiences. Howard and Juárez and Hayes all highlight their criticality heightening at points in their professional teaching careers; and, finally, Giles, de Oliver, and Briscoe highlight their professorial experiences as places of fracture and development of criticality. In addition to this example, that is, the *period* in which we came to acknowledge or learn to articulate the developing aspect of our criticality, the critical autoethnographies demonstrated differences in the following areas:

1. How we came to embrace criticality;

2. Our identification of our positioning within oppressive power relations and who, we identified as enacting those power relations;

3. *How* we resisted and/or even continued to live with oppression; and

4. The perduring impacts of oppression on our personal/professional lives

Indeed, these differences are not exhaustive. But in this chapter we choose to focus on trends and similarities from which we can learn. We hope that the collective experiences and trends we identify might rather serve as a starting point that begins the discussion of the immense value in broader lessons that emerge from critical autoethnographic works. It is also our hope that autoethnographers, teachers, researchers, students, and professors all make use of the patterns and trends that we identify in this chapter.

Why Is "Sensemaking" Important?

Identifying patterns is our way of sensemaking of the autoethnographies and, we submit, is a crucial untapped resource for qualitative and critical researchers. The sensemaking process contributes to the knowledge of critical autoethnographers as they embrace their criticality in the research process. As Kincheloe and McLaren (2002) note, "critical theory retains its ability to disrupt and challenge the status quo" (p. 87), and "scholars saw in critical theory a method of temporarily freeing academic work from these [i.e., *oppressive, post-Enlightenment*] forms of power" (p. 88). These critical autoethnographic stories center such voices and legitimize this type of research. Our own stories disrupt the power and oppression we face. Our sensemaking considers what Weick, Sutcliffe, and Obstfeld (2005) have written regarding the process:

> Viewed as a significant process of organizing, *sensemaking* unfolds as a sequence in which people concerned with identity in the social context of other actors engage ongoing circumstances from which they extract cues and make plausible sense retrospectively, while enacting more or less order into those ongoing circumstances. (p. 409)

For us, this sensemaking process of identifying the critical patterns that emerged from the autoethnographies contributes to the existing body of research that critiques the status quo as it pertains to issues of power and justice. Many forms of research do not critique power and injustice, something that is central to the voices in this book.

Unique Aspects of the Research Data

Uniquely equal power relations shaped the contents of this book. Qualitative research asks for low-inference descriptors when describing the experiences of others (e.g., Johnson & Christensen, 2012). Contributors have had a far more equal say in the results reported than participants traditionally do in qualitative research. That is, until these last two chapters, the data described in their stories have not been excerpted, reconstructed, or interpreted by anyone other than those who lived the stories. In addition, authors sequence their life stories in the order they feel best represents their experience. Thus, each chapter is at the lowest level of inference possible. The entirety of each of the autoethnographic case studies is in the words of the individual participants. These scholars use their own words to relate their stories of becoming critical, making their own choices about what to leave in or take out of their contributions (given the constraints of making them into a chapter length). These critical autoethnographies, as a data set, are directly available to readers. Thus, individual readers can consider them separately and collectively, drawing the same (or different) lessons that we did.

These counter-narratives brought us to tears at times—either in horror at the circumstances experienced by the contributors or in joy at their ability to persevere, negotiate such circumstances, and even thrive. Many of the authors have communicated to us the difficulty of writing these autoethnographies as well as the cathartic and liberating feelings they experienced upon the completion of their chapters. Every one of the diverse collection of authors in this book has been subject to the historical and ongoing forces of racism, sexism, and/or classism. Furthermore, none of their parents, guardians, or close relatives was part of the professoriate. Yet all of them are in the professoriate or are in the last stages of earning a research doctorate. Thus, all of the narratives about becoming critical scholars, as Giles noted (Chapter 4), are insider/outsiders in their scholarly perspectives.

Each of these stories is uniquely rich and collectively abundant in meaning. What we derive from these diverse stories does not begin to exhaust their possible contributions. Indeed, the author(s) of the individual case studies suggests other theoretical advances and particular lessons that can be drawn from the individual case studies. We could make compelling cases for other topics, but for pragmatic reasons of time and space those must be put aside for the nonce. We invite future readers to e-mail us with any further questions or comments they may have regarding this book and our collective interpretation of the 11 different autoethnographic chapters at Felecia.Briscoe@utsa.edu and Mkhalifa@msu.edu. The patterns unearthed in these collective voices push critical researchers as well as autoethnographers in new directions, methodologically and theoretically, as they consider trends that we describe below.

Patterns of Similarity

CRITICALITY BORN OF OPPRESSION

The researchers in this book all experienced unique contexts that led to their own criticality. Indeed, both White and minoritized contributors have demonstrated how the oppression of White supremacy led to their becoming critical. Others spoke about how their experiences as women contributed to the development of their criticality. Many spoke of how power relationships they inherited were oppressive to them and at the same time influenced them to be oppressive to others like them. There may be other experiences that caused the authors to become critical. Yet, because they chose to write these particular vignettes, we assume that the experiences captured represent a crucial time period in or aspect of their development as critical scholars— or at least those they are comfortable sharing with the world. As we discuss each of these areas—race/ethnicity, gender, class, ambiguity, intersectionality, and complicity in reproducing oppression—we note that each of us came to develop our criticality because we were in some way oppressed. We were confronted with oppressive power relations that lessened our choices, and indeed our control, over aspects of our lives. In our comprehension of our need to resist (Foucault, 1980; Collins, 2005), we became critical.

Race and Ethnicity. Racialized (Jennings; Griffin-EL; Howard; Giles; Khalifa, Juárez, & Hayes; and El-Amin, Henry, & Laura) and ethnic (Choti, de la Portilla) markers played a significant role in how we were oppressed. The phenotypical, linguistic, and behavioral differences of the people in this book have been oppressively othered in their schools and societies. Scholars argue that these oppressive forces are systemic (Bell, 1995; Collins, 2000; Lipsitz, 2006). This is confirmed in Jennings's autoethnographic account of his time as a young Black student in a racist school context. His being called a "nigger" by a classmate was one of the earliest oppressive events that led to his criticality. But this racial oppression also happens when "supportive," "helpful," or "complimentary" oppressors "playfully" disparage one's ethnicity, race, or gender. When such an exchange happened with de la Portilla with someone who held an academic position of power over her, she decided to temporarily make the trade-offs necessary to continue her studies. However, she also decided to use the lesson later to resist such oppressions when she was in a less precarious circumstance.

Racial oppression impacts various races differently, as shown with our representations of being African-American, mixed-raced, White, indigenous, and Latina/Chicana. Along with various forms of racialization, oppression occurred differently depending on the geographic or economic context. Likewise, some of us realized our criticality by experiencing oppressive structures, while others encountered racist people that enacted oppression on us. Many of us experienced both oppressive structures and racist people. Yet the collective voices here also suggest that the period in our lives during which we encounter the oppression—and how we thereafter became critical—is relevant. Many of the racialized experiences seemed to occur during a period in or around schooling. Some saw their time as teachers as crucial to their becoming critical; others as younger students; and yet others as high school or university students. This may be a clear indication that schools and universities are indeed not only racialized, but are racialized incubators for becoming critical around issues of racism and other forms of oppression. At the same time, many authors spoke of the resources they gained from school that helped them to confront racial and other oppressions.

Gender. Several of the autoethnographies identify gender as a location for oppression and an impetus for criticality. While Khalifa describes the marginalizing contexts and contestations that he experienced as a Black man, some of the autoethnographies illustrate the global systemic oppression of girls and women. Choti spoke of the ways that a colonized culture of female marginalization happened in her homeland of Kenya. The rights and self-determination of women bounded by community practices (exacerbated by colonization) of Kenyan culture were surreptitiously enforced by her grandmother even though a male (in fact, her own father) and her mother resisted their daughters' oppression. Yet appropriating some colonized aspects (religion) of that culture helped her to resist that oppression and led to her criticality.

Similarly, Briscoe spoke of legacies of oppression that accompanied aspects of her upbringing. In addition to her so-called "tainted" bloodline, the location of women in this particular fundamentalist Mormon existence was wrought with oppressive representations of women. She encountered further, but different and fewer, oppressive representations of women in her early educational experiences. The juxtapositioning of these different representations in her early years began her criticality and eventually allowed her to better understand the glass ceiling that she experienced in higher education. Yet for de la Portilla and El-Amin, Henry, and Laura, it was their experiences in university graduate schools that pushed them more deeply along the path of criticality.

These stories collectively illustrate a deeply embedded, systemic bias against women. These biases and invisibilized privileges for men are deeply oppressive toward women. As is the case with race, oppression comes from multiple levels—institutional, societal, structural, cultural, and individual. Such experiences not only led to our criticality, but also in many cases informed much of our research agenda and activism for years to come.

Intersectionality and Ambiguity. Although many of the contributors focused on one or two aspects of their oppression and resistance, most at least mentioned multiple ways in which they were oppressed—and the multiple pathways of resistance that they thereafter formed. Their narratives indicate that the circumstances around power and systematic oppression are rarely of one stroke. Rather, there are often multiple ways that these oppressions repeatedly occur. For example, Briscoe also spoke of being poor and connected that to her narratives of criticality around race, religion, gender, and bloodline. She was neither the only person to write of her intersectionality with class (e.g., Giles and his "working-class" background) nor the only person to speak of religion and spirituality. Several of us wrote of critical spirituality, which is something we discuss in detail later in this chapter. El-Amin and Griffin-El both shared glimpses of how their transcendent values connected to spirituality and how these values contributed to their criticality and resistance.

These collective ethnographies highlight intersecting forces that act on virtually each individual (coercing certain actions, privileging some while simultaneously disadvantaging others), and these intersecting forces collectively contain the seeds to one's criticality. Stereotypes around ethnicity, gender, language, and race often, for example, converge and construct how people in the United States view Latin@/Chican@s (e.g., de la Portilla and de Oliver). Similarly, the intersectionality of being a White, female academic and having access to unique realms of power is another aspect described by both Briscoe and Juárez. This intersectionality was perhaps most salient in de Oliver's critical autoethnography, in which he describes being constructed as Latino, White, a foreigner, a Black athlete, an American Indian, and a host of working/professional identities. Many of these identities were mischaracterized, being at odds with how he viewed himself as well as other assumed identities. These different contexts impelled him to respond to the various identities that U.S. society ascribed to him.

While intersectionality describes the multiple, convergent contexts acting on the oppressed, ambiguity often prevents them from naming or categorizing both their own and others' oppression. Ambiguity refers to a feeling of knowing and recognizing that oppressive forces are acting on us, but not recognizing how, when, or even why. Several of us grappled with ill treatment at one time or another but did not have the language or tools to name or resist oppression at the time it occurred. Griffin-EL, for example, situated his chapter in a Chapellian discourse of whether or not, when, and how forcefully to resist the constant marginalization he met in his graduate program. Khalifa and Briscoe both spoke of being marginalized in their earlier lives, but not understanding how. As Jennings chose to excel in school, the oppressive questions about the authenticity of his Blackness continue to induce him to question himself.

Unaware Reproducers of Oppression? When the systemic nature of oppression as being is understood, it was easier for some of us to identify ourselves as reproducers of systems of oppression. Howard, Khalifa, and Briscoe speak of moments in their lives when they enacted oppressive systems that they inherited. In Howard's case, she was taught that colorblindness was a way to be equal and fair, but experiences in her personal and academic lives led to her becoming critical. Khalifa also found himself, as an actor, in inherently oppressive systems, and he ended up co-constructing nihilistic behaviors and contexts. Briscoe found herself making sexist assumptions about some of the women in her graduate program. Many of us inherited systems of oppression and began to act in accordance with the systems we found. This not only reinforced our own self-marginalization, but also contributed to upholding the systems that oppress countless others.

The autoethnographies all in some way, therefore, locate the oppressions at a systemic level. Institutions of religion, elementary, secondary and post-secondary education, culture and customs, identity, family, and community can all be deeply reproductive of oppressive power relations through our beliefs, behaviors, and norms. The invisiblization of oppression and its integration into organizations and structures within which individuals— often innocently or inadvertently—assume an oppressive role and all too often an oppressive stance toward those in their demographic category(ies).

The Relationship between Ascripted Identities and Space

The relationship between ascripted identities and space was a common strand that emerged from many of the chapters in this book. The central role of space or location proved, for many of us, to be a path to criticality. Why were we viewed differently and treated differently based on the context? Why did we feel and even often act differently based on the spaces we occupied? Were our bodies being ordered differently in these different spaces? These questions drove many of the autoethnographies. For El-Amin, Henry, and Laura, it was the "hyphen" that partially defined what they would be, and when. For Giles, his comfort and familiarity in his urban home community allowed for a different identity and existence than what he found in academic institutions. Briscoe spoke about the overt sexism she encountered in her early fundamentalist Mormon upbringing and the later, less overt, forms sexism took in mainstream society that at first were invisible to her. In part, no doubt, her working class background had not provided her with cultural lenses she needed to readily discern 'softer' sexism found in middle class culture.

de Oliver's autoethnography captured most saliently, however, the fluidity at which identities are both context dependent and context influencing. His narrative revealed the alienation fostered by the broader U.S. society's penchant for categorizing and ascribing identities to people and then enacting a set of assumptions and behaviors toward people based on their ascriptions. de Oliver describes how various situational circumstances led to his being ascribed assorted subaltern identities depending on the social spaces:

> The conjunction of these negations is not an expression of emancipation from constrictive forms, but rather the standardization of alienation irrespective of whether that identity is odious or altruistic, biological or behavioral, real or imagined.

The impact that space had on our identities was noticeable to us and led many of us to criticalize. It did not seem fair to us that we faced maltreatment because of our difference. And given that most of us hold advanced doctorate degrees, what about those people who do not share our ability to traverse boundaries; that is, what of people who are still in the hood, on Fundamentalist Mormon compounds, or who are still graduate students with a fear of speaking out against an oppressive teacher or advisor—especially to those authority figures who may be unaware that they are being oppressive? How would those without ready access to their own *Community Cultural Wealth,* as Giles discussed, negotiate these oppressive forces?

A collective look at the autoethnographies illustrates an imposing narrative: Despite the hurtful and damaging nature of oppression, it can be the catalyst by which a person develops her or his criticality. The arrangements in which we found ourselves were often characterized by our being overwhelmed by systems or individuals who were in a position of power in terms of our existence and the choices that we made. In our resistance to these unequal power relations, we—immediately or through more learning and enlightenment—became critical and resisted.

Self-Questioning and Self-Doubt: A Negotiated Existence

Collectively, these autoethnographies revealed the lasting impact of our experiences, which caused us to question our abilities, our rights to access, our identities, our goodness, and other aspects of our very being. In some cases, we began to accept the metanarratives that the "White, Male, Non–Working-Class imaginative" held of us. The stereotypical assumptions about being a Black athlete (de Oliver) or a White woman (Juárez) impacted how we viewed ourselves and others who looked like us. In some cases, we began to accept the patriarchal norms for women. Our actions were affected by how we were being viewed and judged by peers, classmates, and/or broader society.

Hesitation to resistance. One poignant example of this was Griffin-EL's hesitation to resist what he felt was ill treatment by the members in a class he was taking. Other members in the course—both students and the course professor—marginalized his intellectual views and course involvement. When his views were directly derided, no one came to his defense, causing him vacillate on when and how forcefully he should resist. This is something that many of the critical autoethnographers revealed about themselves—their developing confidence in their ability to speak truth to power and resist oppression. Scholars have mentioned that those in relative positions of privilege and power—and *not* the severely oppressed—are more comfortable resisting oppression (Collins, 2005; Fine, 1994). Many of us languished for years before we built the courage or developed the articulations to name and thus resist our circumstances. Many of the Black male autoethnographers in this book struggled with this, as they constantly self-corrected against a common stereotype—angry, aggressive Black men. This stereotype caused them to hesitate in resisting the oppression they faced and to conform to White niceness (meaning silence about oppression).

Acting White—Acting Black and other Negotiations. Similarly, Khalifa, Jennings, and Hayes—again, Black male autoethnographers in this book— described themselves as almost in a perpetual state of responding to how they might be viewed by their Black or White peers. This caused Khalifa, as a youth, to embrace gangster, criminalized behaviors that were foreign to his immediate family and upbringing. Jennings and Hayes, on the other hand, struggled with the fear of what other Blacks might think if they earned high marks or demonstrated a level of professionalism. In Chapter 5, Hayes worried that "he very well could embody White racial knowledge in ways that collude with and support the ongoing dominance of Whites." This is well articulated by El-Amin, Henry, and Laura as they struggled with straddling the hyphens of the multiple and often even contested identities. Black-female-PhD-spiritual-mothers-spouses-scholars are many of the identities they negotiate, but their identities were not always deemed compatible in the academic world. Thus, they were implicitly and explicitly discouraged from a scholarly exploration of these hyphenated ways of being in the world. Yet the autoethnographers informed us of their perpetual negotiation of their identities, resistance, and the meta-narrative stereotypes of them.

Confronting Power through Resistance

Each autoethnography offers a story of how we responded to oppression by becoming critical and resisting. This resistance happens in multiple, unique ways and is often driven by our desire to stop being oppressed. As has been evident from the narratives in this book, there is a deep, inextricable connection between our *oppression*, our *criticality*, and our *resistance*. Though each of our stories is different, these experiences were common among all of us. In some ways, we co-constructed our identities by co-opting and incorporating aspects of our oppression as a way to resist. Examples of this happened when Khalifa first encountered aspects of the oppressive street culture, only to then begin enacting it as a way to gain validation in a White supremacist society. In other ways, our anger, hostility, or aggression took root and guided our resistance. Contrary to the common belief that visible emotions are poor conduct, we do not see expression of emotion as a negative trait. Rather, we see the expression of such feelings as affirming, honest, valuable, authentic, culturally nuanced, vital, and appropriate in the face of most oppression. To curtail or to constrain our emotions in the academic realm is to render it sterile and dead. Even worse, such emotional constraint helps to invisibilize the oppression experienced by us and our responses to it.

We contend that an important part of these *counter-narratives* is the refusal to separate our emotions from our intellect. But more importantly, incorporating our emotions with our intellects was one of the ways we resisted the lifelong and sometimes crippling dominant meta-narratives we faced. Conveying our particular narratives is a confrontation of oppressive power, a reshifting of dominant knowledge/power relations and voice. It opens a space for recourse that is often denied and allows us and others to criticality reflect on our paths and ultimately to further resist oppression.

Perhaps the most common form of resistance was the *counter-narrative*. Writing our counter-narratives allowed us to tell our truths, empowered us, and centered our realities. The counter-narratives were one way of naming the oppression that we and others had experienced that seemed to be invisible to others. Jennings in Chapter 2 wrote about this process of resistance for him:

> Thus, my counter-narrative resists the master narratives about African-Americans in education in two ways: by countering the academic identity constructed for African-Americans and by countering the image of U.S. schooling as universally beneficial or even neutral with regard to all racialized groups.

The counter-narrative, in fact, embodies the nature of resistance in this book. The collective stories present an alternative view to that offered by the systems of oppressive power/knowledge relations that we autoethnographers faced. The collective stories countered and served as a protest to the oppressive ascriptions and other forms of colonizing oppression we faced. For Jennings and the other contributors, the counter-narrative was a critical resistance.

Resources Used to Develop Criticality

Our particular critical understanding and resistance depended on the depth, type, and contexts of the oppression we faced. While some of us co-constructed identities and behaviors that incorporated the oppressive stereotypical constructs of the White, male, and/or middle-class meta-narratives, others of us expressed anger and developed counter-narratives of our reality. Co-construction as a means of resistance indicates a certain depth and pervasiveness of oppression and our subsequent responses to it. In fact, when oppression is so ubiquitous, oppressed people often find themselves appropriating (appropriation being a form of embracing and owning, but then changing to make it more useful or relevant; e.g., Blacks and the appropriation of the word "nigger/nigga") aspects of the oppression. The oppressed actually co-construct often nihilistic but culturally authentic identities with the oppressors themselves. For example, aggression (or perhaps "resistance") against oppression, contrarily, is often understood as opposing the spirit of collaboration. Yet, should we collaborate in the oppression against us, our anger is rather a natural reaction to oppression against us. After years of oppression, many of us responded with the passion and emotion appropriate to the overbearing situations we faced. We characterize this as speaking back directly to our oppressors rather than internalizing it and, at some moment later, resisting. Thus, Giles, Hayes, Juárez, Griffin-EL, and Briscoe all chose to show direct resistance and protest to what they saw as acts of oppression against them and/or others. This was crucial to our continued development of criticality. At the same time, we often had to endure punitive repercussions to our resistance.

   Spiritual Criticality. Finally, many contributors described using spirituality as a resource for developing critical understandings and as a source of strength and resistance for the contributors. Critical spirituality—or the use of spirituality and altruism as a way to resist (or at least to protest) oppression—was actually a deep source of power for many of us. Giles and Henry pulled on African-American spirituality from Christian traditions, while El-Amin pulled from Muslim traditions. Griffin-EL pulled from the Christian revolutionary and civil rights leader Martin Luther King Jr. In grappling to understand oppressive power constructs he faced, yet using his positive future positionality, Griffin-EL wrote, "*Forgiveness,* as an act of love, requires the oppressed class to understand that they and the oppressor class are human beings, living in constant contradiction." His ability to pull on transcendent values, such as forgiveness and love, added a level to, or perhaps beyond, criticality. Despite the oppression we faced, we were able to dig even deeper, connect with higher forces, and continue with our lives.

Conclusion

This chapter articulates both challenges and opportunities of criticality. At first glance, readers will certainly understand and may even be discouraged by the emergent patterns of oppression that our critical autoethnographies all seem to highlight. While we all encountered personal experiences with individuals who enacted oppression on us, we were all disaffected by learning that the oppression was both personal and systemic. It surprised, hurt, perplexed, agitated, and ultimately angered us when we learned that there were actual institutional barriers—societal (written and unwritten but understood) rules—that unfairly disadvantaged us in multiple, creative, and adaptive ways. Yet, for most of us, this oppression was the impetus for becoming critical in our professions, studies, and lives.

Our stories all seemed to converge on another phenomenon: Where there is oppression, there will be resistance. The methods we chose to confront and resist oppression were diverse and resourceful, yet enacted differentially. For us, the articulation of this trend is encouraging, because it shows a path forward for others who encounter oppression. Despite the fact that we found our criticality in various phases of our lives, we nonetheless all found it, and all resisted the oppression. However, our multiple resistances to oppressions came with a cost. We pulled from ethnic, community, spiritual, and intellectual sources to confront the oppression; we also acknowledge the beneficial changes that often resulted from our resistance.

While many of us were threatened and even punished, our experience pales in comparison to the lifelong emotional and psychological burdens that many oppressed peoples must forever carry and endure. The benefit, if it can even be said to be such, is that we all grew more critical, spiritual, or otherwise aware of how to confront oppression and thereafter live dignified lives. Our paths to criticality and the emergent themes are: 1) The development of critical epistemology (oppression and the questioning and/or self-doubt, and awareness/articulation of oppression); 2) the relation of the critical epistemologies to the enactment of transformative power/knowledge relations (confronting power and the consequences of those confrontations); and 3) the resources used (the development of critical epistemologies and responses to power, such as critical spirituality). We hope that our critical autoethnographies and stories of our paths to criticality have exposed readers to understanding their own selves better. Finally, given that we are all victims as well as producers of oppression (Foucault, 1980), we hope this work might be used as a way for us all to recognize our power and resist our oppression of others. It is here that we believe that critical autoethnography is not only validated and legitimate, but actually one of the best methodologies through which such questions may be answered.

CHAPTER FOURTEEN

Rage, Love, and Transcendence in the Co-Construction of Critical Scholar Identities

...•————•..

Escaping the Iron Cage of Technical-Rationality

FELECIA M. BRISCOE AND MUHAMMAD A. KHALIFA

Some of the ideas in these autoethnographies may seem foreign, strange, or not fit with readers' understandings of the world. This is to be expected if these chapters actually offer new orientations to society and ourselves. Certainly, we, Felecia and Muhammad, learned new ways of understanding our educational system and society as we read these critical counter-narratives. And many of the authors described how writing their own stories helped them to deepen their critical understandings of the educational system. Based on the patterns and divergences discussed in Chapter 13, this chapter develops a model of emerging criticality and explores some of its theoretical implications. In this chapter, we first describe the process we used in developing the model. Then we present the emergent theoretical model of the interrelated processes by which critical scholar identities are co-constructed. We then discuss the theoretical implications of the model itself. Of particular importance are the theoretical implications for the exercise of agency. Next, we relate the model of emerging criticality to today's instrumental and technical-rational system of schooling that continues to exert colonizing forces upon all students to shape them as colonized/colonizer. Finally, we present some practical lessons derived from these autoethnographies.

Today's colonizing and oppressive forces occur under a positivist episte-mology that is instrumental and technical-rational yet purports to be objec-tive. An instrumental technical-rational epistemology uses facts and figures to make "fair" decisions about various students, faculty, and administra-tors within educational systems. Such technical-rational decision making disadvantages historically oppressed groups (e.g., Briscoe & Khalifa, 2013;

Lipman, 2011) and constructs alienated and meaningless lives for more privileged groups (Baudrillard, 2005). Changing our epistemological perspectives may help us escape the neoliberal iron cage of technical-rational accountability. These critical autoethnographies offer epistemological alternatives to the instrumental and technical-rational ones that dominate our schools and lives.

Developing a Model of Emergent Criticality

In developing our grounded theory from these autoethnographies, we sought to determine the significant relationships among the patterns and divergences discussed in Chapter 13. We struggled to determine the most relevant and significant lessons that could be drawn from our sensemaking of these critical autoethnographies (presented in Chapter 13). We struggled because the autoethnographic patterns were so diverse and rich with possible avenues of interpretation. We finally selected the relationships we saw as most relevant to the collected counter-narratives and to our purpose in developing this book. The axis of interpretation that evolved from our multiple reading and discussions integrates the interrelated concepts of colonization, agency, contextual resources, resistance, and emerging identities. Colonizing forces and the resources available to authors mediate their understandings, actions, and thus co-constructed identities.

Much has been written about colonization (e.g., Tuhiwai-Smith, 1999). For the most part when talking about colonizing forces, the literature focuses on the colonized person. We agree with Dei's (2006) description of colonizing forces and the will to resist (see Chapter 1), as these counter-narratives describe how we continue to resist. However, these case studies extend the conception of colonization to include the forces that construct both halves of the colonized/colonizer dyad that make up different aspects of identities. Thus, we integrate Foucault's notions of power relations and identity with the concept of colonization.

We define colonizing forces as the power relations that coerce identities suitable for colonized/colonizer relationships as described by Dei (2006); that is, the power relations simultaneously coerce the subjectivities for colonizer/colonized relationships. Thus, colonizing forces act to develop two aspects of our identities. Some aspects of our identities are ascribed as culturally, morally, and intellectually inferior, while other aspects are simultaneously ascribed as culturally, morally, and intellectually superior. Although we refer to the colonized/colonizer dyad, we do not presume that people can be neatly divided up into the colonized and the colonizer. Rather, we agree with Collins (2009) that most of us have within ourselves both the colonized and the colonizer or, in her words, the oppressed and the oppressor.

Like Collins (2000), we rely

> upon paradigms that emphasize the importance of race, class, and gender as intersecting oppressions in shaping the U.S. matrix of domination."[1] [And this] . . . matrix of domination contains few pure victims or oppressors. Each individual derives varying amounts of penalty and privilege from the multiple systems of oppression, which frame everyone's lives. (p. 287)

Thus, it is just as important to understand and resist the forces that construct colonizer aspects of our identity as those that construct the colonized aspects.

Advances in Critical Social Understandings

The theoretical implications of our findings are organized into six parts. We first present our model of the interrelationships of identity, colonizing forces, agency, contextual resources, resistance, and transformation. The model (see next page) illustrates processes by which critical identities continually emerge and develop. In the next five sections, we explain how our findings relate to the model. In doing so, we make explicit the interrelated dynamics involved in co-constructing critical scholar identities.

The headings of the next five sections correspond to the dynamics depicted in the model: Section 1 extends poststructural understandings of power, identity, and agency; section 2 focuses on some common colonizing forces experienced by the contributors; section 3 examines the relationship between colonizing forces, questioning, awareness, and resistance; section 4 discusses the relationship between contextual resources and the exercise of agency to resist colonizing forces; and, finally, section 5 describes how resistance transforms our identities, our immediate contexts, and ultimately our society.

Identities: Fluid, Inherited, and Historical

The patterns emerging from this collection of autoethnographies highlight the relationship between power, agency, and identity, illustrating the fluid and dynamic nature of power relations enacted around, in, and through identity. The counter-narratives in this book support a poststructural Black feminist understanding of identity. As a number of poststructuralists and postmodernists (e.g., Foucault 1980b) have noted, identity, rather than being static, is fluid and dynamic. The fluid and dynamic nature of emergent critical identities is seen in every autoethnographic case study in this book.

Model: The Dynamics of Emergent and Developing Critical Identity

Interrelated Processes of Critical Identity Development*

↓**Identity** (fluid, historical, and political) at a particular point in time

↑↓**Colonizing forces act upon identity** (often differently in different spaces)

↑↓**Questioning and becoming aware**/articulating knowledge of colonizing forces (begins to alter identity as agency becomes active)

↑↓ **Accessible contextual resources used for resistance**

    ↑↓**Personal Contextual Resources**

        ↑↓<u>Intrapersonal</u> aspects of identity resistant to colonizing forces emerging from experiences and knowledge gained in earlier and/or different context
            Family stories/knowledge/ideologies
            Community culture of those who have been *othered*
            Anti-racist/sexism/classism context

        ↓↑ <u>Intra- and Interpersonal</u> Spiritual Contextual Resources
            From within
            Through the spiritual fellowship of others

        ↑↓<u>Interpersonal</u>
        Sources
            Friends
            Family
            Colleagues
        Types
            Emotional
            Epistemological
            Ideological

    ↑↓**Public Contextual Resources**
        Critical scholarship
        Critical epistemologies

↑↓ **Resistance and emergent critical identity**
    Understanding self, world, and self's relationship to the world differently

    Acting based on those new understandings

    The new actions change the self as well as the world, which in turn acts upon identity

*As indicated by the arrows, these dynamics are interactive and iterative.

Depending on the context (geographic, societal, historical, and individual), contributors all demonstrated changes in their identity enacted through the identities ascribed to them and their resistance to those ascriptions. For example, de Oliver notes the various types of identities ascribed to him, depending upon his geographic, social, or historical context.

The fluid and dynamic nature of identities is related to the political nature of identities. One's identity (as ascribed and/or co-constructed) positions one in relation to other identities (Foucault, 1980a; 1980b). And as Ricouer (1994) and others have noted, in general we strive to construct more positive (or superior) identities for ourselves. Further, power relations are never dormant or held in reserve; they continually act to influence the actions (including discourses) of individuals, from which collectively the macrostructures and societal discourses emerge (Foucault, 1980a). Thus, not only are actions (both the individual's and others) crucial to one's identity, but identities themselves are power relations and induce particular actions. They induce certain behaviors as they prescribe certain actions and proscribe others as appropriate to certain identities; they also influence the understanding of certain identities and thus how they should be treated (Briscoe & de Oliver, 2012).

However, as Foucault (1980a) suggests, power relations are not fixed and do not act unilaterally upon anyone, but rather are negotiated and enacted moment by moment. These autoethnographies illustrate that the power relations imbued in identity are enacted *upon*, *through*, and *by* the individual contributors. The case studies presented in this volume describe the development of critical identities in relation to the oppressive and/or colonizing forces experienced by the contributors as well as their actions and reactions. Furthermore, a reciprocal relationship exists between contributors' actions and their developing critical identities. As one's understanding of oneself in relation to society becomes more critical, one's actions change, which in turn incites further changes in one's identity, and so on.

Jennings' counter-narrative illustrates the fluid, dynamic, and *political* nature of identity. Jennings tells us how he felt when a little White girl ascribed a "nigger" identity to him. This colonizing event induced actions, thoughts, and feelings first for him, and later for his parents when he related the incident to them. His and his parents' combined actions resisted such an ascribed deficit identity both in the (then) present and extending into a more equitable future (at least at that particular school); they were political actions. Furthermore, as they resisted these colonizing forces, their identities became even more critical. Thus, we see captured in Jennings's counter-narrative and those of others the dynamic, fluid, and political nature of identity as well as the reciprocal relationships of actions and identity.

The counter-narratives in this book also illustrate the historicity of identities, as noted by Norton and Toohey (2011, pp. 414–415): "From a poststructuralist perspective, practices, resources, and identities are both produced and inherited." As different aspects of our identities are enacted from moment to moment, they embody vestiges of earlier identities; thus, identities are always, in part, historical. Contributing authors all describe their awareness of various aspects of their inherited identities. These inherited identities come from both their families (e.g., Briscoe) and from society (e.g., de Oliver). Sometimes these inherited aspects were useful in resisting colonizing forces—indeed, we may inherit identities that are already in opposition/conflict with oppression (e.g., Hayes) while not realizing it (e.g., Khalifa). At other times, some of the inherited aspects of their identities were the result of colonizing forces (e.g., Choti). These counter-narratives tell of the dynamic power relationships enacted by us around and through our identities. We resist aspects of our inherited and/or ascribed identities and through our resistance co-construct alternative identities; these actions require the exercise of our agency. Thus, agency is crucial to emerging identities.

Agency

Agency as an aspect of identity has been much discussed. Rozmarin (2013), drawing from Luce Irigaray's collective works, describes agency as the political part of an identity that wills the change or transformation of both ourselves and the world, "both the outcome and the condition of a political life, aimed at creating political transformations" (p. 469). Jensen (2011) also describes agency as the political aspect of identity, "the capacity to act within or up against social structures" (p. 66). Agency has been used to describe actions of resistance (e.g., Doucet, 2011), such as appropriating once-oppressive practices (e.g., Barton & Tan 2010), and posited as that part of us that enables us to resist colonization and co-construct our own identities even in the most oppressive environments (e.g., Briscoe, 2009). Although a number of scholars have written about agency, the actual means through which agency operates have been little examined. Instead, scholarly literature has largely focused upon the evidence for—or the effects of—agency. We argue that agency operates through accessible contextual resources. Collectively, these autoethnographies demonstrate some of the avenues by which agency operates; that is, the means by which contributors used their agency to resist colonization and thereby transform and criticalize their identities. This notion of agency imbues a resistance to colonizing forces and articulates an epistemological approach that incorporates personal, interpersonal, and spiritual aspects of identity that were used to transcend the oppressive forces encountered by the autoethnographers.

Colonizing Forces

Other scholars have written about identity changing or adapting to/with contexts. However, these narratives add even a bit more to our understandings of this phenomenon—as they consider these identity changes in the face of "colonizing" forces. The oppression most mentioned by contributing authors was the ascription of deficit or limiting identities—in other words, colonizing forces. For example El-Amin, Henry, Laura, Giles, and de la Portilla all described the institutional forces that coerced them to limit their actions as researchers and thereby limited both the type of knowledge they produced and their identities as researchers. On the other hand, two autoethnographies by White women (Howard and Juárez) spoke of their criticality being sparked/developed, not by being oppressed themselves, but rather by their growing awareness of the oppression of racialized groups paralleled by their privileging as Whites. The authors' experiences of racism, sexism, classism, and/or other dehumanizing colonizing forces were an important dynamic in their developing criticality.

The no-win strategy of colonizing power relationships

Although the colonizing forces were multiple and different for the diverse contributors, they described a common colonizing strategy—colonizing forces that position them into no-win choices. In these positionings, they were not presented with a good and bad choice—a good choice that would result in academic advancement and help to create a more equitable environment and a bad choice that would stop academic advancement and/or help to maintain inequitable power relations. The only choices available to them were bad choices—bad for their interests and also for society. In other words, they experienced punitive consequences and society suffered a loss, no matter what choices they made and which actions they took. As described in these autoethnographies, the authors sometimes deliberately calculated the possible outcomes and selected what they saw as the best of the punitive options offered to them; at other times, their choices were inadvertent and not consciously made.

For example, Griffen-EL describes the Chapellian contradiction he experienced in graduate school: Confront the class about their marginalizing practices and be ascribed as the angry Black man, or be silenced and seemingly acquiesce to his and other Blacks' marginalization. Hayes encountered a similar no-win context as a professor in higher education. Choti describes the punitive circumstance whereby she had to choose between giving up some of her rights as a woman or be excluded and derided by her schoolmates (who were abetted by her own grandmother). Khalifa notes that the few societal identities available to Black male youth failed to combine masculinity with academic excellence and good citizenship. This dearth of desirable identities coerced him into a no-win choice: He had to choose between being described as academically excellent and law-abiding but lacking in masculinity, or adopting the very masculine identity of a "hood" but in doing so be coerced into the prison pipeline for minorities. de la Portilla vividly describes the no-win bargain she had to make as a doctoral student, wherein she remained silent about denigrating comments "playfully" directed toward her in order to avoid losing one of her few advocates. Briscoe informs us of her punishments in higher education for not acting "feminine" enough, yet those missing "feminine" traits countered the actions needed to advance in academia. Juárez refused to stop her anti-racist teaching and was then excluded from her faculty position in teacher education. She refused to abandon her principles of anti-racist teaching but had to pay a steep price—there was no good choice for her. Jennings had to choose between learning the White culture of power and advancing academically and professionally versus maintaining the vernacular and close ties with other youth in his Black neighborhood. Giles describes the price he continues to pay in terms of his own academic advancement for choosing to maintain his Black collectivist heritage by working intensively with students of color to help them to be academically successful.

These no-win colonizing strategies induced us at times to unknowingly collaborate with our own oppression or that of others. Some narratives poetically describe the despair and guilt associated with discovering that one unknowingly has perpetuated the oppression of others (e.g., Howard). When coerced into no-win choices, we sometimes find ourselves inadvertently sabotaging our own interests and the interests of those like us, including the principles of social equity itself (e.g., Khalifa, de la Portilla, Briscoe, & Griffin-EL in this volume). As Giles describes in his autoethnography, this continual negotiation of no-win choices results in battle fatigue. Psychology textbooks note that being positioned in such no-win contexts induces learned helplessness (e.g., Peterson & Park, 1998). Regardless of the choices we make, in general our advancement is slow compared with those who have not been positioned to experience such a parade of no-win choices. Through these measures, society loses the full benefit of what a person could offer if they did not have to continually resist colonizing forces. Through these coercive measures, we appear to be living up to the deficit identities that historically have been ascribed to marginalized groups—the very ascribed identities we work to resist. Yet, as described by these narratives, we *do* resist. Our acts of resistance transform ourselves and, if Foucault (1980) is correct, the spaces in which we live and work.

The Dual Nature of Oppressive Colonizing Forces: Questioning and Awareness

Based on these autoethnographies, we argue that questioning and developing critical understandings are often central to resisting colonizing forces. The act of doing so transforms us, and as our identities are transformed, we begin changing colonizing contexts into more equitable ones. Furthermore, these very colonizing forces spurred our questioning and developing awareness. Several narratives describe this dualistic nature of colonizing oppression: while colonizing power coerces deficit and limited identities, its very act of coercion presents an opportunity for the oppressed to become aware of those coercive forces; these assaults upon our or others' dignity provide an impetus to resist them. For example, Howard and Juarez resisted not only the attempts to colonize others, but, importantly, also the colonizing forces that acted to construct them as bearers of White privilege. Juárez's resistance to this colonization was not without cost, as she lost her professional position. Howard revisits her past to locate and undo her construction as a privileged White. Their resistance to their ascribed identity of White privilege was central to their developing criticality; their narratives describe their growing awareness, questioning, and rejection of White privilege.

Yet Black feminist thought informs us that

> [a]lthough most individuals have little difficulty identifying their own victimization within some major system of oppression—whether it be by race, social class, religion, physical disability, sexual orientation, ethnicity, age or gender—they typically fail to see how their thoughts and actions uphold someone else's subordination. (Collins, 2000, p. 287)

These counter-narratives illustrate that we are more likely to become aware of the colonizing forces that oppress us than of those that oppress others. Our experiences of oppressive colonizing power/knowledge relations compel us to become aware of those relations. And these experiences incite us to resist them, as we seek to construct more positive and powerful identities. These narratives also demonstrate the historical or inherited aspects of identity; furthermore that, at least "part" of our identities exists *outside* of any colonizing context (e.g., Jennings or Hayes). This transcendent part of our identity asserts its own epistemology, which is a more powerful understanding of one's identity. These transcendent aspects of our identities also help us to develop resiliency and enable us to use our agency to resist oppressive colonizing forces. For example, de la Portilla describes how her early experiences with her mothers and aunts helped her to develop a positive understanding of herself and the ability to negotiate with *las viejas*. These understandings stayed with her and helped her to resist her own colonization in a doctoral program.

It is important to note that our resistance is not necessarily instantaneous, as it is constantly mediated by our developing awareness. Developing successful resistance to the colonizing forces requires being consciously aware of them as oppressive. Awareness is developed with multiple forms of questioning. We painfully question ourselves about whether or not our perceptions are mistaken when we name and/or resist oppressive colonizing forces (e.g., El-Amin, Laura, & Henry). We also painfully question our own complicity in perpetuating colonizing power relations (e.g., Howard). Both of these painful types of personal questioning go along with our questioning of the colonizing forces that act upon us (e.g., Jennings). Choti describes her ambivalence about female circumcision due to her questioning of both herself and the colonizing forces she faced as a young woman. Griffin-EL describes his semester-long questioning of how to deal with the colonizing forces in a "critical" class. Howard describes her questioning as well as those questions she encourages her students to ask about White privilege. Briscoe describes her decades-long questioning and development of her awareness of how sexism manifests in mainstream society. Questioning is integral to our growing awareness of colonizing forces. Yet even when the contributors become consciously aware of colonizing forces, they do not always immediately or actively resist.

What about the Agency of Those Who Seem to Acquiesce?

If oppressive colonization is dualistic, how do we explain people who seemingly acquiesce to their own colonization—who seem to neither resist nor become critical? These autoethnographies suggest a three-part answer to this question. The first part of our answer is that people caught in oppressive colonizing forces are always resisting and they never totally acquiesce to colonizing forces; we may acquiesce for the moment. The fear of punitive consequences induced our silence and/or passive resistance; we seemingly acquiesce to our colonization. For example, de la Portilla remained silent when her mentor said she looked like a "wetback." She feared that speaking out would jeopardize her earning a doctorate from a prestigious university. She knowingly made this "devil's" bargain, believing/hoping that a doctorate would position her better to resist such oppression in the future.

A second part to our explanation of seeming acquiescence to colonizing power relations is the uncontrollable aspect of luck or timing. In Khalifa's case, what would have happened if the police had found the gun? Or if the police had not stopped their car that particular night? How might Khalifa's life be different today, and how much harder would it be for him to resist society's ascribed roles of Black masculinity? In sum, at times colonized or oppressed people have moments in their lives in which it is inopportune or virtually impossible to engage in the type of critical questioning that leads to resistance or criticality.

A third but crucial part to our explanation is that the exercise of agency to resist colonizing forces does not appear out of thin air—we have to draw upon something in order to resist. It is a constant process that may endure for years before a person recognizes that she or he being mired by colonizing forces. For example, only after certain events in our lives, as teachers, did some of us as recognize that we were indeed reproducing colonizing forces. But if an informed observer chronicled our lives at that particular moment in history, they would have surely seen us as acquiescent. These narratives suggest that an important difference between those who quickly resist and those who do not is the contextual resources available to them.

Agency and Contextual Resources Used for Resistance

The counter-narratives in this book illustrate the importance of accessible contextual resources, both in becoming aware of the colonizing forces and in exercising our agency. The authors of these autoethnographies come from myriad nondominant social spaces. The colonizing forces we experienced as well as the contextual resources available to us for our resistance varied. Thus, we drew upon different contextual resources to resist colonizing forces and thereby co-constructed our identities as critical scholars. From these counter-narratives, we found that our exercise of agency was shaped by our context. The personal contextual resources consisted of (1) intrapersonal resources—the aspects of our identity that lay outside colonizing forces; (2) spiritual resources that encompassed both inter- and intrapersonal resources; and (3) interpersonal resources from our friends, families, and colleagues.

Personal Contextual Resources

An important theoretical implication of our findings with regard to these critical autoethnographies is the personal contextual resources that contributors drew upon both to sustain resistant agency and to use that agency more successfully to resist colonizing forces. Overall, contributors drew upon personal (intra- and interpersonal) contextual resources more often than public and intellectual contextual resources in developing their resistance to colonizing forces. These personal contextual resources were central in their intellectual development as critical scholars.

Intrapersonal resources. Perhaps the personal contextual resource that scholars drew upon most often in developing their resistance was the intrapersonal domain of their inherited identities. As identities are in part historical, when colonizing forces beset our identities, we can draw upon those aspects of our identities formed earlier in childhood (e.g., Giles) and/ or in other contexts (e.g., Briscoe) that lay outside the colonizing forces. These intrapersonal understandings of themselves were developed in alternate social spaces and times—most often in their home and community cultures, which were largely communities of color (e.g., de la Portilla, Choti, Hayes, Khalifa, Giles, El-Amin, Laura, & Henry).

For example, we learn from Khalifa that his father presented a counter-model for Black masculinity that he eventually drew upon to resist the White imaginative of Black masculinity. While mothers, extra-familial mentors, or readings such as *The Autobiography of Malcolm X* might be influential resources for other Black boys, Khalifa's Black father was deeply informative in his duality of the forces and resistance. Contributors used their agency to resist, drawing from both personal and public contextual resources.

Spirituality. Spirituality encompasses both intra- and inter-personal resources: Scholars describe drawing from the spirit within themselves (e.g., El-Amin) and from their spiritual fellowship with others (e.g., Choti; Giles). Choti described drawing from the spiritual fellowship of her family to resist falling into an early pregnancy and/or marriage as a way to escape the ongoing stress of a woman seeking an education in a patriarchal society. Likewise, Griffin-EL describes how he drew from his spiritual heritage to confront his classmates about their marginalizing practices in love rather than anger. Acting in love and forgiveness helped some of his classmates to see their own actions as oppressive. Thus, for some contributors, their spirituality was so important in resisting colonizing forces that it became part of their criticality.

Interpersonal contextual resources. A third but key contextual personal resource that contributors often described was the counsel of friends, family members, and colleagues. These interpersonal contextual resources provided the emotional support needed to withstand battle fatigue (e.g., Griffin-EL), provided alternate understandings of the situations (e.g., Briscoe), and suggested strategies for negotiating these forces (e.g., de la Portilla, Howard).

In sum, personal contextual resources were central in the resistance of these contributors. Perhaps this is not surprising. Public educational systems have been modeled on the cultural norms of wealthy White males, not those of people of color, women (e.g., Spring, 2006), or the poor. Thus, public intellectual resources are unlikely to be useful in resisting White male privileging and the colonization of people of color, the working class, or women. Yet there are some useful public intellectual resources.

Transcendence: Merging Public and Private Resources

Our epistemologies become transcendent when we combine public and private in the development of our critical awareness and in our resistance. The personal contextual resources we used in the exercise of our agency were often combined with the intellectual, epistemological, and ideological resources we accessed during graduate school to develop various forms of resistance. The most commonly cited public resource was that of critical scholarship. This public intellectual scholarship and these epistemologies concerned the ways in which racialized groups, lower-income groups, and women had been and were still being oppressively colonized. Some of us learned early from their cultural communities and families, who had developed and shared resistant epistemologies about the oppression they experienced as racialized people and how to best negotiate those forces (e.g., Jennings).

Being able to draw upon their own experiences also helped us to extend critical social theories we learned in graduate school because we are insiders/outsiders. In other words, critical scholars may be transcendent *because* they are insiders/outsiders. Perhaps scholars always have transcended the public and private domain when they produced new ways of understanding the world. However, if such transcendence existed, it has more often than not been invisible, taken for granted, or prohibited by insider scholars. Indeed, traditional positivists look askance or completely exclude knowledge that is "tainted" by the personal domain.

Yet this very transcendence allows these marginalized groups to combine their personal epistemologies with public epistemologies and create new ways of understanding the world that are useful for both minority and dominant groups as we seek to create a more equitable society. At the same time, we note that such knowledge was missing from—and thus not legitimated—in our public P-12 schooling. Worse yet, such knowledge was largely nonexistent in our undergraduate teacher education (e.g., Juárez & Hayes; Briscoe).

Colonizing forces (e.g., critical theory, critical race theory, critical feminist scholarship) appear to be part of the public school null curriculum. At best, racism and sexism were described as something that had occurred in the past, and classism is largely ignored in both the past and present. Many of the authors tell us that the first time they encountered "legitimated" critical understandings concerning past and current colonizing forces was in their doctoral program (e.g., Juárez & Hayes). If critical knowledge and epistemologies are inaccessible unless one is in a doctoral program, this suggests that such critical information is unavailable to the vast majority of people in the U.S. population. More importantly, the groups of people who are most vulnerable to the oppressive colonizing forces do not have access to the information.

In 2012, as calculated from the United States Census (2013), 0.5% of Hispanics, 0.9% of Blacks, 1.8% of non-Hispanic Whites, and 3.2% of Asian Americans over the age of 25 had doctorates. Likewise, 1.1% of women and 2.1% men over the age of 25 had doctorates. Yet critical scholarship was an invaluable public contextual resource in our resistance to colonizing forces. Critical knowledge helped us to better understand and articulate our own experiences, as well as legitimate our understandings to others. Unfortunately, the personal contextual resources, central to our development of transcendent epistemologies and resistance to colonizing forces, are increasingly vulnerable in the neoliberal climate that has come to dominate educational institutions.

Transcendence in the Neoliberal Era?

The neoliberal ethos permeating education acts against friendships as well as cooperative and democratic relations among faculty (e.g., Ambrosio, 2013). Rather, neoliberal culture, policies, and practices in education induce deeply competitive individualistic and entrepreneurial subjectivities (e.g., Briscoe 2012b). Almost all contributors indicated the importance of the personal support of friends, families, and colleagues in their resistance of colonizing forces. de Oliver describes these neoliberal forces as they strip away the enlightened democratic intellectual identity of scholars in higher education, replacing it with more commercial ones. This individualistic, competitive, and self-interested identity acts against the collectivist subjectivities that are encouraged in many homes of color. Giles describes his resistance to the neoliberal colonizing forces in higher education that were coercing him to abandon his humanitarian and collectivist interpretation of his role as a faculty member in favor of a more competitive and self-interested interpretation. Thus, neoliberal policies act against the very contextual resources by which we exercise our agency to resist oppressive contexts. As the culture of education becomes increasingly entrepreneurial, it becomes correspondingly hostile to those from marginalized social spaces.

Resistance ↔ Transforming Ourselves ↔ Transforming our Context and Society

Resistance is a complex of power/knowledge relations (Briscoe, 1993). As we develop an awareness of colonizing forces, we articulate new forms of knowledge. These new forms of knowledge can have multiple effects. They can change our conceptions of ourselves and of our context. The very writing of these counter-narratives is a means of resistance. In writing these counter-narratives, we further developed our understandings and actions toward people who have suffered colonizing forces or who have been constructed as colonizers. As Collins (2000) notes, most of our identities have been constructed as both oppressed and oppressors. These new epistemological formations become resources by which we and others exercise our agency.

Some readers may recognize their own struggles embodied in these autoethnographies. These counter-narratives thus can help us articulate the colonizing forces that we have faced silently and/or unknowingly. We may gain new ways of understanding ourselves and the contexts of our lives. As we develop these new understandings of society and of ourselves, our actions begin to change to align with them. Furthermore, readers may adapt some of the strategies described herein for negotiating and resisting similar forces that they face in different but similar contexts. As we resist those actions that ascribe deficit/privileged identities, we co-construct new, more equitable ones for others and ourselves. For example, Felecia has begun to incorporate Griffen-EL's concept of love in her confrontations of those who enact colonizing power relations. Likewise, Muhammad's deeper and more consistent attempts at decolonizing his teaching came from his considerations of Jennings's work.

Those who do not recognize any of their own struggles embodied in any these counter-narratives may develop a further awareness of the colonizing practices that oppress others in educational institutions—or the ways that we and they have been constructed as colonizers. As we develop such awareness, we may change the way we act. We may recognize our complicity in colonizing power relations. Our loss of "innocence" may encourage us to change our actions and help others to develop further awareness of their complicity. We may begin resisting, rather than accepting or reproducing, colonizing power relations that privilege some while disadvantaging others. For example, although she was unaware of it at the time, Howard's acceptance of a colorblind discourse made her tacitly complicit in colonizing forces enacted during her high school and early college years. Yet as she developed an awareness of some of these colonizing forces, she changed her tacit acceptance of, and complicity with, a colorblind discourse—one that privileged Whites while ascribing deficit identities to people of color. Her autoethnography helps those of us who have innocently but tacitly participated in such colonizing discourses begin to understand how these practices harm ourselves and others. As we develop such understandings, we can begin to actively resist such practices both by ourselves and by others.

Interweaving and reciprocally affecting each other, we transform ourselves, our understandings, our actions (resistance), and our context. All of which, acting together, according to Foucault (1980a) and Collins (2000), can transform our societies and the world. Our lives, our contexts, and our society can become more egalitarian and meaningful with less alienation, sterility, and isolation.

Transcendence and Escape from the
Iron Cage of Technical-Rationality

More than a century ago, Weber (1902/1992) claimed that Western society was headed toward an iron cage of technical-rationality dominated by an accounting mentality (Weber, 1902/1992). This iron cage of accounting technical-rationality would be a "totally administered society" (Horkheimer & Adorno, 1944/2002, p. 20). In such a society, people would no longer make judgments informed on multiple levels, but rather their decisions would be predetermined by technical-rational policies reliant on numbers. Those aspects not subject to being quantified (e.g., mutual respect, caring, dignity) would disappear from people's considerations. Our lives would become increasingly sterile, alienated, and meaningless as technical-rational thinking colonized more and more of our life worlds. We would become robots caught in a machine. Briscoe and Khalifa (2013) found that public school administrators caught in such an iron cage of rationality were coerced first into ignoring the communication they received from the parents of the students in their schools and secondly into making decisions to close schools in Black communities. Secondly, when asked how they came to make the decision, they pointed to all the technical processes and quantified data they used to make and justify their decisions.

Likewise, Habermas (1968) and Collins (2000) both suggest that unequal power relations distort our understandings of the world and ourselves. The historical idea that one kind of person can own and dictate the actions of another type—whether it be Whites owning Blacks or men owning women—has been a pernicious and ever-changing weed. And if Habermas (1968), Foucault (1980a, 1980b), and Collins (2000) are right, this pernicious weed has warped dominant knowledge paradigms in Europe and the United States for centuries. We suggest that the current forms of these persistent and pernicious warpings are producing the accounting mentality that is rife in the technical-rational and neoliberal system that increasingly dominates our educational system (e.g., Briscoe & Khalifa, 2013).

Horkheimer and Adorno (1944/2002) claimed that intellectual resources outside instrumental technical-rationality epistemologies were crucial in diverting society from this iron cage; they suggested that intellectual resources of spirituality, emotionality, and so on that lay outside of technical-rational (commonly thought to be objective) ways of knowing our world offered a way out of the iron cage. If transcendent ideas, such as those emerging from these critical autoethnographies, begin to shape the way we understand ourselves and others, we may begin understanding our world and making decisions in a more personal, spiritual, and caring way. And if society's dominant understandings begin to incorporate the epistemologies and understandings of those who have historically been excluded—such as these autoethnographies—then the commonsensical ideas that populate our mainstream media and educational curricula may change. They may help to curb the apathy spawned by the battle fatigue. Likewise, the meaning-lessness, isolation, and alienation spawned by an "accounting" technical-rational educational system and society and described by Arter Jackson at the beginning of this book may be ameliorated.

Practical Implications from the Lessons Learned

The model presented at the beginning of this chapter represents a theoretical advancement in our understanding of the processes of agency and the development of critical identity. But what does this all mean for future social justice scholars, whether in higher education or in P-12 education? This book also provides a resource for initiating our questioning of both the colonizer and colonized aspects of our identities—as well as the ways in which society constructs the colonized and colonizer identities. Using the foregoing autoethnographies as beginning points, we can question ourselves and examine our practices, policies, and understandings. Following are some practical and concrete questions we can ask ourselves in our classes, meetings, homes, and research:

PERSONAL INTERROGATION

- Have I experienced similar types of colonizing forces? What different types of identities are ascribed to me and to others? In what contexts and in what ways? In our educational curriculums, what types of identities are constructed that relate to people like me or people different from me? In what ways do curriculums, school faculty, or administrations construct U.S. systems as fair, but some people as inferior/deficient and others as superior?

- What other colonizing forces do I or others experience? What types of identities are ascribed to me and to others through images and practices? Are they deficit? Are they privileged? In what ways am I constructed as superior? As inferior? Through what sorts of practices or images are these identities ascribed? What sorts of practices or images act to dehumanize me or others? Do educational curriculums hide or expose forces that construct colonized/colonizer relations in our society?

- What kind of power relationships do I enact in my practices?

  ♦ Through the things that I do or say, what sort of power relations do I enact? Do my practices (discursive or otherwise) enact egalitarian relations of power? In what ways do I enact power relations that maintain my privileges (White? Economic class? Gender? Sexual orientation? Other?) My disadvantages? Are my actions complicit with power relations that colonize others or myself? Do I look the other way when I see practices that dehumanize or strip the dignity from others or me?

PERSONAL AND PUBLIC ACTIONS

- What resources can we use to further resist the effects and begin undoing the constructions of these colonizing forces?

- What resources are in these counter-narratives that can help us to see and articulate ways in which we are constructed as the colonized? What resources in these counter-narratives can help us to see and articulate the ways in which we are constructed as colonizers? What other resources can we use to recognize colonizing forces?

- What steps can I take to resist this oppression?

- In what ways am I or others made to feel deficit? Are the standards (educational and otherwise) used to judge me or others flexible enough to allow for multiple but fair ways of being in the world? Or does it privilege some groups while disadvantaging others?

- How can we work together to help create a more socially just educational system and society?

  ♦ How do we speak to our oppressors to make them confront their oppressive actions? How do we make others aware of policies and practices that dehumanize us, and how do we begin to change them? How do we stifle our defensiveness when others point out our privilege or our complicity in maintaining our privilege?

This book offers a number of strategies by which to recognize and resist the forces that act to colonize us by ascribing deficit identities to our race/ethnic, gender, or economic class. At the same time, it offers a number of strategies for resisting and transforming both the colonizer and the colonized aspects of our identities. We hope that this collection of counter-narratives benefits those who have been and are currently facing oppressive colonizing practices, as well as those who have perhaps unknowingly enacted colonizing practices. We encourage researchers and educators to discover and reflect about their own paths to criticality. Even in the midst of an increasingly neoliberal educational system and society, we will continue to resist. Courage.

References

Abu-Lughod, L. (1988). *Veiled sentiments: Honor and poetry in a Bedouin society.* Berkeley, CA: University of California Press.

Abu-Lughod, L. (1990). The romance of resistance: Tracing transformations of power through Bedouin women. *American Ethnologist, 17*(1), 41–55. Retrieved from http://www.jstor.org/stable/645251.

Ackelsberg, M. (2014). (Feminist) political science as an interdisciplinary exploration. *Polity, 46*(1), 115–121.

Adams, T. E., & Jones, S. H. (2011). Telling stories: Reflexivity, queer theory, and autoethnography. *Cultural Studies ↔ Critical Methodologies, 11*(2), 108–116.

Adiele, F. (2010, March 10). My life in Black and White: Why memoir is the ultimate multicultural act. *YES! Magazine.* Retrieved from http://www.yesmagazine.org/yes53Adiele.

Aguirre, A., Martinez, R., & Hernandez, A. (1993). Majority and minority faculty perceptions in academe. *Research in Higher Education, 34*(3), 371–385.

Alexander, M. (2012). *The new Jim Crow: Mass incarceration in the age of colorblindness.* New York, NY: The New Press.

Almanac of Higher Education. (2012). 2012 faculty salary survey, University of Texas at San Antonio. *The Chronicle of Higher Education.* Retrieved from http://chronicle.com/article/faculty-salaries-data-2012/131431#id=229027.

Ambrosio, J. (2013). Changing the subject: Neoliberalism and accountability in public education. *Educational Studies, 49*(4), 316–333.

Anzaldua, G. (1999). *Borderlands la frontera: The new mestiza* (2nd ed.). San Francisco, CA: Aunt Lute Press.

Anzaldua, G. (2002). Now let us shift . . . the path of conocimiento . . . inner work, public acts. In G. Anzaldua & A. Keating (Eds.), *This bridge we call home: Radical visions for transformation* (pp. 540–578). New York, NY: Routledge.

Anzaldúa, G. (2003). *La conciencia de la mestiza:* Towards a new consciousness. In C. McCann & K. Seung-Kyung (Eds.), *Feminist theory reader* (pp. 179–187). New York, NY: Routledge.

Appaduri, A. (1996). Introduction: Commodities and the politics of value. In A. Appadurai (Ed.), *The social life of things: Commodities in cultural perspective* (4th ed., pp. 3–63). Cambridge, England: Cambridge University Press.

Apple, M. W. (1989). *Teachers and texts: A political economy of class and gender relations in education.* New York, NY: Routledge.

Apple, M. W. (2003). Freire and the politics of race in education. *International Journal of Leadership in Education, 6*(2), 107–118.

Arredondo, G. F., Hurtado, A., Najera-Ramirez, O., Klahn, N., & Zavella, P. (Eds.). (2003). *Chicana feminisms: A critical reader.* Durham, NC: Duke University Press.

Austin, A. E. (2002). Preparing the next generation of faculty: Graduate school as socialization to the academic career. *The Journal of Higher Education, 73,* 94–121.

Ayanga, H. O. (1996). Violence against women in African oral literature as portrayed in proverbs. In G. Wamue & M. N. Getui (Eds.), *Violence against Women: Reflections by Kenyan Women Theologians* (pp. 13–20). Nairobi: Acton Publishers.

Ayers, J., Wheeler, E., Fracasso, M., Galupo, M. P., Rabin, J., & Slater, B. (1999). Reinventing the university through the teaching of diversity. *Journal of Adult Development, 6*(3), 163–173.

Ayers, W., Quinn, T., & Stovall, D. (2009). *Handbook of social justice in education.* New York, NY: Routledge.

Baldwin, J. (1970, October). Why I left America. Conversation: Ida Lewis and James Baldwin. *Essence* (New York, NY: Signet). Reprinted on pp. 409–419 in Abraham Chapman (Ed.), *New Black Voices.*

Baldwin, J. (1985). White man's guilt. In J. Baldwin (Ed.), *The price of the ticket: Collected non-fiction, 1948–1985* (pp. 409–414). New York, NY: St. Martin's Press.

Balibar, E. (1990). Paradoxes of universality. In D. Goldberg (Ed.), *Anatomy of racism* (pp. 283–294). Minneapolis, MN: University of Minnesota Press.

Bamberg, M. (2004). Considering counter narratives. In M. Bamberg & M. Andrews (Eds.), *Considering counter narratives: Narrating, resisting, making sense* (pp. 351–371). Amsterdam, Netherlands: John Benjamins.

Banton, M. (1987). *Racial theories.* Cambridge, England: Cambridge University Press.

Barnes, B. (2009). A look back and a look ahead: How to navigate the doctoral process successfully. In V. B. Bush, C. R. Chambers, & M. Walpole, *From diplomas to doctorates: The success of Black women in higher education and its implications for equal educational opportunities for all* (pp. 161–183). Sterling, VA: Stylus Publishing.

Barton, A. C., and Tan, E. (2010). "We be burnin'!" Agency, identity, and science learning. *Journal of the Learning Sciences, 19*(2), 187–229.

Bastedo, M. N., and Gumport, P. J. (2003). Access to what?: Mission differentiation and academic stratification in US public higher education. *Higher Education, 46*(3), 341–359.

Baudrillard, J. (2005). *The intelligence of evil or the lucidity pact.* New York, NY: Berg.

Beauboeuf-Lafontant, T. (2009). *Behind the mask of the strong Black woman: Voice and the embodiment of a costly performance.* Philadelphia, PA: Temple University Press.

Becker, A. (1990). The role of school in the maintenance and change of ethnic group affiliation. *Human Organization, 49*(1), 48–55.

Becker, A. L. (2009). Ethical considerations of teaching spirituality in the academy. *Nursing Ethics, 16*(6), 69–706.

Behar, R. (1996). *The vulnerable observer: Anthropology that breaks your heart.* Boston, MA: Beacon Press.

Bell, D. (1992). *Faces at the bottom of the well: The permanence of racism.* New York, NY: Basic Books.

Bell, D. (1995). Property rights in whiteness—their legal legacy, their economic costs. In R. Delgado (Ed.), *Critical race theory: The cutting edge* (pp. 75–83). Philadelphia, PA: Temple University Press.

Bell, D. A. (1995). Who's afraid of critical race theory. *University of Illinois Law Review,* 893.

Bennett, L., Jr. (1966). *The White problem in America.* Chicago, IL: Johnson Publishing Company.

Berger, P., & Luckmann, T. (1966). *The social construction of reality: A treatise in the sociology of knowledge.* London, England: Penguin University Books.

Bernal, D. (2002). Critical race theory, latCrit theory and critical raced-gendered epistemologies: Recognizing students of color as holders and creators of knowledge. *Qualitative Inquiry, 8*(1), 105–126.

Bhaba, H. (1986). Remembering Fanon. In F. Fanon (Ed.), *Black skin, White masks* (pp. 1–2). London, England: Pluto Press.

Blackwell, M. (2003). Contested Histories: Las hijas de Cuauhtemoc, Chicana feminisms, and print culture in the Chicano Movement, 1968–1973. In G. F. Arredondo, A. Hurtado, N. Klahn, O. Najera-Ramirez, & P. Zavella (Eds.), *Post-contemporary interventions. Chicana feminisms: A critical reader* (pp. 59–89). Durham, NC: Duke University Press.

Blaisdell, B. (2005). Seeing every student as a 10: Using critical race theory to engage White teachers' colorblindness. *International Journal of Educational Policy, Research & Practice, 6*(1), 31–50.

Bloom, L. (1998). *The vulnerable observer: Anthropology that breaks your heart.* Boston, MA: Beacon Press.

Bonilla-Silva, E. (2001/2003). *White supremacy and racism in the post-civil rights era.* Boulder, CO: Lynne Rienner Publishing.

Bonilla-Silva, E. (2009/2013). *Racism without racists: Color-blind racism and the persistence of racial inequality in America* (3rd ed.). Lanham, MD: Rowland & Littlefield Publishers.

Bordas, J. (2007). *Salsa, soul, and spirit: Leadership for a multicultural age.* San Francisco, CA: Berrett-Koehler Publishers.

Borman, K., & P. O'Reilly (1989). The eighties image of girls and women in the educational reform literature: A review of the issues. In C. M. Shea, E. Sola,

& E. Kahane (Eds.), *The New servants of power: a critique of the 1980s school reform movement* (pp. 175–183). New York, NY: Greenwood Press.

Bourdieu, P. (1984). *Distinction: A social critique of the judgment of taste.* (R. Nice, Trans.). Cambridge, MA: Harvard University Press.

Bourdieu, P. (1986). The forms of capital. In J. C. Richardson (Ed.), *Handbook of theory and research for the sociology of education* (pp. 241–258). New York, NY: Greenwood Press.

Bourdieu, P. (1988). *Homo academicus.* (P. Collier, Trans.). Redwood City, CA: Stanford University Press.

Bourdieu, P. (1991). *Language and symbolic power.* Cambridge, MA: Harvard University Press.

Boykin, W. (1985). The triple quandary and the schooling of Afro-American children. In U. Neisser (Ed.), *The school achievement of minority children: New perspectives* (pp. 57–91). Hillsdale, NJ: Lawrence Erlbaum.

Boykin, W. (1994). Afrocultural expression and its implications for schooling. In E. R Hollins, J. E. King, & W. C. Hyman (Eds.), *Teaching diverse populations: Formulating a knowledge base* (pp. 243–273). Albany, NY: State University of New York Press.

Bragg, A. K. (1976). *The socialization process of higher education.* Washington, DC: The George Washington University.

Briscoe, F. (1993). *Knowledge/power and practice: A Foucauldian interpretation of nineteenth century classrooms* (Unpublished dissertation). University of Cincinnati, Cincinnati, OH.

Briscoe, F. (2005). A question of representation in educational discourse: Multiplicities and intersections of identities and positionalities. *Educational Studies, 38*(1), 23–41.

Briscoe, F. (2009). "They make you invisible": Negotiating power at the academic intersections of ethnicity, gender, and class. *Equity & Excellence in Education, 42*(2), 233–248.

Briscoe, F. (2012a). Unraveling the meritocratic myth: Oppression and conflict in the emergence of critical educator subjectivities. *Vitae Scholasticae, 29*(2), 32–57.

Briscoe, F. (2012b). Anarchist, neoliberal, & democratic decision-making: Deepening the joy in learning and teaching. *Educational Studies, 48*(1), 72–103.

Briscoe, F. (in press). "The biggest problem": School leaders' discursive construction of deficit Latino ELL identities in a neoliberal context. *The Journal of Language Identity & Education.*

Briscoe, F., & de Oliver, M. (2012). School leaders' discursive constructions of low-income and minority family identities: A marketplace racism/classism. *Critical Inquiry in Language Studies, 48*(3), 1–35.

Briscoe, F., & Khalifa, M. (2013). 'That racism thing:' A critical discourse analysis of a conflict over the proposed closure of a Black high school, race, ethnicity, & education. Retrieved from http://www.tandfonline.com/eprint/rC4jiUjvRK-bg8HCnEXer/full#.UcSLmfZAS_0.

Brockman, N. (2009). Kenya. In R. T. Francoeur (Ed.), *The international encyclopedia of sexuality.* New York, NY: The Continuum Publishing Company.

Butler, J. (1988). Performative acts and gender constitution: An essay in phenomenology and feminist theory. *Theatre Journal, 40*(4), 519–531.

Butler, J. (1999). *Gender trouble: Feminism and the subversion of identity*. New York, NY: Routledge.

Butler, J. (2003). Performative acts and gender constitution: An essay in phenomenology and feminist theory. In C. McCann & K. Seung-Kyung (Eds.), *Feminist theory reader* (pp. 415–427). New York, NY: Routledge.

Caboni, T., & Proper, E. (2009). Re-envisioning the professional doctorate for educational leadership and higher education leadership: Vanderbilt University's Peabody College.

Cahnmann, M. (2003). The craft, practice and possibility of poetry in educational research. *Educational Researcher, 32*(3), 29–36.

Calmore, J. (2005). Whiteness as audition and Blackness as performance: Status protest from the margin. *Washington University Journal of Law & Policy, 18*(1/6), 99–128.

Cannela, G. S., & Perez, M. S. (2012). Emboldened patriarchy in higher education: Feminist readings of capitalism, violence, and power. *Cultural Studies ↔ Critical Methodologies, 12*(4), 279–286.

Carter, D. J. (2008). Achievement as resistance: The development of a critical race achievement ideology among Black achievers. *Harvard Educational Review, 78*(3), 466–497.

Case, K. (2013). *Deconstructing privilege: Teaching and learning as allies in the classroom*. New York, NY: Routledge.

Chambers, T. V. (2009). The "Receivement Gap": School tracking policies and the fallacy of the "achievement gap." *The Journal of Negro Education*, 417–431.

Chamboredon, J., & Prevot, J. (1975). Changes in the social definition of early childhood and the new forms of symbolic violence. *Theory and Society, 2*(1), 331–350.

Chang, H. (2011). Autoethnography as method for spirituality research in the academy. *Spirituality in higher education: Autoethnographies*, 11–30.

Chang'ach, J. K. (2012). Impact of teenage pregnancy on the education of the girl-child: A case study of Keiyo South District, Keiyo-Marakwet County, Kenya. *International Journal of Social Science Tomorrow, 1*(1), 1–8.

Chappelle, D. (Writer), & Brennan, N. (Director). (2004). When keeping it real goes wrong. [Television series episode]. In D. Chappelle, N. Brennan, & M. Armour (Executive Producers), *Chappelle's show*. United States: Paramount Pictures.

Church of Jesus Christ of Latter-Day Saints (2012). *Mormons do not practice polygamy*. Retrieved from http://www.mormontopics.org/eng/polygamy?CID=30002&gclid=CL-W6ZKX7bICFS-RPAodkVIAQg.

Ciabattari, T. (2010). Cultural capital, social capital, and educational inequality. *Childhood Education, 87*(2), 119–121.

Clandinin, D. J., & Connelly, F. M. (1994). Personal experience methods. In N. K. Denzin & Y. S. Lincoln (Eds.), *Handbook of qualitative research* (pp. 413–427). Thousand Oaks, CA: Sage Publications.

Cleveland, D. (Ed.). (2004). *A long way to go: Conversations about race by African-American faculty and graduate students*. New York, NY: Peter Lang Publishing.

Climate Institute. (2011). Water. Retrieved from http://www.climate.org/topics/water.html.

Cochran-Smith, M., Shakman, K., Jong, C., Terrell, D., Barnett, J., & Mcquilian, P. (2009). Good and just teaching: The case for social justice in teacher education. *American Journal of Education, 115*, 347–377.

COEHD (n.d.). College Web pages, click department, and then faculty link. Retrieved from http://education.utsa.edu/faculty.

Coghlan, D., & Brannick, T. (2001/2010). Doing action research in your own organization. London, England: Sage Publications.

Cokley, K. (2003). What do we know about the academic motivation of African-American college students? Challenging the "anti-intellectual myth." *Harvard Educational Review, 73*(4), 524–558.

Colesberry, R. F., & Zollo, F. (Producers); & Parker, A. (Director). (1998). *Mississippi burning* [Motion Picture]. United States: Orion Pictures.

Collins, P. H. (1991/2000/2002). *Black feminist thought: Knowledge, consciousness and the politics of empowerment.* New York, NY: Routledge.

Collins, P. H. (1998). *Fighting words: Black women and the search for justice.* Minneapolis, MN: University of Minnesota Press.

Collins, P. H. (2005). Prisons for our bodies, closets for our minds: racism, heterosexism, and Black sexuality. In A. Ferber, K. Holcomb, & T. Wentling (Eds.), *Rethinking Foundations: Theorizing Sex, Gender, and Sexuality* (pp. 115–137). New York, NY: Oxford University Press.

Collins, P. H. (2009). *Another kind of public education: Race, schools, the media and democratic possibilities.* Boston, MA: Simmons College Beacon Press.

Connelly, F. M., & Clandinin, D. J. (1990). Stories of experience and narrative inquiry. *Educational Researcher, 19*(5), 2–14.

Corcoran, M. E., & Courant, P. N. (1985). Sex role socialization and labor market outcomes. *The American Economic Review, 75*(2), 275–278.

Cosby, B., & Poussaint, A. F. (2007). *Come on, people: In the path from victims to victors.* New York, NY: Thomas Nelson Inc.

Coulter, C. A., & Smith, M. L. (2009). Discourse on narrative research—the construction zone: Literary elements in narrative research. *Educational Researcher, 38*(8), 577–590.

Cozart, S. (2010). Becoming whole: A letter to a young, miseducated Black teacher. *Urban Review, 42*, 22–38.

Creighton, S. (2006). Adult outcomes of feminizing surgery. *International Library of Ethics, Law, and the New Medicine, 29*, 207–214.

Crenshaw, K. W. (1997). Color-blind dreams and racial nightmares: Reconfiguring racism in the post-civil rights era. In T. Morrison & C. B. Lacour (Eds.), *Birth of a nation'hood* (pp. 97–168). New York, NY: Pantheon Books.

Crenshaw, K., Gotanda, N., Peller, G., & Thomas, K. (Eds.). (1996). *Critical race theory: The key writings that formed the movement.* New York, NY: New Press.

Cuadraz, G. H. (1992). Experiences of multiple marginality: A case study of Chicana scholarship women. *Journal of the Association of Mexican American Educators, 10*, 31–43.

Cudd, A., & Holmstrom, N. (2011). *Capitalism, for and against: A feminist debate.* Cambridge: England: Cambridge University Press.

Dahlberg, G., & Moss, P. (2005). *Ethics and politics in early childhood education.* London, England: Routledge Falmer.

Dantley, M. E. (2003). Critical spirituality: enhancing transformative leadership through critical theory and African-American prophetic spirituality. *International Journal of Leadership in Education*, 6(1), 3–17.

DeCuir, J. T., & Dixson, A. D. (2004). So when it comes out, they aren't that surprised that it is there: Using critical race theory as a tool of analysis of race and racism in education. *Educational Researcher*, 33(5), 26–31.

Dei, G. J. (2006). Introduction: Mapping the terrain—towards a new politics of resistance. In G. Dei & A. Kempf (Eds.), *Anti-colonialism and education: The politics of resistance* (pp. 1–24). Boston, MA: Sense Publishers.

DeLeon, A. (2010). How do I begin to tell a story that has not been told? Anarchism, autoethnography, and the middle ground. *Equity & Excellence in Education*, 43(4), 398–413. doi:10.1080/10665684.2010.512828.

Deleuze, G., & Guattari, F. (1984). *Anti-Oedipus: Capitalism and schizophrenia.* (R. Hurley, M. Seem, & H. Lane, Trans.). Minneapolis, MN: The University of Minnesota Press.

Deleuze, G., & Guattari, F. (1987). *A thousand plateaus: Capitalism and schizophrenia* (B. Massumi, Trans.). Minneapolis, MN: The University of Minnesota Press.

Delgado-Gaitan, C. (1994). *Consejos*: The power of cultural narratives. *Anthropology and Education Quarterly*, 25, 298–316.

Delgado, R. (1989). Storytelling for oppositionists and others: A plea for narrative. *Michigan Law Review*, 87(8), 2411–2441. Retrieved from http://www.jstor.org/stable/1289308.

Delgado, R. (1991). Affirmative action as a majoritarian device: Or, do you really want to be a role model. *Michigan Law Review*, 89(5), 1222–1231. Retrieved from http://www.jstor.org/stable/1289552.

Delgado, R. (1995). *Critical race theory: The cutting edge.* Philadelphia, PA: Temple University Press.

Delgado, R., & Stefancic, J. (2001). *Critical race theory: An introduction.* New York, NY: New York University Press.

Delgado, R., & Stefancic, J. (2012). *Critical race theory: An introduction.* New York, NY: New York University Press.

Delpit, L. D. (1988). The silenced dialogue: Power and pedagogy in educating other people's children. *Harvard Educational Review*, 58(3), 280–298.

Denzin, N. K. (1989). *The research act: A theoretical introduction to sociological methods.* Englewood Cliffs, NJ: Prentice Hall.

Denzin, N. K. (2003). Performing [auto] ethnography politically. *The Review of Education, Pedagogy & Cultural Studies*, 25(3), 257–278.

Denzin, N. K. (2006). Analytic autoethnography, or déjà vu all over again. *Journal of Contemporary Ethnography*, 35(4), 419–428.

de Oliver, M. (2008). Democratic materialism: The articulation of world power in democracy's era of triumph. *Journal of Power*, 1(3), 355–383.

deOliver, M. & Briscoe, F. (2011). US higher education in a budgetary vortex—1992–2007: Tracing the positioning of academe in the context of growing inequality. *Higher Education*, 62(5), 607–637.

Descartes, R. (1637). *Discourse on the method of rightly conducting one's reason and of seeking truth in the sciences.* Project Gutenberg. Retrieved from http://www.gutenberg.org/cache/epub/59/pg59.txt.

Dillard, C. B. (2000). The substance of things hoped for, the evidence of things not seen: Examining an endarkened feminist epistemology in educational research and leadership. *International Journal of Qualitative Studies in Education*, 13(6), 661–681.

Dillard, C. B. (2006). *On spiritual strivings: Transforming an African American woman's academic life*. Albany, NY: State University of New York Press.

Dillard, C. B. (2006). When the music changes, so should the dance: Cultural and spiritual considerations in paradigm "proliferation." *International Journal of Qualitative Studies in Education*, 19(1), 59–76.

Dixson, A., & Rousseau, C. (Eds.). (2006). *Critical race theory in education*. New York, NY: Routledge.

Dollar. D., & Gatti, R. (1999). Gender inequality, income, and growth: Are good times good for women? (Working Paper Series, No. 1). The World Bank Development Research Group/ Poverty Reduction and Economic Management Network. Retrieved from http://darp.lse.ac.uk/frankweb/courses/EC501/DG.pdf.

Doucet, F. (2011). (Re)Constructing home and school: Immigrant parents, agency, and the (un)desirability of bridging multiple worlds. *Teachers College Record*, 113(12), 2705–2738.

Dowdy, J. (2002). Language and identity. In L. Delpit & J. Dodwy (Eds.), *The skin that we speak. Thoughts on language and culture in the classroom* (pp. 1–14). New York, NY: The New Press.

Dowdy, J. K. (2008). *Ph.D. stories: Conversations with my sisters*. Cresskill, NJ: Hampton Press.

Du Bois, W. E. B. (1903/1989/2008). *The soul of Black folks*. New York, NY: Bantam.

Duncan, G. (2005). Critical race ethnography in education: Narrative, inequality, and the problem of epistemology. *Race, Ethnicity and Education*, 8(1), 93–114.

Dyer, R. (1997). *White*. New York, NY: Routledge.

Dyer, R. (1998). White. *Screen*, 29(4), 30–45.

Earick, M. E. (2009). *Racially equitable teaching: Beyond the Whiteness of professional development for early childhood educators*. New York, NY: Peter Lang Publishing.

Eisenhart, M. (2005). Boundaries and selves in the making of "science." In W. M. Roth (Ed.), *Auto/biography and auto/ethnography: Praxis of research method* (pp. 283–299). Rotterdam, Netherlands: Sense Publishers.

Elenes, C. A., & Delgado Bernal, D. (2010). Latina/o education and the reciprocal relationship between theory and practice: four theories informed by the experiential knowledge of marginalized communities. In E. G. Murillo, Jr. (Ed.), *Handbook of Latinos and Education: Theory, Research & Practice*. New York, NY: Routledge.

Ellis, C. (1997). Evocative autoethnography: Writing emotionally about our lives. In W. G. Tierney & Y. S. Lincoln (Eds.), *Representation and the text: Re-framing the narrative voice* (pp. 115–132). Albany, NY: State University of New York Press.

Ellis, C. (2004). *The ethnographic I: A methodological novel about autoethnography*. Walnut Creek, CA: Altamira Press.

Ellis, C., & Bochner, A. P. (2000). Autoethnography, personal narrative, reflexivity: Researcher as subject. In N. K. Denzin & Y. S. Lincoln (Eds.), *Handbook of qualitative research* (pp. 733–768). Thousand Oaks, CA: Sage Publications.

Evans, A. E. (2007). School leaders and their sensemaking about race and demographic change. *Educational Administration Quarterly, 43*(2), 159–188.

Fairclough, N. (1992). *Discourse and social change*. Oxford, England: Polity.

Fairclough, N. (1995). *Critical discourse analysis: The critical study of language*. New York, NY: Longman.

Fanon, F. (1963). *The wretched of the earth*. New York, NY: Grove Press.

Fanon, F. (1994). *Black skin, White masks*. New York, NY: Grove Press.

Feagin, J. (2010). *The White racial frame: Centuries of racial framing and counterframing*. New York, NY: Routledge.

Feagin, J. (2012). *White party, white government: Race, class and U.S. politics*. New York, NY: Routledge.

Featherstone, H. (1980). *A difference in the family: Life with a disabled child*. New York, NY: Basic Books.

Feldman, M. S., Skoldberg, K., Brown, R. N., & Horner, D. (2004). Making sense of stories: A rhetorical approach to narrative analysis. *Journal of Public Administration Research Theory, 14*(2), 147–170.

Fine, M. (1994). Working the hyphens. *Handbook of qualitative research*. Thousand Oaks, CA: Sage Publications.

Fisch, A. (2007). *The Cambridge companion to African-American slave narrative*. Cambridge, England: Cambridge University Press.

Fischer, M. (1986). Ethnicity and the post-modern arts of memory. In J. Clifford & G. E. Marcos (Eds.), *Writing culture: The poetics and politics of ethnography* (pp. 194–234). Berkeley, CA: University of California Press.

Fishman, J. (1996). What do you lose when you lose your language? In G. Cantoni (Ed.), *Stabilizing indigenous languages* (pp. 80–91). Tempe, AZ: Center for Excellence in Education.

Fitzsimons, P. (2002). Neoliberalism and education: The autonomous chooser. *Radical Pedagogy, 2*(4). Retrieved from http://radicalpedagogy.icaap.org/content/issue4_2/04_fitzsimons.html.

Fleming, J. (1984) *Blacks in college*. San Francisco, CA: Jossey-Bass.

Flinders, D. J., Noddings, N., & Thornton, S. J. (1986). The null curriculum: Its theoretical basis and practical implications. *Curriculum Inquiry, 16*(1), 33–42.

Fordham, S. (1991). Racelessness in private schools: Should we deconstruct the racial and cultural identity of African-American adolescents? *Teachers College Record, 92*(3), 470–484.

Fordham, S., & Ogbu, J. (1986). Black students' school success: Coping with the burden of "acting White." *The Urban Review, 18*(3), 176–206.

Foucault, M. (1972). *The Archaeology of knowledge and the discourse on language* (A. M. Sheridan Smit, Trans.). New York, NY: Pantheon Press.

Foucault, M. (1980a). Power/knowledge: Selected interviews and other writings, 1972–1977. (C. Gordon, Ed., & C. Gordon, L. Marshall, J. Mepham, & K. Soper, Trans.). New York, NY: Pantheon Books.

Foucault, M. (1980b). *The history of sexuality volume I: An introduction*. (R. Hurley. Trans.). New York, NY: Vintage Press.

Foucault, M. (1982). The subject and power. *Critical Inquiry, 8*(4), 777–795. Retrieved from http://www.jstor.org/stable/1343197.

Frankenberg, R. (1993). *White women, race matters.* Minneapolis, MN: University of Minnesota Press.

Franklin, V. P. (1995). *Living our stories, telling our truths: Autobiography and the making of the African-American intellectual tradition.* Oxford, England: Oxford University Press.

Fraser, N. (1989). *Unruly practices: Power, discourse, and gender in contemporary social theory* (Vol. 94, No. 1–3). Minneapolis, MN: University of Minnesota Press.

Freire, P. (1970/2002/2008). *Pedagogy of the oppressed.* New York, NY: Continuum.

Freire, P. (2007) *Education for critical consciousness.* New York, NY: Continuum.

Friedan, B. (1963). *The feminine mystique.* New York, NY: W. W. Norton & Company.

Fries, B., & Kelly, B. T. (2005). Retaining each other: Narratives of two African American women in the academy. *The Urban Review, 37*(3), 221–242.

Gaines, E. (1971). *The autobiography of Miss Jane Pittman.* New York, NY: Dial Press.

Gallegos, S. (2007, July 13). ICE divides. Stop the raids. *Denver Post.* Retrieved from http://www.denverpost.com/headlines/ci_6362565.

Gandara, P. (1995). *Over the ivy walls.* Albany, NY: State University of New York Press.

Gardner, S. K. (2008). Fitting the mold of graduate school: A qualitative study of socialization in doctoral education. *Innovative Higher Education, 33*(1), 125–138.

Gardner, S. K. (2007). "I heard it through the grapevine": Doctoral student socialization in chemistry and history. *Higher Education, 54,* 723–740.

Gee, J. (1996). *Social linguistics and literacies: Ideology in discourses.* London, England: Falmer Press.

Gee, J. (1999). *An introduction to discourse analysis: Theory and method.* New York, NY: Routledge.

Giles, M. S. (2003). *Howard Thurman: A spiritual life in higher education* (Unpublished doctoral dissertation). Indiana University, Bloomington, IN.

Gillborn, D. (2005). Education as an act of White supremacy: Whiteness, critical race theory and education reform. *Journal of Educational Policy, 20*(4), 485–505.

Gilliam, W. S. (2005). *Pre-kindergartners left behind: Expulsion rates in state prekindergarten systems.* Retrieved from http://www.challengingbehavior.org/explore/policy_docs/prek_expulsion.pdf.

Gilligan, C. (1982). *In a different voice: Psychological theory and women's development.* Cambridge, MA: Harvard University Press.

Giroux, H. (2002). Neoliberalism, corporate culture, and the promise of higher education: The university as a democratic public sphere. *Harvard Educational Review, 72*(4), 425–463.

Gluck, S. B., & Patai, D. (1991). *Women's words: The feminist practice of oral history.* New York: Routledge.

Gomez-Peña, G. (1996). *The new world border: Prophecies, poems, and loqueras for the end of the century.* San Francisco, CA: City Lights.

Gonzalez, J. C. (2006). Academic socialization experiences of Latina doctoral students: A qualitative understanding of support systems that aid and challenges that hinder the process. *Journal of Hispanic Higher Education, 76,* 669–700.

Gould, S. (1981). *The mismeasure of man*. New York, NY: Norton.

Gramsci, A. (1971). *Selections from the prison notebooks*. Q. Hoare & G. Nowell Smith (Eds. & Trans.). London, England: Lawrence & Wishart.

Granfield, R. (2010). Making it by faking it: Working-class students in an elite academic environment. In S. J. Ferguson (Ed.), *Mapping the social landscape: readings in sociology* (6th ed., pp. 123–135). New York, NY: McGraw-Hill.

Gregory, A., Skiba, R. J., & Noguera, P. A. (2010). The achievement gap and the discipline gap: two sides of the same coin? *Educational Researcher, 39*(1), 59–68.

Group Mu (Eds.). (1978) *Collages*. Paris: Union Générale.

Group, L. F. (Ed.). (2001). *Telling to live: Latina feminist testimonios*. Durham: Duke University Press.

Guajardo, M., & Guajardo, J. (2002). "Critical ethnography and community change." In Y. Zou & E. T. Trueba (Eds.), *Ethnography in schools: Qualitative approaches to the study of education*. Lanham, MD: Rowman & Littlefield.

Guinier, L. (2004). From racial liberalism to racial literacy: Brown vs. Board of Education and the interest-divergence dilemma. *Journal of American History, 91*(1), 92–118.

Habermas, Jürgen. (1968). *Knowledge and human interests*. (J. Shapiro, Trans.). Boston, MA: Beacon Press.

Hall, C. L. (2009). *African-American journalists: Autobiography as memoir and manifesto*. Lanham, MD: Scarecrow Press.

Hall, J. R. (1992). The capital(s) of cultures: A nonholistic approach to status situations, class, gender and ethnicity. In M. Lamont & A. Fournier (Eds.), *Cultivating differences* (pp. 257–285). Chicago, IL: University of Chicago Press.

Hall, J. R. (1996). Introduction: Who needs "identity"? In S. Hall & P. du Gay (Eds.), *Questions of cultural identity* (pp. 1–17). Thousand Oaks, CA: Sage Publications.

Haman, E.T., & England, W. (2011). Hyphenated identities as a challenge to nation-state school practice. In S. Vandeyar (Ed.), *Hyphenated selves: Immigrant identities within education contexts* (pp. 205–213). Pretoria, South Africa: UNISA Press.

Hamera, J. (2005). Exposing the pedagogical body: Protocols and tactics. In B. K. Alexander, G. L. Anderson, & B. P. Gallegos (Eds.), *Performance theories in education: Power, pedagogy, and the politics of identity* (pp. 59–78). Mahwah, NJ: Lawrence Erlbaum Associates Publishers.

Haraway, D. (1991). *Simians, cyborgs, and women: The reinvention of nature*. New York, NY: Routledge.

Harris, A., Carney, S., & Fine, M. (2001). Counter work: Introduction to "Under the covers: Theorising the politics of counter stories." *International Journal of Critical Psychology, 4*, 6–18.

Harris, C. I. (1992). Whiteness as property. *Harvard Law Review, 106*, 1707.

Harvey, D. (2005). *A brief history of neoliberalism*. London, England: Oxford University Press.

Hayes, C. (2006). *Why we teach: Storying the lives of a Black family of Mississippi educators* (Unpublished doctoral dissertation). University of Utah, Salt Lake City, UT.

Hayes, C., Juárez, B. G., & Cross, P. T. (2012). What we can learn from big mama? *Critical Education*, 3(1), 1–24. Retrieved from http://m1.cust.educ.ubc. ca/journal/index.php/criticaled/issue/archive.

Heidegger, M. (2008). *Being and time*. (J. Macquarrie & E. Robinson, Trans.). Oxford, England: Harper Perennial Modern Classics.

Helfenbein, R. J., & Taylor, L.H. (2009). Critical geographies in/of education: Introduction. *Educational Studies*, 45(3), 236–239.

Hemmings, C. (2011). *Why stories matter: The political grammar of feminist theory*. Durham, NC: Duke University Press.

Hill, D. (2009). *Rethinking education in the era of globalization*. New York, NY: Routledge.

Holt, N. L. (2003). Representation, legitimation, and autoethnography: An autoethnographic writing story. *International Journal of Qualitative Methods*, 2(1), 18–28.

hooks, b. (1989). *Talking back: Thinking feminist, thinking Black*. Boston, MA: South End Press.

hooks, b. (1990). *Yearning: Race, gender, and cultural politics*. Boston, MA: South End Press.

hooks, b. (1992). *Black looks: Race and representation*. Boston, MA: South End Press.

hooks, b. (1994). *Teaching to transgress: Education as the practice of freedom*. New York, NY.: Routledge.

hooks, b. (2003). Eating the other. In S. Hesse-Biber, C. Gilmartin, & R. Lydenberg (Eds.), *Feminist approaches to theory and methodology* (pp. 179–194). New York, NY: Oxford University Press.

hooks, b. (2005). *Sisters of the yam: Black women and self-recovery*. Cambridge, MA: South End Press.

Hoover, E. (2013). Minority applicants to colleges will rise significantly by 2020 in *The Chronicle of Higher Education*. Retrieved from http://chronicle.com/article/ Wave-of-Diverse-College/136603/.

Horkheimer, M., & Adorno, T. W. (2002). *Dialectic of enlightenment: Philosophical fragments*. Redwood City, CA: Stanford University Press.

Horowitz, E. L., & Horowitz, R. E. (1938). Development of social attitudes in children. *Sociometry*, 1, 301–338.

Howard, G. A. (1999). *We can't teach what we don't know: White teachers, multiracial schools*. New York, NY: Teachers College Press.

Howard, K. J. (2012, forthcoming). We hear what we know: Racial messages in a southern school. In J. Lester & R. Gabriel (Eds.), *Performances of research critical issues in K-12 education*. New York, NY: Peter Lang Publishing.

Howard, T., & Flennaugh, T. (2011). Research concerns, cautions and considerations on Black males in a "post-racial" society. *Race Ethnicity and Education*, 14(1), 105–120.

Hughes, S. A. (2008). Maggie and me: a black professor and a white urban school teacher connect autoethnography to critical race pedagogy. *Educational Foundations*, 22(3), 73–95.

Hume, D. (1888, 1967 printing). *A treatise of human nature*. (L. A. Selby-Bigge, Trans.). Oxford: Clarendon Press.

Huntington, S. P. (2004, April). The Hispanic challenge. *Foreign Policy*. Retrieved from Harvard University Foreign Policy Web site: http://cyber.law.harvard.edu/blogs/gems/culturalagency1/SamuelHuntingtonTheHispanicC.pdf.

Hurtado, A. (1996). *The color of privilege: Three blasphemies on race and feminism*. Ann Arbor, MI: University of Michigan.

Irigaray, L. (1985, Eng. trans. 2002). *To speak is never neutral*. New York, NY: Routledge.

Irvin, George (2008): *Super rich: The rise of inequality in Britain and the United States*. Cambridge, England: Polity Press.

Jackson, J., & O'Callaghan, E. (2009). What do we know about glass ceiling effects? A taxonomy and critical review to inform higher education research. *Research in Higher Education, 50*(5), 460–482.

Jackson, S., & Johnson, R. G. (Eds.). (2011). *The Black professoriat: Negotiating a habitable space in the academy*. New York, NY: Peter Lang.

Jenkins, K. (1999). *Why history?: Ethics and postmodernity*. London, England: Routledge.

Jensen, S. (2011). Othering, identity formation and agency. *Qualitative Studies, 2*(2), 63–78.

Johnson, B., & Christenson, L. (2012). *Educational research: quantitative, qualitative, and mixed approaches* (4th ed.). New York, NY: Sage Publications.

Jones, S. H. (2005). Autoethnography: Making the personal political. In N. K. Denzin and Y. S. Lincoln (Eds.), *Handbook of qualitative research* (3rd ed.) (pp. 763–792). Thousand Oaks, CA: Sage.

Jorgensen, D. L. (1989). *Participant observation: A methodology for human studies*. Newbury Park, CA: Sage Publications.

Joy, L. (1998). Why are women underrepresented in public school administration? An empirical test of promotion discrimination. *Economics of Education Review, 17*(2), 193–204.

Juárez, B. G., & Hayes, C. (2010). Social justice is not spoken here: Considering the nexus of knowledge, power, and the education of future teachers in the United States. *Power and Education, 2*(3), 233–252.

Juárez, B. G., & Hayes, C. (2012). An endarkened learning and transformative education for freedom dreams: The education our children deserve. *The Journal of Educational Controversy, 6*(1), 1–17. Retrieved from http://www.wce.wwu.edu/Resources/CEP/eJournal/v006n001/a007.shtml.

Juárez, B. G., Smith, D. T., & Hayes, C. (2008). Social justice means just us White people: The diversity paradox in teacher education. *Democracy & Education, 17*(3), 20–26.

Kamerman, S. (2006). *A global history of early childhood education and care. EFA Global Monitoring Report 2007*. United Nations Educational, Scientific and Cultural Organisation. Retrieved from http://www.researchconnections.org/childcare/resources/1170.

Kennedy, R. (2002). *Nigger: The strange career of a troublesome word*. New York, NY: Pantheon.

Kenya Decides 2013. The Kenya Decides Web site. Retrieved from http://kenya-decides.co.ke/county/kisii/.

Khalifa, M. (2012). A Re-new-ed paradigm in successful urban school leadership principal as community leader. *Educational Administration Quarterly, 48*(3), 424–467.

Khalifa, M. A. (2011). Teacher expectations and principal behavior: responding to teacher acquiescence. *The Urban Review, 43*(5), 702–727.

Kim, M. (2000). Women paid low wages: Who they are and where they work. *Monthly Labor Review, 27,* 26–30.

Kincheloe, J. L., & McLaren, P. (2002). Rethinking critical theory and qualitative research. In Y. Zou & E. T. Trueba (Eds.), *Ethnography and schools: Qualitative approaches to the study of education* (pp. 87–138). Lanham, MD: Rowman & Littlefield.

King, J. E. (1991). Dysconscious racism: Ideology, identity, and the miseducation of teachers. *The Journal of Negro Education, 60*(2), 133–146.

King, Jr., M. L. (1964). Letter from Birmingham jail. In A. F. Westin (Ed.), *Freedom now!* (pp. 10–21). New York, NY: Basic Books.

King, M. (1967). *Where do we go from here?* The Martin Luther King Jr. Research and Education Institute. Retrieved from http://mlkkpp01.stanford.edu/index.php/kingpapers/article/where_do_we_go_from_here/.

King, M. L. (2010). *Strength to love.* Minneapolis, MN: Fortress Press.

Kuhn, T. S. (1962). *The structure of scientific revolutions.* Chicago, IL: University of Chicago Press.

LaCapra, D. (2001). *Writing history, writing trauma.* Baltimore, MD: Johns Hopkins University Press.

Ladson-Billings, G. (1999). Preparing teachers for diverse student populations: A critical race theory perspective. *Review of Research in Education, 24,* 211–247.

Ladson-Billings, G. (2000). Fighting for our lives: Preparing teachers to teach African-American students. *Journal of Teacher Education, 51*(3), 206–214.

Ladson-Billings, G. (2004). Just what is critical race theory and what's it doing in a nice field like education? In G. Ladson-Billings & D. Gillborn (Eds.), *The RoutledgeFalmer reader in multicultural education* (pp. 49–68). New York, NY: RoutledgeFalmer.

Ladson-Billings, G. (2005). The evolving role of critical race theory in educational scholarship. *Race, Ethnicity and Education, 8*(1), 115–119.

Ladson-Billings, G., & Tate, W. (1995). Towards a critical race theory of education. *Teachers College Record, 97*(1), 47–69.

Lamont, M., and Lareau, A. (1988). Cultural capital: Allusions, gaps and glissandos in recent theoretical developments. *Sociological Theory, 6*(2), 153–168.

Lareau, A. (2000). *Home advantage* (2nd ed.). Lanham, MD: Rowman & Littlefield.

Lee, W. Y. (2009). The success of Black women in higher education and its implications for equal educational opportunities for all (Afterword). In V. B. Bush, C. R. Chambers, M. B. Walpole, W. Y. Lee, & K. Freeman (Eds.), *From diplomas to doctorates: the success of black women in higher education and its implications for equal educational opportunities for all.* Sterling, VA: Stylus Publishing.

Lensmire, T. (2008). How I became White while punching de tar baby. *Curriculum Inquiry, 38*(3), 300–322.

Leonardo, Z. (2005). *Race, Whiteness and education*. New York, NY: Routledge.

Levidow, L. (2002). Marketizing higher education: Neoliberal strategies and counter-strategies. In K. Robins and F. Webster (Eds.), *The virtual university? Knowledge, markets and management* (pp. 227–248). Oxford, England: Oxford University Press.

Lewis, A. (2001). There's no "race" in the schoolyard: Color-blind ideology in an (almost) all-White school. *American Educational Research Journal*, 38(4), 781–811.

Lewis, A. (2003). *Race in the schoolyard: Negotiating the color line in classrooms and communities*. New Brunswick, NJ: Rutgers University Press.

Lincoln, Y., & Cannella, G. (2009, January 1). Ethics and the broader rethinking/reconceptualization of research as construct. *Cultural Studies/critical Methodologies*, 9(2), 273–285.

Lipman, P. (2011). *The new political economy of urban education: Neoliberalism, race, and the right to the city*. New York, NY: Routledge.

Lipsitz, G. (2006). *Possessive investment in Whiteness: How White people profit from identity politics*. Philadelphia, PA: Temple University Press.

Lomax, L. E. (1966). The unpredictable Negro. In A. F. Westin (Ed.), *Freedom Now!* (pp. 22–25). New York, NY: Basic Books.

Lorde, A. (1984). Age, race, class, and sex: Women redefining difference. In A. Lorde (ed.), *Sister Outsider*. Freedom, CA: The Crossing Press.

Luke, C., & Gore, J. (1992). Feminisms and critical pedagogy. New York: Routledge.

Lynn, M., & Parker, L. (2006). Critical race studies in education: Examining a decade of research in U.S. schools. *The Urban Review*, 38, 257–334.

Lyotard, J. (1984). *The Postmodern condition: a report on knowledge*. (G. Bennington & B. Massumi, Trans.). Minneapolis, MN: University of Minnesota Press.

Lyotard, J. (1993). *The Postmodern Explained: Correspondence 1982–1985*. University of Minnesota Press, Minneapolis.

Mackeracher, D. (2004). *Making Sense of Adult Learning* (2nd ed.). Toronto, ON: University of Toronto Press.

MacNaughton, G., Davis, K., & Smith, K. (2010). Working and reworking children's performance of "Whiteness" in early childhood education. In M. O'Loughlin & R. Johnson (Eds). *Working the space in between: Pedagogical possibilities in rethinking children's subjectivity*. Albany, NY: State University of New York Press.

Margolis, E., & Romero, M. (1998). The department is very male, very white, very old, and very conservative: The functioning of the hidden curriculum in graduate sociology departments. *Harvard Educational Review*, 68(1), 1–32.

Martin, E. (1994). Introduction: problems and methods. In E. Martin, *Flexible bodies: the role of immunity in American culture from the days of polio to the age of AIDS* (pp. 1–19). Boston, MA: Beacon Press.

Martinez, P. (2011, April 11) Minority professors' satisfaction at Cornell drops. *The Cornell Daily Sun*. Retrieved from http://cornellsun.com/node/46591.

Marx, S. (2006). *Revealing the invisible: Confronting passive racism in teacher education*. New York, NY: Routledge.

Marx, S. (2008). Critical race theory. In L. Given (Ed.), *Sage Encyclopedia of Qualitative Research Methods, 2*, 163–167.

Massey, D. B. (1994). *Space, place, & gender.* Minneapolis, MN: University of Minnesota Press.

Mattis, J. S. (2000). African American women's definition of spirituality and religiosity. *Journal of Black Psychology, 26*(1), 101–122.

McCarthy, C. (1988). Rethinking liberal and radical perspectives on racial inequality in schooling: Making the case of nonsynchrony. *Harvard Educational Review, 58*, 265–279.

McDonald, M., & Zweichner, K. (2009). Social justice teacher education. In W. Ayers, T. Quinn, & K. Stovall (Eds.), *Handbook on social justice in education* (pp. 595–634). Florence, KY: Taylor & Francis.

McIntyre, A. (1997). *Making meaning of Whiteness: Exploring racial identity with White teachers.* Albany, NY: State University of New York Press.

McLaren, P. (1997). *Revolutionary multiculturalism: Pedagogies of dissent for the new millennium.* Boulder, CO: Westview Press.

McLaren, P. (1999). Unthinking Whiteness, rethinking democracy: Critical citizenship in Gringolandia. In C. Clark & J. O'Donnell (Eds.), *Becoming and unbecoming White: Owning and disowning a racial identity* (pp. 10–55). Westport, CT: Praeger.

McLaren, P. (2006). *Life in schools: An introduction to critical pedagogy in the foundations of education* (5th ed.). New York, NY: Allyn & Bacon.

Medina, C., & Luna, G. (2000). Narratives from Latina professors in higher education. *Anthropology & Education Quarterly, 31*(1), 47–66. Retrieved from http://www.jstor.org/stable/3196270.

Meneley, A., & Young, D. J. (2005). *Auto-ethnographies: The anthropology of academic practices.* Ontario, Canada: Broadview Press.

Merchant, C. (1980). *The Death of nature: Women, ecology and the scientific revolution.* New York, NY: HarperCollins.

Meyer, D. (2006). Bush, the decider in chief, in *CBS News.* Retrieved from http://www.cbsnews.com/news/bush-the-decider-in-chief/.

Meyer, K., & Firestone, J. (2005). Has the chilly climate warmed? Perceptions about unequal treatment of men and women at the University of Texas at San Antonio. *All Academic Research.* Retrieved from http://citation.allacademic.com//meta/p_mla_apa_research _citation/0/1/9/4/8/pages19483/p19483-2.php.

Mills, C. (1997). *The racial contract.* Ithaca, NY: Cornell University Press.

Milner, H. R. (2008). Critical race theory and interest convergence as analytical tools in teacher education policies and practices. *Journal of Teacher Education, 59*(4), 332–346.

Ministry of Education (2009). *Primary and secondary schools enrollment.* Nairobi: Government Printer.

Mintz, S. (2004). *Huck's raft: A history of American childhood.* Cambridge, MA: The Belknap Press of Harvard University Press.

Mirowski, P. (2013). *Never let a serious crisis go to waste: How neoliberalism survived the financial meltdown.* London, England: Verso.

Misra, J., Lundquist, J. H., Holmes, E., and Agiomavritis, S. (2011). The ivory ceiling of service work. AAUP. Retrieved from http://www.aaup.org/article/ivory-ceiling-service-work#.Un2pqpFofMo.

Mohanty, C. T. (2003). "Under western eyes" revisited: Feminist solidarity through anticapitalist struggles. *Signs, 28*(2), 499–535.

Muhammad, K. G. (2010). *Condemnation of Blackness: race, crime, and the making of modern urban America.* Cambridge, MA: Harvard University Press.

Muller, S., & Dennis, D. (2007). Life change and spirituality among a college student cohort. *Journal of American College Health, 56*(1), 55–59.

Muller, N., & O'Callaghan, C. (2013). Feminisms. *The Year's Work in Critical and Cultural Theory Crit Cult Theory, 21*(1), 23–42.

Mutua, R. (1978). Women's education and their participation in the changing societies of East Africa. In A. O. Pala, A. Awori, & Krystall (Eds.), *Participation of women in Kenya society* (pp. 160–169). Nairobi, Kenya: Kenya Literature Bureau.

Nash, K. (2012). Blinded by the White: Foregrounding race in a literacy course for preservice teachers. (Unpublished doctoral dissertation). University of South Carolina. Nashville, TN.

National Association for Education of Young Children. (2009). *Developmentally appropriate practice in early childhood programs serving children from birth through age 8.* Position statement of the National Association for the Education of Young Children. Retrieved from http://www.naeyc.org/files/naeyc/file/positions/PSDAP.pdf.

Nelson, L. (1993). The psychological and social origins of autobiographical memory. *Psychological Science, 4*, 7–14.

Ngo, B. (2008). Beyond "culture clash": Understandings of immigrant experiences. *Theory Into Practice, 47*(4), 4–11.

Njue C., & Askew, I. (2004). Medicalization of female genital cutting among the Abagusii in Nyanza Province, Kenya. Retrieved from http://www.popcouncil.org/pdfs/FRONTIERS/FR_FinalReports/Kenya_FGC_Med.pdf.

Noble, J. B. (2006). *Sons of the movement: FTMS risking incoherence on a post-queer cultural landscape.* Toronto, ON: Women's Press.

Noguera, P. (2003). *City schools and the American dream: Reclaiming the promise of public education* (Vol. 17). New York, NY: Teachers College Press.

Norton, B., & Toohey, K. (2011). Identity, language learning, and social change, *Language Learning, 44*(4), 412–446.

Núñez, A. M. (2014). Employing multilevel intersectionality in educational research: Latino identities, contexts, and college access, *Educational Researcher, 43*(2), 85–92.

Nystrom, P. (1929). *Economic Principles of Consumption.* New York: The Ronald Press Company.

Ogbu, J. (2004). *Black power: Radical politics and African-American identity.* Baltimore, MD: Johns Hopkins University.

Oikarinen-Jabai, H. (2003). Toward performative research: Embodied listening to the self/other. *Qualitative Inquiry, 9*(4), 569–578.

Olneck, M. R. (1990). The recurring dream: Symbolism and ideology in intercultural and multicultural education. *American Journal of Education*, 98(2), 147–174.

Oloo, H., Wanjiru, M., & Newell-Jones, K. (2011). Female genital mutilation practices in Kenya: The role of alternative rites of passage; a case study of Kisii and Kuria districts. Retrieved from http://www.feedtheminds.org/downloads/FGM%20Report_March2011.pdf.

Olsen, Deborah, (1991). Gender and racial differences among a research university faculty: Recommendations for promoting diversity. To Improve the Academy. Paper 225. Retrieved from http://digitalcommons.unl.edu/podimproveacad/225.

Omi, M., & Winant, H. (1986/1994). *Racial formation in the United States from the 1960s to the 1980s*. New York, NY: Routledge.

Omwoyo, S. (2008). The impact of coffee production on Abagusii women in Kenya. In C. Wawasi Kitetu (Ed.), *Science and Technology: Perspectives from Africa* (pp. 156–157). Dakar, CODESRIA Gender Series Volume 6. Retrieved from http://www.codesria.org/spip.php?article1382.

O'Reilly, P., and Borman, K. (1984). Sexism and sex discrimination in education. *Theory Into Practice*, 26(2), 110–116.

Parker, L., & Lynn, M (2002). What's race got to do with it?: Critical race theory's conflicts with and connections to qualitative research methodology and epistemology. *Qualitative Inquiry*, 8(1), 7–22.

Payne, R. (1998). *A framework for understanding poverty*. New York, NY: Aha Process, Inc.

Peffley, M., & Hurwitz, J. (1998). Whites' stereotypes of Blacks: Sources and political consequences (pp. 58–99). *Perception and prejudice: Race and politics in the United States*.

Pennington, J. (2007). Silence in the classroom/whispers in the halls: Autoethnography as pedagogy in White pre-service teacher education. *Race & Ethnicity*, 10(1) 93–113.

Pennycook, A. (2001). *Critical applied linguistics: A critical introduction*. Mahwah, NJ: Lawrence Earlbaum Associates.

Perez, E. (1999). *The decolonial imaginary*. Bloomington, IN: Indiana University Press.

Perry, Imani. (1988). A Black student's reflection on public and private schools. *Harvard Educational Review*, 58(3), 332–336.

Peshkin, A. (1988). In search of subjectivity—one's own. *Educational researcher*, 17(7), 17–21.

Peterson, C., & Park, C. (1998). Learned helplessness and explanatory style. In D. F. Barone, M. Hersen, & V. B. Van Hasselt (pp. 287–308). *Advanced Personality*. New York, NY: Plenum Press.

Picca, L. H., & Feagin, J. R. (2007). *Two-faced racism: Whites in the backstage and frontstage*. New York, NY: Routledge.

Policastro, J. (2010, March 15). Warning: Parts of Mexico dangerous for Americans. Retrieved from http://www.wishtv.com/dpp/news/national/warning-parts-of-mexico-dangerous-for-americans.

Pollock, M. (2005). *Colormute: Racetalk dilemmas in an American school*. Princeton, NJ: Princeton University Press.

Rabinow, P. (Ed.). (1984). *The Foucault Reader*. New York, NY: Pantheon Press.

Rains, F. V. (2000). Is the benign really harmless? Deconstructing some "benign" manifestations of operationalized White privilege. In J. Kincheloe (Ed.), *White reign: Deploying Whiteness in America* (pp. 77–101). New York, NY: St. Martin's Press.

Rapley, John (2004) *Globalization and Inequality: neoliberalism's downward spiral.* Boulder, CO: Lynne Rienner Publishers, Inc.

Ream, R. (2003). Counterfeit social capital and Mexican-American underachievement. *Educational Evaluation and Policy Analysis, 25*(3), 237–262.

Ricoeur, P. *Oneself as another.* (K. Blamey, Trans.). Chicago, IL: University of Chicago Press.

Roediger, D. (2005). *Working toward whiteness: How America's immigrants became white: The strange journey from Ellis Island to the suburbs.* New York, NY: Basic Books.

Rogers, R. (2002). Through the eyes of the institution: A critical discourse analysis of decision making in two special education meetings. *Anthropology & Education Quarterly, 33*(2), 213–237.

Rogers, R., & Mosley, M. (2008). A critical discourse analysis of racial literacy in teacher education. *Linguistics and Education, 19*(2), 107–131.

Romero, M. (2002). *Maid in the USA: 10th anniversary edition.* New York, NY: Routledge.

Rosaldo, R. (1993). *Culture and truth: The remaking of social analysis.* Boston, MA: Beacon Press.

Roth, W. M. (Ed.). (2005). *Auto/biography and auto/ethnography: Praxis of research method.* Rotterdam, Netherlands: Sense Publishers.

Rousseau, J. J. (1762/1979) *Emile.* (Allan Bloom, Trans.). New York, NY: Basic Books.

Rozmarin, M. (2013). Living politically: An Irigarayan notion of agency as a way of life. *Hypatia, 28*(3), 469–482.

Ruder, K. (2010). *The collective leadership storybook: Weaving strong communities.* Seattle, WA: The Center for Ethical Leadership.

Russel y Rodriguez, M. (1998). Confronting anthropology's silencing praxis: Speaking of/from a Chicana consciousness. *Qualitative Inquiry, 4*(1), 15–40

Saldivar-Hull, S. (2000). *Feminism on the Border: Chicana gender politics and literature.* Berkeley, CA: University of California Press.

Samier, E. (2002). Weber on education and its administration: Prospects for leadership in a rationalized world. *Educational Management and Administration, 30*(1), 27–45.

Sanders, P. (2009). *The resurgence of the soul's inner wellspring of knowledge: Remembering, reclaiming, and embracing cultural and spiritual wisdom and truth for the soul's journey* (Unpublished doctoral dissertation). California Institute of Integral Studies, San Francisco, CA.

Sandoval, C. (2004). U.S. third world feminism: The theory and method of differential oppositional consciousness. In S. Harding (Ed.), *The feminist standpoint theory reader: Intellectual & political controversies* (pp. 195–210). New York, NY: Routledge.

Sartre, J. P. (1958) [2003]. *Being and nothingness.* (H. E. Barnes, Trans.). London, England: Routledge.

Shadle, B. L. (2003). *Bridewealth and female consent: Marriage disputes in African courts, Gusiiland, Kenya. Journal of African History, 44*(2), 241–162.

Shadle, B. L. (2006). *Girl cases: Marriage and colonialism in Gusiiland, Kenya, 1890–1970.* Portsmouth, England: Heinemann.

Shepler, S. 2003. Educated in war: The rehabilitation of child soldiers in Sierra Leone. In E. Uwazie (Ed.), *Conflict resolution and peace education in Africa* (pp. 57–76). Lanham, MD: Lexington Books.

Shujaa, M. (1994). *Too much schooling, too little education.* Baltimore, MD: Africa World Press.

Shujaa, M. J. (Ed.). (1994). *Too much schooling and not enough education: A paradox of Black life in White societies.* Trenton, NJ: Africa World Press.

Silberschmidt, M. (1992). Have men become the weaker sex? Changing life situations in Kisii District, Kenya. *The Journal of Modern African Studies, 30*(2), 237–253.

Silberschmidt, M. (1999). *Women forget that men are the masters: Gender antagonism and socio-economic change in Kisii District, Kenya.* Copenhagen, Denmark: Nordiska Afrikainstitutet.

Silberschmidt, M. (2001). Changing gender roles and male disempowerment in rural and urban East Africa: A neglected dimension in the study of sexual and reproductive behavior in East Africa. Retrieved from http://www.engagingmen. net/files/resources/2010/RaymondBrandes/ Changing_gender_roles_and_male_ disempowerment.pdf.

Simmel, G. (1978/2004). *The philosophy of money.* London, England: Routledge.

Smith, B., & Sparkes, A. C. (2008). Narrative and its potential contribution to disability studies. *Disability & Society, 23*(1), 17–28.

Smith, L. T. (1999/2007). *Decolonizing methodologies: Research and indigenous peoples.* London, England: Zed Books Ltd.

Smith, M. A. and Kollock, P. (Eds.). (2000). *Communities in Cyberspace.* London: Routledge.

Smith, S. (1993). *Subjectivity, identity, and the body: Women's autobiographical practices in the twentieth century.* Bloomington, IN: Indiana University Press.

Smith, W. A. (2004). Black faculty coping with racial battle fatigue: The campus racial climate in a post-civil rights era. In D. Cleveland (Ed.), *A long way to go: Conversations about race by African-American faculty and graduate students* (pp. 171–190). New York, NY: Peter Lang.

Soja, E. (2010). *Seeking spatial justice.* Minneapolis, MN: University of Minnesota Press.

Solorzano, D., Ceja, M., & Yosso, T. (2000). Critical race theory, racial microaggressions, and campus racial climate: The experiences of African American college students. *The Journal of Negro Education, 69*(1/2), 60–73.

Solórzano, D. G. (1997). Images and words that wound: Critical race theory, racial stereotyping, and teacher education. *Teacher Education Quarterly, 24,* 5–20.

Solorzano, D. G., & Yosso, T. (2002). Critical race methodology: Counterstorytelling as an analytical framework for education research. *Qualitative Inquiry, 8*(1), 23–44.

Sparkes, A. C. (2000). Autoethnography and narratives of self: Reflections on criteria in action. *Sociology of Sport Journal, 17,* 21–43.

Speight, S. L. (2007). Internal racism: One more piece of the puzzle. *Counseling Psychologist, 35*(1), 126–134.

Spring, J. (2006). *Deculturalization and the struggle for equality: A brief history of the education of dominated cultures in the United States.* New York, NY: McGraw-Hill Company.

Spring, J. (2010). *The American school, a global context: From the puritans to the Obama administration.* New York, NY: McGraw Hill.

Spry, T. (2001). Performing autoethnography: An embodied methodological praxis. *Qualitative inquiry, 7*(6), 706–732.

Stacey, J. (1991) Can there be a feminist ethnography? In S. Berger Gluck & D. Patai (Eds.), *Women's Words: The Feminist Practice of Oral History.* New York: Routledge, 111–119.

Stephens, S. (1995). *Children and the politics of culture.* Princeton, NJ: Princeton University.

Stepto, R. (1991). *From behind the veil: A study of African-American narrative.* Chicago, IL: University of Illinois Press.

Stewart, C. F. (1999). *Black spirituality & Black consciousness.* Trenton, NJ: Africa World Press Inc.

Stover, J. (2005). *Rhetoric and resistance in Black women's autobiography.* Gainesville, FL: University Press of Florida.

Strathern, M. (1987). An awkward relationship: The case of feminism and anthropology. *Signs, 12,* 276–292.

Sue, D. W., Capodilupo, C. M., Nadal, K., & Torino, G. C. (2008). Racial microaggression and the power to define reality. *American Psychologist, 63*(4), 277–279.

Sugrue, T. J. (2005). *The origins of the urban crisis: Race and inequality in postwar Detroit.* Princeton, NJ: Princeton University Press.

Tamale, S. (1996). The outsider looks in: Constructing knowledge about American collegiate racism. *Qualitative Sociology, 19*(4), 471–495.

Tatum, B. D. (1994). Teaching White students about racism: The search for White allies and the restoration of hope. *Teachers College Record, 95*(4), 462–477.

Taylor, E. (1998). A primer on critical race theory: Who are the critical race theorists? And what are they saying? *Journal of Blacks in Higher Education, 19,* 122–124.

Taylor, E. (2009). The foundations of critical race theory in education: An introduction. In E. Taylor, D. Gillborn, and G. Ladson-Billings (Eds.), *Foundations of critical race theory in education* (pp. 1–13). London, England: Routledge.

Taylor, E., Gillborn, D., & Ladson-Billings, G. (Eds.). (2009). *Foundations of critical race theory in education.* New York, NY: Routledge.

Taylor, L. H., & Helfenbein, R. J. (2009). Mapping everyday: Gender, Blackness, and discourse in urban contexts. *Educational Studies, 45*(3), 319–329.

Teitler, J. (2008). *Toward a developmentally and culturally appropriate early childhood classroom: The teacher experience* (Doctoral dissertation). Retrieved from Pro-Quest Dissertations and Theses (304416981).

The Waukesha Freeman (1882). The U.S. outlaws polygamy. Retrieved from http://dailyperspective.newspaperarchive.com/history/2008-12-31/us-outlaws-polygamy.

The Woodrow Wilson National Fellowship Foundation. (2005). *Diversity and the PhD: A review of efforts to broaden race and ethnicity in US doctoral education.* Retrieved from http://www.woodrow.org/images/pdf/resphd/WW_Diversity_PhD_web.pdf.

Thompson, A. (2003). Caring in context: Four feminist theories on gender and education. *Curriculum Inquiry, 33*(1), 9–65. Retrieved from http://www.jstor.org/stable/3202137.

Trainor, J. (2005). "My ancestors didn't own slaves": Understanding White talk about race. *Research in the Teaching of English, 40*(2), 140–167.

Tuck, E., & Ynag, K. W. (2013). R-words: Refusing research. In D. Paris & M. T. Winn (Eds.), *Humanizing research: Decolonizing qualitative inquiry with youth and communities.* Los Angeles, CA: Sage Publications.

Tuhiwai-Smith, L. (2012). *Decolonizing methodologies: Research and indigenous peoples.* Dunedin, NZ: University of Otago Press.

Ture, K., & Hamilton, C. V. (1967). *Black power: The politics of liberation.* New York, NY: Vintage Books.

Turja, L., Endepohls-Ulpe, M., & Chatoney, M. (2009). A conceptual framework for developing the curriculum and delivery of technology education in early childhood. *International Journal of Technology and Design Education, 19*, 353–365.

Turner, C., & Thompson, J. (1993). Socializing women doctoral students: Minority and majority experiences. *Review of Higher Education, 16*(3), 355–370.

Turner, C., Gonzalez, J., & Wood, J. L. (2008). Faculty of color in the academe. What 20 years of literature tells us. *Journal of Diversity in Higher Education, 1*(3), 139–168.

Turner, V. (1969). *The ritual process: Structure and anti-structure.* Ithaca, NY: Cornell University Press.

Tyson, K., Darity, W., & Castellino, D. (2005). "It's not a Black thing": Understanding the burden of acting White and other dilemmas of high achievement. *American Sociological Review, 70*, 582–605.

UNICEF (2007). Early gender socialization. Retrieved from http://www.unicef.org/earlychildhood/index_40749.html.

United States Census (2013). Educational attainment. Retrieved from http://www.census.gov/hhes/socdemo/education/data/cps/2012/tables.html.

UTSA (2012) About UTSA. "UTSA's mission." Retrieved from http://www.utsa.edu/about/creed/.

Van Ausdale, D., & Feagin, J. (2001). *The first r: How children learn race and racism.* Lanham, MD: Rowman & Littlefield.

Villalpando. (2003). Self-segregation or self-preservation? A critical race theory and Latina/o critical theory analysis of a study of Chicana/o college students. *Qualitative Studies in Education, 16*(5), 619–646. DOI: 10.1080/0951839032000142922.

Walby, S. (2011). *The future of feminism.* Cambridge, MA: Polity Press.

Wall, S. (2008). Easier said than done: Writing an autoethnography. *International Journal of Qualitative Methods, 7*(1), 38–53.

Wangila, M. N. (2007). *Female circumcision: The interplay of religion, culture and gender in Kenya*. New York, NY: Orbis Books, Maryknoll.

Weber, M. 1902/1992. *The Protestant ethic and the spirit of capitalism*. (Talcott Parsons, Trans.). New York, NY: Routledge.

Weick, K., Sutcliffe, K., & Obstfeld, D. (2009). Organizing and the process of sensemaking. *Handbook of Decision Making, 16*(4), 83.

Weidman, J. C., & Stein, E. L. (2003). Socialization of doctoral students to academic norms. *Research in Higher Education, 44*, 641–656.

Weisbuch, R. (2005). President's preface. In The Woodrow Wilson National Fellowship Foundation, *Diversity and the PhD: A review of efforts to broaden race and ethnicity in US doctoral education*. Retrieved from http://www.woodrow.org/wp/wp-content/uploads/2013/06/WW_Diversity_PhD_web.pdf.

West, C. (1993). *Prophetic thought in postmodern times*. Monroe, ME: Common Courage Press.

Wheeler, E. A., Ampadu, L. M., & Wangari E. (2002). Lifespan development revisited African-centered spirituality throughout the life cycle. *Journal of Adult Development, 9*(1), 71–78.

Whitely, W. H. (1960). *The tense system of Gusii*. Kampala, Uganda: East African Institute of Social Research.

Wilbur, S. P. (1997). An archeology of cyberspace: virtuality, community, identity. In D. Porter (Ed.), *Internet Culture* (pp. 5–22). New York: Routledge.

Winant, H. (2000). Race and race theory. *Annual Review of Sociology, 26*, 169–185.

Wolcott, H. (1990). *Writing up qualitative research*. London, England: Sage Publications.

Wolcott, H. F. (1994). *Transforming qualitative data: Description, analysis, and interpretation*. Thousand Oaks, CA: Sage Publications.

Wright, R. (1954). *White man, listen!* New York, NY: Anchor Books.

Yosso, T. J. (2002). Toward a critical race curriculum. *Equity & Excellence in Education, 35*(2), 93–107.

Yosso, T. J. (2005). Whose culture has capital? A critical race theory discussion of community cultural wealth. *Race, Ethnicity and Education, 8*(1), 69–91.

Young, S. L. (2009). Half and half: An (auto)ethnography of hybrid identities in a Korean American mother-daughter relationship. *Journal of International Intercultural Communication, 2*(2), 139–167.

Zine, J. (2004). *Staying on the "straight path": a critical ethnography of Islamic schooling in Ontario* (Doctoral dissertation). University of Toronto, Ontario, Canada.

Professional Biographies of Contributors

Listed in Alphabetical Order

Dr. Aisha El-Amin, is a grant manager at University of Illinois at Chicago (UIC) in the College of Education and an adjunct professor at Concordia University. As a Diversifying Faculty in Illinois Fellow, she earned a PhD from UIC in 2011. Her research interests include educational justice with a focus on marginalized intersecting racial and religious identities. Aisha is part of the leadership body of Teachers for Social Justice, a school board member for Community Consolidated Schools #168, the public school coordinator for Council of Islamic Organizations of Chicago (CIOGC), and co-developer of *Muslim Cultural Sensitivity in Public Schools* Resource Guide approved by, and distributed to, Chicago Public School personnel.

Dr. Felecia M. Briscoe earned her doctorate in the social foundations of education from the University of Cincinnati in 1993. Since then, she has had a position at Concord University for seven years and, most recently, for 15 years at the University of Texas in San Antonio. She has published more than 20 journal articles and book chapters, including three in 2013: " 'The Biggest Problem': School Leaders' Discursive Construction of Deficit Latino ELL Identities in a Neoliberal Context" in *The Journal of Language, Identity & Education*; "Racism? Administrative and Community Perspectives in Data-Driven Decision Making: Systemic Perspectives versus Technical-Rational Perspectives" in *Urban Education*; and " 'That Racism Thing': A Critical Discourse Analysis of a Conflict over the Proposed Closure of a Black High School" in *Race, Ethnicity, & Education*.

Dr. Damaris Moraa Choti comes from Kenya and wrote her autoethnography as a doctoral candidate in the Department of K-12 Educational Administration at Michigan State University, East Lansing. She has since then earned her doctorate. Her dissertation was on women in school leadership in Kenya. In Kenya, women school leaders face numerous challenges, some of which are rooted in the way girls and boys are socialized. This state of affairs discourages many women seeking school leadership roles. Dr. Choti's interest in women in school leadership was motivated by her desire to understand what nonetheless enables some women leaders to succeed. She holds a master's degree in K-12 educational administration from Michigan State University and a bachelor of science degree (biology/chemistry) from the University of Eastern Africa, Baraton, Kenya. She and her husband, Jonathan Choti, have two daughters, Dorcas Ogake and Elisabeth Osebe.

Dr. Elizabeth de la Portilla is an associate professor and the coordinator of the anthropology program at San Antonio College in San Antonio, Texas. San Antonio College is a community college that serves students from a cross-section of economic and ethnic backgrounds. She previously taught at the University of Texas at San Antonio after graduating with a doctorate from the University of Michigan at Ann Arbor as a cultural anthropologist with specialties in medical anthropology and ethnobotany. Dr. de la Portilla's research interests are Curanderismo, ethnobotany of the Southwest, identity theory, and the language of race as used in medical science research. She is the author of *"They All Want Magic": Curanderismo and Folk Healing*, published by Texas A&M Press.

Dr. Miguel de Oliver is an associate professor of geography (PhD, Pennsylvania State University) and has been at UTSA since 1992. In keeping with his genealogy, Dr. de Oliver's interests are multifaceted. Much of his research centers on demographic disparities in the postmodern urban landscape. A particular interest has been consumerism and the manifestations of social inequality in the North American built-environments. Representative of this interest, his article "Multicultural Consumerism and Racial Hierarchy: A Case Study of Market Culture and the Structural Harmonisation of Contradictory Doctrines" appeared in *Antipode*. The postmodern dimensions of anti-immigration policy inspired him to write "Nativism and the Obsolescence of Grand Narrative: Comprehending the Quandary of Anti-Immigration Groups in the Neoliberal Era," published in the *Journal of Ethnic and Migration Studies*. Additional recent interests address the impacts of neoliberalism with respect to the problematic trajectory of democratic governance in the world economy ("Democratic Materialism: The Articulation of World Power in Democracy's Era of Triumph," *Journal of Power*). Also, the impact of neoliberalism on academia resulted in "US Higher Education in a Budgetary Vortex—1992 to 2007: Tracing the Positioning of Academe in the Context of Growing Inequality," *Higher Education*.

Dr. Mark S. Giles is an associate professor in the Department of Educational Leadership and Policy Studies, director of the African-American Studies program at the University of Texas at San Antonio, and president of the Critical Race Studies in Education Association (2012–2013). He earned a bachelor of arts degree in Afro-American Studies from the University of Cincinnati, an master of science degree in College Student Personnel from Miami University–Ohio, and a PhD in Educational Leadership and Policy Studies, with a minor in 20th-century United States history, from Indiana University. Prior to joining UTSA, he served as an Assistant Professor in the Department of Educational Leadership at Miami University–Ohio. His scholarship and teaching interests include 20th-century African-American educational history, African-American spirituality and ethical leadership, and critical race studies. He has extensive professional experiences in urban community affairs, post-secondary academic support services, and diversity-focused administrative positions. In addition, Dr. Giles has experience working with middle-school students' college aspirations, nontraditional college students, and urban educational issues.

Dr. Nosakhere Griffin-EL is currently a lecturer at the University of Cape Town Graduate School of Business. Dr. Griffin-EL's research and teaching agenda focuses on working with oppressed and non-oppressed people to build dreams that are personally authentic, intellectually sound, socially relevant. He holds a PhD in Social and Comparative Analysis in Education from the University of Pittsburgh. He and his wife Eliada Griffin-EL shared a life's work together and are the proud parents of two boys.

Dr. Cleveland Hayes is an associate professor of education at the University of La Verne, La Verne, California. Dr. Hayes teaches elementary and secondary methods courses as well as research methods. His research interests focus on applying a Critical Race Theory lens to examine the lived experiences of Latino and Black educators and students, historical and contemporary issues within Black education, and the role of Whiteness within teacher preparation programs. His work has appeared in journals including *Qualitative Studies in Education*, *Democracy and Education*, and *Power and Education*.

Dr. B. Genise Henry is a project director for the Middle School Matters (MSM) Initiative at the Meadows Center for Preventing Educational Risk (MCPER) at the University of Texas at Austin. (The now) Dr. Henry provides technical assistance and professional development to districts as a part of this initiative, assisting in the school-wide implementation of effective instructional practices in reading instruction and intervention. She has provided many years of coaching and instructional support to secondary and elementary schools in the areas of language and literacy. At the time of writing she was a doctoral candidate at Texas State University–San Marcos in the school improvement program, where she was named a David L. Clark scholar. Her research interests include educational leadership and social justice in education.

Dr. Joy Howard, at the time of writing, was a doctoral student in the Social Foundations of Education program at the University of South Carolina. She has since then earned her doctorate in the social foundations of education. Her primary research interests include using critical social theories to investigate race in education. She is also interested in diverse qualitative methodologies, particularly ethnographies in/of education and schools.

Dr. Michael E. Jennings at the time of writing served as an Associate Dean in the College of Education and Human Development (COEHD) at the University of Texas at San Antonio. In this capacity, he oversees the Consortium for Social Transformation, an innovative administrative unit that seeks to promote diversity and interdisciplinary scholarship, with an emphasis on education and human development. He also serves as a tenured associate professor in the Department of Educational Leadership and Policy Studies, where his research focuses on (a) cultural and racial diversity; (b) critical race theory; and (c) narrative/autobiography. His graduate training was completed at the University of North Carolina at Chapel Hill, where he received a master of arts degree in political science (focusing on political theory) and a PhD in the Social Foundations of Education.

Dr. Brenda G. Juárez is a faculty member of the Gender Studies at the University of South Alabama in Mobile, Alabama. Her current research explores the intersection of race and place applied to contemporary Black education and racial diparities in educational outcomes, opportunities, and experiences. She has published numerous articles on multicultural teacher preparation, culturally responsive teaching practices, and perspectives of exemplary Black educators. She is the co-author of *Black Children, White Parents: Experiencing Trans-Racial Adoption*.

Dr. Muhammad A. Khalifa is an assistant professor in the Department of Educational Administration at Michigan State University. He has worked as a public school teacher and administrator in Detroit. His research focuses on culturally responsive leadership in urban schools and demonstrates the necessity of school leaders to enact a nuanced school leadership unique to the sensibilities and histories of the local community. He also has prepared school leaders in a number of international locations in Asia, the Middle East, and Africa. He argues that principals must be culturally responsive in not only promoting school culture, but also in how they even enact instructional, transformational, and transactional leadership. His research has been published in *Educational Administration Quarterly*, *Urban Review*, *Journal of School Leadership*, *Race Ethnicity and Education*, *Urban Education*, and *Education and Urban Society*. He has two forthcoming edited books: *On Becoming Critical* and *The Handbook on Urban School Leadership*. He has recently been helping school leaders and state-level education officials with conducting equity audits in local school districts to effectively confront achievement and discipline gaps in school. The demand has been so great that he developed an online equity audit tool that principals can use to conduct equity audits in their buildings.

Dr. Crystal T. Laura is an assistant professor of Educational Leadership at Chicago State University in the Department of Doctoral Studies. She received a PhD from the University of Illinois at Chicago in Policy Studies of Urban Education in 2011. Crystal researches, teaches, and organizes in Chicago to dismantle the school-to-prison pipeline for youth everywhere. Her first book, *Being Bad: My Baby Brother and the Social Ecology of Discipline*, is under way.

Index